Stay
Black
and
Die

Stay
Blac

Duke University Press   *Durham and Lond*

I. Augustus Durham

ON MELANCHOLY
AND GENIUS

k and Die

23

© 2023 DUKE UNIVERSITY PRESS. All rights reserved
Printed in the United States of America on acid-free paper ∞
Project Editor: Bird Williams
Designed by Courtney Leigh Richardson
Typeset in Warnock Pro, Canela, and Fengardo Neue
by Westchester Publishing Services

Library of Congress Cataloging-in-Publication Data
Names: Durham, I. Augustus, [date] author.
Title: Stay black and die: on melancholy and genius / I. Augustus Durham.
Description: Durham : Duke University Press, 2023. | Includes bibliographical
references and index.
Identifiers: LCCN 2023008296 (print)
LCCN 2023008297 (ebook)
ISBN 9781478025528 (paperback)
ISBN 9781478020745 (hardcover)
ISBN 9781478027652 (ebook)
Subjects: LCSH: American literature—African American authors—History and
criticism. | Melancholy in literature. | Melancholy in music. | African American
authors—Aesthetics. | African Americans in literature. | African Americans—
Race identity. | BISAC: SOCIAL SCIENCE / Ethnic Studies / American / African
American & Black Studies | SOCIAL SCIENCE / Gender Studies
Classification: LCC PS153. B53 D874 2023 (print)
LCC PS 153. B53 (ebook)
DDC 810.9/896073—dc23/eng/20230825
LC record available at https://lccn.loc.gov/2023008296
LC ebook record available at https://lccn.loc.gov/2023008297

Cover art: *Mother to Son*, 2021. 30 inches × 22 inches. Mixed media.
© Ernest Shaw. Courtesy of the artist.

To Daniel and Maxine,
objects who were never lost to me;

and to Imri,
the subject who found me.

CONTENTS

In order for me to speak a truer word concerning myself, I must strip down through lay-ers of attenuated meanings, made an excess in time, over time, assigned by a particular historical order, and there await whatever marvels of my own inventiveness. The personal pronouns are offered in the service of a collective function. —HORTENSE J. SPILLERS, "Mama's Baby, Papa's Maybe: An American Grammar Book"

Why be sad when being melancholy is so much more poetic? —CARRIE HAWKS, *black enuf**

The Race of Melancholy

I recall, at a very young age, my parents preoccupying my siblings and me with truth-telling, that is, lying was always taboo. But as children are prone to do, when I entreated, "I need *x*," my mother, almost always, responded, "All you *need* to do is *stay black and die*." To say this verity made sense in my youth would cause me to fib and yet, I ponder: From the start, was she preparing me for a "finish" through/with blackness as if its staying correlated to *leaving*, even this world? In retrospect, my mother did not compel my *end*, but the discernment of life and death, under the guise of "need," intertwining with blackness—the totality of the death drive: "an ingenious concept from a theoretical viewpoint. It seems to concern death . . . allows one to deal with death, but without having to deal with the threatening elements in it, to discuss it and at the same time to abstain from such discussion. The essence of death, the frightening element in it, is not ignored, but rather directly countered." These ideations, appearing contradictory, are directly linked: "This aphorism . . . is an odd phrase. . . . Yet, this tellingly simple and straightforward statement says exactly what it means . . . staying black and being dead formed a singular relationship."[1] Does blackness maintain a staying, that is living, and dying power, a (counter)point to psychoanalytic mourning and melancholy? And does the performance of the phrase catalyze genius as endowed by and through the black feminine/maternal?[2] This autobiographical gesture implicates me and *Stay Black and Die: On Melancholy and Genius* as I speak "a truer word" about blackness and the poetics of melancholy. The term's etymology commences this reading.

From the ancient Greek μελαγχολια, the condition of having black bile, the word is a portmanteau of μελαν—of the combinatory form melano-, that is "forming words with the senses dark-coloured and (*Biol.* and *Med.*) 'of or relating to melanin'"—and χολη, or bile.[3] The inextricability of this illness with pigmentation, generally manifested at the epidermis, indexes a mode of *race-ing* a priori to being "raced": "a term . . . for modulating acts of identity as a measured motion or rhythm that is affectively attuned to place, race, and being."[4] To "race" doubles as a mobile act and a prescriptive/descriptive initiation, desired or not, into sociality. At the same time, this once-internal malady, refracted through melanin to gauge "health," marks a prognosis for an inimitable saga cultivated through bygone circumnavigations. If this occasion of race(-ing) is one or the byproduct of melancholy, does said condition mobilize black persons whereby they "stay black" and someday "die"? Or, in a highly speculative mood, does black bile produce symptoms like yellow bile (e.g., jaundice, which [dis]colors the skin)?

Some semblance of a response arrives through *Loss: The Politics of Mourning*. In "Mourning Remains," David L. Eng and David Kazanjian chart how the classical humors—"blood, yellow bile, black bile, and phlegm"—portend race-ing logic:

Indeed, the role classical humoral theory played in the emergence of the modern, Western category of "race" during the eighteenth century makes such a task [how "loss takes effect by materializing as—or as materialized—social constraint"] ever more urgent . . . as eighteenth-century Britons began to produce knowledge about "human variety," they blended humoral theory and Christian beliefs with new scientific thought about anatomy, blood circulation, the senses, and psychology.... The first edition of the *Encyclopedia Britannica* (1771) draws on such syncretism in its definition of complexion: "Among physicians, the temperament, habitude, and natural disposition of the body, but more often the colour of the face and skin."

Humoral discourse—the internal discharge of these vapors being determinative of "character"—tracks with the modernist construction of race; the "biological" and "social" undergo a cultural shift before and during this era. An apparatus like the spirometer, which "produced Black bodies as defective and monstrous" based on "measures [of] lung capacity," projects that "syncretism."[5] These notions, coterminous with the Transatlantic slave trade and the encyclopedic systematizing of knowledge, highlight how the somatic rumbles with the psychic with still extant ramifications. Such "scientific" measures are metaphors for *Stay Black and Die* as the resurfacing of that childhood anecdote obliges grappling with whether blackness is enduringly melancholic or melancholy is immemorially "black," and brings on line genius.

The interrelation of melancholy and genius has persisted from antiquity to the contemporary. For example, in *Problems*, Aristotle ponders, "Why is it that all those who have become eminent in philosophy or politics or poetry or the arts are clearly of an atrabilious temperament, and some of them to such an extent as to be affected by diseases caused by black bile.... ?" Hence, "the humoral theories [serve] to link normal dispositions and temperamental variation with states of apparent disorder and to support the assumption that brilliance and achievement are associated with melancholy ... the *explicit association of melancholia and genius* ... that later dominated western cultural history up until the romantic period is found for the first time in *Problema* [*sic*]."[6] With humoral theory and race-ing as categorizing protocols, melancholy and genius provoke a Western thought project. Yet eliding blackness engenders how *Stay Black and Die* addresses these sociocultural developments to reimagine "brilliance and achievement."

Langston Hughes supplies this reimagination in "Necessity":

Work?
I don't have to work.
I don't have to do nothing
but eat, drink, stay black, and die.
This little old furnished room's

so small I can't whip a cat
without getting fur in my mouth
and my landlady's so old
her features is all run together
and God knows she sure can overcharge—
Which is why I reckon I *does*
have to work after all.

Boycotting work, "I" embraces the facts of life—eating, drinking, staying black, dying. Then "I" has an immediate consciousness check, taking inventory of the surround: the small dwelling filled with worldly goods; a feline proximity prescient to Jacques Derrida; the Methuselan landlady who prices rent *too damn high*.[7] These events flip that initial stance. Though the cessation of work charges "I" to "stay black, and die," reckoning that life necessitates work equally summons that charge; Hughes chronicles living and dying "black" as the poem's summation—the "all" of it—and the ultimate accomplishment as rehearsed in my memory ("All you need to do is . . ."). In so doing, he improvises as the beginning and ending of "Necessity" pitch the chorus and the middle is *made up*: "If the blues as a form was nevertheless somewhat limited in terms of its improvisational potential, compared to, for example, a long 'blowing' solo in the form associated with be-bop and post-bop jazz, then Hughes also was able to use the blues as part of a larger repertoire of improvisational techniques in order to fully capture the movements of life."[8] Sounding "the blues" foreshadows the introduction, and my speculation has legs: If the (over)abundance of "black bile" catalyzes performance, one could be melancholy and later enact genius. Melancholy, not sadness, best channeling one's poiesis summarizes *Stay Black and Die* as it sutures those affects together by situating black aesthetics as prime sites for such comprehension.[9] All the more, inventiveness awaits.

As seen in the Hughes analysis, I employ two discursive practices often bestowed in theological circles: exegesis and eisegesis. I am attentive to hermeneutics being shaped by an (un)quenchable yearning; one undertaking being devoid of desire (exegesis), and the other being rife with it (eisegesis), imbues a hierarchy of interpretation. Though these twinned analyses are not explicitly assigned value judgments, one approach being "honest" indicts the other being "deceptive."[10] These are the hurdles of exegesis and eisegesis *in color*, or "reading while black": the arrival of a text, and the reader to it, only to experience bewilderment that one is here yet nowhere to be found. Said another way, "As opposed to exegesis, [eisegesis] re-figures the relationship between the *act* of reading and the reading as activated through the force of that double antithetical genitive 'of.' Any act 'of' reading is never a simple one-way activity . . . the difference [of exegesis and eisegesis] being between a radical objectivism and a radical subjectivism . . . *any* act of reading is seen to tremble at the moment of positing a univocal interpretation."[11] If such an omission, while reading, causes an occasion to "tremble," said absence makes the heart grow *colder*. Though some believe one perusing act is truthful, I historicize how people tell untruths, misconstruing their eisegesis for exegesis. Validating who we are and/or what we believe often invalidates those never known and/or believed, diagramming violent spaces declared "intellectually curious." Yet there is *good news*.

In homiletics, "[Eisegesis] was usually a sign that a group member had genuinely encountered God and the text and was now wrestling with how best to process that in the sermon . . . preachers contend with an awkward secret: eisegesis is needed when attempting exegesis."[12] I welcome that awkward secrecy: To pull out and peer in, the definitive and desirous—all are requisite. I read in front of *and* behind texts to the extent that "there will come a point in interpretation when the reading, if pushed far enough, will run into an aporia, a no-through road, at which moment a decision will have to be made. The critic's reading at this point is always an eisegesis. Because at that moment the logical becomes alogical. When the exegesis is pushed to its limit, it becomes eisegesis, a catachrestic positing in the void, a *monstrous* inter-pretation or a leap from an abc to an *X*."[13] Understanding *Stay Black and Die* as an expedition for the lost and found, which will be expounded upon momentarily, means I, and hopefully you, know precisely what that X marks. Still, I also differentiate eisegesis from critical fabulation. Owing much to the fabulist tradition, as deployed via "the archive," I speculate based on what these thinkers narrate; instead of projecting that they "shut up," I encourage them to keep talking, keep performing.[14] My hermeneutical regard for and inclusion of said thinkers requires explanation.

Through the works of Frederick Douglass, Ralph Ellison, Marvin Gaye, Octavia E. Butler, and Kendrick Lamar, *Stay Black and Die* examines black masculinity in the United States (even as these figures dabble in diaspora) across three centuries. Besides Butler, whose male protagonist arrives in chapter 4, each person is ostensibly a "race man": "a black male leader who has stood up to the white power structure and has stood by the assaulted black masses in order to man the front line of the race war . . . the logic of black exceptionality—the idea that only one *man* has the right to speak for the race—might tend to intensify this dominant paradigm."[15] Though I do not argue that these men vie for that top spot, they perform "manning" in multiplex ways in their given epochs. Marlon B. Ross portrays the race man as muscling the vicissitudes of his people on his back, dashing foes in fail swoops. But what this book counters, amid Ross's provocation, is: Who or what carried said man to the battlement? Who or what prepared him for bellicosity, for death, ahead of wielding his exacting *weapon*? A preliminary response arrives when Olaudah Equiano converses with James Baldwin:

> We have fire-arms, bows and arrow . . . we have shields also which cover a man from head to foot. All are taught the use of these weapons; even our women are warriors, and march boldly out to fight along with the men . . . among others my mother was there, and armed with a broad sword. . . . As I was the youngest of the sons, I became, of course, the greatest favourite with my mother, and was always with her; and she used to take particular pains to *form my mind*. I was trained up from my earliest years in the *art of war*; my daily exercise was shooting and throwing javelins; and my mother *adorned me* with emblems, after the manner of our greatest warriors.

and

> To be androgynous . . . is to have both male and female characteristics . . . there is a man in every woman and a woman in every man. . . . But love between a man and a woman . . . would not be possible did we not have available to us the spiritual resources of both sexes. . . . Freaks are called freaks and are treated as they are treated—in the main abominably—because they are human beings who cause to echo, deep within us, our most profound terrors and desires.
>
> Most of us, however, do not appear to be freaks—though we are rarely what we appear to be. We are . . . visibly male or female, our social roles defined by our *sexual equipment*.
>
> But we are all androgynous . . . because each of us . . . contains the other—male in female, female in male. . . . We are a part of each other. Many of my countrymen appear to find this fact exceedingly inconvenient and even unfair, and so, very often, do I. But none of us can do anything about it.[16]

Prior to expressing how "an end was put to [his] happiness" from enslavement, Equiano confesses what his literary descendant later critiques. Though shields encompass male bodies, he defrocks the militaristic sartorial when his mother transmogrifies into that armament, tutorial and affective, for him. The maternal "pains" toward his mental formation accompany her *will to adorn* the "greatest favourite" before their separation. Moreover, such language heralds Sigmund Freud, over a century on, as well as my recent and forthcoming argument: "[Freud] himself spoke of the inestimable, the virtually magical, advantage that came to him from his mother's special regard—'a man who has been the *indisputable favourite of his mother* keeps for life the feeling of a *conqueror*, that confidence of his success that often induces real success.'"[17] Equiano, then, mimics his mother's tutelage in that, after catastrophe, she is always with/in him.

Contrastingly, Baldwin's introduction negates his conclusion, distancing himself from and drawing near to his "countrymen," many of whom were also race men. (Baldwin as such is complicated due to commonplace intentions to excise his work from his sexuality, no different than recent recuperations and refutations of Malcolm X. In turn, the "race man" is a decidedly hetero-normative and classist office, among other things; or, one *funks* it through drag.[18]) Unacknowledging that "inconvenient and even unfair" androgyny, the metonymic femininity of masculinity, deters categorization as an "abomination," despite the twosome providing "spiritual resources," energy from digesting the exigent gumbo of "profound terrors and desires." This fear, which is filiation for Equiano, of "social roles defined by our sexual equipment" undignifies the interpenetration, in thought and deed, of "a man in every woman and a woman in every man" as an act of "love," the proverbial "freak" *coming out*. The race man does not want a *rival,* let alone it being the black feminine/maternal.[19]

While Baldwin's contextual rhetoric may make some readers wince, namely his biological turn to the gender binary, an aspect of his argument premises *Stay Black and Die*: to deconstruct (and in one case "destroy"?) the "race man"—as "race" stands in for "slave" (Douglass), "invisible" (Ellison), "trouble" (Gaye), "pregnant" (Butler), or "flying" (Lamar)—to evidence the "echo," the other "deep within." (Though one is unsure whether Gayatri Chakravorty Spivak read Baldwin, it is kismet that "to echo, deep within" is interlocutory to the "Narcissus-Echo relationship" such that her essay "is an attempt to 'give woman' to Echo, to deconstruct her out of traditional *and* deconstructive representation and [non]representation, however imperfectly." Is this Baldwin's imaginatively predative contention?[20]) Yet I want to impress upon this further.

This book toes the line between lostness and evasion. Because each chapter investigates the echo, the search-and-rescue is sometimes readily apparent so that the one "deep within" is not wholly missing; I signify on psychoanalytic rhetoric because it is easy to find the reverberant. But in other chapters, that sonic embodiment is lost inasmuch as some thinkers relegate their echoes to that very status, engaging in evasive acts to fortify their manhood. In turn, this book certainly wrestles with the haunting and hosting of genius and how it materializes; and it argues that the melancholic ambivalence some men harbor for the one deep within—as "'ambivalence' remains not only the privileged and arbitrary judgment of a post-modernist imperative, but also a strategy that names the new cultural situation as a *wounding*"—is why they psychoanalytically identify with, and etiologically abstract, the echo.[21]

The revelation of melancholy and genius stages a visitation with Baldwin's dragon, later called a *monstrosity*, to encounter what it means to stay black and die.

Writing *Stay Black and Die: On Melancholy and Genius* has been revelatory, namely the realizations, among others, that I have not only been melancholy for most of my life—how obvious!—but I have also been in some state of mourning over the last twelve years, in particular a series of losses almost every Spring during that period. Such confessions are not how I roll, let alone in a space like this where I have no control over who and how many people will read that admission. However, I want to begin these acknowledgments by thanking whomever or whatever has guided me thus far on the journey to now; and to say, albeit peculiarly, that I am proud of me for somehow waking up every morning over this long *durée* and working through catastrophe. That said, by acknowledging my melancholy and mourning, I take responsibility for bringing about those feelings in others. For those named and unnamed here, I apologize.

Beginning in Connecticut seems appropriate since that is where my love of learning commenced. There are so many memories, and so many people who are no longer here whom I still see, as if sitting in my living room, and whom I still hear, as if laughter fills our silences. I remember most every classroom teacher from the Montessori School in Bridgeport, Connecticut to those from first through eighth grade at Washington Science-Tech Magnet and Carrigan Middle Schools, but particularly Principal Delilah T. Gomes at Washington who regarded my intelligence seriously at five, and gave me a local platform to recite the "I Have a Dream" speech from memory at school, only to later do it for the chapter of The Links in Milford, Connecticut. That same oratory was first given regard by the West Haven Black Coalition, then led by Mrs. Carroll E. Brown, and landed my face on the cover of the Monday edition of *The Connecticut Post* when I was just tall enough to see over the kitchen counter. As a preachers' kid, First Baptist Church in Milford and Shiloh Baptist Church in Bridgeport exposed me to the Power and the Personality. People like Aunt Ruby (and her wet kisses) and Mr. Barrington (who shook my hand and made it heavier); or Reverend and Mrs. Kenney (her macaroni and cheese) and Aunt Dot (her caretaking)—they, and more, were integral to my early upbringing. And while the transition from Carrigan to Choate Rosemary Hall involved its own growing edge, I know the years spent at "our school upon the hillside" set me on a trajectory that prepared me for a vast and troubling world, yet also afforded me immaterial wealth. I want to acknowledge Miss Connie Matthews for talking me off many a cliff; the late Mr. Konthath Menon for telling me I had the potential but needed to apply myself; and Mr. Reginald Bradford and Mrs. Eera Sharma for constantly encouraging me.

The University of Pennsylvania and Princeton Theological Seminary (PTS) allowed me to hone my intellectual pursuits in community without fear of being isolated. A formative moment at Penn was being a Ronald E. McNair Scholar, which links directly to the life I currently lead, just as winning the Edler Garnet Hawkins Memorial Award, funded by Geddes Hanson who taught my mother when she attended PTS, helped to build my library. In both spaces, respectively, I encountered people who let me flourish and supported my endeavors: Marc Lamont Hill, Janice Curington, Charles Howard, Maria Paz Gutierrez, Connie Gordon, Crystal Wyatt, the McNair Office staff, Bernadine Abad, Valerie Ross, Mary Gordon, Audrey Mbeje, Ndela Ntshangase, Sandra Sanneh, and Steve Kocher, Bonita Grubbs, the late Donald Capps, Yolanda Pierce, Cleophus LaRue, William Stacy Johnson, Mark Lewis Taylor, Jan Ammon, Martin Tel, Chester Polk Jr., and Carol Lynn Patterson.

The doctoral work I completed at Duke University, and my subsequent President's Postdoctoral Fellowship at the University of Maryland, College Park, provided discursive and financial backing to complete the book now held in your hands. Various arrangements of community validated this project in big and small ways; whether chapter workshops for the Duke African and African American Studies Department, chaired by Thomas DeFrantz, or the Hurston-James Society, coordinated by Alisha Hines; or paper presentations for a Summer Institute and Fall Workshop at the University of North Carolina, Chapel Hill, spearheaded by Juliane Hammer and Cemil Aydin, early critiques of the work spurred it to completion. Likewise, gratitude to Alexander Weheliye who read a dissertation chapter as a noncommittee member and provided copious notes; and J. Kameron Carter who saw the germ of a book chapter as a seminar paper. Moreover, that very seminar paper was indebted to Fred Moten who let me free-write for a semester and met with me weekly, outside of class or office hours, to hash out my arguments. For two consecutive years while at Duke, I presented chapters from the book at MoPOP in Seattle so thanks to Charles Hughes and Antonia Randolph for the invitations. To my Duke English cohort, here's to making a way out of no way. To my Duke professors and people, many of whom also glimpsed early gestures to *Stay Black and Die* or let my work be all over the place but still saw something there or kept me fed or employed, especially during the summers, or showed up on my behalf or said a kind word—Kathy Psomiades, Robyn Wiegman, Karla Holloway, Ranjana Khanna, Wahneema Lubiano, Ian Baucom, Rey Chow, Antonio Viego, Paula McClain, Jasmine Nichole Cobb, Karen Jean Hunt, Michaeline Crichlow, Patrick Douthit, Thavolia Glymph, Kerry Haynie, Charmaine Royal, Stephen Smith—and to staff who made sure my paperwork was right and every check arrived— Maryscot Mullins, Tyra Dixon, Kenya Harris, Doris Cross—thank you. To my dissertation committee: Tsitsi Jaji, thank you for chairing the dissertation and modeling for me that the music and the theory were never separate and worthy of me performing them out loud, as well as saving me from precarity through a phone call; Maurice Wallace, thank you for advocating for me when I was made invisible and preparing the way in your absence; Priscilla Wald, thank you for watching me and inviting me to be suspicious of my own words; and Nathaniel Mackey, thank you for listening to me and convincing me that the prose and the poetry were equally deserving of my attention, and that I could be a gumshoe.

While at Maryland, the President's Postdoctoral Fellowship gifted me two years of uninterrupted care for this book. Thank you to Dean Bonnie Thornton Dill and Associate Dean Daryle Williams who welcomed me to campus and made it possible for me to dedicate that kind of time and energy to the project; and to Blessing Enekwe who directed us, the Fellows, with poise and sobriety amid the world collapsing. To the Fellows with whom I shared those two years, here's to our success in whatever situations we choose. Being housed in the English Department also meant joining a cadre of interlocutors. To those who extended kindness to me during my tenure there—within the department, Amanda Bailey, the chair, Ralph Bauer, Shannon Bobbitt, William Cohen, Nia Crawford, Amanda Dykema, Oliver Gaycken, Valerie Hornsby, Matthew Kirschenbaum, Robert Levine, Randy Ontiveros, Sangeeta Ray, Dennis Winston, Edlie Wong; and outside of the department, La Marr Jurelle Bruce and Marlon Ross through conversation, Soyica Diggs Colbert and Robert Patterson through the Black Thought Collective, and Katherine McKittrick through writing—thank you. I want to especially thank those department members who convened a manuscript workshop for me at the end of my first year and led me, with honesty, to the necessary revisions foundational to this book: GerShun Avilez, Tita Chico, Merle Collins, Julius Fleming, Jr., Chad Infante, and Zita Nunes. The shift from colleagues to friends was easy and for that, I am grateful. In advance of completing the fellowship and starting at Lehman College, I also had the fortune of having people not affiliated with Maryland read aspects of my project, if not the whole thing, or discuss it with me or show me immense kindness—kudos to Keith Clark, David Eng, Michael Boyce Gillespie, LaWanda Isreal, Jessica Marie Johnson, Kinohi Nishikawa, Jenisha Watts Osei, Kevin Quashie, Guthrie Ramsey, Shana Redmond, Robert Reid-Pharr, Ed Roberson, Britt Rusert, P. Khalil Saucier, Lisa Thompson, Tyrone Williams, Ronaldo Wilson, and Dagmawi Woubshet; and to E. Patrick Johnson for hearing me at that symposium and inviting me to present at Northwestern, and to Walton Muyumba for that chance encounter over refreshments at ASAP. Speaking of Lehman, I want to thank Dean James Mahon for championing me and the work; the two English Department chairs under whom I have served, Paula Loscocco and David Hyman, for leaving me to my own devices, generatively; my English colleagues, particularly those in my cohort of hires, Eve Eure and Matthew Frye-Castillo; Mary Phillips, for seeing me and wanting to converse; and Lehman Art Gallery, for letting me design a program and present a chapter from the book.

I count it a privilege to have mentors I can reach out to who will answer; I know not everyone has that luxury so if I may luxuriate momentarily. In addition to those currently at Duke, I must acknowledge Luke Powery, whose locational trajectory I mirrored and who, like Howard Thurman, compels me to ponder what I want, really—for hearing me all those years ago, thank you. To Mark Anthony Neal, who shared his space with me to write and his classrooms with me to teach and his insights with me to grapple—for suffering this fool, thank you. To Margo Natalie Crawford, who told me to publicly celebrate myself so that others could celebrate with me—in the spirit of Lucille Clifton, thank you. To Mary Helen Washington, who told me that the biggest barrier to my success was getting in my own way, even on the page—for being right, thank you. Also right was my editor, Ken Wissoker, who heard my 2017 MoPOP paper and sought me out. Since then, he has been tireless in his support of this project by giving me the room to let it sit and transform, not forcing work to arrive that was not there yet. His patience and candor have made this moment possible; and thanks to Ryan Kendall for her aid. Also worthy of acknowledgments are my readers, with special regard for Reader 1, who likely wrote the most adept reader report I have ever seen, for their immense engagement with the work and instructive criticism for its improvement; the staff at Duke Press who pushed the project to completion through marketing and production; Derek Gottlieb for his care with the index; and Ernest Shaw Jr., the designer of the cover art, who so graciously blessed my "child" with his own.

To my friends, some of whom are long-standing interlocutors—Gloria Ayee, Brenna Casey, Eldrin Deas, Kita Douglas, Jessica Issacharoff, Peace Lee, Mary Caton Lingold, Mark Kushneir, Sonia Nayak Kushneir, Marina Magliore, Khwezi Mkhize, Dani Parker Moore, Matthew Omelsky, Sasha Ann Panaram, Xavier Pickett, Danielle Purifoy, Christopher Ramos, Antonia Randolph, Shontea Smith, Daniel Stark, Jessica Stark, Joseph Winters; some of whom are from way back—Amber Harris, Tiffany Major, Carminia Muñoz, Amara Omeokwe Davis, Crystal Wyatt, Mikal Anderson, Bryce Pollard, Chavon Sutton, Chidinma Nwakanma Eguzouwa, Tiffany Ford, Jamille Tinsley, Rasika Chakravarty, Rachel Patterson, Roy Prather, Gerren Price, Antoinette Bailey, Nakeisha Blades, Jeanette Curtis, Martyn Griffen, Camille Hardiman, Dominique Harris, Ukamaka Izuchi, Kristal Prather, Malaika Simmons, Stefanie Thomas, Jidekene Iruka, Gabrielle Banks, Jon Howard, André Isaacs, Jared Watson, Petal Samuel, Sean Méndez Catlin, my Inspiration family, Aretha Campbell, Whitney Fauntleroy, Andrew Hudson, Liam O'Donnell, Anthony Riley, Andrew Scales, Len Scales, Shirley Thomas, Susan Tindall, Angela Moses, Jalea Moses, Christopher Bruce, Natalie Bullock Brown, Timothy Anne Burnside, Archana Gowda, Camille Jackson, Ayanna Legros, Jessica Namakkal, StacyNicole Robinson, dp Smith, Thomas Williams; some of whom are recent arrivals—Marcus Board, Jr., Aryn Bussey, Derrais Carter, Jared Clemons, Cameron Davis, David de León, Brandon Donahue-Shipp, Jessica Gatlin, Randi Gill-Sadler, LaMont Hamilton, Emerson Zora Hamsa, George Henry Harris, Steven Jefferson, Rodney Jones, William Mosley, Tyrone Palmer, Emily Sahlin, Jasmine Smith, Dennis Tyler, Julian Wamble; and some of whom were there when my life was low—Darian

Agnew, Sophia Aladenoye, Aissa Bautista, Mitchell Burgess, Jodine Gordon, Enchanta Jackson, Regina Langley, Janée Moses, Oluwatomisin Oredein, Ewurama Sackey, Matthew Sahlin, Nura Sediqe, William Scott Terrell—thank you for every moment.

And to my family, my departed grandparents, Edwin and Senna, John L. and Agnes, and Edna, who would likely hold this book and marvel, and to my extended relatives, the Smiths and the Durhams—thank you for being people in search of a life that confirmed, or exceeded, every prayer and dream. I want to particularly thank my Aunt Bert for watching me and my siblings when we were little; my Aunt Mary, who most every summer sent back-to-school materials; my Aunt Willa, who single-handedly kept me fed when I was living in Durham, North Carolina; my Aunt Pat and Uncle Johnny, whose house was always open to me; my Uncle Leo, who helped me furnish my home; and my cousins, particularly Tonya, Michael, and Corwin, who supported in word and deed; Marcus, who was always transparent and compelled the same from me; Tia and Floyd, who gave me shelter and conversations into the wee hours; and Eric Lorde, who always had the music. To my godmother, Terri, I can say you are one of a few people who has always been there, from Bridgeport Hospital that Thursday night to now, documenting my life and the lives of those I love—thank you for the eclecticism and the protection. To my siblings, Phoebe, Tabitha, and Simeon, also known as Flopsy, Mopsy, and Cottontail, Peter loves you like a rabbit loves crumb cake. To my parents, my mother, who gave me the classical tradition, and my father, who gave me vernacular—Mommy, every word in this book's gonna be about you because at every apex and every abyss, you are there and if what I learned on April Fools' 2022, the very day I sent the draft of this book to the press, means anything, I know that I was loved; and Daddy, in the wake of Mommy, thank you for living for the four of us because I know there were days you did not want to get up yet you modeled how to brave catastrophe if love is central. And to Imri, you are love. You are my best thing. You are my melancholy. You are my genius. InI.

In the absence of women on board,
when the ship reached the point where no landmass
was visible in any direction
and the funk had begun to accrue—
... —who
commenced the moaning? ...
In the absence of women, of mothers,
who found the note that would soon be called "blue,"
... Who knew
what note to hit or how? In the middle
of the ocean, in the absence of women,
there is no deeper deep, no bluer blue.
—ELIZABETH ALEXANDER, "Absence"

Yet, the blues often transcend racism in their lyrical expression of life's contradictions. In
the blues there is an adult sensibility of an unfair and unforgiving world in which one, nev-
ertheless, must take stock and bear responsibility. This theme of looking into the contradic-
tions and absurdity of life, of being born into a world of suffering, is indication of an insight
from ancient times that has taken new forms in the modern world. ... We encounter, then,
the theme of the cathartic realization of life and its relation to suffering.
—LEWIS R. GORDON, "When I Was There, It Was Not"

Kind of BlueBlack
The dead bears the dead.
The dead buries the dead.
The living-dead channels the dead.
The living-dead heralds the living-dead.
The living-dead troubles the deadly living.[1]
Love melancholy.

Stay Black and Die: On Melancholy and Genius is, in its own right, a symphony. Featuring a quintet of "race men"—Frederick Douglass, Ralph Ellison, Marvin Gaye, Gan from Octavia E. Butler's "Bloodchild," and Kendrick Lamar—this composition is at once harmonious and cacophonous. The aforementioned phrases further imply the symphonic nature of *Stay Black and Die* by acting as a series of luftpauses, the musical notation of an apostrophe (') that "indicates the end of a phrase," throughout this introduction as it examines psychoanalysis via melancholy, or "the blues," and consumption, then meditates on affect theory and abstraction to outline genius, or "blues music"; these notations also play on aesthetics as an apostrophe is a poetic device to address the absent.[2] With these declarations providing theoretical *rest*, equally acknowledging who, or what, dwells in absentia requires exposing the premise of this book: the modulation of objects lost to subjects found. Let's begin!

In *The Death-Bound-Subject: Richard Wright's Archaeology of Death*, Abdul R. JanMohamed shares his text's mission vis-à-vis its interlocutors: Toni Morrison (*Beloved*) and Hortense J. Spillers ("Mama's Baby, Papa's Maybe: An American Grammar Book"). Its critical gaze epitomizes "the gradual shift . . . this tradition of African American *literary* meditation about the death-bound-subject evinces a fascinating transformation," via Frederick Douglass and Harriet Jacobs, and "reaches its climax generally in the work of Toni Morrison . . . which . . . raises that aporetic structure of the death-bound-subject to its excruciatingly painful and profoundly illuminating climax."[3] The salience of *Beloved* is notable as the legacy of the slave-narrative-cum-autobiography to the historical fiction novel illumines the canonizing of black letters, their theoretical/formal innovations in black stud(y/ies), and the influence of such ideas.

Transmuting blackness as a paradigmatic comprisal of "people with problems to problem people" provokes an "effort to 'fix' black people," resulting in "their own elimination as a condition of progress. The negative path has produced . . . a form of subjectivity conditioned by a suprastructural expectation of its elimination—namely, a death-bound subjectivity." Morrison pens, at the micro- and macrocosmic level, a work wherein that suprastructure compels an act that "is beyond control, but is not beyond understanding": Sethe locally condemns slavery when discontinuing her third-born, the ominous mimicry of her own plight.[4] Yet the novel also positions her, and happenings in Cincinnati and at Sweet Home, as a ripple inaugurated from the cumulonimbic vantage of *Beloved*—the punished and punishing—as she travels the Maafa: "I AM BELOVED and she is mine. . . . I would help her but the clouds are in the way . . . the men without skin bring us their morning water to drink . . . small rats do not wait for us to sleep . . . we are all trying to leave our bodies behind . . . the little hill of dead people . . . the men without skin push them through with poles . . . they fall into the sea which is the color of the bread." Beloved is death-bound long before her infantile body connects with wall planks in that instant of maternal hand-eye coordination.[5] The mother as lost ("Sethe's is the face that left me") and found ("You rememory me? Yes. I remember you. You never forget me? Your face is mine."); the daughter in the sky, asea, in the shed—Beloved represents *the repeating body*. This signifies that though race-ing charts "progress" through black extermination, death-bound-subjectivity can redress "fixed" endings ranging from precarious ("what is caused by the social world requires a change in the social world for it, too, to change. We live, however, in a world that demands the change of individuals instead of a changed society.") to preferred (Sethe as "postulate of destructive threats from nonsexual forms of aggression").[6]

JanMohamed next invokes Spillers's body-flesh duality and rereads Giorgio Agamben's "bare life" where flesh is "close to the zero degree of subjectivity in that it is defined as readily killable" although it is "still *alive*"; borrowing her formulation "allows us to define the zone inhabited by 'bare life' or the death-bound subject as that between flesh and meat."[7] Like Morrison, Spillers should be ruminated on if the coincidence of 1987, the year her essay and *Beloved* are published, orchestrates these works as soloists in JanMohamed's concerto. Said differently, "If we think of the 'flesh' as a primary narrative . . . its seared, divided, ripped-apartness, riveted to the ship's hold, fallen, or 'escaped' overboard," is Beloved "the fallen"—out of the clouds, the killable alive nestled between flesh and meat—who, having been submerged for an undisclosed period, enunciates, "I come out of blue water after the bottoms of my feet swim away from me I come up I need to find a place to be the air is heavy I am not dead I am not"? If this "primary narrative" provokes 3, Beloved, the deletion in that spitefully venomous Ohio address, 124 Bluestone Road, does Sethe constitute the 0 (degree); and, by extension, are we the infinite numbers succeeding 4, that being Denver?[8] And are the novel's dedicated "Sixty million and more" those *left behind*, those to the left of, 1 and its invisible predecessor—reinventions of what mathematicians deem "imaginary numbers," the coefficients *i*? Nonetheless, that death-bound-subjective admission gains legibility:

I am not.

Subverting Agamben repositions "bare life" through a black feminist lens to account for those epistemically inscrutable. Yet something else happens when these thinkers evoke "the departed."

Whether an apparition is expressed in that "Grammar Book," in "The Idea of Black Culture," Spillers opines, "And it is precisely that split of motives between current systems of thought . . . and those spaces of *habitation* that are organized and unfolded as if in an autonomy of values that is going to *haunt* any discussion of social formations that are assigned a cultural valence." And Morrison calls *Beloved* a novel wherein "*haunting* is both a major incumbent of the narrative and sleight of hand . . . to keep the reader preoccupied with the nature of the incredible *spirit world* while being supplied a controlled diet of the incredible political world."[9] When "making" or "doing" culture, one simultaneously inhabits while being inhabited, holds physical space while something takes a psychic hold. Attentive to the diction of those to whom *The Death-Bound-Subject* is indebted—"habitation"; "haunt"; "haunting"; "spirit world"—one notes these theorists inciting the ghost.[10] If the death-bound-subject/bare-life purveyor occupies that zone between flesh and meat, this limbic personality experiences that transition in four steps: One kills flesh, killed flesh transforms, killed flesh dies, dead flesh becomes meat. *Stay Black and Die* holds intrigue for the *ontos* in the secondary and tertiary positions: Is that the black feminine/maternal who is "haunted, with death constituting the unseen but always-felt-backdrop of the quotidian"?[11] A necessary conversation on psychoanalysis and consumption ensues.

Sigmund Freud offers one of many entry points for theorizing melancholy in the twentieth and twenty-first centuries. In the 1917 essay "Mourning and Melancholia," he narrates the psychic toll of those titular affects; their similarities and differences are pertinent:

Mourning is regularly the reaction to the loss of a loved person, or to the loss of some abstraction which has taken the place of one, such as one's country, liberty, an ideal, and so on. In some people the same influences produce melancholia instead of mourning and we consequently suspect them of a pathological disposition. . . . This picture becomes a little more intelligible when we consider that, with one exception, the same traits are met with in mourning. The disturbance of self-regard is absent in mourning; but otherwise the features are the same . . . it is evident that melancholia too may be the reaction to the loss of a loved object.[12]

These explanations of mourning and melancholia provide insight for affect as experiential. They have the same economy with differing comportments as revealed through life and death; the innerworkings of loss can invite states of unwellness as enacted by the psyche, the self, the other. Elicited by the psychic loss of the loved object, melancholia is egocentric whereas in mourning, when said object effectively dies, "the ego becomes free and uninhibited again"—an expedition that keeps one psychically and physically bound fast at an infinite crossroads.[13] Mourning forging the road to freedom, and melancholia cementing the thoroughfare to bondage, since it "has been deemed undesirable, pathological, and mentally or emotionally disabling because of its potentially infinite duration," drives "stay black and die" as a life-and-death sentence, syntactically and otherwise.[14] My interest instantiates itself by recognizing who the "lost" is.

While Freud references the "loved object" in the essay, Julia Kristeva, and other theorists, argues that the object is the mother; her loss substantiates melancholy and its potentiation toward mania. She also assesses the mother as "death-bearing":

For man and for woman the loss of the mother is a biological and psychic necessity, the first step on the way to becoming autonomous. *Matricide is our vital necessity.* . . . The lesser or greater violence of matricidal drive . . . entails . . . its inversion on the self; the maternal object having been introjected, the depressive or melancholic *putting to death of the self* is what follows, instead of matricide. In order to protect mother I kill myself while knowing . . . that it comes from her. . . . I make of *Her* an image of Death so as to not be shattered through the hatred I bear against myself when I identify with Her . . . it is She who is *death-bearing,* therefore I do not kill myself in order to kill her but I attack her, harass her, represent her.[15]

Matricide-cum-suicide lays bare how melancholy compels autonomy: The (death-bearing) object births the (death-bound-)subject. In spite of questing to end the person one eventuates to be, the "suicidal" child is spurred to life by the mother through psychic subterfuge; she protects one from oneself. Representation sets the terms for revelation—the murderous one is a maternal avatar. But a "dilemma of melancholy" surfaces: Expressed in language, melancholy has a "profound mistrust of representation per se" so that the affected passes off the self "not as a representation of the lost thing but as that lost thing itself . . . the secret name of the dead." The passed-on has capital(ization) at the usage of pronouns; Kristeva confers the "fantasy of feminine immortality," even as *Her* "death" occurs through heady filial happenstance.[16] And yet another dilemma emerges: Black maternity as the origin of melancholy and mania underwrites age-old pathology (e.g., "The Moynihan Report")—if the lost (black) mother enables melancholy, living in Her child's "immediate environment," can She be "recovered"?[17]

Considering JanMohamed's "bare life" formulation, one contemplates the relevance of "meat" in the aftermath of maternal loss: "The ego wants to incorporate this object into itself, and, in accordance with the oral or cannibalistic phase of libidinal development in which it is, it wants to do so by *devouring* it . . . attributing to this connection the refusal of nourishment met with in severe forms of melancholia."[18] What psychoanalysis unknowingly proposes, over and against the known propositions constituting death-bound-subjectivity, is the death-bearer is integral to "bare life." Mourning and melancholia are corollaries of meat and flesh: "Killing" mother to accelerate independence supposes that digestive endpoint happening through mourning. But parental fungibility as a melancholic phase confirms the economic similarity of these affects. Another perspective for discerning the death-bound-subject, and its mother hunger, rehears Kristeva's psychoanalyzing ahead of a dietetic roadblock.

The lost loved object is the immortalized feminine to the point of divinity, appearing as the *host* of communion lore. Whether She offers Herself or is offered to the affected, the echoing mantra is to take and eat, this is a body broken for melancholy—do this in remembrance of Her; and as often as the affected eats, or drinks, one proclaims Her death until She comes (again). This pericope invites the intelligibility of Langston Hughes's poem "Necessity." If the "I" does "nothing / but eat, drink, stay black, and die," this subject subverts Freud's essayed muses: The lyrical listing boycotts "sleeplessness and refusal to take nourishment," symptomatic of melancholia; and "I" forgoing work, despite the nihilistic reversal in the end ("I reckon I *does* / have to work after all"), symbolizes mourning as "free and uninhibited." Eating, drinking, staying black, and dying are sacraments for consuming the lost. Although dubious whether "I" mourns or is melancholic for the maternal, one's interest piques that the other poetic beings, the landlady and cat, code as archetypically feminine.[19] Nevertheless, what resides in that inhabited zone, cognizant of transubstantiation, is something like bread, or wine, to signify *you are what you eat*. The affected (re)claims Her because if the mother is the first occasion of "food," then death becomes Her, and Her child—"readily killable" flesh who degenerate to meat.

The dead bears the dead.

This carries over to the "stay black and die" imperative as certain choreographies of that performance "require" "regulation"—"libidinal development" as materialized bloodthirst, the consumptive life of race-ing, that is, lynching; apartheid; forced sterilization; "whistling"; "reckless eyeballing"; four little girls attending Sunday School; urban blight; white flight; gerrymandering; redlining; coordinating a government-sanctioned public works crisis down to the waterworks office; calling "citizens" "refugees" in their natal "home" as broken levees mark godly judgment for "sin"; walking home from the convenient store when "neighborhood watch" employs the Castle Doctrine; knocking on a door for help because your car crashed; swimming at the local pool or in a friend's gated community; turning that shit up at a gas station; eating an "African woman" cake to simulate female genital mutilation; holding Bible study; lounging on the couch when someone forcibly enters your apartment for lack of "paying attention"; jogging down the street and marveling at the house under construction; being spat at or coughed on in a pandemic; in- and out-of-school suspension, even on Zoom; high infant mortality rates; legalized brutality when lying in bed with your pregnant girlfriend and annually having your gravestone pockmarked with bullets or sleeping on the living room sofa near your grandmother or loitering in Walmart with an unloaded weapon or taking the BART to celebrate a new year you will not see or selling loosies on a corner or bootleg CDs at a convenient store or laughing with your friends when a bullet enters your skull or being folded onto yourself in a police van like a rag doll or playing by yourself in the park or driving with a broken tail light or forewarning your second amendment right while reaching for your ID as your fiancé sits in the driver's seat and her daughter sits in the backseat or running away or looking like a demon and Hulk Hogan all at once or playing with your nephew when a "wellness check" ensues or having a no-knock warrant visited upon you and the person you love while slumbering and sustaining fatal injuries labeled "None" or being trans or the rumormongering of a forged check equivocated for a counterfeit twenty-dollar-bill or being thrown off your balcony or falling asleep in your car at Wendy's to evade a DUI ahead of your daughter's eighth birthday party only to be treated as taxidermy while bleeding out that goes against "the rules" or a "traffic stop" for a dangling modifier (read: an air freshener festooning your rearview mirror) only to discharge a 9mm confused for a taser or . . . ; and . . . —the "controlled diet" of necropolitical terror, *ditto* in perpetuity.[20] These deathly constancies interanimate the transmogrification from flesh to meat as the death-bearing object and death-bound-subject are continuously *lost*, the two-way foci of mourning and melancholy.

The dead buries the dead.

The death-bound-subject in that flesh-meat waiting room exhibits how bare life qualifies worth: "Just as mourning impels the ego to give up the object by declaring it to be dead and offering the ego the inducement of continuing to live . . . after the object has been abandoned as valueless. . . . The conflict within the ego, which melancholia substitutes for the struggle over the object, must act like a painful wound which calls for an extraordinarily high anti-cathexis."[21] That one is, and eats, the lost, appraised "valueless," solidifies that roadblock. Losing the love object, and expediting melancholy, augments repression: The registry of a "painful wound" as cerebral calligraphy for a troubled mind permits the disavowal of invested energy to deduce how and why that flesh is "killable" in the first place, especially if suture is the purposive end of "injury" because "[i]f we think of the cultural situation of [blackness] as a *wounding*, or a writing in [the] blood, the ground of such conjecture traces back to those branded and marked bodies that [one] 're-members.'" Or not. This palimpsest precedes repetitive death and furthers the repressive in that supposedly after devastation, the body, mental and material, always reverts to "normal."[22]

The lost object, in that naked intercession where Her pupil is death-bound, meets a "violent end" through disparagement and denigration: the degree of Spillers-cum-JanMohamed's *zero*. Death-bound-subjectivity is "a systematic and thorough archaeology . . . of the subject who is formed, from infancy on, by the imminent and ubiquitous threat of death." My childhood aphorism pronounces this deathly nearness, this truthfulness fully misunderstood until now. The one who loses the loved object converges with the death-bound-subject because both preoccupy themselves with kindred existential crises; the "gradual shift" from "narcissistic object-choice to narcissism" feels like a series of "conscious and deliberate decisions," while each "single struggle of ambivalence" presents "extremely sharp intuitive, often unconscious choices."[23] Though the death-bound-subject initiates a project of archaeology, the lost-loved-object as death-bearing mother fleshes a genealogy. This incites my improvisation, fomenting psychoanalysis and showcasing the interventions of *Stay Black and Die.*

These ruminations hitherto on blackness and melancholy, vis-à-vis consumption, intuit a critical position that is the interweave of lost-loved-objectivity and death-bound-subjectivity, the intergenerational reflex of the old and new. These constructs situate loss as anathema to death; love as the possibility to incessantly bind; objectivity and subjectivity as conspiring vehicles for behavior. This perspective, read through the prevailing adage, mediates between Afro(-)pessimism and black optimism. The affective and intellectual postures associated with these reading practices produce polarization. Afro(-)pessimism catalogues the ubiquity of anti-blackness as a "world-making" enterprise; black optimism upends said trauma to chronicle black "agency" in the cause of "freedom." These admittedly brief descriptions imply the ontic difficulty and ease of the centering admonition in application. The difficulty—loss: of the loved object, of innocence, of self—reifies the mantra to brave a subjugating world. It is melancholy. But it is genius because it fosters, à la W. E. B. Du Bois, a spiritual striving, an aleatory ease that grasps for personhood, attempting to halt overtaking. My analysis is necessarily, and irrespectively, an optimistic *and* pessimistic stance; because "melancholy is the difference and indistinguishability between optimism and pessimism," this phrase, "stay black and die," generatively collapses melancholy and genius.[24] This provokes a concept: the "blues idiom."

Albert Murray defines this as "an attitude of affirmation in the face of difficulty, of improvisation in the face of challenge. It means you acknowledge that life is a low-down dirty shame yet confront that fact with perseverance, with humor, and above all, with elegance." This resonates with the death drive as a counter to direct realities. All the more, he tracks the lingo on a continuum where the blues—"depression, *melancholia*, despair, disintegration, sadness"—evolves into blues music. Deducing that "[Negroes] invented the blues; Europeans invented psychoanalysis. You invent what you need," Murray contrives blues music as "a way of making an aesthetic statement with sound. . . . Conventional Americans think Negroes are crying when they're singing the blues. They're not; they're getting ready to have a good time!"[25] The Negro-European dichotomy relates to the performative and theoretical inasmuch as what the European "needs," or patents, may not be what the Negro, even in diaspora, *wants.*

The blues idiom bespeaks the capacity for translation in that through aesthetic gravitas, one locates the lost through performance; the onlookers' perception of the blues as tears is the performer, through psychic retrieval, tripping the black fantastic: "The evidence of our history continued to argue for some association between color and death . . . cultural practices—music, literature, and visual arts—all used the facts of black death and dying as their subject . . . an overlap of fiction and fact, artistic subject and streetscape, lyric and conversation . . . captured black melancholy." The abject-aesthetic melisma emblematizes the blues idiom, shading psychoanalysis in blueblack and riffing on "slavery . . . as one of the richest displays of the psychoanalytic dimensions of culture before the science of European psychoanalysis takes hold." This describes the blue, or melancholic, black thinking in that epistemic frame prior to its creation; and if the "effectiveness of power depends partly on its ability to produce forgetful subjects," black nonpresence in psychoanalysis, and discourses more generally, is consequential of "amnesiacs" silencing the objects they cultivate through antecedent disregard, confirming that chronology. Is it the case, then, that "the success of psychoanalysis . . . diminishes because of its inbuilt and characteristic incapacity to handle patients more complex, more experienced, or more adventurous than the analyst himself"?[26] Still, Spillers's slavery idiom segues to section four of her essay that concludes with the black feminine/maternal. This may connote that, the Negro, dispersed, psychoanalytically "needs" *She*; this would surely be the case as Her baby.

The living-dead channels the dead.

To jumpstart this process, one narrates Her loss: "1) the captive body becomes the source of an irresistible, destructive sensuality; 2) at the same time— in stunning contradiction—the captive body reduces to a thing, becoming *being* for the captor; 3) in this absence *from* a subject position, the captured sexualities provide a physical and biological expression of 'otherness'; 4) as a category of 'otherness,' the captive body translates into a potential for pornotroping and embodies sheer physical powerlessness that slides into a more general 'powerlessness,' resonating through various centers of human and social meaning."[27] Further denigrated, She experiences a peculiar form of consumption during slavery. Her "object" residency manipulates the "subject position" being unimaginable by exemplifying thingification, dwelling in an "unlocalized space that is neither here nor there."[28] Is this the crucible of bare life? Exerting a power over others She cannot wield, and providing "pleasure" at the cost of Her pliability, or lack thereof, this captive body—animalized as "so many live sardines" and "gendered" as a "black male"—is a "monstrosity" by the grammar lesson's end.[29] What was taught is twofold: The monster educates us about our own *monstrous intimacies*; and through a process of following the crumbs of the material trace, one debunks the saga of a lost object to complete the trek toward a "found subject": the black feminine/maternal who inculcates Her "son" with aesthetics that produce genius—this is *Stay Black and Die: On Melancholy and Genius*.[30] (Heretofore and subsequently, language regarding "the subject" stands to be addressed. Subject-object relations expose an ongoing treachery as some strains of black stud[y/ies] remain suspicious of subjecthood in modernity because of the enduring reducibility of blackness to objecthood, meriting the inquiry: Who wants to be a subject?[31] Yet I invoke the status precisely because of intramural concerns, namely how black persons engage one another in quotidian acts of deference and disregard, under or apart, maybe, from the dominant gaze, wherein generally understood objects rotate in and out of a subject position of their own conjuration as easily [?] as those persons stay black and die. Dissecting the "I"/"i" specimen encompasses those offices, that is, can "the blacks " "do both"?) Reimagined through blueblackness, melancholy rebuts Western sentimental modes; black femininity/maternity as a psychoanalytic locus achieves similar ends. Locating the lost in the performative, that idiomatic transition of "the blues" to "blues music," establishes the black psychosocial lifeworld: The lost-loved and death-bound are always and in all ways interconnected, affirming a theorem of yore, double consciousness, even as it has a black feminine precursor: Anna Julia Cooper, particularly in *A Voice from the South*.

Expanding on the intimation that "the Negro is the only *original and distinctive genius* which has yet come to growth—and the feeling is to cherish and develop it," she theorizes:

> Everything to this race is new and strange and inspiring. There is a quickening of its pulses and a glowing of its *self-consciousness*.... Something like this ... is the enthusiasm which stirs the *genius of young Africa in America*; and the memory of past oppression and the fact of present attempted repression only serve to gather momentum for its irrepressible powers.... What a responsibility then to have the sole management of the primal lights and shadows! Such is the colored woman's office. She must stamp weal or woe on the coming history of this people.[32]

Proposing an intellectually imbricated diaspora, she singularly supervises the lights and shadows, imploring other colored women to take up such cinematography. She anticipates a "coming history" that only succeeds with the black feminine imprimatur; escalating "momentum," she institutes the race-ing of the race. Cognizant of that turn-of-the-century optic swap that readies the twentieth century to deal with its "problem," and critically aware of Cooper as a prototypical "race woman" who, shaping black thought, experiences obfuscation through echoic elision by "race men," I propel her metaphor to further "find" the "lost": For Cooper, the "memory of past oppression" and "present attempted repression" are false starts, examples of premature "loss" due to eagerly mediocre opponents, hence why her collective "genius" has new and strange and inspiring, quickened and pulsating and glowing, self-consciousness. (Du Bois is quite derivative on this point: "If, however, the vistas disclosed as yet no goal . . . the journey at least gave leisure for reflection and self-examination; it changed the child of Emancipation to *the youth with dawning self-consciousness, self-realization, self-respect.*") If "blues music is like a mother tree which branches off" into more art, Cooper sings synecdoche: "this trueness to one's habitat, this appreciative eye and *ear* for the tints and *voices* of one's own *little wood* serves but to usher us into the eternal galleries and *choruses* of God. It is only through the unclouded perception of our tiny 'part' that we can come to *harmonize* with the 'stupendous whole.'"[33] Might *Stay Black and Die* be one of those branches? Nonetheless, the historical-cultural import of blueness elaborates this.

Being "blue" was a British phenomenon as early as 1616, denoted by the term "blue devils to designate baleful demons"; however, this timing posits that fallacious beginning since blueness "long held mournful associations for West African cultures who used deep blue dye from the indigo plant for mourning ceremonies."[34] In like manner, "blue" enters the vernacular almost coeval with the Maafa when persons were bartered for indigo (as profits in the 1700s "outpaced those of sugar and cotton," and it had a value comparable to gold). The nineteenth-century pluralization, "the blues," related to "apparitions seen or experienced during delirium tremens." The blues conjured the boogeyman. Cited in work by Washington Irving and Thomas Jefferson, "blue devils" may have been subsumed as a black communal necessity to exorcise evil(doers).[35] But hunger still lingers as imparted through a West African tale related to indigo:

> when the heavens hung closer to the Earth, there was a woman who lived in the land through which the Niger River flows. She felt a great loneliness for God and a hunger for beauty. . . . She yearned for hair as blue as thunder, for cloth that was not simple white cotton. She wanted to become one with the sky. Now, in those times, bits of sky could be eaten, but eating sky could be dangerous business. Her hunger was

stronger than her fear for what she knew had been forbidden, and she *devoured* more and more until she became *drunk* with it. As punishment, God pulled the sky higher . . . the people of the land . . . and their children for generations to come, each filled with their own great hunger, were set on a trail of infinite desire. Their longing was the material in the bluest of God's blues and garments dyed in indigo.[36]

This woman, desiring empyrean oneness, craves being not so far from the holy Other. If God is lonely, mirroring this black feminine, the devouring decision to rendezvous with the Creator is because melancholy loves company. But there is a stunning consumptive reality: Psychoanalytic identification, when the ego internalizes the lost object, is concomitant to the "libidinal development" of psychic feeding. With eighteenth-century "blues" indicating alcohol withdrawal, not only is this sky-digesting woman portentous of the "oral or cannibalistic phase" of melancholia in the African mind, but also the "color" is an intoxicant ("she became drunk").[37] If this "infinite desire" for blueness, real or imagined, by "generations to come" synchronizes with celestial introjection, slave ships would have transported said appetite and fostered a "New World hunger," a famishment producing mirages where any looming landmass perceived as home amounted to an *Island of Hallucination*: "Some of the people of the ship used to tell me they were going to carry me back to my own country . . . and thought if I should get home what wonders I should have to tell. But I was reserved another fate, and was soon undeceived when we came within sight of the English coast." This is what Elizabeth Alexander intimates in that "[b]efore the head rag, the cast-iron skillet, / new blue awaited on the other shore, / invisible, as yet unhummed."[38]

Aboard a death-dealing and death-wielding wooden flotilla, where heavenly obstruction occurred in the hold, the genius of young Africa in the Americas, melancholy colored, occasions the ineffable at which we marvel: A vessel from the Dutch Gold Coast, now Ghana, heads to Suriname. The forty slaves stowed away—dark-skinned, slender, given to appearing quite ill, solemn, having difficulty standing, blinking in the sunlight—convey a surprise when ascending from the hull: Shaven, these "naturalized" "African Americans" have "patches of hair shaped like stars and half-moons." Gauging if the scarification was torture or entertainment by the crew against "the bounty," the capitalist, awaiting the vessel at its final destination, asks the captain "why he cut the niggers' hair like that"; he "disclaims all responsibility. 'They did it themselves,' he says, 'the one to the other, by the help of a broken bottle and without soap.'" The locative counterbalance: "On New Year's Day in 1738, the

Dutch West India Company vessel *Leusden* found itself in trouble" off the Suriname coast; "the captain ordered the crew to put its cargo in the hold and nail down the hatches. The cargo . . . was 680 women, men, and children bound for slave markets in the Americas. Nearly all of them lost their lives that day in the most fatal of such incidents during the slave trade . . . the wreck has never been found." Such flashpoints, follicular and feckless, of death-bound-subjectivity index "the ocean archive" as the deep incites blueness for those who stay black then die.[39]

Inserted in these repetitions of the nadir, and the messiness of an enterprise where blood was indiscriminately shed "without soap," that former cargo—regarded as and *en route* to being "readily killable" in the expanse of the voyage—performs in darkness the rememory of lunar luminescence and starlight. Does this naval gazing, coupled with that folklore, concede that it may not be that black flesh becomes blue but some are *born that way*—predisposed to melancholy, they are "delivered" to a destination, between the astronomic and aquatic, as said birth breaches below the navel or when "citizens" disembark in their new "home"? Are black folk "blues people"? Does LeRoi Jones/Amiri Baraka validate this when recounting Frances Anne Kemble discussing Isaac, "'the only exception . . . among our boat voices to the high tenor which they all seem to possess,'" whom she reports is "'a basso profundo of the *deepest dye*'"? If the oceanic stranded "sang" themselves to their killability, did ships, namely their *bellies*, harness acoustics akin to great edifices? Is the hold an engulfed cathedral? Is Isaac phonating "Absence" whereby he rang out "the first blue note from one bowel, one throat, / joined by dark others in gnarled harmony," while rowing the "diarist"? Does he sound, or *look*, like indigo?[40]

Though rethinking the "birth" trope can envision this black aesthetic as "assembly"—"unadorned, unmarked by the self-conscious creation of meaning, they found common cause in the essentially human act of aesthetic self-fashioning . . . uprooted Africans engaged in an act of *bricolage*: they used what was at hand . . . to cobble together the beginnings of an African American culture . . . not so much born but assembled"—I commingle these possibilities because blueblacks are the prototypes of both/and. Born-assemblages, the "acculturated," and those who dwell in *Stay Black and Die*, somehow compose "song" in a strange land after displacement from a known one (lost-loved-objectivity); and corporealize the fabric of a nation that tatters and discards said material (death-bound-subjectivity). Cedric J. Robinson substantiates this: "Resistances were formed through the meanings that Africans brought to the New World as their cultural possession; meanings sufficiently distinct from the foundations of Western ideas as to be remarked upon over and over by the European witnesses of their manifestations . . . that tradition almost naturally assumed a theoretical aspect as well."[41] This narrativization peculiarly foresees how *from a broken bottle traces of perfume still emanate* as "perfume" neologizes "performance" when the rapacity for blueness, under unfathomable conditions, is mimetic of She, the Ancestor, "the equivalent of the Godhead, if not exactly synonymous to it."[42]

This preoccupation with the blues, or melancholy, entangles the psychoanalytic ideal in blackness. The blues idiom invites reflexivity to confront loss, whether the maternal or "some abstraction," regardless of adjacency to practical death and theoretical dislocation. If melancholy engenders "music," that "good time" is genius: a black feminine/maternal signifier that clears space for the affected to enunciate how it feels to be, or have, a problem.[43] The thinkers in *Stay Black and Die* live, move, and have their being under the guise of *blueprints*. It is advantageous to comment here where JanMohamed begins: Richard Wright.

A proponent of "the idea of black culture," Wright cites "1) the Negro church; 2) and the folklore of the Negro people" as archetypes for Marxist productivity, the "Blueprint for Negro Writing." He continues drafting the second prospect: "It was, however, in a folklore moulded out of rigorous and inhuman conditions of life that the Negro achieved his most indigenous and complete expression. Blues, spirituals, and folk tales recounted from mouth to mouth; the whispered words of a black mother to her black daughter on the ways of men; the confidential wisdom of a black father to his black son; the swapping of sex experiences on street corners from boy to boy in the deepest vernacular; work songs sung under blazing suns—all these formed channels through which racial wisdom flowed."[44] Disregarding his religious hesitance, Wright praises these "sources" and supplicates that if Negro writing is to have any power, it must be charismatic like worship, lined and metered like melody or the speechifying cadence of the everyday. Meanwhile, I depart from his same-gendered parentage commentary because this book confirms whispered words and confidential wisdom between black mothers and sons, that is, "Well, son, I'll tell you: / Life for me ain't been no crystal stair."[45] This blues intimacy, "mouth to mouth," foreruns Angela Y. Davis: "Sexuality after emancipation could not be adequately expressed or addressed through the musical forms existing under slavery. . . . The blues . . . articulated a new valuation of individual emotional needs and desires. The birth of the blues was aesthetic evidence of new *psychosocial* realities with the black population . . . it both reflected and helped construct a new black *consciousness*." And like my hermeneutic, "there is no all-consuming *pessimism* in the blues, blues consciousness also eschews the *optimism* so evident in the spirituals." In chronological lockstep, the blues of the Harlem Renaissance also standardizes a practice through which writers "archive, evoke, and celebrate musical and oral vernacular practices." And when Hughes, and others, "formalizes the blues on the page, he invents a new literary genre; he thus expands the possibilities of literature while also valorizing the blues as a poetic form."[46] The blues idiom: erotic, aesthetic, theoretical.

The blues become "musical" in the improvisation of astral-coiffed craniums—a formalism still practiced in black barbershops—or an idiomatic tic that makes much out of little. Affectively and effectively, *Stay Black and Die* worries the line through the preponderance of "black psychoanalysis," a discursive disposition wherein "theories of psychoanalysis are useful, then, only insofar as they reveal the human situation. They contain no inherent truth and are, themselves, susceptible to change as the human condition changes."[47] Though less concerned with "the human"—like subject-object conversations, I do not parse whether one's self-identification as such is valid, but rather theorize how one navigates said self-identification—I take seriously the consternation blackness poses to thought, especially by those who never regarded people who are darker than blue, thus complicating psychoanalysis proper whereby the psychic jumps out in the performative vis-à-vis the meronymy of black femininity/maternity to the de(con)struction of race manhood.[48] Likewise, while there can be discomfort attaching "black" to any paradigm, I do not (re)entrench the episteme by assessing it "cultural capital" but contend that "the blacks" "do" "psychoanalysis" whether it receives such nomenclature.[49]

Stay Black and Die supplants that prior "roadblock" to unpack the "symbolic deadlock": "Rather than seeing the deadlock that projects for emancipation encounter as purely a stumbling block to be negotiated, one might embrace the deadlock as itself a political position. A properly psychoanalytic politics would transform it from an obstacle into a point of *identification*. . . . The ultimate contribution of psychoanalytic thought to politics is its ability to provide a basis for an emancipatory politics of the limit. The fundamental symbolic deadlock . . . involves the binary signifier, or the signifier of the feminine." The death-bound-subject secures "emancipation" by inhering the binary signifier on the grounds of Her negation as disorder(ly); or, as Selamawit Terrefe argues, "Embracing the monstrous may entail *interrupting* desire as much as it pertains to its construction."[50] While melancholy has been dichotomized as a "kind of consumption"—"a condition of endless self-impoverishment . . . [that] is also nurturing . . . [t]he melancholic eats the lost object—feeds on it, as it were" as "a *legislation* of grief"—I assert one dines on the lost to disrupt hunger, that melancholic famine. (And though this "cannibalism" speeds up echoic effacement, might the procedural act before "Supper" be *saying grace* in gratitude for "nourishing" and "strengthening" "the body"?)[51] Thus, JanMohamed subscribes to a "controlled diet" of Morrison and Spillers in their collective morphology from "an obstacle into a point of identification," a calculus to "recover," dare one say *love*, the lost. To "stay black and die" problematizes psychoanalysis by amalgamating racial preservation—life—with the "death drive"—loss—as elemental, Hughes's "Necessity" toward "work."[52]

The living-dead heralds the living-dead.

Given the theorizations of the mother in black stud(y/ies), this book inserts itself into that compendium.[53] Just as that archive pressures Western constructs of femininity/maternity, this phrase—because of who said it, and this text being deferential to that utterance—accomplishes a similar end in the realm of psychoanalysis. I reckon with the "staying" of blackness and its "dying" through the corporate internalization of that aphorism, embracing the deadlock through a speech act; *Stay Black and Die* consumes that terse buffet of words as a cathexis for the journey because "[n]ot yet caught in paint or stone, and as yet feebly depicted in the poem and the novel, the Negroes' most powerful images of hope and despair still remain in the fluid state of daily speech." And when Margo Natalie Crawford sounds melancholy in contemporary black thought as "a new kind of resonance; the word itself begins to sound more like the mood of a black interior than the residue of Freud's pathologizing of melancholy that he sets apart from what he saw as healthier acts of mourning," this book joins that legacy, revering folk speak and congealing affective polarities to expose melancholic genius.[54]

Examining literature, specifically (auto)biography, music, and visuality, I reveal radical-aesthetic practices (re)generating the black feminine/maternal, regardless of those acts being (c)overt to Her "offspring." This "points to how melancholy not only lives a life of the mind but . . . culture as well. These rituals are conversational because they place the past and present in dialogue. They are also conversational because they grow out of competing melancholic states."[55] "Competing," then, is not rac(e-)ing in *Stay Black and Die*, but a sketching of continuous and reciprocal affective performances that sustain the haunting of the past and present—"the internalization of loss does not remain fixated on itself. It finds its coherence in an ability to reinvent itself in external space."[56] This ghosting is not a (post)modern undisclosed absence, but an understudied presence where the cameos of She, in the work of Her "son," convene being astounded by Her second coming.

"Everybody knows I'm a motherfuckin' monster.": Our Beautiful Dark Twisted Fantasy

Genius is a slur.—FRED MOTEN

Un génie, qu'est-ce que c'est?[57]

This provocation encapsulates qualifying said category. A note extends the query: "Derrida's question insists upon the fact that the French word *génie* is invariably singular in number and masculine in genre, despite its feminine 'e' ending." Producing a variegated explanation, the word supplies ocular doublespeak as masculinity drives the concept while femininity brings up the caboose. This correlates to its classical Latin origin—a "male spirit of a family, existing in the head of the family and subsequently in the divine or spiritual part of each individual"; the ending is "a formation in—*ius* (suffix chiefly forming adjectives) on a base ultimately related to that of *gignere* to beget)," and has syntactical linkage to "genital."[58] This etymologic seesawing, for the eye and tongue, conjugates gendered, parental, and racial complexity—should the black feminine/maternal commune with those unaccustomed to her voice? A brief historicity of genius formats this discussion.

Immanuel Kant presumes genius to be "the talent (or natural gift) which gives the rule to Art"; it "opens paths for artists of lesser accomplishment to follow, whether they be male or female"—inspiration from genius is not gender exclusive. But like melancholy, where and how genius originates is humoral: the "understanding of character for centuries characterized males as 'hot and dry' but females as 'cold and moist,' and the vapors that arise from the uterus . . . cloud the mind and dim the ability to apprehend Truth, thus restraining the female artist from ascending to the insight of genius."[59] Tying humoral theory to mental capacity in this era, when women are melancholic (later hysterical) and men maniacal, presets the institutionalization of psychoanalysis in late nineteenth-century Europe: The "psychic life" is already gaining traction as "thought." Humors deem "intellect"; Kant pens "enlightened" prose; racialization is being benchmarked—genius converges as a *classificatory* endeavor, a paradigm born at intersections to exclude those on the outskirts.[60] (Aristotle foreruns this epochal bracketing when he concludes that "[s]laves and females are told that they lack [the "deliberative faculty of the soul"], and so are forewarned that, in a world dominated by humans, their tenuous links to "human" will be their demise in social and political life, if not an accelerant toward their biological death"—the black feminine/maternal stays black only to die.[61])

These ideals double down on falsified beginnings because as the womb of the female artist somehow holds a "universal law" in abeyance, people equivocate genius by substituting the symbol "in the flesh" and excising the source "in theory": Genius allots itself to someone as a tutelary god or attendant spirit; it is not the someone. It can also be "two spirits," in embodied contradistinction, "accompanying a person throughout his or her life"; the father and mother are presumably that quintessential duo, shepherding their progeny.[62] But when adjectives like "good" and "bad" characterize said spirits, such adjectivizing tracks with D. W. Winnicott and his "(not-)good-enough mother": "The good-enough 'mother' (not necessarily the infant's own mother) is one who makes active adaptation to the infant's needs . . . according to the infant's growing ability to account for failure of adaptation and to tolerate the results of frustration. Naturally, the infant's own mother is more likely to be good enough than some other person . . . in fact, success in infant care depends on the fact of devotion, not on cleverness or intellectual enlightenment." Winnicott, crafting the mother as a composite possibility, implies that to be "good-enough," she must perform "failure," inflict "frustration," as virtue signals of being *daft* not *deft*, cleaving not clever. Perplexity continues because along with this (not-)good-enough concept, as her "specified level of natural ability or aptitude" devolves into codependence with her actively needful child, "adaptation" renders itself via the breast.[63]

The breast supplies a ravenous symbiosis between mother and child; considering the obsolete and rare usage of genius as a person's appetite, the previous allusion to the mother as "food" is appropriate. If the child is genius based on hunger, the mother polices that whetting, making her more than devout. Winnicott employs peculiar verbiage:

> The object-relating of the pure female element establishes what is perhaps the simplest of all experiences, the experience of *being*. . . . Henceforth, on the male element side, identification needs to be based on complex mental mechanisms, mental mechanisms that must be given time to appear, to develop, and to become established as part of the new baby's equipment. On the female element side, however, identity requires so little mental structure that this primary identity can be a feature from very early, and the foundation for simple being can be laid (let us say) from the birth date, or before, or soon after. . . . The male

element *does* while the female element (in males and females) *is*. . . .
The breast here is a symbol not of doing but of being.[64]

Parental identity, namely maternity, is put on notice. In this household, the "male element" requires heavy lifting, *doing,* to have the infant identify with him; but the "female element" mimics periodized thought: "what made a human being great was what made him distinctively *not-female* . . . the Romantic concept of genius is gendered: the term was forged at the point where two modes of misogyny meet . . . the creative and the procreative. . . . The role of the woman within the society is like the role of her womb: she provides a suitable environment within which the best individuals . . . can flourish and perfect human civilisation."[65] This requisite host inaugurates Romantic *queerness* in that while genius is a "noun in bourgeois aesthetics because it reinforces a myth of individualism," the ruse of its singularity is undone ("Male geniuses had feminine traits") simultaneous to the zeitgeist citing said male geniuses as having "close relations" with sodomites based on their "feminine" proximity, which is to say, these chronotopic follies precede the oncoming "trends" of the long nineteenth century as the psychoanalytic preoccupation with sexuality bears out near its end.[66]

Projecting that the mother, diametrical to the father, solely "is," that she imprints "little mental structure," infects what she "does" through (pro)-creation. Acknowledging her negatory disordering—she who *is* and *does* (not)—is prolegomenous to he who reacts in this spirited bond. This "foundation," "laid" as it were, is metaphysical regarding these processes because if losing "some abstraction" creates melancholy, the abstracted thing could be genius, she who begets. Yet psychoanalysis determines blackness as the unthought position insomuch as the black breast presents a paradigmatic thought exercise: If the mother "is" black, such a reality could disrupt her "being" and transform to "doing" against her with headlines like "female body . . . bleeding from the breast on any given day of field work because the 'overseer,' standing the length of a whip, has popped her flesh open"; or *Young Woman with Milk Stolen.*[67]

Installed at the Tate Modern in London, *Fons Americanus,* or "Fountain of America," by Kara Walker curates black-breasted complexity: "She has built a twisted counterpart to the Victoria Memorial—a fountain whose jets emerge from the nipples and open jugular of a Venus figure 40 feet up, feeding a basin populated by sailors and sharks." A sculpture flanking the obelisk is "'Queen Vicky,' a caricatural African figure carrying a coconut, whose skirt shelters a figure Ms. Walker calls 'Melancholy'" (fig. 1.1). The consumptive life of race(-ing) is mobile *and* troublingly erotic—this zenith squirts, as water runs like milk and blood for the suckling and vampiric crowd, an erected simulacrum Moses Grandy attests to when an "overseer" reprimands black women "with raw hide so that the blood and the milk flew mingled from their breasts": Does Walker's Venus, and Queen Vicky, depict that monstrosity?[68]

The Winnicottian breast, as identificatory and adaptive pivot, is a conundrum: The appetitive child cannot be "genius" in the nursing performance of failure and frustration if the mother, and her body part, is up for consistently undeserved flogging. The black mother as "not-good-enough" is disingenuous—was the inverse available? Claudia Tate explains, "While things 'white' signify entitlement, liberty, and power, things 'black' signify penalty, lack, and defect. Such racialized allotments of *good and bad* are omnipresent ... blackness becomes for many 'a focal point for projections of all that we find most unacceptable,' while we unconsciously equate whites and whiteness with 'safety, goodness and abundance.'"[69] These prescriptions of whiteness and blackness impose the unthought as only legible antithetical to "the thinking." Ruminating on something unworthy of rigor, one subordinates the thingified through "disciplining" to legitimate "good" and "bad"— the former "kills" the latter to simulate what constitutes *life*.[70]

Delineating the (not-)good-enough, Winnicott "set out to understand ... what resources were available to the infant and the child that could make up for the deficits in the mothering he needed to sustain the continuity of his development? He found that the paradox of these childhood solutions was that they enabled the child to survive, but with the unconscious project and hope of finding an environment in which development could start up again. A life could be lived, that is to say, in suspended animation." Blackness rebukes this "life": The "crime" of being "not-good-enough," and subsequently birthing a deficit-laden child, coincides with being strung up from a tree limb—*strange fruit* in "suspended animation"—while blood-milk sprays from the wean-on site. Yet the mammary hope of the "good-enough" "gives the infant the *illusion* that there is an external reality that corresponds to the infant's own capacity to create."[71] This survival, this "external reality," requires draping that "hope" in black as an effect of melancholy. Joseph R. Winters cautions the uncritical espousal of the affect: "the discursive reproduction of ['the rhetoric of progress' with 'reassuring tropes, ideals, and fantasies'] results in the conflation of hope and optimism, a process that cultivates expectations of a better future by marginalizing or downplaying dissonant memories and attachments. These dissonant attachments ... are necessary to challenge current configurations of power"—what is more dissonant than (en)forced

FIGURE I.1. Details of *Venus* (above) and *Queen Vicky* (right) from Kara Walker's *Fons Americanus*, 2019. (Courtesy of Matt Greenwood and Tate Modern.)

detachment from the place one supposedly latches on to for "bonding"? If blackness is the "recalcitrant dimensions of that past and present that resist closure and the eagerness to 'move forward,'" despite the powerful behaving monstrously and defining the powerless like so, the "capacity to create" persists.[72]

The living-dead troubles the deadly living.

Stay Black and Die addresses black femininity/maternity as a psychoanalytically underdetermined category. That is, "[t]he association between being Black and having a Black mother was critical to maintaining the biopolitical ordering of slavery and continued as a question for consideration and redefinition through and in the wake of Reconstruction . . . one could rearticulate the problem of the color line in terms of reproduction, such that one substitutes the question of what it feels like to be a problem with what it means to have a Black mother."[73] She is a singular problem for the multiplicity; the sums and differences pre- and post-Reconstruction, in frottage with the genesis of European psychoanalysis, feel like ironic orders of operation as black maternity (re)fashions the psychosocial order, the reception and treatment of her and her kin. So, when race-ing this "good-enough mother," (dis)counting that historicized "suspension," is she black, as in, "[She] nourished the dream nothing could smother / Deep in [her] breast—the Negro mother"?[74] Given her critical aporia, this revision elicits naïveté. And if developmental environment changes catalyze "hope," should she parent at all having exposed her baby to cruelty? Though these questions, facetious, refer to the social and historical, there is a provocative aesthetic response when on his 1961 album, *Charles Mingus Presents Charles Mingus* (the split ego!), Mingus names the ultimate record on the project "All the Things You Could Be By Now If Sigmund Freud's Wife Was Your Mother."

Before his countdown to the track's indulgent chaos, Mingus states, "We have a special treat in store for you; it's a composition dedicated to all mothers, and it's titled 'All the Things You Could Be By Now If Sigmund Freud's Wife Was Your Mother,' which means if Sigmund Freud's wife was your mother, all the things you could be by now, which means nothing. You got it?" Mingus is *playing the dozens*: "The big-mouth brag, as much a sort of art form as a strategy of insult, the dozens takes the assaulted home to the backbone by 'talking about' his mama and daddy . . . bloodless because it is all wounding words and outrageous combinations of imagery, and democratic, because anyone can play and *be* played, it outsmarts the Uzi—not that it is pleasant for all that—by re-siting (and 'reciting'?) the stress."[75] He recites the stress by repeating the title with his particular verve, only to re-site it by making "things" seem "good," or better yet hopeful, then turning them "bad" under closer examination—is Freud's wife-as-mother (not-)good-enough? (1961, like 1987, is a coincidental year: Hughes too plays the maternal dozens when publishing *Ask Your Mama: 12 Moods for Jazz.*[76]) Mingus's affect enlivens a quandary of *Stay Black and Die*: If the blues idiom initiates "black psychoanalysis," is playing the dozens integral to blackness in relation to affect theory?

Freud dictates that melancholia is the "the loss of some abstraction which has taken the place of [the loved person], such as one's country, liberty, an ideal, and so on."[77] The "so on" indeterminately imparts a ubiquity akin to *The Affect Theory Reader* when it displays the lost through melancholic comportment. The introduction, "An Inventory of Shimmers," commences by posing a question and a statement: "How to begin when, after all, there is no pure or somehow originary state for affect? Affect arises in the midst of *in-between-ness*: in the capacities to act and be acted upon"; the paragraph ends, "[A]ffect is persistent proof of a body's never less than ongoing immersion in and among the world's obstinacies and rhythms, its refusals as much as its invitations." The book effaces itself *in media res*, a place of anoriginal in-betweenness; this is the abstraction that has been lost. However, through continued perusal and psychoanalytic pontificating, one realizes the "lost object" in the *Reader* is race—is this affect theory's death-bound subject such that it acts on it as it reacts in haunted silence?[78]

The quibble is not with the elision; after all, *Stay Black and Die* deals in psychoanalysis. The aim is also not to "make everything about race," even if. . . . Rather, how does a primer argue for its interpretive apparatus toward accumulation—"swells of intensities that pass between 'bodies' (bodies defined not by an *outer-skin envelope* or *other surface boundary* but by their potential to reciprocate or co-participate in the passages of affect)"—yet remain unaware of the "bodies" said primer populates on its psychoanalytic "kill list"?[79] It is not the obscurantism alone that causes impolite staring, but the altruism to transmute "outer-skin" or "other surface" for obtuse "shimmers." Those unspecified "bodies" belong to "the blacks," particularly the black feminine/maternal, whose envelopes and boundaries insinuate their "potential to reciprocate or co-participate in the passages of affect"; and to such a degree that if "[a]ffect, in psychoanalysis and deconstruction, then, becomes an ethics of hauntology," one imaginatively capitalizes "passages" as an addendum to Gwendolyn Brooks's hauntological lyric:

Self-shriveled Blacks.

Begin with gaunt and marvelous concession:

YOU are our costume and fundamental bone.[80]

The melancholy of the "loss of some abstraction" is the loss of abstraction itself—the "so on."

Blackness is not afforded abstraction for the sake of abstraction. Instead, the world abstracts it to commodify and draft its own obstinacies and rhythms, furthering its unthought positioning. Yet I also insist that blackness is counterintuitively the thinking person's (un)thought. If melancholy is abstraction lost, then reparation, psychoanalytically, is the recuperation of the abstract(ed)—is this not blackness: "a mode of genericization whereby the specificity of . . . historical experience . . . has been precluded from the representational field, and its value and significance thereby tacitly rejected"?[81] Here, the black feminine/maternal is the focal point where a dialogue may occur about her, within her earshot, even if no one knows her name; and if perchance one does know it, a conscious effort is cathected to not ask her opinion, or the conception she has none at all. The thinking (un)thought. The *Reader* introduction reifies this anecdotally, elucidating "stay black and die." At a conference, Bruno Latour "asked everyone to write down the antonym of the word 'body'. . . . ones that Latour found most intriguing were 'unaffected' and '*death*'. . . . 'If the opposite of being a body is dead [and] there is no life apart from the body . . . *to have a body is to learn to be affected*, meaning "effectuated," *moved, put into motion by other entities, humans or nonhumans*. If you are not engaged in this learning, you become insensitive, dumb, you drop dead.'"[82] This exposits a fact of blackness as conference attendees do not (cannot?) give credence to this "bare life."

Though death is not central in *Stay Black and Die*, instead holding living and dying in tension, that recent monster epitomizes "in-between-ness" as the black feminine/maternal is the ontic conduit for the bookends of feast and fatality: "She became instead the principal point of passage between the human and the non-human world . . . the focus of a cunning difference—visually, psychologically, ontologically—as the route by which dominant modes decided the distinction between humanity and 'other.' At this level of radical discontinuity in the 'great chain of being,' black is vestibular to culture. In other words, the black person mirrored for the society around her what a human was *not*." Is this plasticity, "a mode of transmogrification whereby the fleshy being of blackness is experimented with as if it were infinitely malleable lexical and biological matter, such that blackness is produced as sub/super/human at once, a form where form shall not hold: potentially 'everything and nothing' at the register of ontology"? Having Spillers and Zakiyyah Iman Jackson converse, I contend that although Jackson cites Saidiya Hartman as the ground for her plastic idea—"the plasticity of race as an instrument of power"—those sentences from "Interstices: A Small Drama of Words" are predative as I extend the thought genealogy and ponder Spillers's plasticizing:

> Ontologized plasticization...is a conceptualization of form itself rather than a conceptualization of how a form is taken up within the logics of law, economic markets, or political economies. In other words, it's not a conception of the commodity and its uses, but I am interested in property, but I'm interested in the properties of form. . . . I think typically in black studies, the conversation is usually that of being treated like an animal or being in between human and animal or being partially human and partially animal, and I'm actually not saying any of those things . . . these appearances are undergirded by a demand that tends toward the fluidification of state or ontology . . . the demand is that blackened humanity be all forms and no form simultaneously.[83]

What Jackson intimates might contradict my claim; yet despite her "between," Spillers, and her syntactical agility, concedes that if the human-nonhuman worlds contrive a Venn diagram, that "She," that "principal point of passage," is the eye of an ever-present tornado, the optical zero (degree) of plasticity that later embodies form as fungible "other." Fluidification occurs on that "route" called "cunning difference," a tempestuous triad where in that nexus of overlaps, drawn by "dominant modes" through "the properties of form," She, centrifugally and centripetally, torques as neither-nor-both-and-either-or: the all and nothing of all. Blackness, the contranym. I forgo polemic to verify Spillers arguing this in 1984 as Latour "(un)thoughts" her, perhaps through outer-skin and other surface dislodging, in 2004. Affect theory elides the Middle (Passage) that shapes the social and theoretical. It also begs why the "learned" are perpetually death-bound, a faux pas for banter in "polite company," yet the "unlearned"—insensitive, dumb, drop-dead worthy—define others, lauded for the gift of gab, and live life more abundantly . . .

The *Reader* unthinks race, presenting the absent, even as a category like "blackness" would seem to concretize the "theory" insofar as "[a]ffect, rather than presenting itself as that which is expressed by the subject, instead appears as a self-touching and auto-affection that both instantiates and questions the stability of the subject." That said, if black stud(y/ies) engages affect theory, it is as "affect theory." Luxuriating in limbo deters investigating how we got here, why we are still here, and where we go from here; this book, then, deals in "self-interrogation" or "interior intersubjectivity." The intersubjective is self-reflexive; such interplay fuses the inner (psychoanalysis) and outer (affect), prototypical of Cooper's genius, Du Bois's black folk.[84] The "historical burden": "respond to what came before, to what [we] inherited, and it [has] little or nothing to do with [us] as *individuals*, although it [is] as *individuals* in concert with others that [we are] compelled to respond." Hence, I employ an "African discursive and social practice" where "[g]iven this elaborate schematization, there is, in effect, 'no one'—in a rather different sense from the 'nothing' and 'no one' of Western philosophical/psychoanalytic discourse . . . 'one' is nothing more or less than a link through which ['the world of the social,' 'the intermediary world of the genies, the spirits . . . and malevolent and benevolent forces,' and 'the Spirits elect, the Ancestors, the Godhead'] reverberate"—the individual-one is conductive of the echo. (This is germane to genius because "representative capacities of genius gradually shifted [from 'ambivalent conceptual, psychological, and historical space between the individual and social collectivity']: toward collectivities other than the nation, and toward an increasingly detailed, psychologized, and sexualized notion of the individual genius: the genius as pathological subject."[85] To deem genius "in black " "pathological" undergirds paradigms unaccountable for/to blackness, understandably; here I am less interested in that "subject" than the designation-conferring episteme. The "individual genius" shift—a ruse for the Western "one," thus the isolationist "space" between person and society transforming to supranational collectivities where, coincidentally, everyone "looks" the same—compels complicating [self-]mastery, oneness.) The "individual" and the "one" may be antonymic; while "stay black and die" is often voiced "one-to-one," it resonates for the individual-cum-collective.[86] But I also want to address a tidbit regarding *all the things this text could be by now.*

Spillers's intersubjective-interrogative heuristic is formative to this undertaking on race and psychoanalysis (and affect theory!), especially if said heuristic, purposed now through autobiographical concern, "is predicated, then, on *speaking*. . . . To speak is to occupy a place in social economy, and, in the case of the racialized subject, his history has dictated that this linguistic *right to use* is never easily granted with his human and social legacy but must be earned, over and over again, on the level of the personal and collective struggle that requires in some way a confrontation with the principle of language as *prohibition*, as the withheld"; but there may be dissonance in the vein of "personality," even for an academic monograph. Spillers, self-proclaimed "democratic idealist," hence the hurdle of *that* designation *that* one time in *that* book, deduces, "I have no evidence that what are for me, at least, the major topics of [psychoanalysis] are not stringently operative in African-American community: (1) self-division . . . (4) the paradox of the life-death pull . . . (7) the paradox of the negative." This book transits in these numerary figurations while realizing that Spillers herself was "speaking": If I time her essay correctly, she, akin to "the Negro of the Antilles," penned it as "the Negro of Ithaca," where "the nearest black person [she] knew" was "a car-ride away" in the wake of the "frenzy" surrounding Rodney King and/or O. J. Simpson; I, too, confess my locativity while writing this as "the Negro of the Eastern Seaboard," once racially profiled at the university library, let alone in my capacity as an instructor of record, because I did not "look my age" to a security guard who could have been a distant uncle. Oh, the melancholy! But that is it: Listening intently to the Ivy ether, her "ear" preludes her "mouth" so that like the chronological conjunction of reading and shade, this text narrates what occurs when one hears *then* speaks, in the cause of futural "vision" (see: Samba C., the loquacious baobab, and his "devil"-peer Malik), only to abstract that originary voice as if the eventual outcome is, quite literally, *self*-evident. Put another way, Spillers, questioning Frantz Fanon's *Black Skin, White Masks*, answers in the conditional affirmative regarding what I, like the Martinican, may be up to: If "the intramural" is worthwhile terrain, is the phobogenic objecthood of the black feminine/maternal enumerated not only in her "first impression" with "them," but also when her "son," told to "send go," leaves "home" to be "groomed" a "man of the people," yet returns, having gained "wisdom," and deems her *nothing* in both "tongue" and temperament? Spillers, then, may be Lacanian despite the overwhelming historical record, if Rodney King is a benchmark, that black utterances, (intra-/extra-)murally, do not merit that we can "all just get along."[87] Thus, this book (re)searches (for) the echo.

If psychoanalysis and affect theory are our "historical burdens," *Stay Black and Die* gauges blackness's facticity such that "the blacks" have been conditioned, without qualification, that when, where, why, and how we "stay" is a life matter that could manufacture death. If we dwell in the in-between, this book too surveys how, sans a didactic roadmap, staying black imbues a *regard for flesh* ahead of haphazard tenderizing as meat over yonder. Extending this play, in *Beloved*, Baby Suggs encourages, "The dark, dark liver—love it, love it." Affectively valuating that bile-producing organ, she may propose enamor with its black material.[88]

Love melancholy.

Mingus's dozens playing now finds relief: Freud's wife-as-mother, meaning nothing, points to "You" as *Nobody*. This nothingness move—"he follows along the lines of his own cryptic signature, 'Nothing. It means nothing.' And what he proceeds to perform on the cut is certainly no thing we know. But that really is the point—to extend the realm of possibility for what might be known, and, not unlike the dozens, we will not easily decide if it is fun"— maintains an outcome that may be mirth: Nobody, You Could Be, By Now, Right Now, Somebody.[89] Serendipitous to that *Reader* rationale, in the faint recesses of the mind, Martin Luther King, Jr. asks, "Where Do We Go from Here?":

> The tendency to ignore the Negro's contribution to American life and to strip him of his personhood is as old as the earliest history books and as contemporary as the morning's newspaper . . . the Negro must rise up with an affirmation of his own Olympian manhood. . . . *As long as the mind is enslaved, the body can never be free* . . . the Negro must boldly throw off the manacles of *self-abnegation* and say to himself and to the world, "*I am somebody*. I am a person. I am a man with dignity and honor. I have a rich and noble history. . . . Yes, I was a slave through my foreparents and I am not ashamed of that. I'm ashamed of the people who were so sinful to make me a slave." Yes, we must stand up and say, "*I'm black and I'm beautiful*," and this *self-affirmation* is the black man's need, made compelling by the white man's crimes against him.[90]

Being somebody, even in its masculinism, might unveil a salient moment in the black radical tradition. The mind, engaged in self-work, comports itself in such a manner that King's "rise up" and "stand up" could be preceded by being brought to his knees in a reverential fit: "My final prayer: O my body, always make me a man who questions!" Through Fanonian theorization, the body, hooked up to an inquiring mind, apparently finds deification, residing in that divine office of the *paradox*: It incites questions as it questions, sharpening a hermeneutic to be suspicious of one's own words due to "the black male psyche as always divided, in conflict with itself. And not only at war, but trapped in a racial drama which is both necessary and unavoidable."[91] But a juxtaposition of King and Morrison emerges, inviting a new reading of (the) twelve.

Critical of "Black is Beautiful," Morrison surmises the phrase as "an accurate but wholly irrelevant observation if ever there was one . . . the slogan provided a psychic crutch for the needy and a second (or first) glance from whites . . . a full confession that white definitions were important to us." As she continues, echoes of King, and Murray for that matter, surface, an ostensible negation of her recent musings: "When the strength of people rests on its beauty, when the focus is on how one looks rather than what one is, we are in trouble. When we are urged to confuse dignity with prettiness, and presence with image, we are being distracted from what is worthy about us: for example, our intelligence, our resilience, our skill, our tenacity, irony or spiritual health." This agonism compels her to compile *The Black Book*. Morrison, prone to literarily decenter whiteness, seemingly counteracts that affinity if King's pronunciation happens for and to the self before unleashing that cerebral monologue—is he seeking the "white glance"? Is his "we" obvious orating to the SCLC? To whom is her "worthy" declaration being logged? And if the King-Morrison copulative is at hand, is *Stay Black and Die* a *Black Book*, "made up of all the elements that distinguished black life (its peculiar brand of irony, oppression, versatility, madness, joy, strength, shame, honor, triumph, grace and stillness) as well as those qualities that identified it with all of mankind (compassion, anger, foolishness, courage, self-deception and vision)"?[92] Though our current moment renders "black resilience," or blackness as a cypher for humanity, gauche, moves not disagreed with, I perpetuate playing the dozens, even in this book: Responding to affect theory and psychoanalysis, this project contends in part that "[t]he game of living, after all, is played *between the ears*, up in the head. Instead of dispatching a body, one straightens its posture; instead of offering up a body, one sends his word." But if this book is that *Book*, could I also be *the blue clerk* in that "at the same moment that the melancholy came it was quickly brushed aside by the thought that [Douglass, Ellison, Gaye, Butler, Lamar, and others were] my library"?[93] Either way, rebutting the self as suspect, or invested solely in style, one might send word where shame was. Yet Mingus behooves an insurgent provocation: What are All the Things You Could Be By Now If A BlackFem Was Yo' Momma?

I imagine You Could Be *Anything* . . . even if that meant *Nothing*.

Through a theoretical microscope, I record how these quintet members produce abstraction; if abstraction becomes abstraction*ism*—"the resolute awareness that even the most realistic representation is precisely a *representation*, and that as such it necessarily exists at a distance from the social reality it is conventionally understood to reflect"—*Stay Black and Die* plays abstractionist hide-and-seek, excavating representations by "race men" of the black feminine/maternal inasmuch as "[s]he—herself a corporeally splintered body—is a pivotal figure in revealing and reworking antinomic blackness, which is to say, her representation reproduces the borders between a black self, endowed with an interiority, and racial blackness, as it is always and only given by the social."[94] C. Riley Snorton's doubling riffs on Cooper's "the commonplace and vulgar" twinning with "the elegant and the refined." This split screen exhibits the psychoanalytic and affective because during melancholy, "one part of the ego sets itself over against the other, judges it critically, and . . . takes it as its object. . . . What we are here becoming acquainted with is the agency commonly called 'conscience'"; this can be prelusive to mania or "circular insanity." This circularity is obvious being born of a mother who spatializes nihilism as one ponders: "How could something come from nothing?"[95] Yet Freud disrupts this: "all states such as joy, exultation or triumph, which give us the normal model for mania, depend on the same economic conditions. . . . All such situations are characterized . . . by increased readiness for all kinds of action—in just the same way as in mania, and in complete contrast to the depression and inhibition of melancholia." Melancholia does not solely necessitate mania—do "all such situations" apply to blackness if it is melancholic genius?[96]

Whereas mania was the *du jour* external reality of people more invested in "estate planning" than establishing parity, for others, internal conversations foresaw premonitions. The mental garret: where one carves out loopholes through thought.[97] This suggests "all kinds of wanting, wishing, yearning, longing, and striving—conscious and particularly unconscious. . . . While desire is constitutive of loss, desire also *generates by-products* even as it makes deficiency conspicuous." This aleatory heft is the blues idiom, giving entrée to "possessing genius."[98]

If the various productive labors of the black feminine/maternal were never given their due, perhaps she inculcates her acuity through what she could "possess": the child, whether through blood ties or fictive kinship. This is simultaneous to such relation during enslavement (and post-emancipation) being "false because the female could not, in fact, claim her child, and false, once again, because 'motherhood' is not perceived in the prevailing social climate as a legitimate procedure of cultural inheritance."[99] Reread psychoanalytically: How does one "kill the mother" who is not one? Is there anything to kill because, having "stayed black," she is already "dead"? Yet on par with "fettered genius," irrespective of fashioning shackles or the African American poetic bard tradition, does the black feminine/maternal combine "the aesthetic power and social validity of traditional formalist artistry with the complexities of . . . experience, culture, and heritage to produce a full and sufficient . . . artistic and cultural self"—is this captive maternity?[100] If so, this twisted gifting, this odd present, foreruns how the suffering locates the lost through throwback. This trace exceeds the womb whether one carries to term or employs terms of endearment. A work, ironically called "Crazy," exemplifies that "special quality":

> What a paradox: Kept inside, the pain is poison, but when artists, especially Black artists, let it out, it's genius. But genius is not a typical state with normal expectations; it's acceptable for a genius to act (or actually be) crazy. . . . While we are afraid of the darkness that the artist appears to create from, but we love the creation. . . . And when we are solving a mystery, the answer—sometimes obvious, sometimes inconceivable—is often not as interesting once we understand it. We don't want to understand them, to see them, because to be unseen is to be unknown, and that mystery is the birth of cool. So we give a wide berth around Black artists' mystery. . . . We don't want to undercover their secrets fully, to see the faces beneath the masks.[101]

This passage projects "cool" being *born*, genius "let out." The homophonic nature of b(i/e)rth reckons with the mystery of life—apparent, inconceivable, but conceived. The darkness allusion syncs with this text as said state is where one would "stay black."

Though this crazy description is how Rachel M. Harper understands the poet that is her father, Michael S., if one wonders where the mother is, she answers: beneath the masks as the genesis of "cool," a homographic-anachronistic re-siting of the humoral. Harper elongates the trope: "[Black artists] turn our loss, our heartache, into art—*we give it life*. So it then *exists beyond our own bodies* (our own selves), becoming timeless and universal. . . . What, in the end, is more cool than that? . . . We look at those artists [Morrison, James Baldwin, John Coltrane, Richard Pryor, or Jean-Michel Basquiat] as we *look upon our mothers during childbirth*: We don't want them to suffer in order to bring us into the world, but we are damn happy to be alive."[102] Harper induces ambivalence: Does "suffering" engender "happiness"—joy, exultation, triumph—as if the best output accomplishes itself in the worst situation? As if the race is not to the swift nor the battle to the strong but to one who endures the race(-ing) until the end, harboring victorious spoils having been crowned "good-enough"?[103] While her platitude is hackneyed, regardless of the black masculine/paternal becoming a surrogate vehicle, recalibrating her sentiment entreats: In "Crazy," is "black cool" *black jouissance*, a juxtaposition to that of brown?

Amber Jamilla Musser theorizes, "These forms of otherness—excess forms of embodiment—are central to what I call *brown jouissance*. In contrast to an ecstasy that imagines transcending corporeality, brown jouissance is a reveling in fleshiness, its sensuous materiality that brings together pleasure and pain." Explicating Lyle Ashton Harris's *Billie #21*, where he cosplays Billie Holiday, she continues, "In Harris's explicit manipulation of his body, we see that pleasure and pain emerge from the history of black female fleshiness. This is summoned by the citation of Holiday, as well as the pleasures, pains, and possibilities that lie within his own body.... Fleshiness is inseparable from processes of objectification *and* the production of selfhood."[104] While this hearkens to Kristeva's matricide-autonomy tendency, and my provocation of the death-bound craving the death-bearing, Musser and I diverge and converge here, situated at the infinitesimal line-crossing of a separate Venn diagram.

She reads Harris's citation as a "form of hunger . . . that coalesces—even as it gnaws at the edges—in this state of openness and insatiability . . . to move toward an embodiment of hunger. . . . This is not the desire born of subjectivity in which subject wishes to possess object, but an embodied hunger that takes joy and pain in this gesture of radical openness toward otherness."[105] If Harris's Holiday consumption is a "form of hunger," do others exist, namely that of "subjects" who *do* wish to possess "objects"? I wonder if Harris's form-of-hunger-as-embodiment is because Holiday is not his "mother": He does not "lose" an object that does not "belong" to him, thus disclosing himself as a "motherless child." Instead, he engages in *bricolage*, poaching Holiday's likeness to portray *brown jouissance* as flesh reverie. Yet the "pleasures, pains, and possibilities" of Harris's body align with Harper's "cool": Without reportage of the image as Harris-cum-Holiday, one may mistake the masquerade. The poacher births the prey—the hunted, hungered-for, thing—with precision, no different than "motherly" artists; he performs "cultural melancholy" because "the specter of the lost mother haunts blackness."[106] Is suffering, then, not a precursor to happiness, to "black cool," to *black jouissance*, but to after-mathematic investments, cathexes, in the aforementioned *suture*, an uneasy decision to subsume "fun" for function, the realization of a "painful wound" once, or "socially constructed" to be, repressed—is this *grace*?

If this is genius as relayed by the maternal, when wondering "if melancholy can be passed down through generations, not just culturally but at the level of our DNA?" in born-assemblage fashion, one answers: "if melancholy sometimes feels like a vast enveloping grief, then perhaps music and the consolation it brings can help us to grieve. The melancholic note in popular music—the 'blue' note . . . —heals, soothes and, if we allow it, can transform our suffering into this kind of knowing and accepting melancholia."[107] Though maternal vocation does not require being a "musician," this proposition legitimates an earlier intimation: The blues idiom is an inventive endeavor that enables. *Stay Black and Die* ruminates on such things as revealed in the ambiguity of "so on," clocking hidden figures unchecked through time. That said, there is the calculation that "Black affect, then, is *unthinkable*, falling within the epistemological closure of Man's episteme; buried beneath an overdetermined discourse that reads the expression and performance of Black affect as always already excessive, inadequate, or both."[108] By extension, the questions this text poses are: Though one knows (with certainty?) the unthinking, (why) do they matter (so much)? And is "the opposition" possible? While affect theory and psychoanalysis do not, or cannot, interpolate blackness, if *Stay Black and Die* contends with the interior intersubjective, the self-interrogating, it traces what occurs if "opposing counsel" *thinks*, with variations of regard for those who dominate unthought, even if their thoughts land in unthoughtful hands. Hence, Freud does not occupy a hinge for this book so as to imply he is central to the *techne* through which it walks. Rather, he is a straw man so that if, when reading, he is summarily *lost*, a full story can still be told—what might this mean for Man's episteme?

This study is also not vying for "recognition" in psychoanalysis or affect theory. On the contrary, as has already been pronounced and hopefully discerned, blackness as critical vantage was already *working* ("readiness for all kinds of action") either before or through (dis)engagement with/ignorance of ahistorical and categorically flimsy argumentation. Further, secondary sources do not explain Freud then "evidence" blackness—the quintet members are his interlocutors. With his oeuvre being additive and limiting, I experiment with whether I can impose his enunciation in the blues idiom, as seen in this introduction. This is similar to June Jordan on "Black English": "You cannot 'translate' instances of Standard English preoccupied with *abstractions* or with *nothing/nobody evidently alive*, into Black English. That would warp the language into uses antithetical to the guiding perspective of its community of users. Rather you must first change those Standard English sentences, themselves, into ideas consistent with the person-centered assumptions of Black English." Might Freud race, compete, on the terms of "Black English" ("All you need to do is . . .") in an allegedly *Black Book* as I, the *blue clerk*, spin out the "surplus"?[109] Vis-à-vis "black psychoanalysis"-"affect theory," these chapters haunt—they do not elicit tears, perhaps, but rather the intimacy of good and bad times.

The first chapter, "Read | Frederick," examines Frederick Douglass embodying "ART" and "FACTS," a conceptual duo from the second autobiography, *My Bondage and My Freedom*. In its introduction, James McCune Smith considers whether Douglass receives his intellect from his rumored white father or black mother, Harriet Bailey. She is "the *only* one of all the slaves and colored people in Tuckahoe" who could read. Douglass traces his perspicacity to her literacy; this occurs alongside the recollection of her likeness being similar to the drawn bust of an Egyptian pharaoh. Likewise, Betsy Bailey, his grandmother, "could so intelligently *read* a river or the furrow of a field" despite her "illiteracy." Using *The Narrative of the Life of Frederick Douglass, An American Slave, Written by Himself* and the aforementioned, I argue that these works forward him as the literary manifestation of his matrilineage such that his writings formally arrive as maternal elegies, in the same way elegies about him project maternity. Surmising him to precede ideations of mourning and melancholia, I contend Douglass is not only, and obviously, his mother's child, but also, via these women, otherworldly.

In "The Little Man at Chehaw Station: The American Artist and His Audience," Ralph Ellison refers to "the little man behind the stove," a figure at the crossroads of process and performance. Miss Hazel Harrison, Ellison's Tuskegee piano teacher, imparts this riddle after he fails his instrumental recital. This teachable moment is double: She uses kinship language during the lesson, and the classroom is her basement studio. Basements and/or the under(-)ground are vital to Ellison, especially in the *Invisible Man* prologue, as he plots fascinating yet isolated narrativizations of a "mother," using vernacular, sharing the location with her "son." I propose in "Travel | Ralph" that these moments are not isolated, but quasi-autobiographical/-allegorical. This assertion attends to the women in Ellison's life—Mrs. Ida Ellison, his mother; Mrs. Zelia N. Page Breaux, a "beloved schoolteacher"; and a host of others—who insert him within a tradition that marks him a man of letters, despite his admission of white male authors as "ancestors." Hence, (other)-maternal figures foreshadow his flourishing: Each woman is the originary trope of the "invisible man," giving him the groove.

Marvin Gaye's "Trouble Man" elicits dual amazement: its presentation, performed primarily in falsetto, and the moment of a primal scream. "Man | Marvin" enacts a "close listening" in that the opening lyrics engender confusion as to what he sings. This aural puzzle formats how Gaye's queer childhood is foundational to the recording as he becomes his "mother," in manifold manners, and "father," even as his "father"—a pastor and disciplinarian—becomes his "mother" through drag. The chapter examines how Gaye's life demonstrates the body-flesh dichotomy à la Spillers. Moreover, when learning that George Gershwin became a muse while writing the eponymous film soundtrack, I listen for which composition Gaye sampled and speculate through sonic registers to hear "Trouble Man" as a sonic reimagining of opera and black female vocality.

"Woman | Gan" addresses feminism and womanism through the lens of "gender trouble" and "science fiction" by convening a dialogue among Alice Walker, Judith Butler, and Octavia E. Butler. Because feminist and womanist discourses pressure the constitution and ratification of "the Law" in its myriad iterations, I run with that logic to suggest that a man can be "womanish" due to his matrilineage having peculiar interactions with "legal" modes. This occurs through a short-story case study: In Octavia E. Butler's "Bloodchild," the protagonist, Gan, is a boy impregnated by a female alien to incubate her offspring for future survival.

Traversing multiple musical registers, Kendrick Lamar's 2015 album *To Pimp a Butterfly* charted in a time of ongoing unrest. In a section I coin the "middle passage," four successive records highlight this existential journey: "u," "Alright," "For Sale? (Interlude)," and "Momma." Read together, the titles outline how Lamar declares the "evils of Lucy." In a recurring meditation on the album, he admits that though evils are "all around" him, he keeps "running for answers"; he finds them when he comes "home," arriving there on the record "Momma." I assert in "Love | Kendrick" that "Lucy" is a "mocking double." Although listeners cite "Lucy" as Lucifer, I close read the album's lyrics and watch its music videos to convey Lamar—a mocking double himself of Milkman in Morrison's *Song of Solomon*—as exorcising evil and seeking the "eternal feminine": the oldest human fossil located in Ethiopia in 1974, "Lucy." The conclusion, "Study | Us," tackles the promise of blackness and lying.

Having invoked the Romantic, I want to clarify that I do not sentimentally approach the black feminine/maternal; the category ranges from an ephemeral object mourned by her child prior to maturity to ones there and not there to a dueling presence who proliferates sexual and gender indeterminacy in childhood that foreshadows adulthood creativity to a persona who entertains her oppressor amid harvesting ammunitioned beauty for her brood to someone the child never "knows" yet lives in his imagination. In all, the book setup is strategic: Having narrated losing and finding the black feminine/maternal in this introduction, the forthcoming chapters chart how ordinary, or better still, melancholic beginnings have spectacular ends. Thus, when considering "genius," I, as per Dionne Brand, am not enthralled in "doing," or for that matter "praising," the black spectacular, despite testifying to and having gratitude for certain outbursts of such.[110] This is because we are often too easily enamored with the output yet harbor boredom for the origin. Thus, genius is as simple as reading, a riddle, a song, an arm, or flight.

If this makes communing with the black feminine/maternal real, I invite you to *Stay Black and Die* as such an event is nothing less than a monsters' ball.

. . .

this man, this Douglass, this former slave, this Negro
beaten to his knees, exiled, visioning a world
where none is lonely, none hunted, alien,
this man, superb in love and logic, this man
shall be remembered. . . .
—ROBERT HAYDEN, "Frederick Douglass"

The Art and the Fact

In the beginning of Frederick Douglass's *My Bondage and My Freedom*, the
second of his three autobiographies, two moments encourage the reader seeing and believing to remark on the ensuing origin story. The first calculation,
posed by an EDITOR who remains unknown, hints at the text's mythopoetic
nature, attuning our eyes to the modus operandi in which we will partake:

> If the volume now presented to the public were a mere work of ART, the
> history of its misfortune might be written in two very simple words—
> TOO LATE. The nature and character of slavery have been subjects
> of an almost endless variety of artistic representation; and after the

brilliant achievements in that field, and while those achievements are yet fresh in the memory of the million, he who would add another to the legion, must possess the charm of transcendent excellence, or apologize for something worse than rashness. The reader is, therefore, assured, with all due promptitude, that his attention is not invited to a work of ART, but to a work of FACTS—Facts, terrible and almost incredible, it may be—yet FACTS, nevertheless.

Dictating that the autobiography subsumes ART for FACTS, the undisclosed writer deploys a phenomenology: The lived experience of blackness elucidates itself as a literal artifact (read: art-I-fact).[1] This chapter hopes to encounter the "I," somewhere in between art and fact, with the eye(s): Frederick Douglass, a figure invested in his subjectivity.

While this preface obliges reading the nameless EDITOR's words as FACTS, the second instance of sight and belief veers toward ART, even the speculative, as a methodology. James McCune Smith authors the autobiography's introduction; he lauds Douglass as a man to whom "mankind [should] pay him the tribute of their admiration" because "he raises himself from the lowest condition in society to the highest." Receiving "[t]he cordial and manly greetings of the British and Indian audiences in public, and the refinement and elegance of the social circles in which he mingled," Douglass is regarded "not only as an equal, but as a recognized man of *genius*." As the introduction ends, McCune Smith locates him at that artifactual nexus: "I asked William Whipper . . . whether he thought Mr. Douglass's power inherited from the Negroid, or from what is called the Caucasian side of his make-up? . . . he frankly answered, 'I must admit, although sorry to do so, that the Caucasian predominates.' . . . I almost agreed with him; but, *facts* narrated in the first part of this work, throw a different light on this interesting question. . . . In the absence of testimony from the Caucasian side, we must see what evidence is given on the *other side* of the house."[2] This (new) historicism sweeps the "house that race built" considering the "absence" on the "other side" of the nuclear household. Born Frederick Augustus Washington Bailey to "Harriet Bailey, daughter of Isaac, a freeman, and Betsey Bailey," he "was ignorant of the most elementary facts of his birth."[3] McCune Smith moves past his artful question to initiate a racialized fact-finding mission as Douglass leaves clues about the "other side" that is his mother.

This is perhaps the first encounter one has in the search, with Douglass, for that personal pronoun; ignorance of his nativity is most apparent when he frames his biological "house":

I say nothing of *father*, for he is shrouded in a mystery I have never been able to penetrate. Slavery does away with fathers, as it does away with families. Slavery has no use for either fathers or families, and its laws do not recognize their existence in the social arrangements of the plantation. When they *do* exist they are not the outgrowths of slavery, but are antagonistic to the system. The order of civilization is reversed here. . . . My father was a white man, or nearly white. . . . There was a whisper, that my master was my father; yet it was only a whisper, and I cannot say that I ever gave it credence. Indeed, I now have reason to think he was not; nevertheless, the fact remains, in all its glaring odiousness, that, by the laws of slavery, children, in all cases, are reduced to the condition of their mothers.[4]

"The Author's Parentage" showcases Douglass unpacking the byproducts of slavery through the (extra)ordinarily familial. This inanimate ideology "does away" with those its "laws" rhetorically purport to *serve and protect*. Disembodied, it enacts oppression through embodied agents, achieving personification by way of its "treacherous hand."[5] This bodying permits slavery skinning itself to effectively "kill" the paternal actor and his next of kin. Hence, Douglass, working through the nuances of vulnerability, infuses his discourse on enslavement with (a)scientific language and defers to the "Almighty."

The divine inoculates the oppressed with "germs of affection"; "in his wisdom and mercy," He "arms the helpless infant against the ills and vicissitudes of his lot" to ward off the perpetual illness of servitude; He dispenses "the tenderest affection . . . as a partial compensation to the mother for the pains and lacerations of her heart" when irrevocably severed from her progeny. This ART and FACTS approach diagrams how the institution "touches" him and those he loves; despite being "vaccinated," he concedes the extant catastrophe: "There is not, beneath the sky, an enemy to filial affection so destructive as slavery. It made my brothers and sisters strangers to me; it converted the mother that bore me, into a *myth*; it *shrouded* my father in *mystery*, and left me without an *intelligible beginning* in the world."[6] While these admissions are integral to Douglass's "I," dwelling on the maternal myth occasions an opportunity for "truth."

Nathan Irvin Huggins's biography of Douglass exemplifying a slave and citizen—him "bondaged," him "freedomed"—summarizes this autobiographer and the art he produces after facts. But such a titular dichotomy also engenders possibility in that his hybridity, and the (un)intelligibility of his unavailable-to-testify citizen-father, signals his mother as the default who

gifts him intellect. This "I" journey is double: If the autobiographical artifact is emblematic of the source, in this case Douglass, one excavates the
source of the source, an absence crafted by that very aesthetic imagination
as mythic: Harriet Bailey. His literary proclivities impute her hand *guiding*
his, even as he textualizes her life and his grandmother's, such that the autobiographies are maternal elegies.[7] Examining race and psychoanalysis in the
nineteenth century whereby Douglass theorizes said discourses; and tracing
his acuity through affect, "science fiction," and iconography when he emerges
as "sublime" and otherworldly in excess of his fight with Mr. Covey, I situate
him as an obvious "momma's boy" and her artifactual return.

"We, 'Other [Black] Victorians'" and Psychoanalysis

Despite African diasporic peoples' psychic lives predating its late nineteenth-
century European inception, psychoanalysis has privileged sexuality over
race as *the* subjectivizing analytic, disregarding the imbrications of black
life.[8] While these moves first isolate themselves in a part of the world Douglass only ever visits, his writing traffics in psychoanalytic sentiment, thus
making him protoFreudian; or, better still, Sigmund Freud becomes an apos-
tle of Douglass. That recent passage on slavery and its obliterative relations
among bondspersons typifies how mourning and melancholy relate to the
black psychosocial lifeworld. Douglass proves not only that his thinking is
precursory to said paradigms, but also that he enacts a counternarrative for
matrilineal reclamation. He presciently *blackens* psychoanalysis; his coloring
exposits the aporia.

Melanie Klein describes "melancholia" as "depression" in the index of *The
Psychoanalysis of Children* as "the change between high spirits and extreme
wretchedness, which is a characteristic of melancholic disorders, is regularly
found in children."[9] While I do not perpetuate her conflation, that "wretchedness" nod inaugurates itself long before Klein, or Frantz Fanon, via David
Walker: "the result of my observations has warranted the full and unshaken
conviction, that we, (coloured people of these United States,) are the most
degraded, *wretched*, and abject set of beings that ever lived since the world
began." Roughly a century prior to Klein, Walker, in his 1829 *Appeal*, surmises "high spirits" becoming abjection with relation to the pre- and postco-
lonial plight of black people in the States. He lays bare a racial psychoanalytic
through absolutist language: The "American project" of enslavement, under
which this "set" live, differs from foreign and bygone versions of servility
because this national "name and form of slavery" suspends the oppressed in

a constant state of limbo.[10] Douglass continues this "wretched" legacy when writing about the beating of his Aunt: "The scene here described was often repeated in the case of poor Esther, and her life, as I knew it, was one of wretchedness." Ironically experiencing such terror as a child, Douglass fore-runs Klein and concretizes the fear that his Aunt's fate "might be [his] next."[11] This predates Freud's "Mourning and Melancholia" in that "the loss of some abstraction which has taken the place of [a loved person], such as one's country, liberty, an ideal, and so on" brings on Douglass's, and others,' affection. Walker, then, describes black adults, and children, one could hesitantly claim as "depressed," regardless of Klein.[12] But to understand twentieth-century psychoanalysis, the thoughts of the nineteenth deserve airing. That is, before occupying "the modern," on either side of the pond, one must *address* where "'other [black] Victorians'" live.[13]

Douglass is a Victorian-era icon: The *My Bondage and My Freedom* frontispiece "illustrates Douglass's sublime and black aesthetic: there is an incongruity between his black body and his white hands; between the rich details of his body and the rough sketch of his fists; between the majestic orator and someone who rejects words for blows. His black aesthetic is also a characteristic male pose; his clenched fists suggest not only the defiance of the former slave but the self-sufficiency of the Victorian male" (fig. 1.1). The image records subjectivity—an ego split yet inseparable—and portends psychoanalytic introjection as he will identify with his mother through photographic anamnesis.[14] Douglass is similarly Victorian via his autobiography and George Eliot's *Daniel Deronda*.

While the epigraph of book 1, chapter 1 in Eliot's novel—a metaphor regarding time and science whereby the in-between of these polarities is "the less accurate grandmother Poetry"—conflates ART and FACTS, another moment gives pause: At the end of *Daniel Deronda*, one learns of the protagonist's "mixed-race" parentage; born to Jewish parents (a mother who "loved the life of [her] art," singing and acting, a "money-changing and banking" father, and a grandfather touted as a "clever physician"), he is raised by and as an Englishman. But his parental narration is telling: "'You lost your father and mother when you were quite a little one; that is why I take care of you.' Daniel then straining to discern something in that early twilight, had a dim sense of having been kissed very much, and surrounded by thin, cloudy, scented drapery, till his fingers caught in something hard, which hurt him, and he began to cry." This ostensibly mimics Douglass: "I never saw my mother, to know her as such, more than four or five times in my life; and each of these times was very short in duration and at night. . . . I do not recollect of ever

FIGURE 1.1.

seeing my mother by the light of day. She was with me in the night. She
would lie down with me, and get me to sleep, but long before I waked she
was gone." Speculatively, 1876 Eliot could have encountered 1845 Douglass
since the latter's autobiography trafficked in Europe: A second edition of *The
Narrative of the Life of Frederick Douglass, An American Slave, Written by
Himself* was "published in Dublin by Webb and Chapman in 1846, with a new
preface and appendix," as well as an 1860 translation of the second autobiography into German titled *Sklaverei und Freiheit*.[15] Nevertheless, this may
glimpse the lives of "'other Victorians.'"

This Foucauldian paradigm is a historiography that sits with the nation-
state conferring pockets of the populace to misery. *The History of Sexuality,
Volume I* wrestles with the repercussions of bodies being "outed," riffing on
the libidinal in psychoanalysis—"The loss of a love object is an excellent op-

portunity for the ambivalence in love-relationships to make itself effective and come into the open."[16] By sussing out nuclear (war)fare under one roof, espousing the gravity of "love-relationships," one spatializes the home as the hub of melancholy:

> For a long time, the story goes, we supported a Victorian regime, and we continue to be dominated by it even today. Thus the image of the imperial prude is emblazoned on our restrained, mute and hypo-critical sexuality. . . . Codes regulating the coarse, the obscene, and the indecent were quite lax compared to those of the nineteenth century. It was a time of direct gestures, shameless discourse, and open transgressions. . . . Sexuality was carefully confined; it moved into the *home*. The conjugal family took custody of it and absorbed it into the serious function of reproduction. . . . silence became the rule. The legitimate and procreative couple laid down the law. The couple imposed itself as model, enforced the norm, safeguarded the truth, and reserved the right to speak while retaining the principle of secrecy.[17]

The puerile melancholy of Kleinian discourse may be a generational curse. The penumbra cast by the shining of Victorian regimentation finds its sunset in compulsory missionary work routinized in humble abodes: This diction— "codes," "regulating," "lax," "confined," "moved," "conjugal," "custody," "the rule," "the law," "imposed," "enforced," "safeguarded," "the right"—marks the home as a phantasmagoric small-scale prison industrial *duplex*. Put another way, "*Home*: Women-headed households, serial monogamy, flight of men, old women alone, technology of domestic work, paid homework, re-emergence of home sweat-shops, home-based businesses and [pre-]tele-commuting, [non-]electronic cottage, urban homelessness, migration, module architecture, reinforced (simulated) nuclear family, intense domestic violence"; or the informatics of domination.[18] Silence and secrecy as social modes affirm public texts becoming private bodies, forwarding family units as "mad"—the *déjà-là* of death. This alludes to Freud because "[t]he most remarkable characteristic of melancholia . . . is its tendency to change round into mania."[19] This framework for Victorian psychosis obliges the laboring subject, the mother, to develop an odd bond with the fruit of her womb as an act of *labor power*.

Though this Marxist motif expresses an individual's capacity for capitalist productivity, changing the diction around "labor" evokes the generative in that "the most ancient system in which the idea of blood-relationship was embodied, was a system of kinship through females only."[20] Despite the claim of feminine consanguinity being foundational to the building and propagation of "family ties," these homebound affections are simultaneous with and microcosmic of the greater scheme to contrive the nation-state. Slavery's "treacherous hand" transmogrifies to tentacles: the "plantation is a *little nation of its own*, having its own language, its own rules, regulations and customs. The laws and institutions of the state apparently *touch it nowhere*. The troubles arising here, are not settled by the civil power of the state. The overseer is generally accuser, judge, jury, advocate and executioner. The criminal is always dumb. The overseer attends to all sides of the case." Douglass indicts the plantation as an autoincorporated potentate in miniature, localizing and extending itself as the extrajudicial instrument of bondage's tactility. The overseer thus registers as *the hand of the king*, if not the king himself. Race-ing this discourse, one notes black women's labors: "the lines of division between the market and the household which distinguished the public and the domestic and divided productive and reproductive labor for propertied whites does not hold when describing the enslaved and the carceral landscape of plantation. Reproduction is tethered to the making of human commodities and in service of the marketplace." Slaves' productive labor—"work"—interlocking with their reproductive labor—"giving life"—"colors" psychoanalysis as the black feminine/maternal was, and still might be, "the belly of the world."[21]

In spite of the nation-state employing "citizenry" on the frontlines of mass production, said bodies must first be *conceived*, thus the "master forcibly coupled men and women with the aim of producing the maximum number of healthy child-slaves . . . the profound traumas the black woman must have experienced when she had to surrender her child-bearing to alien and predatory economic interests."[22] And while the suggestion is that these concepts shifted from "open transgressions" to being "carefully confined" in the home, the black woman experiences imaginative prolapse—what was interior is exterior, protruding out as an architectural exoskeleton, an open floor plan. Her home, corporeal and residential, not only is rendered violable, penetrable by the highest bidder under the strictures of that marketplace, but also what she produces out of it is commodified in that selfsame public sphere. This is a newfangled interpretation of *home economics*—"the slave exists out of the world and outside the house."[23]

The formulations surrounding these political and sexual abuses of power solidify that although the "erotic" finds shelter in the "comfort" of the homestead during the nineteenth century, in the slave economy, the public conveyance of privacy projects children being born of human-subhuman *knowing*, "the unexceptional liaison of enslaved women having babies with their zookeepers," that is, enslaved bodies, prior to and following the seventeenth century, "'made a display of themselves,'" and to the extent that this "taint of abnormality" did "pay a penalty" for the exposure.[24] Douglass comprehends this: "Men do not love those who remind them of their sins— unless they have a mind to repent—and the mulatto child's face is a standing accusation against him who is master and father to the child. What is still worse, perhaps, such a child is a constant offense to the wife. She hates its very presence, and when a slaveholding woman hates, she wants not means to give that hate telling effect."[25] Signaling the coming to light of what happens "in the dark," these slaves composite a theory: As problems of social and sinful excess, this flesh provokes a perplexing negation because in their occupation as spaces of limit(ation), they are not self-possessed, even if what they produce *in* and *through* labor fosters the chronotope of modernity, a space of limitlessness as human possibility. This is symptomatic of *habeas viscus*: "The conjoining of flesh and habeas corpus in the compound . . . brings into view an articulated assemblage of the human (viscus/flesh) borne of political violence, while at the same time not losing sight of the different ways the law pugnaciously adjudicates who is deserving of personhood and who is not (habeas)."[26] This disallows the "laboring" body the privilege to "enjoy" its productivity because "[w]hen the commodity labour power no longer exists, the human container that would have possessed this labour power endures as an empty shell . . . an inert fleshy materiality that marks the lack of labour power, a purely physical existence without a subjectivity . . . the phenotypical attribute comes to mediate and determine the form of social existence of this human container once it is integrated into the class relation . . . 'blackness' comes to naturalise this lack."[27] All of this requires locating Douglass's matrilineage collectively experiencing generational object losses.

Given this recent zoology, those liaisons suppose that "[t]he bastard offspring of enslaved black mothers and obscure white fathers/masters . . . fashion nonoedipal dramas of slavery which reveal nuclear relations as a less significant matter to the slavocracy than the bourgeois imperatives of ownership, dominance, commodity, and (re)production . . . the bastard/mulatto status . . . would appear to figure also as a trope for the constitutional illegitimacy of African American subjecthood."[28] Douglass theoretically ("[slavery] shrouded my father in mystery") and practically ("slavery does away with fathers") charts this bastardizing (and knowing the religiocultural framework existent in his life, this account is equally the ethnographically ethnic redux of Egyptian Hagar and her son Ishmael—a child *sired* by a Hebrew who preferred not to openly confront his "sin"; and his wife who hated that newborn's presence, enacting hatred toward mother and child with telling effects). Yet if psychoanalysis intimates maternal (in)significance expediting autonomy, is this rumored bastard/mulatto legible regardless of living "without an intelligible beginning in the world"?[29] His narrativizing alludes to his precursory psychoanalytic, providing some semblance of a response to this provocation.

In the first two chapters of *My Bondage and My Freedom*, Douglass sustains a reading of slavery superimposing the grandmother as maternal proxy. Betsey Bailey rears him during his early childhood, and he later discusses leaving her custody to live on another plantation: "This I refused to do, preferring to stay with grandmamma. I could not help feeling that our being there boded no good to me. Grandmamma looked sad. She was soon to *lose another object of affection*, as she had lost many before. I knew she was unhappy, and *the shadow fell from her brow on me*, though I knew not the cause."[30] The threat of separation from the maternal stand-in elicits anxiety as Douglass internalizes and externalizes her affective posture. Attentive to this lexical display, one testifies to Freud as Douglassonian: The autobiographer already channels a lost love object but construed in reverse—he, the child, arrives to be "some abstraction" under the aegis of the "visible institution," which is to say, "In its depiction of traumatic events, African American literature often inverts the melancholic scenario: not only may the survivor become melancholic for a lost object, but the lost object, or a personified history, can become melancholic for the survivor." Douglass foretells a narrative tic that will pervade black writing in the twentieth and twenty-first centuries, no different than him heralding psychoanalysis before it projects its own limiting shadow.[31] And speaking of "the shadow," he casts what Freud will pen: "The object cathexis proved to have little power of resistance and was brought to an end. But the free libido was not displaced on to another object; it was withdrawn into the ego . . . to establish an *identification* of the ego with the abandoned object. Thus the **shadow of the object** fell upon the ego, and the latter could henceforth be judged by a special agency, as though it were an object, the forsaken object." In this discussion of object-choice, wherein the affected one's investment of libidinal energy is the hinge for how one reconciles loss, this psychic labor power, this "special agency," completes itself ahead of enacting "revenge on the original object" as an offshoot of melancholy.[32] Yet Douglass undoes the future-as-episteme because by identifying with, introjecting, his grandmother's umbra, he does not seek revenge but relationship, albeit one that centers love; he realizes he will be forsaken, melancholy, when that natal sever occurs.

Grandmamma may not constitute grandson's "intelligible beginning," but their disruptive departure strikes an intractable ending he deems "unhappy." The shadow moves reciprocally, not in one direction, as this love must survive amid wretchedness, that is, Douglass's veiling conjures him a *man half in shadow*—a reflection from one side of the house, his rumored-about master-father; and the other from the black feminine/maternal, his psychoanalytic ground. And if the death drive "splits the very ego into one component that is unaware of such drive while being affected by it (that is, its unconscious component) and another component that struggles against it (that is, the megalomaniac ego that negates castration and death and fantasizes immortality)," does this shadow legitimate that frontispiece where whiteness (the unconscious) wrestles blackness (the megalomaniacal)? Under that tenor of intelligibility, my Victorian periodizing may be salient in that by "charting the vicissitudes of . . . manhood and imitation, we can start by asking what is the link here between a desire to identify, assumed to be already as the root of a drive to copy and assimilate, and the desire to be a black man? Does this lead to white and black identities becoming *distorted, imagistic equivalents* of one another? A projected screen where phobias and fantasies meet?"[33] This outlines the labor of slavery.

A hostile personage that quantifies and qualifies loss, the institution, in and through its own wicked engagement, manipulates black flesh to *love folks to death*: The slave, kept alive to accomplish the erection, financial and social, of the system, is disposable, a perishable good ripe for being discarded after meeting a prescribed end; said discarding can be an "exchange" between plantations as Douglass jars his love for Grandmamma, an affective preserve for his psychic experience of her "death," albeit premature. This hastens mourning and melancholy because the enslaved emerges through declension as an interchangeable part since the administrators of this "little nation" "got a buncha ideas, and really horrible crap between them and anything meaningful."[34] They cannot translate their thoughts except as nonsense because as taskmasters, they manage the on-the-job training of themselves. Some learn to litigate; others love to lose. Thus, as a de facto psychoanalyst, one diagnoses Douglass's melancholy-cum-death drive as compounded by loss because

> [t]he symbol is established through the negation (*Verneinung*) of the loss, but a disavowal (*Verleugnung*) of the symbol produces a psychic inscription as close as one can get to hatred and a hold over the lost object. That is what one deciphers in the blanks of discourse, **vocalizations,**

rhythms, syllables of words that have been devitalized and need to be restored by the analyst on the basis of an apprehended depression. . . . It is indeed a production of the split ego, made up of fantasy and fiction—in short, the **level of imagination**, the **level of writing**—which bears witness to the hiatus, blank, or spacing that constitutes death for the unconscious.[35]

This "hatred and a hold over the lost object," with psychic inscription as a close complement, does not necessarily, or solely, reveal the maternal for Douglass. Rather, the program that makes his mother a myth is the culprit for his hatred and proliferates his affective "hold": slavery—the "hand" he abhors as it handles him. Yet what follows is an attempt at the recuperation of objects by choice. A restoration of vocalizations, rhythms, and syllables of words that are fantasy and fiction made real as melancholy invites the performative. Douglass's level of imagination bearing witness to the black aesthetic and black feminine/maternal that were given hiatus, blanked out, spaced out, by the false Almighty. A conscientious effort to think the unconscious to death and begin again, revealing his genius as imparted through maternity.

Look Like an Egyptian; or, Frederick Douglass, the Pan-African Machinist

Frederick Douglass has the blues. While calling him a bluesman is certainly anachronistic, his "blues criticism" foreruns said work across genre, including that of Langston Hughes, Ralph Ellison, LeRoi Jones/Amiri Baraka, James H. Cone, Angela Y. Davis, and Daphne A. Brooks. His blues transforming to blues music, his blues idiom as per Albert Murray, amplifies "wild songs," even as he sings "to drown [his] sorrow." (He further confesses his vocality: "[Covey] was a poor singer, and *mainly relied on me for raising the hymn* for the family, and when I failed to do so, he was thrown into much confusion." Douglass, the crooner.)[36]

At the end of chapter 2 in *The Narrative of the Life of Frederick Douglass, An American Slave, Written by Himself,* he speaks about how "fellow-slaves," "peculiarly enthusiastic" to receive their "monthly allowance" at the Great House Farm, "would make the dense old woods, for miles around, reverberate with their wild songs, revealing at once the highest joy and the deepest sadness." He continues theorizing this wilderness wildness:

I did not, when a slave, understand the deep meaning of those rude and apparently incoherent songs. I myself was within the circle; so that

I neither saw nor heard as those without might see and hear. . . . they were tones loud, long, and deep . . . The hearing of those wild notes always depressed my spirit, and filled me with ineffable sadness. . . . and while I am writing these lines, an expression of feeling has already found its way down my cheek. . . . Those songs still follow me, to deepen my hatred of slavery, and quicken my sympathies for my brethren in bonds. . . . The songs of the slave represent the sorrows of his heart; and he is relieved by them, only as an aching heart is relieved by tears. . . . The singing of a man cast away upon a desolate island might be as appropriately considered as evidence of contentment and happiness as the singing of the slave; the songs of the one and the other are prompted by the same emotion.[37]

Douglass voices and names his object-driven hatred. Yet this odium affectively demonstrates him being a harbinger of psychoanalysis: "Douglass positions himself as both subject and object of slavery, both *analyst and analysand*, by differentiating between two forms of signification, located in the spaces both 'inside' and 'without' the 'circle' of song." This shapely invocation is intriguing since Freud later intuits mania, brought about by melancholia, as "circular insanity."[38] But when Douglass stands from without, apart from, the circle, he gains insight, testifying to the sinister nature of his subjection. However, it may not be that he steps outside the circle, that being, his spectating does not depend on his ontic status; rather, the border is porous, letting him, and the reader-as-analyst, play in and out of that space to erode the shape usually unbroken.[39]

Douglass envisions the sonic wild from within and without; his auricular memory brings him back to that penetrable barrier as he cries to keep from languishing. Metaphorizing the enslaved as a kind of castaway, while rehearing "[t]hose African persons in the 'Middle Passage' were literally suspended in the oceanic," he weds "contentment and happiness" with sorrow singing.[40] While it is befuddling whether this rhetorical matrimony is signifying ("I have often been utterly astonished, since I came to the north, to find persons who could speak of the singing, among slaves, as evidence of their contentment and happiness. It is impossible to conceive of a greater mistake. Slaves sing most when they are most unhappy.") or similitude, if the latter is correct, is Douglass *playing the fool*, that is, is this "same emotion," the economy of melancholy-turned-mania, a portent of Freudian "joy," Lacanian *jouissance*— "the pleasure made available to the subject through the mediation of discourse, the pleasure availed this subject by his or her ability to ground a psychic sense of the self as coherent, autonomous, and self-controlled through the use of the mechanisms of language and fantasy"?[41] This might clarify the permeable partition because affectively encircled, he literally writes himself out of that circuitously lunatic hole, presaging in the nineteenth century what Édouard Glissant in the twentieth calls "poetics of relation." Invoking the circular, Douglass scores the *shape of blackness*, and its aesthetics, in that "[t]he circle opens up once more, at the same time that it builds in volume . . . aesthetics, by means of which we make our imaginary concrete, with the opposite intention, always bring us back from the infinities of the universe to the definable poetics of our world. . . . Thus, we go the open circle of our relayed aesthetics, our unflagging politics. We leave the matrix abyss and the immeasurable abyss for this other one in which we wander without becoming lost."[42] Douglass, transitioning from the "dense old woods" to the presumptive desk where he writes while weeping, mobilizes the abyss as replete, voluminous, with poesy—this is *blues epistemology*.

This theorem is "a longstanding African American tradition of explaining reality and change. This form of explanation finds its origins in the processes of African American cultural construction within, and resistance to, the antebellum plantation regime . . . the blues epistemology is embedded, necessary, and reflective. It is a self-referential explanatory tradition."[43] To be an acolyte of this thought process is to be aware of one's interior while critical of one's surroundings. Douglass's blues idiom outlines a distinct experience colored by that couplet of spatial peculiarity and affective retort; this duo parallels what has been expressed as a "bloc"—an "alliance, a bargain, or a contract between disparate ethnic, gender, class, and other elements." Two blocs comprise the blues epistemology, mutually feeding each other in the cause of convening collectivities: the plantation and blues blocs. With the intersection of common sensibility and artful pragmatism, these blocs are black working-class expressions of lofty goals. And if "[t]he blues are the cries of a new society being born," such an outburst validates the guise of the maternal and performative.[44] Douglass's first autobiography is a foreword, is progenitive, to this episteme. The blocs are artifactual, circling us back to the black feminine/maternal as the autobiographer's imagination bears out restoring his lost object(s).

The artistic and factitious impose a force on *My Bondage and My Freedom*; the performance that proceeds from such is discernible through McCune Smith's introduction. Evidencing the other side of the genetic house, he cites Douglass speaking about the "power and spirit" of his grandmother. Then in the middle of the paragraph, quoting Douglass, he recounts, "'I learned, after my mother's death, that she could read, and that she was the *only* one of all the slaves and colored people in Tuckahoe who enjoyed that advantage. How she acquired this knowledge, I know not, for Tuckahoe is the last place in the world where she would be apt to find facilities for learning.'" Last, he references Douglass viewing a drawn bust in James Cowles Prichard's *The Natural History of Man* (fig. 1.2) that resembles his mother. And right as the introduction concludes, McCune Smith *changes the joke and slips the yoke*:

> The head alluded to is copied from the statue of Ramses the Great, an Egyptian king of the nineteenth dynasty. . . . The nearness of its resemblance to Mr. Douglass' mother, rests upon the evidence of his memory, and judging from his almost marvelous feats of recollection of forms and outlines recorded in this book, this testimony may be admitted. These facts show that for his energy, perseverance, eloquence, invective, sagacity, and wide sympathy, he is indebted to his negro blood. The very marvel of his style would seem to be a development of that other marvel,—how his mother learned to read. The versatility of talent which he yields, in common with [Alexandre] Dumas, Ira Aldridge, and Miss Greenfield, would seem to be the result of the grafting of Anglo-Saxon on good, original, negro stock. If the friends of "Caucasus" choose to claim, for that region, what remains after this analysis—to wit: combination—they are welcome to it. They will forgive me for reminding them that the term "Caucasian" is dropped by recent writers of Ethnology; for the people about Mount Caucasus, are, and have ever been, Mongols. The great "white race" now seek paternity, according to Dr. Pickering, in Arabia—"Arida Nutrix" of the best breed of horses &c. Keep on gentlemen; you will find yourselves in Africa, by-and-by. The Egyptians, like the Americans, were a *mixed race*, with some negro blood circling around the throne, as well as in the mud hovels.[45]

This virtuosic passage foments that Negroid versus Caucasian brouhaha as McCune Smith rebukes his logic, and Whipper's: The black maternal is the locus of intellect and its afterglow. Inserting Douglass in the genealogical line of African Diasporic genius invokes transnationalism, citing the cradle of epistemic civilization to confirm geological and anthropological discourses regarding mitochondrial DNA; the Mount Caucasus construal foretells the Afro-Asiatic man in the politics and theology of the Nation of Islam; and the mud-hovels convention propagates Egypt as the site where the once-and-future king—drawn from the Nile, exposed as a child of *the help*, and

FIGURE 1.2. "Ramses II" in James Cowles Prichard, *The Natural History of Man; Comprising Inquiries into the Modifying Influence of Physical and Moral Agencies on the Different Tribes of the Human Family,* 1843.

Rameses. It is thought by Mr. Martin * to resemble the second Egyptian type described by Blumenbach, namely, that which approaches the Hindoo.

Fig. 48.

Head of Rameses.

In this figure, it is observed that "the general expression is calm and dignified; the forehead is somewhat flat; the eyes are widely separated from each other; the nose is elevated, but with spreading nostrils; the ears are high; the lips large, broad, and turned out, with sharp edges; in which points there is a deviation from the European countenance."†

* See Mr. Martin's "Natural History of Mammiferous Animals," &c. 8vo. Plates. London, 1841.

† Ibid.

put upon to make bricks without straw—entreats his former office, "Let my people go!" Hence, "[a]s the Exodus-inspired title . . . might suggest, [Douglass] crafts his identity as a black Moses."[46] This self-collapsing into that Hebrew-cum-Egyptian overlays his travels to Egypt thirty-plus years after the second autobiography.

A multicity journey with a Rome layover, the trek metanarrates romantic antiquity and confirms the West having "important resources in Africa . . . he presents a more progressive narrative of all roads leading both to and from Africa." However, Rome, not Egypt, is where he reifies McCune Smith's "mixed-race" categorization. Though this scenario marks certain hypotheses as "facts," he falls into "condescending" readings of Egypt; this unease offers Africa as an otherland, not the motherland, "a horizon of alterity against which Douglass's sense of himself as a patriotic American can be calibrated." This Americanness vis-à-vis royal Africanity characterizes him as a "'Representative American man' . . . continually transforming himself."[47] With this African voyage, the completion of his *birthright*, preceding twentieth-century contrivances, discursive and otherwise, of "Diaspora," he conveys all roads leading from and to America and projects a designation still-contested: being African(-)American.[48]

Nonetheless, Douglass's mother's readerly potential for leaving a legacy facilitates his "I" between art and fact. He enjoys an "advantage" through this forebear who, in the absence of goo-goos and ga-gas, vocalizes still small feet that travel some twelve miles—one way, under lunar shimmer—as the original route summary. The "very little communication" Harriet has with Frederick when she arrives may have been her retelling of once-read bedtime stories; or, like the reverberations in the dense woods, she may have tuned her marathon with lullabies rehearsed ahead of putting her child to sleep.[49] This foreshadows not only Douglass's affinity for words, but also the renovation of the "other side" of the house blueprinted by architect McCune Smith. If this cultural Egyptology is the impetus to read his genius through her literate singularity, unearthed by a detour through aural memories and an image—ART and FACTS—a new query arises: What side of the chromosomal house unveils itself when Douglass "reads" Covey? To examine which side of Frederick Bailey surfaces, we first peruse a chance meeting.[50]

After suffering Covey's brutality one Friday afternoon, Bailey flees to the woods and "falls in" with his friend Sandy Jenkins on Saturday: "He told me, with great solemnity, I must go back to Covey; but that before I went, I must go with him into another part of the woods, where there was a certain root, which, if I would take some of it with me, carrying it always on my right side, would render it impossible for Mr. Covey, or any other white man, to whip me." When Bailey returns Sunday, Covey speaks to him "very kindly" and charges him to do his "necessary work," making him "half inclined to think the ROOT to be something more than [he] at first had taken it to be." The root reroutes punishment as a *phantom link*—"a 'conjure doctor,' with a strong attachment to folk traditions and an African heritage," Jenkins reveals a Pan-African retention, psychosomatic and homeopathic. But Monday, "the virtue of the ROOT [is] fully tested" to prove if "escape" happens with impunity.[51]

Though Huggins abridges the particularities of this tussle, the autobiographies relay it being "nearly two hours"; Covey enlists his cousin, William Hughes; and those who "refused to help," Bill Smith and Caroline, are also slaves.[52] Though Bailey subdues Covey while his "property" stand by idly, "his move from being crushed by slavery to asserting his rights as a man was a communal victory as well as an individual one."[53] Still, Bailey recalls (fig. 1.3):

> Covey sneaked into the stable, in his peculiar *snake-like way,* and seizing me suddenly, he brought me to the stable floor. . . . I gave a sudden *spring,* (my two day's rest had been of much service to me,). . . . The fighting *madness* had come upon me, and I found my strong fingers firmly attached to the throat of my cowardly tormentor; as heedless of consequences, at the moment, as though we stood as *equals before the law.* The very color of the man was forgotten. I felt *as supple as a cat,* and was ready for the snakish creature at every turn. . . . Covey and I had now been skirmishing *before daybreak,* till now, that the sun was almost shooting his beams over the eastern woods, and we were still at it.[54]

All of this incites numerous ponderings. To begin, is this the "transcendence" of race through the erasure of "the very color" of one's adversary, and the self-cum-challenger? Also, this title match is timed toward the dawn, the moment night is at its darkest and a new day is on the precipice of breaking (free). Bailey performs, akin to Langston Hughes, dream variations, flinging his arms wide in some place of the sun, dancing and whirling till the quick day has begun.[55] Personifying the sun and gendering it male, like the Almighty, he presumes Nature to be in control as it beholds those out of it. Meanwhile, the darkness, the blackness, of night, and its movements, has theoretical traction as an elegy requires our attention.

In "Frederick Douglass: 1817–1895," Hughes pens:

> Douglass was someone who,
> Had he walked with wary foot

FIGURE 1.3. "An Original AoM Comic: Frederick Douglass—How a Slave Was Made a Man," 2013. (Courtesy of Ted Slampyak and "The Art of Manliness" website.)

And frightened tread,
From very indecision
Might be dead,
Might have lost his soul,
But instead decided to be bold
And capture every street
On which he set his feet,
To route each path
Toward freedom's goal,
To make each highway
Choose *his* compass' choice,[56]

Transiting from "indecision" to his decisiveness to "be bold," from anxiety to anticipation vis-à-vis peripatetic action—"Had he walked with wary foot / And frightened tread" eventuating to "capture every street / On which he set his feet"—mirrors his mother's nocturnal ambulation. He is not only her cypher, but also an exemplar for those who read the poem "in *Liberator* in 1966 at the height of the civil rights movement."[57] Hughes retroactively elongates a protest tradition that traverses chronological boundaries to showcase Douglass's self-making as a telos of liberty, marking the publishing venue as kismet. Reading that fighting darkness persists.

Bailey the cat is occupationally disposed in the blackness of a morning yet birthed when a snake interrupts his labor; "Covey had 'the cunning of the serpent' and the craftiness of the fox. . . . Among blacks he was known as 'the snake.' . . . A few inches shorter than Frederick, he was thin and wiry, with small green-gray eyes that were set deep into his forehead. Instead of hissing, he spoke from the side of his mouth in a low growl . . . like a dog 'when an attempt is made to take a bone from him.'" Further citation of him as "well versed in the 'art' of slave discipline" exposes the breadth and depth of Bailey's literacy through his use of allusion and simile to account for the reptilian.[58] The institution of slavery, latitudinous in power, may be more *visual* than visible. The economy of optics/photography wholly relates to the forthcoming reading as everything hinges on the spring.

Bailey "springs" to action against the serpentine because although rejuvenated from a two-day respite, he *senses* a rally to madness in the nascent light of day. This cat reacts "in a flash." Under the auspice of a dream, he, the *Revenant*, is a hypothetical interlocutor for the photographic method: From the vantage of the *Spectator*, we also become the *Operator*, a reading public engendered to deconstruct this *Spectrum*.[59] Visualized in this momentous wrestling is Jacob's tropology to Israel as "[t]he paradox of subjection implies a paradox of referentiality: namely, that we must refer to what does not yet exist . . . we seek to account for how the *subject comes to be*. That this figure is itself a 'turn' is, rhetorically, performatively *spectacular*; 'turn' translates from the Greek sense of 'trope.' Thus the trope of the turn both indicates and exemplifies the tropological status of the *gesture*."[60] Conceding the literal turning in this fight, and the black literary hermeneutic to relate the Bible to these historiographies, one regards this conversion apropos as Bailey grasps for, provides a glimpse of, his "Black freedom." Years after this struggle, which hastens his "I" in that "[t]he battle with Mr. Covey was the turning-point in my career as a slave . . . the *triumph* was a full compensation for whatever else might follow, even death itself," Bailey becomes Douglass, reportage of what the subjected "comes to be."[61] (Despite this self-determinative naming, a series of events prior to it are expedited by Douglass's first wife, Anna Murray; born free, she sews a sailor's disguise for his train to New York City, which she likely funded, and there they get married under the gauze of "freedom."[62])

This turning is coincident with Jacob-cum-Frederick's nomenclatural lineage since his grandfather's name is Isaac, the only "father figure" Douglass would have known whose kinship bond mirrors that of his daughter: "As a sawyer working at various jobs away from his wife's cabin, where the children lived, Isaac may have appeared there only at night, leaving at dawn, becoming a fleeting presence in a little boy's memory."[63] There is also an eye-minded transition that rehearses the revenant: When Douglass acquires literacy and contracts melancholy, he admits, "I have often wished myself a beast. I preferred the condition of the *meanest reptile* to my own." Later becoming a cat, strangling "Satan [who] ain't nothin' but a snake in the grass," he shape-shifts through the ruse of animality—genius at work, reminiscent of another oneiric variation as night comes gently, tenderly, the precedent to daylight when he lands a cow yard TKO. A moment when "[e]ducation brings the slave, who is death, back from death, back from the undiscovered country, back to life."[64] "Seizing [him] suddenly," Covey elicits his turning as a slave blending in with the dark—is he an *invisible man*?—becomes a cat staging a sun dance.

This feline talk feels serendipitous, given the heading for this chapter section, insofar as Egyptians deified cats because of their "peculiar 'aloofness.'" During a 1979 Brooklyn Museum Expedition, trekkers beheld a statue of the animal, sacred to the goddess Mut, at the deity's Karnak precinct: "this seated animal could represent either a lion or a cat, but in the partly preserved hieroglyphic inscription the word *myt* (cat) can be read, so that it is reasonably sure that it originally represented a cat." Douglass calling himself a cat links precisely to its Egyptian reverence. The proximity of that hiero-glyphic inscription, *myt*, to what he calls his mother, *myth*, reveals the "hold over the lost object" producing that inscription, psychic and physical. An addendum to this mythos analogizes feline-human relations: "When a man smells of myrrh his wife is a cat before him. When a man is suffering his wife is a lioness before him."[65] The wife as feline shape-shifter translates to the mother who occupies similar states for her shape-shifting son as he requires a lioness when he succumbs to melancholy and a cat when he reeks of genius.

This ocular attention, reading Douglass's words in the typical sense as he *reads* Covey in the contemporary sense, aligns with affective photography in a sublime mode:

> Douglass attacked slavery and racism by championing the picture-making proclivity of all humans. In so doing he emphasized not only humanity's common origins, but the *superiority of imagination to reason*. The "full identity of man with nature . . . is our chief distinction from all other beings on earth and the source of our greatest achievements." While "dogs and elephants are said to possess" the capacity of reason, only humans sought to recreate nature and portray both the "inside soul" and the "outside world" through such "artificial means" as pictures. Making pictures required imagination. . . . The power of the imagination . . . was "a sublime, prophetic, and all-creative power." It linked humans to "the Eternal sources of life and creation," and allowed them to create and appreciate pictures as accurate representations of some greater reality. The power of the imagination helped people realize their sublime ideals in an imperfect world.[66]

Notice that a dog—Mr. Covey, as designated previously—has the "capacity of reason," but cannot impart the interior-exterior duality as a matter of *wholeness*; a cat-as-man presumably can. Though Douglass likely did not read Immanuel Kant, they synchronize rhetorically because the "superiority of imagination to reason" is what the philosopher would call objective finality.[67] For Douglass, to be a slave-made-man occurs over and against American racecraft. Certain not to imbricate the textual with the photographic, I surmise the pictures he captures with his words exhibiting his calculus of what it means to be, with its limits and excesses, "human." Said differently, instead of "Douglass . . . getting out of animality *by going through it*" or, contingent on an 1873 speech, his "hierarchized conception of feeling and capacity, even in its deployment as empathetic identification with animals, actually rehears[ing] the assumptive logics of racial subjection," what if *My Bondage and My Freedom*, and the first-autobiography occasion when he learns to read, actually conveys: You have seen how a man was made an *animal*; you shall see how an animal is made a "man"—embrace animality, animalize your maker?[68]

Frederick Augustus Washington (Bailey) Douglass is chimeric—cat, invisible, slave-made-man. Listen as he deploys his imagination: "Douglass found a mechanical analogy that explained how time itself was out of joint.... 'The cause [of our troubles] is deeper down than sections, slaveholders, or abolitionists. These are but the hands of the clock. The *moving machinery is behind the face*. The machinery moves not because of the hands, but the hands because of the machinery. To make the hands go right you must make the machinery go right."[69] As Douglass convicts his "home" of its limiting machinic impulses, I subvert his quotation: While deciding that like the elusive EDITOR, there is an investment in *deep time*, a specter "out of joint," who constitutes this "machinery"?[70]

If Douglass "clocks" the United States, broken or not, who in his oratory would have been moving the hands of the apparatus but the enslaved—what Harriet Jacobs, juxtaposed to Shana L. Redmond, coins "God-breathing machines": "chattel property . . . made to do double duty as man and machine through relations of intimacy and violence as well as facility and brute labor"—no matter what "the face" conveyed? Essentially, "whites simply treated their 'slaves' like pieces of machinery. But machinery that could be whipped if it didn't produce enough. Fast enough. Machinery that could be mutilated, raped, killed, if the desire arose. Machinery that could be cheated, cheerfully, without a trace of guilt."[71] Reduced to mechanisms on a conveyor belt, pushing this American project along to "completion" only to cycle back around and repeat the same process, regardless of wear and tear, these laborers are employed under hazardous work conditions. Like a womb, this *assembly line* operates as "a factory (producing blackness as abjection much like the slave ship's hold and the prison)" while also manufacturing worldly goods—is this not ART and FACTS, even as the marking of time happens TOO LATE, and the confirmation of interchangeable parts?[72] This clockface machinery could be doublespeak in that one should not easily presume Douglass is talking about "the brain" of the object alone. He could be referring to its "eye," individual and collective, despite occupational austerity. Extending this optometric consciousness, his eyes once recalled pharaonic royalty in an anthropological text and announced: I see me as her, the king.[73]

Related to this self-fashioning, the root Douglass carries is relegated to his right side, the site of authority in Judeo-Christian lore.[74] This poultice pierces his internal man of Kantian "perfection," endowing his body indefatigability. And yet, this cat, after the struggle, uses linguistic "tools" to "dismantle" the "master's house" in the cause of his own revival: "It was a resurrection from the dark and pestiferous tomb of slavery, to the heaven of comparative freedom. . . . I had reached the point, at which I was not afraid to die. This spirit made me a freeman in *fact*, while I remained a slave in form. When a slave cannot be flogged he is more than half free . . . and he is really '*a power on earth.*'"[75] Melismatic of Philippians 2:5–8 (New Living Translation)—"You must have the same attitude that Christ Jesus had. Though he was God, he did not think of equality with God as something to cling to. Instead, he gave up his divine privileges; he took the humble position of a slave and was born as a human being. When he appeared in human form, he humbled himself in obedience to God and died a criminal's death on a cross"—Douglass, death-driven, self-identifies as "divine":

> William C. Coffin, a New Bedford abolitionist, called upon a young black man from town to stand and tell his story. Frederick Douglass stood and addressed the crowd. He was an arresting figure, in his early twenties, over six feet in height, robust in frame, forceful and direct in manner. He was physically attractive, but it was what he had to say that galvanized his audience. . . . What was possible for him was also *potential* within other black men and women. Furthermore, it revealed in him—a black man, a slave, the man farthest down—the spark of liberty, of humanity, of what some would call *divinity* . . . one could glimpse human potentialities, and indeed *human perfectibility*, a testament for an American faith.[76]

This is what McCune Smith calls the "charm of transcendent excellence." While the revelation of his physical appearance is worth discussing, there is something more perplexing in this commentary: What is to be made of Douglass, a cypher for the national atonement of slavery, bearing witness to and being the prototype of American faith, of democracy? Is this faith national self-aggrandizement as that supposed City on a Hill; or a faith in the possibility that said nation "produces" Douglass and almost two centuries on bears another "hero" in the person and works of a Pan-African named Barack Hussein Obama? (An aside: US "democracy" interpolates Douglass when he becomes the ambassador to Haiti. But the appointment "served to tarnish the latter days of Douglass's venerable career" as he was often a "Black prop"—does this sound familiar?)[77] Is this testament to "potential" and "human perfectibility" the "survival" of the African in America and not the faith in America, by America, to make that survival possible? More is at play here as we return to Hughes's elegy and discuss more soon.

His homage ends intertextually and may offer answers to these recent ponderings:

> To all the world cried,
> *Hear my voice!* . . .
> *Oh, to be a beast, a bird,*
> *Anything but a slave!* he said.
>
> *Who would be free*
> *Themselves must strike*
> *The first blow,* he said.
>
> He died in 1895.
> *He is not dead.*

The ending of this elegy "might have been a rallying cry for all those who worried that full freedom and equality might never be a reality. . . . While the poem calls attention to the strength and determination of Frederick Douglass, it also calls on African Americans not to be afraid to 'strike the first blow' against white oppression."[78] Such striking takes on metapoetic whimsy.

Hughes, appropriating a practice like Robert Hayden in "Middle Passage," cites Douglass who himself quotes Lord Byron from *Childe Harold's Pilgrimage* (canto 2, stanza 76). Douglass incorporating these words is deft:

> we can imagine the intervention of poetry into the text as being private, allusive, domestic, fraternal, random, calculated, perhaps market-driven. . . . But without these lines, the chapter on Covey (chapter XXI) in *My Bondage and My Freedom*, for example, would end: "I had made up my mind to do him serious damage, if he ever again attempted to lay his violent hands on me." The difference in the chapter's conclusion without the verse is the notable lingering residue of violence, Douglass dangling from his sentence as the direct object, the singular objective pronoun, the experience closed linguistically yet open rhetorically and psychologically like a gaping wound still without its suture of final anodynic meditation. The verse is that suture. It fashions a reader, including her or him without didactic direction into the imagination of the creation . . . Verse here is an intervention, a mediator . . . Byron's lyrics are the textual segue between chapter (entitled "My Last Flogging," . . .) and the title/subtitle of the succeeding chapter, "My Life as a

Freeman"/"Liberty Attained." It is precisely the lyric's ability to behave as an adjective in this instance by means of its fragmentation of the narrative experience, which allows the narrative to become "forget-ful" and to start therefore again, ever so slightly outside of the time in which it was originally rendered.[79]

The utility of Byron in *My Bondage and My Freedom* supports earlier pre-monitions about blackness and Victorianism whereby Douglass is a centurial icon intertwined with transnational poetics, even at the level of imitability; by adjoining the lyrical "blow" to the text, the words photograph an enjamb-ment that simultaneously performs like a landing strip:

RESULTS OF THE VICTORY.   249

but I could never bully him to another battle. I had made up my mind to do him serious damage, if he ever again attempted to lay violent hands on me.

"Hereditary bondmen, know ye not
Who would be free, themselves must strike the blow ?"

K*

Repeating the Lord extends the journey's grammar: Douglass the modifier, dangling, affixes a cushion for his direct object in the first person singular—"me"—to accomplish that "blow," arriving safely at the soon-coming destina-tion: "Life as a Freeman"/"Liberty Attained."[80] Byron's words—intervening, mediating, segueing—poetically hyphenate Douglass's "highway." If such words suture, in excess of claiming insight into the "imagination of the creation," they collapse ascendingly into a *North Star*, "*his* compass' choice," as Douglass, es-tranged from his mother, stitches the fragments of his maternal memoriam and (un)consciously routes each path to freedom's goal with her footsteps sourcing the affective trail.

The motivations for ending a chapter with such lyricism, in preparation for a subsequent one beginning, hint at the sublime because "[w]hatever is fitted in any sort to excite the ideas of pain and danger, that is to say, whatever is in any sort terrible, or is conversant about terrible objects, or operates in a man-ner analogous to terror, is a source of the *sublime*; that is, it is productive of the strongest emotion which the mind is capable of feeling . . . ideas of pain are much more powerful than those which enter on the part of pleasure."[81] The pleasure of a longed-for freedom, preceded by the pain of the Last Flogging, prioritizes the syntactic precision of Douglass when he quotes Byron again in his 1863 speech, "Men of Color, to Arms! A Call by Frederick Douglass";

however, when repeating the lyric, he performs the remix: "Who would be free themselves must strike the blow."[82] Shifting from the interrogatory to the declamatory, he explicates that the issue is not whether the force will occur, but rather that someone is audacious enough to catalyze such defense-offense having experienced incessant severity prior to landing physical remonstrance as justifiable indignation. Moreover, a stunning occasion of *the spirit of revolt*: In Byron's wake, the sublime pervades mid-Atlantic zeitgeist, particularly when, in a town once called Jerusalem, Thomas R. Gray transcribes ten iterations of "blow" in *The Confessions of Nat Turner*, the earliest instant being in his preamble "TO THE PUBLIC": "[Turner] was not only the contriver of the conspiracy, but gave *the first blow* towards its execution." Recalling Reverend J. W. E. Bowen, who recites Byron's initiating phrase from a pulpit in 1892 Washington, DC, when pondering "What Shall the Harvest Be?," one registers that "no human community is admitted to fellowship, or the essential right to 'self-determination,' without undergoing the ways and means of confrontational violence."[83] Between verb and direct object, action and act, Douglass, and others, cry out, "Hear my voice!" as orality outlives the death knockout. He contradicts slavery and calls people to arms, whether as Hughes's beast or bird or, as argued here, a cat—the an*i*morphic residue of the black feminine/maternal.

Douglass awakes Monday morning with *all power in his hands*, nontraditionally scripting his renaissance a day later. Suffering "symbolic-death," he returns as an (autobiographical) risen savior, that is, "If the work of mourning consists in killing the dead, then symbolic-death is closer to that state in that it too is predicated on the 'acceptance' of the dead as dead, on the affirmation of oneself as, in some sense, a dead being. . . . [Douglass's] terminology of resurrection and redemption clarifies the fundamental difference between mourning and melancholia . . . and symbolic-death . . . the latter, unlike the former, entails a rebirth, a radical transformation of the subject."[84] The *Revenant* again prefigures Freud. Due to a panacea Africana, he transfigures and shape-shifts, contriving himself as one of the *untouchables*. Confronted in a cow yard by and triumphant over Covey the snake, this Pan-African is not simply Negroid and Caucasian, animal and invisible man, machined and majestic:

Fantastically, Frederick Douglass is a cyborg.

Maternity and the Elegy

Whatever the makings of the cyborg in the person of mid-nineteenth century masc-racial-abolitionist Douglass, they forge a peculiar synchronicity with the late twentieth century sci-techno-socio-feminist project while positing noteworthy complications for the "black cyborg" of contemporary affectations. Though my cyborg proposition is backdated, it demands retracing our footsteps to behold where we have come, over a way that with tears has been watered, as a reading of the *other side of the house*:

> "women of colour" might be understood as a cyborg identity, a potent subjectivity synthesized from fusions of outsider identities and in the complex political-historical layerings of her *"biomythography"* . . . *literacy is a special mark of women of colour*, acquired by *US black women as well as men* through a history of risking death to learn and to teach reading and writing. . . . Cyborg writing is about the power to survive, not on the basis of original innocence, but on the basis of seizing the tools to mark the world that marked them as other. . . . But it is this *chimeric monster* . . . that crafts the erotic, competent, potent identities of women of colour . . . because of her ability to live on the boundaries, to write without the founding myth of original wholeness, with its inescapable apocalypse of final return to a deathly oneness that *Man has imagined to be the innocent and all powerful Mother, freed at the End from another spiral of appropriation by her son.* . . . This is not just literary deconstruction, but liminal transformation. These cyborgs are the people who refuse to disappear on cue . . . by *writing.*[85]

Does Frederick achieve "perfectibility" through Harriet? If this son reads his mother as a myth, alongside categorizing the black woman cyborg as a biomythography (and making Zami her new name à la Audre Lorde), it may mean that like things beget like things.[86] This is to say, him comprehending himself as a product of said myth, in advance of being a symbiotic *myt*, would inaugurate a new genre: autobiomythography, the amalgamation of ART and FACTS. This chimera, born of a "chimeric monster," signals that a child introjecting that black feminine/maternal monstrosity is inculcated with the potential to "read" and "write." In other words, she invites contemplation, when coupled with the cyborg being a "creature in a post-gender world," by grounding the nexus of the race-gender commingle, a realization supplied when one "pictures" the mother.[87]

Arguing that Douglass is a contemporary of other nineteenth-century race ethnographers, Michael A. Chaney thinks on the image from Prichard's text. The offering exposes the inescapability of the black-white binary, acknowledging Douglass's "bastard/mulatto status." The preoccupation with race gives little to no hearing to the *fact of gender.* This is not to say that Chaney does not address it, but to say he deduces that "there is some indication that Douglass's notion of Ramses II may well have been connotative of femininity." I push this rationale: If one accedes to *My Bondage and My Freedom* as an "auto(bio)ethnography," Chaney's formulation, is the bust remembrance connotative of Douglass's femininity since he, and his ocular proclivities, is only made possible by the mother?[88] When he views Ramses II, is he not looking at himself—a portrait of the pharaoh of the mud hovel and the throne converging with the "slave-made-woman" Bailey? I count it quite spectacular and ripe for query that despite citing Prichard's pagination, Douglass would have come across images of female Egyptians because they exist in that selfsame text.[89] Although this cyborg, and his chosen maternal depiction, offers not only an exploded racial vision, but also an irruptive bombast for a gendered world, I inject perplexity with that death-driving frontispiece as a looming specter.

Invoking the work of João Costa Vargas and Joy A. James suggests there are black cyborgs and there are "black cyborgs"; saying this may contrive Douglass as the unwieldy signification of both. Thinking about the death of Trayvon Martin, they insist, "Yet the gravity of Martin's last wrestle with his opponent, the 'mortal combat' against an enemy backed by white supremacy's judicial, police, and media machineries, is a compelling story, one about a youth who refused blackness-as-victimization, without any guarantee of redemption." If the Covey fight is precursory to that fatal Florida event, complexity abounds because Douglass does impress, self-guarantee, redemption when cosplaying "the Christ," that is, "Part divine, part mechanical, part biological, black rebel cyborgs demand not democracy but freedom" (see the autobiography title). Such black cyborgian rebellion, perhaps regionally phenomenological, opposes other black cyborgs who "view the emergence of the nation-state from the ash of the colony (ghetto) burning down as the consummate victory. . . . Some endowed with the superhuman powers of governmental or corporate entities reproduce existing structures with modifications."[90] Having recounted his governmental inclusion, I acknowledge Douglass as a *both/and* black cyborg: Is one tasked now with preferring that black cyborg—combative for his freedom, blow-striking—over the one attempting to facilitate, albeit passively, the bondage of others? Does this further legitimate the frontispiece, no longer emblematizing the death-drive but rather "democracy"-dealing, as the unconscious and megalomaniacal blur? Or is one ambivalent whereby if Bailey is a black cyborg, she bears Douglass, a black cyborg, even as he, with age and access, departs from it, compelling (in)visible scare quotes around the category? I am unsure if there is a "clean" resolution except to say this may be how to best "Read | Frederick."

If one now toys with Douglass's twoness, a desiderated cyborgian affect might be extant in that due to circumstance and the technology of the day, by not appropriating a maternal image but proffering her "likeness" to a rich young ruler, Douglass shields Bailey from acts of capture prototypical of the West and its spiraling End. Though he never concedes she "wrote," he characterizes her as "remarkable" and "extraordinary," that he is "quite willing . . . to attribute any love of letters [he possesses] . . . to the native **genius** of [his] sable, unprotected, and uncultivated *mother*"—routine platitudes for an excellent performer.[91]

Cognizant of its facticity, *My Bondage and My Freedom* artfully presents a poetics, whether Douglass's pastoral battle or his overall hermeneutic. That said, even with their liminal presences in the work, mother and daughter Bailey spur the genre of the autobiographies, namely the second, as elegy. And if Douglass, somehow, tracks the "new birth of our republic," Betsy Bailey being born on the precipice of ratified states, united, conveys republican formation paralleling his matriarchy: "This extraordinary woman was unlettered, but evidently possessed a mind capable of making finely logical connections. . . . Douglass proudly claimed that his mother was literate. If this was so, Harriet Bailey's intellectual achievement, like Frederick's, probably owed much to the encouragement of Betsy, who could so intelligently *read* a river or the furrow of a field."[92] If Grandmother reads topographies and Mother reads texts, then (Grand)Son is primed to critique "Nature" more generally and the "nurture" of the slave economy specifically. In this way, *My Bondage and My Freedom* artifactually offers matrifocal revelations.

The elegy is an aesthetic practice that resonates with "Mourning and Melancholia" in that the genre produces substitutionary material for those eponymous affects:

> By representing the loss of the other, the poet establishes a distance between the original object and the arbitrary verbal signs that convey its loss. This distance is essential to the work of mourning . . . because it helps the grieving poet understand the difference between the dead and the living, a profoundly simple difference between those who no longer speak or write and those who do. Although the mourner wants to cling to the lost object and deny this difference, the act of "figuring" the loss brings about the "elegist's reluctant submission to language itself." This submission . . . marks the successful completion

of mourning at the same time it signals that the lost one has transcended death by achieving aesthetic immortality in a timeless literary *artifact*.[93]

I cohere Douglass with McCune Smith, and Freud, through this poetic form to rethink the autobiography in relation to this recent argumentation. The elegy is a living testament that will "outlast death" as "[t]his resolution converges with the elegist's assessment and affirmation of his surviving powers, one of the most important of which is his continued use of language."[94] If maternal mourning incites Douglass to language, written and/or spoken, these works console him in place of his long-lost mother(s). He occupies that Almighty office as he prescriptively self-medicates through his autobiographies to combat the gravity that "never having enjoyed, to any considerable extent, her soothing presence, her tender and watchful care, [he] received the tidings of [his mother's] death with much the same emotions [he] should have probably felt at the *death of a stranger*"; or his plantation separation from Grandmamma.[95] Thus, we return to Prichard's bust to make legible how he, more than she, operationalizes a shifting cyborg identity.

Though the contrast in Douglass's writing between the first two autobiographies has been deemed an "oversimplification" of his "national politics" because his Ameri-centric scope shifts to a transnational one through incorporating Africa, his maternal theorizing offers a complexity that inserts his pen in a larger canon: "Douglass makes no such comparison in the 1845 *Narrative* between his mother and an Egyptian masculine figure. Deborah McDowell offers a gender-focused argument that 'Douglass's account of his mute mother remembered as a white man captures emphatically the discursive priorities of masculinity and its gendered relation to the feminine.' One could make the case along the lines of [Eric] Sundquist that Douglass claims a lineage of patriarchal nobility via his mother's physical features that situate him as the 'Franklinian' man with connections in high places."[96] Based on this argument, one contemplates: What exactly makes Ramses II "white"—is it the medium through which the rendering itself circulates, or how its renderer believes the "Egyptian" to look? Note that the image caption itself dictates that Ramses II is a "deviation from the European countenance." If McCune Smith and Douglass are correct, pharaoh is "mixed race"—he is, allegedly, as "white" as he is "black." In either case, the gender component of McDowell's critique may clarify this puzzle, even if the visual scene invites a differing approach now.[97]

If Douglass prioritizes his masculinity through his "fatherly" mother, then her flesh is "ungendered," regardless of "her" citation as the genesis of "his" intellect. And if Douglass's father is "white," and Caucasians will find themselves in Africa "by-and-by," then the (black) mother as (Egyptian) royal is sensible—Douglass is no less a global "renaissance man" than Benjamin Franklin vis-à-vis his "Englishness"/"Frenchness."[98] However, "shrouded in mystery," the patriarch installs imaginative *différence*: The "white" bust potentiates to be, with all the intentions of the pun and the locative anthropological citation, a "black" *mummy*! Douglass's mélange brings about his "constitutional illegitimacy," where "constitutional" counterintuitively means "chromosomal."[99] Yet parentage lingers uncannily.

Anna Murray's death, and Douglass's subsequent marriage to Helen Pitts, stages a point of conflation regarding embodied and aesthetic replacement:

> Anna died in 1882. She was almost seventy years old, Douglass sixty-four. For years she had been suffering from severe rheumatism, which kept her immobile and at times paralyzed. In her last months, she received "faithful constant care" from nurses, and she died quietly. "*Mother*," as Douglass now called her, "was the post in the center of my house and held us together." Eighteen months after Anna died, Douglass married Helen Pitts, a college-educated white woman who was twenty years his junior and worked as his secretary. News of the marriage outraged many whites and blacks, including family members, partly because he did not explain it well. While Anna had been "the color of my mother," Helen was "the color of my *father*," he said, which suggested to some people that he was now drawn to the white part of his identity.[100]

These intersecting configurations bring McCune Smith to mind again in that what was thought a single-unit residence is mixed-use as Douglass, romantically and otherwise, subtends the two sides of his "house"; the elegy extends past the page, pervading the private palimpsest that is his life. Post-Reconstruction, he "represented himself as a free man, but relinquished the ideal of racial equality. His sublime black aesthetic was replaced by a desublimated, beautiful white one."[101] Douglass's endearing relationships affirm this intriguing *race play*: As Murray replaces Bailey in this amorous saga, Pitts replaces Murray replacing Bailey; or, if Murray is "Mother," is Pitts "Father" due to (de)racialization? Having first married the "maternal" "myth," he chooses the "paternal" "shroud" as posthumous follow-up. If the elegiac form is an interpretive prelude to Freud related to replacement measures revealed through mourning, that psychoanalytic category of the lost object, usually the mother, may be the father for Douglass, or both parents as witnessed by his helpmeets. A minor detour: Given Douglass's presumed parentage, Edward Blyden described "mulattoes" as "'always restless and dissatisfied' in their desire for complete racial assimilation with whites . . . genuine blacks must be defended against those dissatisfied types. . . . Even though he found exceptions—of Douglass he wrote, "He is strongly Negro, although of mixed blood. His *genius* and power come evidently from the *African side* of his nature"—Blyden's at times ludicrous notion of race instinct or ancestry only serves to fuel . . . a "paranoid hatred of mulattoes."'" Though Blyden aligns with McCune Smith regarding "blood work," does Douglass "live into" that dissatisfaction hypothesis by way of Pitts? These circumstances become more tantalizing when noting that Ottilie Assing, German translator of *My Bondage and My Freedom*, regarded herself as Douglass's "'natural' wife"; when he married Pitts, she committed suicide.[102] This nuptial saga highlights my caution calling Douglass a "feminist," though he "converts" to it via Elizabeth Cady Stanton and supports suffrage. Nevertheless, though Assing had "agency," there was also Lucy Ellen Moten: "refused the position of principal of Washington's Minor Normal School because the all-male Board of Trustees felt that the tall, elegant mulatta 'cut too fine a face and figure' for the job," Moten petitioned Douglass, a trustee; he would only advocate for her "if she agreed to give up dancing, playing cards, going to the theater, entertaining gentleman callers—and her fine clothes." Agreeing to these terms, she is hired for the position. These stories, among others, distill Douglass's private and public personality regarding women.[103]

If the writer substitutes what is lost with the poetic, the new thing enacts "*legitimacy* at the expense of [the lost object's] separateness and well-being."[104] Heretofore, Douglass employs rotational dynamics during his life by performing elegy as a mode of genius. Yet I assert that elegies written about him equally entertain ART and FACTS, even in their (un)witting testimony to the black feminine/maternal, as Douglass too may be "Mother."

The epigraph for this chapter, Hayden's sonnet "Frederick Douglass," was "[o]riginally . . . intended . . . for *The Black Spear* dealing with several of the outstanding figures in the antislavery struggle, and 'Douglass' was to be the culminating, climactic poem in the series." Reverential of figures like William Lloyd Garrison, Abraham Lincoln, Harriet Beecher Stowe, Sojourner Truth, and Douglass, he never published the collection, yet the Douglass poem appeared in *The Atlantic Monthly* in 1947. Perhaps the first noteworthy tidbit is Hayden dedicated the unfinished work to his mother—"Frederick Douglass" would have been included in a collection that was itself composed of a series of elegies wherein Hayden, born Asa Bundy Sheffey, paid homage to "G. Ruth Scott," the moniker assigned to his mother, Ruth Sheffey. Like Douglass to his aunt, Hayden renames a woman in his life having been "named" by her, just as his birth name is secondary to its new spelling. While he intimates that of the sonnets about the aforementioned actors, "Douglass was the only one [he] liked, and so in time [he] discarded the others," how this favored poem wrestles with time plays upon the clock metaphor and the undocumented EDITOR's admonition of the autobiography being "TOO LATE."[105] As fascinating is the convergence of Hayden's life with Douglass's, namely his upbringing—William and Sue Ellen Hayden "raised the boy as their own, giving him their name, along with almost equal portions of love and guilt. His foster mother never let the boy forget her charity, his ingratitude, and his natural mother's unworthiness. His foster father devoted his hard-shell Baptist morality toward an upright raising of his son; Hayden thus oscillated among love, gratitude, recrimination, guilt, and downright emotional confusion." An anecdote: In his forties, he attempts to procure a passport and learns "he did not exist as Robert Hayden"; he was living "under an assumed name" since the Haydens never legally adopted him. Hence, *The Black Spear* dedication could signify him as synonymous with melancholy, and genius, in that he is a lost "object of affection," even to his estranged mother, and ostensibly "without an intelligible beginning in the world."[106]

Though the first version of the sonnet from 1945 marks Douglass as the *Revenant* from that "pestiferous tomb"—"Such men are timeless, and their lives are levers / that lift the crushing dark away like boulders"—the 1947 version "opens with immediacy and engagement" through the use of the word "when":

> When it is finally ours, this freedom, this liberty, this beautiful
> and terrible thing, needful to man as air,
> usable as earth; when it belongs at last to all,
> when it is truly instinct, brain matter, diastole, systole,
> reflex action; when it is finally won; when it is more
> than the gaudy mumbo jumbo of politicians. . . .[107]

Through repetition, "[t]he cumulative effect of clauses in the opening unit commencing with *when* emphasize the conditional quality of unachieved freedom and create suspense within the reader." The reader and Douglass again play within and without that previously invoked circle pervaded with poesy. Suspicious and full of suspense, conditioned through tense and to be tense, one wonders if Douglass will undo seeming disjointedness—chronological (TOO LATE), technical (hands of a clock), ontological (intelligibility)—as slavery is like "a contagious disease, a malignancy that spreads to destroy its perpetrators as well as its victims."[108] Will Douglass's bondage be quarantined and eradicated by his desirous freedom?

Though Hayden might have read parts of Douglass's autobiographies, specific to his incorporation of liberty ("this freedom, this liberty, this beautiful / and terrible thing") beside passages from *My Bondage and My Freedom*, I am piqued by him discerning the work of the sonnet in juxtaposition to the cow yard fight: "'The poem is tightly constructed, taut and wound up *like a spring*. It doesn't let go of the reader until he comes to the final line.'"[109] The poem rhetorically embodies how Douglass (re)acts to Covey. The sonnet becomes flesh insofar as one realizes that it exerts a power more beautiful and more terrible, liberty-inducing one might say, than whatever subjection imposed through the flexibility of page-turning, hand-writing, wrists. Hayden also implicates himself:

. . . this man
shall be remembered. Oh, not with statues' rhetoric,
not with legends and poems and wreaths of bronze alone,
but with the lives grown out of his life, the lives
fleshing his dream of the beautiful, needful thing.[110]

He "claims Douglass will not be remembered with poems, yet what is Hayden here doing . . . this apparent contradiction . . . seems evident. The poet is not naïve enough to assume that his conception of freedom 'has arrived,' but he hopefully longs for a time and a reality of freedom when his poem, and other tributes to Douglass like it, simply will be superfluous."[111] If the sonnet's power is ephemeral, as the palms of hands, tethered to eyes, seek the vertical vowel between ART and FACT, it marks a melancholic shift toward aspiration.

That adverbial repetition enacts metronomic potential as Douglass transcends time *when* he premises a graphic novel, *when* he populates the spaces between comic strip gutters, *when* he haunts a TV commercial for black hair during *the hippest trip in America, when* he professes *Lessons of the Hour*. Hayden "performs" the poem to obliterate its future necessity, espousing instead "a time and a reality" that will be full of that "thing, needful to man as air"; the sonnet, then, is "about . . . the kind of difficult love of community that is not about answers, per se, and not about heroes, solely, but rather about the hard processes of living, facing struggle, and imagining strategies, the kind of heroism that is not about pedestals. Poetry is always implicitly enacting, 'I don't want to forget this,' which in the end works the same as the grander 'This must be remembered.'"[112] This engenders a twofold response.

If melancholy is the loss of "one's . . . liberty," the poem portrays how "Douglass's gift for abstract logic helped move his vision closer to reality. . . . Douglass will be remembered *when* freedom is real rather than abstract." As well, "[t]he real heritage left by Douglass is not fame commemorated or maintained with artifacts, but rather the living progeny of his example."[113] The move from abstraction to reality concretizes itself not only in Douglass crafting theory and applying it to his and others' lives, but also in the sonnet revering him as an ancestor, like Harriet Bailey, through "fleshing his dream"—a reminiscence of "The Negro Mother":

God put a dream like steel in my soul.
Now, through my children, I'm reaching the goal.
. . .
I had only hope then, but now through you,
Dark ones of today, my dreams must come true:
. . .
Oh, my dark children, may my dreams and my prayers
Impel you forever up the great stairs—
For I will be with you till no white brother
Dares keep down the children of the Negro mother."[114]

Is Hayden the "living progeny" of Douglass? Is he, are we, the dream and the hope of the cyborg? Though this chapter maintains artifactual investments, this fleshy exposé proves that the material can be superimposed with the maternal. Whether Douglass is the maieutic of liberty—akin to Shiphrah and Puah who save male Hebrew newborns from slaughter, catalyzing the recovery of Moses from the bulrushes—or Lady Liberty himself, this "needful thing" is paramount.[115] Another elegy is as provocative along the race-gender commingle.

Three stanzas in Paul Laurence Dunbar's 1895 sonnet "Frederick Douglass" induces one's interest in the black feminine/maternal:

A hush is over all the teeming lists,
    And there is pause, a breath-space in the strife;
A spirit brave has passed beyond the mists

And vapors that obscure the sun of life.
And Ethiopia, with bosom torn,
Laments the passing of her noblest born.

She weeps for him a mother's burning tears—
    She loved him with a mother's deepest love
He was her champion thro' direful years,
    And held her weal all other ends above.
When Bondage held her bleeding in the dust,
He raised her up and whispered, "Hope and Trust."
. . .

Oh, Douglass, thou hast passed beyond the shore,
    But still thy voice is ringing o'er the gale!
Thou 'st taught thy race how high her hopes may soar
    And bade her seek the heights, nor faint, nor fail.
She will not fail, she heeds thy stirring cry,
She knows thy guarding spirit will be nigh,
And rising from beneath the chast'ning rod,
She stretches out her bleeding hands to God![116]

Structured in ABABCC(DD) rhyme and lined in iambic pentameter, these couplets convey something like kinship based on the nature of the poem and its poet. This conceit is sustained when recognizing that the collection that houses this poem, *Majors and Minors*, is dedicated to Dunbar's mother: "As my first faint pipings were inscribed to her, I deem it fitting, as a further recognition of my love and obligation, that I should also dedicate these later songs to MY MOTHER."[117] The maternal shadow cast on these poems, similar to *The Black Spear* in incompletion, testifies to the motherly dedication to the filial from the beginning. Note too that Dunbar refers to his poems as "songs," undergirding the elegy considered here as "blues music."

The irony of the collection being dedicated to Mother Dunbar is that she receives elation regarding her son meeting his muse; when he encounters Douglass in Chicago at the World's Columbian Exposition, he pens a letter to her: "'[Douglass] got up and came tottering into the room, "and this is Paul Dunbar" he said shaking hands and patting me on the shoulder. "Paul, how do you do? I've been knowing you for some time and you're one of my boys." He said so much Ma that I must wait until I am with you before I can tell you all. He had me read to him my "Ode to Ethiopia."'" The ostensible history between the two—as if Douglass had known Dunbar long before this occasion, likely because he was his employee in Chicago at the Haitian Building where they meet—achieves sentimentality when the written-on labels the writer his "boy." Though one agrees that "the elegy has tended for men to enact a rite of passage between men . . . the generic pattern of the transmission of male authority" so that "[i]n mourning the loss of Douglass for the black community, [Dunbar] is also stating his aspirations as a poet that he might become a black writer of significance," the rehearsed stanzas counter this gesture and make the case that "family matters."[118]

Ethiopia is a site-specific pivot for all persons involved. This *Revenant* son has a new home. Put upon to read the first stanza through the hypothetical lens of Grandmamma, one notes how the sonnet-ized subject *misti*fies and *evapo*rates before our very eyes in a manner consistent with black nature.[119] The shadow portrayed in the first stanza suggests the loss of another object of affection—the Ethiopian mother's "noblest born"—as she mourns him by covering household mirrors with a black veil. These poetic devices convey the maternal no longer as an Egyptian pharaoh, but the Queen of Sheba. In this way, "Dunbar summons Douglass, this figure whose life has now [passed], as a way of both recalling an African past and predicting a pan-African future." Is Douglass no longer TOO LATE, but rather RIGHT ON TIME, a black cyborg *clocking* a "humanity that fabricates time and measures freedom and enslavement by teaspoons"?[120] Dunbar reading "Ode to Ethiopia" to Douglass, let alone at the World's Columbian Exposition in a space called the Haitian Building in the Windy City, convokes diaspora whereby the muse as "African American" "father" and Ethiopia as "the mother, intimating the language of Africa as the motherland, calling attention to the structure of the heterosexual family as a network of identity," presume Dunbar as an Africana prince.[121]

The poetic child championing his mother "thro' direful years" provides a truncated synopsis of the 1855 autobiography. Pre- and post-Emancipation, as Douglass undertakes a transnational tour to utter the ills of the hated institution, he writes about his mother with a level of care mimicked by Dunbar as he eulogizes in verse this son "loved with a mother's deepest love." The allusion to the mother "bleeding in the dust" riffs on the cyborg's intention to "subvert the apocalypse of returning to nuclear dust in the manic compulsion to name the Enemy" in that Dunbar calls out the perpetrator of said scarification and sedimentation—Bondage—by capitalizing upon the ideal through personification. This son, with an inessential father, whispering "Hope and Trust" about his essential "other side" beckons elegiac hymnody:

Faith of our mothers, loving faith
Fount of our childhood's *trust* and grace

O may thy consecration prove
Source of a finer, nobler race
Faith of our mothers, living faith
We will be true to thee till death.[122]

Inasmuch as Douglass abides by such melodic endearment, Dunbar generationally repeats it toward this "father" who once reckoned himself his mother.

This musicality enlists itself in the final stanza when Dunbar signals that the voice of his eponymous subject rings "o'er the gale." Likewise, the black feminine no longer has allocation to Ethiopia but has been totalized as the race: It is the pupil of Douglass ("Thou 'st taught thy race how high *her* hopes may soar"). Blackness is that "living progeny" as Douglass—teacher, "faithful mother"—is the "Source of a finer, nobler, race." Under the tutelage of that "stirring cry," blackness returns us to Douglass's circle, listening no longer to his melancholy, but to his thunderous encouragement to strive for that terrible thing. And by evoking the "chast'ning rod" in this "elegy, praise-poem, jam session," Dunbar, prior to James Weldon Johnson in 1899 and Hughes in 1967, calls us—members of this race gendered she—to Lift Every Voice and Sing![123]

This is "her" story; this is "her" song. She has no recourse for penitence under the rubric of utter depravity; her "machinist grandeur" teaches the body something about the flesh—metalloid, hybrid: She endures big and little bangs. She challenges myths that, like the inessential father, *shroud* the begotten—the child who carries her spitting *imago*—under a veil of difference. Her child attends (to) these plenary sessions because she has pored over information to instill that "[t]he fact of domination *is* alterable only to the extent that the dominated subject recognizes the potential power of its own 'double consciousness.' The subject is certainly seen, but she also *sees*. It is this return of the gaze that negotiates at every point a space for living, and it is the latter that we must willingly name the counter-power, the counter-mythology."[124] No different than Frederick to her, Harriet is her mother Betsey's child, just as Betsey is the daughter of Jenny.[125] Douglass sees as an adult what he hears as a child: the "counter-power," the "counter-mythology." The ART of FACTS, the FACTS of ART.

If this son's literacy, read through his mother's, teaches anything, it is that the child's regard for her opens the affective possibility of changing one's mind: "If slavery creates one kind of mother, freedom creates another. There remains no absolute or innocent mother for him to recover, no impersonal or absolute reality to which he must submit and conform. There are simply two competing mothers, one Douglass knows when a slave, the other he knows when free. And the difference between these two mothers is fundamentally sentimental and political rather than natural and given."[126] Douglass, "slave and citizen," first interprets his mother through the narrative of an American slave, written by himself; then again, altogether differently, through the bound-made-free. This may prove why the last autobiography is, simply, *The Life and Times*, that is, "If *My Bondage and My Freedom* consists of so many facts about slavery, one wonders if the artistic temperament of *Narrative of the Life of Frederick Douglass* (1845), Douglass's first and, arguably, the literary's defining ex-slave autobiography, did not, in fact, require the latter one's urgent facticity."[127] While this concession is agreeable, the second autobiography accomplishes that ART-FACTS twinning, just as the first. This troubles Bailey as a lost object because though her son presences her in the first autobiography, he possesses her in the second—a sober choice to locate the echo.[128] This shift exemplifies Douglass's artifacts, his autobiographies, reclining into a timeless posture that confirms their being birthed, generations removed, by *literate* mothers from "Tuckahoe, near Hillsborough, and about twelve miles from Easton, in Talbot county, Maryland."[129]

Pointing to a past her son gives a glimpse into when "dancing" a nightmare as a dream variation. Eternally roaming the universe as her family artifact transforms from microfiber on a shelf to a digital upload on the web worldwide, concretizing the nature of being a cyborg with "little hope for Western democracy's ability to embrace black life. [Her] reflections from . . . the grave reveal a rebel who relinquishes the unachievable goal: striving for a socially recognized 'humanity' that is constructed on the antithesis resting on her hip."[130]

Harriet Bailey, "this [wo]man / shall be remembered. . . . "

I first encountered Ellison through the scrim of Larry Neal's 1970 essay "Ellison's Zoot Suit,"
so I knew what I needed to read for—the invaluable critical propositions about African-
American culture, the dazzling enactment of blues vernacular in modernist prose, artistic
achievement steeped in reference to the music and an eye capable of discerning what Zora
Neale Hurston described as the distinctive symmetry and angularity that were the most
striking manifestations of black style and the will to adorn. I also knew what I had to read
past—the cult of the masculine hero and an aesthetic project that "restores to man his full
complexity" and to the native son truth and revelation, while abandoning the daughter to
the chaos of the underworld. —SAIDIYA HARTMAN, "Ralph Ellison's Letters Reveal a
Complex Philosopher of Black Expression"

#travelnoire: Reading an American Grammar Book; or, a Theoretical Layover at Chehaw

"The Little Man at Chehaw Station: The American Artist and His Audience"
by Ralph Ellison conceals as much as it illumines; its anecdotal wisdom provokes questions and provides answers:

> It was at Tuskegee Institute during the mid-1930s that I was made aware
> of the little man behind the stove. At the time I was a trumpeter major-
> ing in music and had aspirations of becoming a classical composer. . . .

I had outraged the faculty members who judged my monthly student's recital by substituting a certain skill of lips and fingers for the intelligent and artistic structuring of emotion that was demanded in performing the music assigned to me. . . . I had sought solace in the basement studio of Hazel Harrison, a highly respected concert pianist and teacher. . . .

"But, baby," she said, "in this country you must always prepare yourself to play your very best wherever you are, and on all occasions." . . .

"All right," she said, "you must *always* play your best, even if it's only in the waiting room of Chehaw Station because in this country there'll always be a little man hidden behind the stove."

"A *what*?"

She nodded. "That's right," she said. "There'll always be the little man whom you don't expect, and he'll know the *music*, and the *tradition*, and the standards of *musicianship* required for whatever you set out to perform!"

Speechless, I stared at her. . . . I was in no mood for joking. But no, Miss Harrison's face was quite serious. So what did she mean? . . . and as I stood beside Miss Harrison's piano, visualizing the station, I told myself, *She has GOT to be kidding!*[1]

The word "Chehaw" elicits onomatopoeia to my senses. Whenever someone states it or it passes the eye, it conjures the sounds twin boys made while tending their family's land amid the dew: "gee" and "haw" were directional maneuvers that informed mules to move left (GEE!) or right (HAW!) in fields conditioned to harvest a bounty for those in the homestead.[2] A generous metaphorizing would be that just as an ass understands African American Vernacular English, Chehaw Station was, and presumably is, a site where language holds no bounds. "[A] lonely whistle-stop where swift north- or southbound trains paused with a haughty impatience to drop off or take on passengers; the point where . . . special coaches crowded with festive visitors were cut loose, coupled to a waiting switch engine, and hauled to Tuskegee's railroad siding," the station projects a "melting pot," "function[ing] as a point of arrival and departure for people representing a wide diversity of tastes and styles of living."[3] A panoply of persons would travel this "expressway" to the institute; onomatopoeically, those from the *left* and *right* side of the tracks mingle in a banal railroad car to inscribe a ubiquity across class, gender, and race. Yet Ellison positing essentialist claims on his titular muse induces limits.

His theorization of the little man behind the stove connotes him as autochthonous to Chehaw; this bucks the reality that all who linger at the whistle-stop, including its primary laborer, take some form of transportation to "get there." All the more, he cognizes "haunting, blues-echoing, train-whistle rhapsodies" and not the "classics."[4] Translation: Given his locative status, and the preconception of his ability to "throw down" in a kitchen, this man fries chicken on par with Gus's in Memphis and knows the proper measure of water for a fabulous peach cobbler, but has no semblance of the *joy of cooking* to prepare a bouillabaisse or make a mean baklava! This melting-pot nod gives entrée to play.

Ellison provides options for deducing what the little man does occupationally by placing him "behind" the stove. Such appliance proximity does not necessitate gastronomy; he may vend tickets to the institute or heat the station by filling the stove with coal in the winter, thus him being "the little stove warmer." But he is also "the seemingly homeless, seemingly ignorant man who sits *in* the stove at the train station."[5] The epithetical turn, "in" instead of "behind," signifies dubiousness: Is he the cook or coal wielder, a meal or the folkloric coal-turned-diamond? This mirth furthers the comical: "Ellison affirmed that in America, the absence of class and the easy, trickster-like play on identity mean that anyone can be anything at any time . . . one never knows whether the person with whom you are interacting might be a connoisseur of music, fine art, or the Classics." I would add "cuisine" to the list to insist on "the impossibility of fixing individuals within a single tradition." Hence, whether in *Juneteenth* or "The Little Man at Chehaw Station," Ellison eats in the diaspora.[6] Jocular and semantic, this little man is a "teachable moment."

When Ellison italicizes the text in his essay, emphasizing what Miss Hazel Harrison shares about the little man, he focuses on what he produces but not his know-how *to* produce: "Music." "Tradition." "Musicianship." All receive his deliberate slant, disregarding that the little man knows these things to augment his relevance. His aesthetic knowledge foretells his taste, or lack thereof as believed by this young musician who conceives progress outweighing process. Perhaps this scene occurs during Ellison's second year at Tuskegee because his rhetoric then appears immensely sophomoric now; or, as Cheryl A. Wall expresses, "The young man who seems to represent the narrative present is more laughable than laudable."[7] His italics tells the story: a dubious "what?" before a speechless stare; a caps-lock "got" that supposes inner-monologic yelling or a raised tone. Harrison does not invite "solace" to her studio; he arrives seeking it, believing she will assuage his waning strokes of genius, simulated through digital and labial dexterity, superseding the music department's precision requisites, that is, the question is not can one play, but rather play *well* as the difference between mechanics and histrionics when the strictness of one incites the freedom of the other.

This freedom notion reminisces on the relationship of blackness and materiality as the intangible and tangible have an abiding relationship: "This presence of the commodity within the individual is an effect of reproduction, a trace of *maternity*.... Of equal importance is the containment of a certain personhood within the commodity that can be seen as the commodity's animation by the *material trace* of the maternal—a palpable hit or touch, a bodily and visible phonographic inscription." What one ostensibly produces, and performs, is bound up with the (re)producer: the mother. In theory and praxis, she constantly marks her territory with material residue trailing behind her because

> enslavement—and the resistance to enslavement that is the performative essence of blackness (or, perhaps less controversially, the essence of black performance) is a *being maternal* that is indistinguishable from a *being material*. But it is also to say something more. And here, the issue of reproduction (the "natural" production of natural children) emerges right on time as it has to do not only with the question concerning slavery, blackness, performance, and the ensemble of their ontologies but also with a contradiction at the heart of the question of value in its relation to personhood that could be said to come into clearer focus against the backdrop of the ensemble of motherhood, blackness, and the bridge between slavery and freedom.[8]

Although this instantiation of "follow the leader" reads like aimless wander, could it be a preconditioned-postpartum travelogue toward freedom? The assertion seems to be that the black feminine/maternal (re)produces (un) naturally in that what she imparts is not aphoristically by blood alone but also *water,* especially if what she instills breaks through in the aftermath of what enslavement wrought via the oceanic. If this "bridge" is the maternal-material connection that necessitates personhood, the "aquaculture" beneath that superstructure is integral to the larger ecosystem: This water is *the flow* or, better still, *the groove*.[9]

This maternal-material dyad in black stud(y/ies) has psychoanalytic resonance as some thinkers speculatively toy with Sigmund Freud, namely his essay "A Note Upon the 'Mystic Writing-Pad'": "If I distrust my memory . . . I am able to supplement and guarantee its working by making a note in writing . . .

a *materialized* portion of my mnemic apparatus, which I otherwise carry about with me *invisible*. I have only to bear in mind the place where this 'memory' has been deposited and I can then '*reproduce*' it at any time I like, with the certainty that it will have remained unaltered." Materiality, invisibility, and reproductivity collaborate toward the "possession of a 'permanent memory-*trace*'"; this Freudian technology mimes the mneme: "devices to aid our memory seem particularly imperfect, since our mental apparatus accomplishes precisely what they cannot: it has an unlimited receptive capacity for new perceptions and nevertheless lays down permanent—even though not unalterable—*memory-traces* of them." This Mystic Writing-Pad, also known as a "Printator," is "a writing-tablet from which notes can be erased by an easy movement of the hand . . . a slab of dark brown resin or wax with a paper edging; over the slab is laid a thin transparent sheet, the top end of which is firmly secured to the slab while its bottom end rests on it without being fixed to it. . . . The upper layer is a transparent piece of celluloid; the lower layer is made of thin translucent waxed paper." An anachronistic iPad, it is outfitted with a "stilus" that "presses the lower surface of the waxed paper on to the wax slab, and the *grooves* are visible as dark writing upon the otherwise smooth whitish-grey surface of the celluloid," a "'protective shield against stimuli.'"[10] The Pad produces that visible inscription; while not phonographic, despite the "grooves," it emblematizes penmanship, a fluid digital motion whereby scrutability sings the clarity of memory. Wax paper touching dark brown resin presents this protection as shielding "blackness." With this technology accounting for the material, the maternal belies itself when discerning "memory-traces."

While the celluloid "receives the stimuli, namely the system *Pcpt.-Cs.*," or Perception-Consciousness, an ephemeral sketching, the *Ucs.*, or Unconsciousness, beckons the trace.[11] In "Mourning and Melancholia," Freud determines that when experiencing melancholia, "the relation to the object is no simple one; it is complicated due to ambivalence . . . countless separate struggles are carried on over the object, in which hate and love contend with each other. . . . The location of these separate struggles cannot be assigned to any system but the *Ucs.*, the region of the memory-traces of *things* (as contrasted with *word*-cathexes)." Resulting from hate ("to detach the libido from the object") and love ("to maintain this position of the libido against assault"), this ambivalence is apt considering the *Pcpt.-Cs.-Ucs.* triangulation and the maternal-material, all acting as an affective itinerary for our upcoming travels with Ellison.[12] These unconscious "struggles" compel the one who suffers that object loss to consciously repurpose the libido through the security of an outlet: writing, a love-hate act in which one "mustn't assume that aesthetic expression is the prime motive for writing; it is really only a means to the more profound end. So don't worry about it if you write out of sadness or hate or love—fear—or fascination, the important thing, if you wish to do it, is to write."[13]

Though "*word*-cathexes" counterpose "memory-traces," the shift between these Freudian essays presumes the Writing-Pad as a conduit through which an investment of linguistic energy as affective surplus lifts off or, rather, is *penned down*. Celluloid consciousness could reveal the unconscious maternal as a retention under the guise of permanence. Ellison flexes his anamnestic muscle, if one doubles back to that piano studio moment, because his reaction to Harrison exhibits the ambivalence he harbors toward black femininity/maternity, a posture that pervades the journey ahead as we navigate free interchanges to track the maternal trace in his materials. As well, these ideations equally offer an intriguing turn in Ellison's essay and his body of work generally: It is precisely the spatiality of basements/the under(-)ground where the black feminine bestows the groove as memory-trace, where her vernacular gifting proves the "slow flow's remarkable."[14] Excavating the maternal-material in Ellison's corpus, I ponder: If this trace tars a path to freedom, to Perception-Consciousness, is it always already invisible/unconscious; or, if the trace manifests as material, is its progenitor—the black feminine/maternal—the originary *invisible man* such that I repeat a query posed to an Ellison nether-dweller: "'Old woman, what is this freedom you love so well?'"[15] Answering these questions will have necessarily sobering ramifications for the artist and audience in concert.

How Ralph Got His Groove Back

A telling aspect of the little man essay is the incredulity Ellison imposes on Harrison, the person to whom he retreats to proverbially lick the wounds from his instrumental misstep with the hope she has adequate dressing.[16] Based on his demeanor, he cannot handle her truth, neglecting her own aesthetic wanderings prior to Tuskegee: "Miss Harrison had been one of Ferruccio Busoni's prize pupils, had lived (until the rise of Hitler had driven her back to a U.S.A. that was not ready to recognize her talents) in Busoni's home in Berlin, and was a friend of such masters as Egon Petri, Percy Grainger, and Sergei Prokofiev." As "[a] social recluse on campus and an insatiable practitioner of her craft (she wore down to the wood the keys of a brand new Steinway in four years). . . . The incredible black [pianist] of her generation . . .

tempered the provinciality of campus life with her international flair."[17] Harrison joins a cadre of black expatriates who travel to Germany to obtain new perspectives on their putative homeland.[18] Yet as an accomplished pianist, she provokes from Ellison the assumption of not having contact with the little man ("I told myself, *She has* GOT *to be kidding!*"). But her historical flashpoints convey that based on her excursions prior to returning stateside, she probably ran into him. It would have undoubtedly been difficult wheeling her piano on the railroad car to perform a sonata, but is it plausible that when "setting the mood" while stove-warming, he opted for such ambient music as Rachmaninoff's *Piano Concerto no. 3 in D minor, Opus 30*? Nonetheless, Harrison returns home and confronts being an ambassador, a prophet, without honor in her own country and among some of her peoples. She, like the little man, is an archetype of the "human riddle."[19]

Working as a "recluse" in that basement, she legitimates Saidiya Hartman's "native daughter" as she entertains the "chaos" of an "underworld," even if said tumult centers on a lackluster student performance following her own transnational inanity. Ellison's prose also surveys the little man as a "masculine hero" given "full complexity": "as I leaned into the curve of Miss Harrison's Steinway and listened to an interpretation of a Liszt rhapsody . . . the little man of Chehaw Station fixed himself in my memory. And so vividly that today he not only continues to engage my mind, but often materializes when I least expect him."[20] Years after receiving the riddle, he endows this (im)material essence with a power that meets us at the essay's outset—ambivalence transforms into acceptance. In the bend of a grand piano, this baby-grand pupil internalizes the little man and learns excellence, genius, after melancholy. Though this bildungsroman recounts itself in 1978, more than forty years after the fact, these narrative instances compel consideration for Ellison's magnum opus.

The events that shaped the writing of *Invisible Man* converge in the 1981 "Introduction" to commemorate its thirtieth anniversary. Locative polarities catalyze novelistic inspiration:

> It all began during the summer of 1945, in a barn in Waitsfield, Vermont, where I was on sick leave from service in the merchant marine, and with the war's end it continued to preoccupy me in various parts of New York City, including its crowded subways: In a converted 141st Street stable, in a one-room ground-floor apartment on St. Nicholas Avenue and, most unexpectedly, in a suite otherwise occupied by jewelers located on the eighth floor of Number 608 Fifth Avenue. It

was there . . . I discovered that writing could be just as difficult in a fellow writer's elegant office as in a crowded Harlem apartment. There were, however, important differences, some of which worked wonders for my shaky self-confidence and served, perhaps, as a catalyst for the wild mixture of elements that went into the evolving fiction.

These words situate Ellison spending as much time above ground as he does *under neath*. This up and down, in and out, above and below proffers a "negating negation" with relation to spatial forms architecturally understood as section drawings.[21] When intimating another negation as seen in the sanctity of workplaces, the elegant Fifth Avenue office versus the crowded Harlem apartment, he attends to networks that shelter collectivities. This is simultaneous to *Invisible Man* being regarded as one of "the Classics," "a 'subterranean thing'—their presence *under the ground*, as it were, *as material as the black soil*."[22] Piecing the Chehaw realities with the crowded subway car, one reads how the peopling of transportation systems permits this writer-passenger to move above- or under(-)ground with fellow travelers toward a prescribed destination.

While Ellison's "selfish gain" constitutes authorial liberty, he recognizes "important differences" spatially: "Thus actually and symbolically the eighth floor was the highest elevation upon which the novel unfolded, but it was a long, far cry from our below street-level apartment and might well have proved disorienting had I not been consciously concerned with a fictional character who was bent upon finding his way in areas of society whose manners, motives and rituals were baffling . . . most of the novel still managed to get itself written in Harlem."[23] Yearning for "home," below street level, presents a conundrum. Elevating oneself, to obtain natural light and solitude, so disorients that it can be vertiginous. Writing the bulk of *Invisible Man* in Harlem, that concrete jungle, signifies him being *grounded* as he finds camaraderie in a precursory undercommons, a place where the novel "drew much of its substance from the voices, idioms, folklore, traditions and political concerns of those whose racial and cultural origins" he shared.[24] Chehaw is a portable melting pot that materializes for him secondarily in that borough.

As Ellison exposes the groundwork of *Invisible Man*, clues about his muse materialize:

The narrative that was upstaged by the voice which spoke so knowingly of invisibility . . . focused upon the experiences of a captured American pilot who found himself in a Nazi prisoner-of-war camp in which he was the officer of highest rank and thus by a convention of war the designated spokesman for his fellow prisoners. Predictably, the dramatic conflict arose from the fact that he was the only Negro among the Americans, and the resulting racial tension was exploited by the German camp commander for his own amusement . . . for my pilot there was neither escape nor a loved one waiting. Therefore he had either to affirm the transcendent ideals of democracy and his own dignity by aiding those who despised him, or accept his situation as hopelessly devoid of meaning; a choice tantamount to rejecting his own humanity.

This is "signatural Ellison—the high moral seriousness, conceptual elegance, and, above all, the staunch conviction of American 'exceptionalism.'"[25] The lattermost ideal regards nationalistic chutzpah in the face of harm when captured behind enemy lines. He conceives the distressed Negro as exemplary of the democratic and cultural maintenance of loyalty and valor for country and compatriot (despite that allegiance being "rendered absurd by the prevailing mystique of race and color").[26] This recalls that commodity formulation and requires a material referendum.

Engaging this recent quotation, alongside that overarching trace, one tracks the Tuskegee piano teacher's global imprint insofar as the Negro American pilot could be construed as Harrison. A rereading: She is in Nazi Germany as it ascends to the apex of "ethnic cleansing"—a different little man with an all-too-terrible, and terribly different, fascination with stoves—but instead of marking territory via footprint residue, she carries exculpatory evidence on herself as a *fact of blackness*. A predisposition to PTSD: post-traumatic skin disorder. One contemplates the typography of ellipses in *Invisible Man*: They are "ambivalent, enigmatic, paradoxical—the presence of absence [or vice versa] that like the blackness of blackness 'is and ain't.'"[27] In Berlin, Harrison solidifies the indirection of who she "ain't"—her artistry as irreducible to her personhood—being illegible based on who she "is"—a black person far from "home." Ellipses "figure affective excess: they mark the place where language struggles to create, and fails. This *place* can be figured as the gap of the asymptote. . . . One can speculate *into* this gap . . . in the fissures of possibility created when those who fall or are pushed into that impossible gap are figured as representative. What can they represent, and how?" This scene of speculation interprets Harrison through a hermeneutic of overreading.[28] She, in "that impossible gap," is the connective tissue to understand Ellison, and by extension invisible man; the bridge called her back, in ensemble with motherhood and blackness, is the allusive thruway "between slavery and freedom" as one strolls the troubling path of representation to realization.

Mining this gap exposes how one cannot object to the circumstances to which one is the subject(ed), yet somehow still projects poise. Not only does Ellison's muse "find support for his morale in his sense of individual dignity and in his newly awakened awareness of human loneliness," but also "[t]he crowning irony of all this lay in the fact that neither of his adversaries was aware of his inner struggle."[29] The rank of pilot is a malapropism for Harrison's routinization as a pianist with basic training in classical music; she is the only Negro among the Europeans in Busoni's "encampment" and its adjacent "outposts." She must "find [her] way within a crowd of other lonely individuals" on this unprecedented trek; her "passionate rejection of native and foreign racisms while upholding those democratic values which [s]he held in common with [her fellow] white [musicians]" is laid bare.[30] Is this unconscious permanence?

A stranger in a strange land, Harrison is a meandering synecdoche. Unsure of the dismissals, or escapes, of other musicians housed under that roof, one concedes her exile likely not being encouraged for other tickling fingers. Her life and artistic dedication have peculiar value—if she remains a migrant to Germany, the race-gender double jeopardy could have meant she would "go first." She was "of lesser value than the lives of whites making the same sacrifice" for their art; she must flee. She has asylum Nowhere, a crossroads where the social construction of race and the material trace mark displacement as her perpetual address. She reifies the "pseudoscientific sociological concept which held that most Afro-American difficulties sprang from our 'high visibility.' . . . Thus despite the bland assertions of sociologists, 'high visibility' actually rendered one *un*-visible."[31] Regardless of Busoni's abode as a European Chehaw, that Germanic melting pot becomes a cauldron, threatening this Gretel *in color* when traversing the crumby trail. Harrison's decision to "stay black" in Berlin may have been the death of her.

This affective ado is melancholy: The inability to hone one's talents in foreign community manipulates said person as "some abstraction" who experiences "the loss of . . . liberty, an ideal, and so on." But do these occurrences invert themselves in that studio when *conjuring* is a defense mechanism she shares with her student? Ellison is clear that the little man is Harrison's "riddle" so that although he theorizes him as a "[c]onnoisseur, critic, trickster . . . like Brer Rabbit," the initial griot is indeed the woman atop the stool, whether it belongs to the bar at Chehaw or under her Steinway, as she performs genius.[32] Invoking that bygone cultural archivist enables further speculation as to the Harrison-Ellison relationship.

When encountering her protégé to rehash his instrumental assessment, Harrison addresses him endearingly: "'But, *baby*,' she said, 'in this country you must always prepare yourself to play your very best wherever you are, and on all occasions.'" This utterance verifies a bond that was once musical, even material, but may in fact be maternal:

In African-American communities, fluid and changing boundaries often distinguish biological mothers from other women who care for children . . . othermothers—women who assist bloodmothers by sharing mothering responsibilities—traditionally have been central to the institution of Black motherhood. . . . Motherhood . . . can be invoked by African American women as a *symbol of power*. Much of Black women's status in African-American communities stems not only from actions as mothers in Black family networks but from contributions as community othermothers. . . . *Black mothers also pay the cost of giving up their own dreams of achieving full creative ability*. . . . Many Black women blues singers, poets, and artists manage to *incorporate their art into their daily responsibilities* as bloodmothers and othermothers.[33]

Harrison is Ellison's othermother, and her kinship language demonstrates nomenclatural power. Her status surfaces via her creativity being squelched across the pond. Such assistance by those (un)bound by blood highlights that (un)natural association as water maintains a sanguine thickness—riding the flow, fording the groove.

One corroborates Harrison's othermotherhood because of another woman in Oklahoma City (OKC): Mrs. Zelia N. Page Breaux, Ellison's music teacher at the Douglass School, was "charmed" by him during his performance of "a nursery song." He reciprocates the enamor: "'It was Mrs. Breaux who introduced me to the *basic discipline required of the artist* . . . and it was she who made it possible for me to *grasp the basic compatibility of the mixture of the classical and vernacular styles* which were part of our musical culture. . . . Mrs. Breaux was a sort of *second mother*.' . . . Ralph opened himself to Breaux. In the process, he found the *embryo* of his life's work."[34] This first othermother, who implements vernacular as the "seed" of Ellison's eventual career, sparks interest partly because of the rhetorical arc of their story; this narration sounds like that of Oedipus Rex. Either way, at Tuskegee, "Ellison introduced himself to Harrison, whom he took piano from that fall. . . . Harrison became Ellison's confidant and wise matron in place of Breaux, offering the talented youngster advice and instilling in him the importance of practice and discipline." Ellison seeks the (other)maternal wherever he travels; Harrison is a third-order "mother." Yet the overarching application of "(other)mother" in his lifeworld has pushback: "[Harrison's] status as artist is undermined by Ellison's insistence on placing her in maternal relation to him. . . . If the maternal Breaux introduces 'basic discipline,' Ellison must defy her rules in order to discover the jazzmen who become his exemplars. In this instance, too, Ellison marginalizes his female mentor. Neither Harrison nor Breaux [rises] to the level of the literary ancestors or cultural exemplars Ellison valorizes." Though the othermaternity of Harrison, as well as Breaux and others subsequently, extends what Wall rightfully argues, Ellison's motherly default is one of the few ways he *values* the women in his life (as one uncannily hears the lost object coding as "valueless").[35] Signifying on his ostensible condescension, I perform my intention, mirrored in the thesis of said women as the tropic "invisible man," to inject them into the ancestor/exemplar category: "(other)mother," and its permutations, is shorthand for *genius*.

Harrison divulges the necessity of study as her pedagogical responsibility when students like Ellison arrived at her studio to therapize their mundane presentations at ground level, aping the mediocrity of "others." She imparts knowledge then does her work, leaving her otherchild to do as she says *and* does. But this consult happening after a recital failure showcases a genealogy of persons seeking comfort amid chaos—Harrison's European departure is localized for Ellison. That is, this sequence of events portrays him as the beneficiary of an othermothering legacy when Chehaw comes to Harlem, when black aesthetics visit where he is *living with music*.

In an eponymous essay, published in a December 1955 issue of *High Fidelity*, Ellison posits his writing theretofore, no doubt inclusive of *Invisible Man*, as a consequence of sound. Though Alexander G. Weheliye contrives "Living with Music" as symbolic of consuming sonic technologies, I conceive that technological consumption as affective.[36] Mainly, "a drunk of legend" debilitates Ellison's productivity: "he would shout to the whole wide world one concise command, 'Shut up!' . . . The writer's block which this produced was indescribable . . . but in all that *chaos of sound* I sympathized with his obsession, for I, too, *hungered and thirsted* for quiet. Nor did he inspire me to a painful identification, and for that I was thankful. Identification, after all, involves feelings of guilt and responsibility." In that "tiny ground-floor-rear apartment in which [he] was also trying to write," he inheres those vagabond utterances as drafty, seeping into his domicile and his person like steady streams of air.[37] His quietude quest lingers like an unquenched appetite. While he disidentifies, thankfully, with the man, he affectively identifies with him because his drunken words engender blockage: "Shut up!" pronounces both hush and the inertia of his fingers.

This aural deployment takes place via not only the town lush, but also "a singer who lived directly above us; you might say we had a singer on our ceiling." Describing her as not having "the objective of . . . jazzmen," namely those from OKC, Ellison confesses that "she was intensely devoted to her art" and "presented a serious ethical problem: Could I, an aspiring artist, complain against the hard work and devotion to craft of another aspiring artist?"[38] Sonically accosted on every side, he implies that in this interstice, proximate to the street and beneath the chanteuse's residence, he dwells in *middle-earth*, a chaotic under-world; he imaginatively co-occupies that region with that previously abandoned "daughter."[39] (Is he she?) Meanwhile, the forthcoming plot points to the Harlem wino and singing persona as seers of a sonic past when Ellison rehearsed his own creation of racket.

He juxtaposes these incessant silence requests with a "sense of guilt" over his critique of the songstress because during his hometown maturation as a fledgling trumpeter, he subjects his neighbors to "great distress," instrumental bleating that "terrorized a good part of an entire city section." Through nostalgia, Ellison elicits our attention for a notable moment: "I'd give whole summer afternoons and the evening hours after heavy suppers of black-eyed peas and turnip greens, cracklin' bread and buttermilk, lemonade and sweet potato cobbler, to practicing hard-driving blues. Such food oversupplied me with bursting energy, and from listening to Ma Rainey, Ida Cox and Clara Smith, who made regular appearances in our town, I knew exactly how I wanted my horn to sound." Craving an instrument to sound like a woman's voice seems a specific autobiographical trope of trumpeters, tautologized by Miles Davis; he recounts "them spook-filled Arkansas back roads" where he hears a black churchwoman singing at "about six or seven": "Shit, that music was something, especially that woman singing. . . . That *kind* of sound in music, that blues, church, back-road funk kind of thing, that southern, midwestern, rural sound and rhythm . . . started getting into my blood." In these soundscapes, these bluesmen traffic in a listening practice enabled by the black feminine wherein "[t]o hear the voice is to witness the history. To embody the voice, to play it, to represent it, is to bear witness to that history."[40] Ellison, dining in diaspora, receives a double portion of sustenance from that summer menu through the (other)maternal-material, even if his satiation subjects the neighborhood to an inquietude he later feels in Harlem.

This seasonal soul food is a foretaste of performative digestion: the blues dictated by blueswomen as itinerant "parents." This *prix fixe* service spurs

Ellison to devour what he loves and has presumably "lost."[41] One equally acknowledges this smorgasbord being spread by the woman behind/in the stove in OKC: Mrs. Ida Ellison, his mother. When the black maternal feeds an empty stomach, she unequivocally nourishes a starving mind. Nevertheless, wanting his horn to replicate "sirens"—black feminine vocal instrumentality as sonic dreams deferred—substantiates a mixed metaphor for the listener and listened to: "'Son, let's hear you try those "Trouble in Mind Blues." Now try and make it sound like ole Ida Cox sings it.' And I'd draw in my breath and do Miss Cox great violence."[42] This "violence," perhaps confessional code for *performance anxiety*, should be unpacked psychoanalytically to gloss the groove.

Ellison's "bursting energy" endows a mode of psychic identification:

> One or two things may be directly inferred with regard to the preconditions and effects of a process such as [identification]. On the one hand, a strong fixation to the loved object must have been present; on the other . . . the object-cathexis must have had little power of resistance . . . this contradiction seems to imply that the object-choice has been affected on a narcissistic basis, so that the object-cathexis, when obstacles come in its way, can regress to narcissism. The narcissistic identification with the object then becomes a substitute for the erotic cathexis, the result of which is that in spite of the conflict with the loved person, the love-relation need not be given up.

The trumpetic braconnage of Cox's voice reads as pubescent hubris—object-choice preceding object-cathexis, hastening narcissism—or an aspirational pull where the once-starving-now-full artist has a "strong fixation to the loved object," the (other)mother, due to melancholy.[43] (I view this "Living with Music" plot line as quasi-mimicked by Spike Lee in *Mo' Better Blues*. While these scenes are not exactly similar, "noise" ambivalently manifests in Brooklyn as in OKC: Although in the opening scene, the filmic mother forces her son, Bleek, to practice the trumpet, which he "hates," the instrument becomes, apropos to the culinary allusion, his *bread and butter*; it feeds him, and his soul, in adulthood. Yet when deciding who would portray Bleek's mother, the casting director chooses Abbey Lincoln. If the desirous move for an instrument to sound like a blueswoman fulfills itself, the trumpet is maternal-material—the queer happening of music.[44]) If any obstacle exists, it is the "little power of resistance" by community members to urge this impressionable musician to make his horn sing, over and against "those who complained and cried to heaven for Gabriel to blow a chorus so heavenly and sweet and so hellishly hot that I'd forever put down my horn."[45] If Ellison cohabitates in that underworld, his blaring ushers the sonic-sick to Hades. Still, he supplicates to black women's vocality for trumpetic melodiousness.

Pivoting again to the vocalist on his roof, one testifies to the psychoanalytic:

> I was forced to listen, and in listening I soon became involved to the point of *identification*. If she sang badly I'd hear my own futility in the windy sound; if well, I'd stare at my typewriter and *despair* that I should ever make my prose so sing. . . . Yet it was ironic, for after giving up my trumpet for the typewriter I had avoided too close a contact with the very art which [Kathleen Ferrier] recommended as a balm. . . . Now in this magical moment all the old *love*, the old fascination with music superbly rendered, *flooded back*. When she finished I realized that such music in my own apartment, the *chaotic* sounds from without and above had sunk, if not in silence, then well below the level where they mattered. Here was a way out. If I was to live and write in that apartment, it would only be through the grace of music.[46]

Obligated to wrestle with the environmental clamor, Ellison stops being swayed by the noise of a street caveat, instead channeling music that metes out an amazing grace. He contracts melancholy, a despair closely related to Freud's "so on," when rotating brass warbling out for banal word processing. Yet his moodiness also depends on his neighbor's vicissitudinal phonating as she unconsciously admonishes his striving toward a *blueprint for Negro writing*, namely the "blues, spirituals, and folk tales recounted from mouth to mouth," or diaphragm to digit. He syncs with Richard Wright's "architecture" when he narrates this singer as "a purist committed to French art songs and a few American slave songs sung as if *bel canto*." The blueprint is pertinent because when he stages this phonographic cacophony with the singing ceiling, he plays "Marian Anderson . . . Bessie Smith to remind her of the earth out of which we came . . . Ellington's 'Flaming Sword' . . . or Satchmo scatting, 'I'll be Glad When You're Dead.'"[47] To qualify (re)capturing music as a "balm"—salve for a wound—is quasi-Freudian: Literally under the influence of what he overhears, he proposes that "identification is the expression of there being something in common, which may signify *love*."[48] That "old love" gives him new wings, a chance to get his mojo back; and it is kismet that in advance of my forged kinship between blood and water, the fascination of "this magical moment" washes over him as a deluge. Ellison shuts the craze up, and employs a natural law: He does not destroy noise but transforms it to an alternate state where he comprehends "the idea of music as defense against chaos . . . reaching 'the unconscious levels of the mind' and working 'its magic with mood and memory.'"[49] This sonic reclamation constitutes "a way out" for him and us.

These aural transitions outline the politics of noise versus sound. In spite of Ellison being flummoxed by the alcoholic and the vocalist, "because he is able to choose the music and the technology of transmission, it is a sonic intrusion, that is noise, to his neighbors, for they are now subjected to El-lison's system of sound and not their own"—he behaves like the noisemakers he detests. While Weheliye contends this interplay perpetuates masculinity, this technological judo equally foregrounds the affective, even along gender lines. This is a sonic fairytale: When Ellison declares this stereophonic "battle of the sexes," this "war of decibels," the music as proverbial beauty appears to "release the beast" in him.[50] Given the concession that "[b]ecause music's meaning is *embodied* in its physical quality, we cannot separate music's rhe-toric—its 'words'—from its physical reality, its 'delivery,'" Ellison embodies the sound of music spun by his neighbor through identification, just as he disembodies the art of noise pervading that urban tundra from the nontee-totaler. He receives deliverance from his writer's block, blasting a "music/noise continuum . . . a collective space to be shared."[51] Is he not the reaction catalyzed by the woman up above his head? Does she *deliver* him to a com-munalism that feeds the tenement soundscape as opposed to creating noise pollution? Is this the maternal-material?

If these affectively consumed sonic technologies hold up, one re-sounds the first sentence of "Living with Music": "In those days, it was either live with music or die with noise, and we chose rather desperately to live"—the intoxicated noisily reaps a dying injunction with aesthetic repercussions, a "social death" revealed in an inability to put typewriter to paper as the meter of every line on the apparatus potentially succumbs to arrhythmia; yet the ceiling woman invests Ellison with genius, a vivacity wherein "music will not only calm, it will ennoble," making visible, material, that which is invisible to forerun writing the *Great American Novel*.[52] Thus, "sound technology for El-lison provides opportunities for a listener to learn to listen differently, more acutely, and more intentionally . . . a modern listening enhanced through the intentional play between the ear, the body, and technology . . . not merely for notation of sounds, but also for sound thinking, or thinking through listening . . . it is listening that enables—sometimes wholeheartedly and sometimes ambivalently—the reconstitution of a fractured racial self."[53] Though "Living with Music" elides certain tidbits, namely the epidermal makeup of the two others in this sounding trio, presumptive as we might be, replacing "racial" with "affective" imbues that acute listening, and reading, as Chehaw erects itself at its northeasternmost exposure.

This sonic neighbor knows the music, tradition, and musicianship, compelling Ellison to dig in his crates to convene that phonographic pugilism. While this "little man," unnamed and feminized, is only seen once—"on the stoop a few weeks after [Ellison's] rebellion"—she, like her mythic Tuskegee counterpart, is primarily heard (of), implying her invisibility beside phonic intelligibility.[54] But music having the physicality of *delivery* means while traveling with Ralph, realizing that the maternal-material is the spatial-aural in his life, then basements, and the women confined there, are sites for regenerating the affective fracture.

The Tragedy of Happy Accidents

Remember in "The Little Man at Chehaw Station" when Ellison vibes with Harrison's riddle as she masters Liszt. He fixates on the performance as the being behind the stove transforms from a myth to a man right before his very ears; the stove warmer's psychic implantation occurs in the curvature of the pianistic womb for the otherchild via his othermother. In the prologue of *Invisible Man*, the basement as "womb" enacts a natal return when the protagonist hears the feminine "phonographically":

> the invisible man's first descent into his memory, history, and imagination comes by way of song . . . descending from Armstrong's conscious world into the unconscious realm of the black mother, Ellison's character descends into a preternatural site rife with sacrament and mystery. . . . His return to the space of the maternal—the movement toward the maternal is always a "return," since the maternal is antecedent to human life—obviates the simple trope that would make of Ellison's descent and prospective ascent a rescinding of the West's normative negation of black being. Ellison's return to the womb of the maternal is, rather, a complex return to the very embrace of human life that idealizes *agape* love, makes *eros* possible, and holds *thanatos* . . . at bay. Again . . . the descent into the womb, while seemingly a remanding of a daemonic place, is a prolegomenon, a propaedeutic to the world that love demands.[55]

The Harrison-Ellison relation confirms that *agape,* an ideal for living shared between a teacher and her recently faltering student; Ellison casting invisible man as propaedeutic replays his prior instruction when his mentor conceives for him a fictional man in her studio. The descent into "memory, history, and imagination," and ascent toward problematizing Western conceptions of blackness, suggests that as invisible man "spirals down" in this textual world, he can be "lifted up" in the under neath. Notwithstanding the musical parallels of both experiences, to be tackled momentarily, an immediate interest is how mixed genres in the novel elicit multiplex meanings.

The notion of "Ellison's 'Usable Past'" argues for the novel as (auto)biography.[56] For example, during a scene in *Invisible Man*, when "blind Homer Barbee" gives "a speech or sermon" that "doesn't matter" generically, "the master speech of this type is given . . . in an evocation of the founder, perhaps modeled, in its symbolic import, on Booker T. Washington." Barbee—"playing upon the whole audience without the least show of exertion," carrying his listeners into the "presence" as they teem with their senses on edge during could-be Convocation or Founder's Day—potentially exerts this homiletical prowess on the lawns of a Tuskegee-like institute. Another interpretation presumes this oratory being "modeled on an actual speech delivered in chapel at Tuskegee Institute. . . . Major Robert Moton, president of the college, delivered an oration during the fall of Ellison's freshman year in which he described a dying Booker T. Washington summoning Moton to his bedside and saying "Major, don't forget Tuskegee.""[57] This historicity inserts the protagonist as a possible loiterer at a terminal akin to Chehaw, meeting the man-myth-legend behind the stove on his way to college or crossing paths with someone like Harrison after his monthly examination in the fictional music department. With this (auto)biographical mapping at hand, one is further intrigued that Ellison crafts watershed moments in under(-)worlds. Is it plausible, commingling his and Louis Armstrong's instrumentality, that *en route* to Harrison's studio, he set his jaunt to a groove? That having been afforded self-reflection, he entreats the pianist: *What did I do to be so black and blue*?[58] If she is the othermother to whom the otherchild runs, is she an "invisible man" based on her location?

This spatial specification riffs on the mythos, rendered circuitously, of the novel: "the 'truth' for invisible man is mobilized in a return to a *racial source*. . . . The first order of circularity . . . The second order is entirely memorial on the part of the 'author'. . . . The third order of circularity . . . is imposed on the second and consists of commonly identifiable symbols of authority. . . . For mythic studies, the archetype becomes an indispensable figure since the myth is ordained by a *common ancestral meaning*." These "architectonics" rely on the schema of section drawings; cutting these "live-work spaces" open makes their interiority fully apparent.[59]

The fiction preoccupies itself with a power subsumed in that black feminine/(other)maternal formulation: If this exit underground initiates the return to a womb or common ancestor, one is invested in the authority who speaks, and the authorized who listens, there. Although "we tend to forget that the place or situation of the narrative has not shifted from underground," the source material hints at the novel's psychoanalytic as it contends with mourning and/or melancholia: "with one exception, the same [distinguishing mental features of melancholia] are met with in mourning. . . . Profound mourning . . . contains the same painful frame of mind, the same *loss of interest in the outside world.* . . . It is easy to see that this inhibition and *circumscription of the ego* is the expression of an exclusive devotion to mourning which leaves nothing over for other purposes or other interests. It is really only because we know so well how to explain it that this attitude does not seem to us pathological."[60] One addresses the words at the end of the quotation first since in the novel and theory, "[w]hat this mental survey shows are the layers of conflict and renewal which invisible man must work through in a reversed order of things."[61]

The nonpathological removal of oneself from the "outside world" assesses the invisibility of this man above ground, and his self-reflexive visibility under it, as a stage of long-form mourning through devotion to a routine. He inhibits access to exterior threats, ordering the interior self, whether his skull or lair, to be bound within a circle as ego circumscription. This "profound" mourning signaling melancholy crafts this unseen figure as the locus of these themes. Yet what is mourned/makes him melancholic—"the patient is aware of the loss which has given rise to his melancholia, but only in the sense that he knows *whom* he has lost but not *what* he has lost in him"—obliges circling back to the racial source inaugurating this chapter.[62]

When Ellison meets Harrison in her piano studio, he is in a haze, rather than a blaze, of glory for he has been equipped with performative tools for excellence he willingly compromises for fleeting visions of grandeur: "Above ground, the dreaming mind, intruded upon by reality, does not dominate, except at peril to the individual"—Ellison is content with the lightning bug when he could have the lightning.[63] While Harrison's underground labor is not because she confuses stardom with sobriety, that being a clear head, she has seen the peril of individuality when her upper-room dreams in Berlin rerouted themselves to her basement tenure at Tuskegee. He seeks her comfort because someone in another life inculcated him with a tradition to show him what is good and what is required of him: the light(n)ing!

Ellison, in Harrison's workplace, stands in contradistinction to invisible man. It is no wonder the latter siphons "a power line," to illumine 1,369 lightbulbs, "into the building and [runs] it into [his] hole in the ground" from Monopolated Light & Power—he wants the light(n)ing.[64] This power obsession is not because it is inaccessible to those underneath the pavement; rather, it cements the bedrock for a darkness visible, a "creativity [that] goes into dimensions of Black culture that are relatively protected from the incursions of the dominant group." This energy-cum-communal conglomerate, a power grid so to speak, no different than that celluloid skin, propagates the black counterfeit tradition of the "protection": "such symbolic retreat resembles *Invisible Man*'s hideout in [the] book's prologue: 'Please, a definition: A hibernation is a covert preparation for a more overt action.'"[65] Possessing the light(n)ing is flirting with the (c)overt, a dark exercise ahead of letting one's little light shine. And if the women in Ellison's life supply that power and protection, both qualities relate to the phonograph in invisible man's lair. The contraption lets him into a space of dark matter where the groove takes up residence by any means necessary. Deploying acoustemology—"the study of sound, an exploration of sonic sensibilities—how sound enables us to make sense of reality"—indexes that for Ellison, the basement is an especially soniferous space because how sound becomes sensate makes it a location where acoustics, and by default noise, generatively run amok.[66] Is *Invisible Man* potentially more allegory than (auto)biography? We keep listening.

Invisible man drifts on a memory toward a sonorous encounter as the reefer casts its spell; one inquires, à la Farah Jasmine Griffin, who set invisible flowin':

Invisibility . . . gives one a slightly different sense of time, *you're never quite on the beat.* . . . Instead of the swift and imperceptible *flowing* of time, you are aware of its nodes, those points where time stands still or from which it leaps ahead. And you slip into the breaks and look around. . . . So under the spell of the reefer I discovered a new *analytical way of listening to music.* . . . *That night I found myself hearing not only in time, but in space as well.* I not only *entered* the music but *descended*, like Dante, into its depths.[67]

Tapping into the nadir, he wrestles with the phonograph's defective needle, its never-quite-on-the-beat-ivity, to re-member the self. This is counterfactual to the codification of melancholia's twin, mourning: "In what, now, does the work which mourning performs consist? . . . Reality-testing has shown that the loved object no longer exists, and it proceeds to demand that all libido shall be withdrawn from its attachments to that object. This demand arouses understandable opposition . . . so intense that a turning away from reality takes place and a clinging to the object through the medium of a *hallucinatory wishful psychosis.*"[68] This hazy account undoes the spatiotemporal in that this listening party for one colloquially heals all wounds.

Ellison situating these sounds in invisible man's underground lair is him hooking up the sonic particularity of the fictional women to the phonation of his nonfictional othermothers, mainly Harrison at Tuskegee and/or the singing-ceiling neighbor in Harlem; having *lived* with music, he drafts a character who *listens* to it differently. Said women are the resurrected composite of the no-longer-existing loved object, reworked fantastically through maternal figures who sing and wail; ingesting reefer to heighten the hallucinatory is the libidinous rebuttal to withdraw maternal attachment. Hearing those women "is related to cognition because we have to make sense of what we hear . . . hearing is not limited to the ears, as perceiving is intimately connected to the body, requiring a physiological reaction involving our brains, heads, and nervous system . . . particular sounds are often linked to particular spaces and locations, further enabling us to sense and locate that sound in time and space."[69] If this acoustical reading is valid, the relationship of women and the under(-)world to Ellison's "usable past" is, quite literally, the prologue! Moreover, black mo'nin,' or mo(ur/a)nin(g), revealed in ephemera from Emmitt Till's death, inscribes itself anew: One sits with the sound of the *phono*graph, machined and embodied ("'I moan this way 'cause he's dead,' she said."), preceding that of the developed-and-published *photo*graph and the perceptual noise of a wailing mourner, even if that tragedy—the loss of a son—is purveyed by his mother, that is, Can you stay BLACK and *Listen* to This?[70]

Invisible man, this blueblack essence, is indeed listening, albeit circularly, in this women-populated descent; in those depths, there is "a still lower level on which [he] saw a beautiful girl the color of ivory pleading in a *voice like [his] mother's* as she stood before a group of slaveowners who bid for her naked body."[71] This "mother," skinned as an othermother, is heard in the ontic basement, That Bitter Earth, where she vocalizes and corporealizes the strange fruit it bears. The spatiotemporal *flows* like a needle on vinyl; the othermother's ivory complexion affirms the hewed reality of a piano while haunting the protagonist: Does this girl's acoustic pleading *curve* like Harrison's Steinway into which Ellison once leaned? He seemingly exposes that "the project of defining black manhood within a modernist idiom would necessitate an encounter with the figure of the black maternal as *a character and as the ground of nonbeing* that engenders black manhood."[72] This is the bodily and visible phonographic inscription, the palpable hit or touch—the black feminine/(other)maternal trace. This counterintuitive modality encourages identifying whether she is a man invisible.

One accedes that "the 'little man' is a type of 'invisible man,' unprecedented and unlocatable, though this address to 'him' travels through the terminus of Chehaw."[73] This dubious *him* surrounded by scare quotes—or, in another grammatological posture, inverted commas to further mark territory—indicates wonder about the trickster. Regarding gender, the mantra of return to a "racial source" reconceptualizes Ellison's essay whereby one happens upon not only othermotherhood, but also otherparenthood. That being, when the eye scans the first paragraph of Hortense J. Spillers's standard-bearing essay and reads, "My country needs me, and if I were not here, I would have to be invented," that same eye peruses nearly a decade earlier, "But out of a stubborn individualism born of his democratic origins, [the little man] insists upon *the cultural necessity of his role*, and argues that *if he didn't exist he would have to be invented. If he were not already manifest in the flesh*, he would still exist and function as an idea and ideal . . . a manifestation of the *idealistic action of the American Word* as it goads its users toward a perfection of our revolutionary ideals."[74] This excerpt bequeaths a tracking device to retrace the theoretical residue of otherparentage: Ellison is Spillers's otherfather (and I would argue her othermother is Professor Elizabeth Phillips who shares the lightning quip). This inventory of inventions, and that fleshly categorization, generates a legacy that circulates like phonographic shellac, transmitting cross-generational speech acts—melismas—to recapitulate the patented parents' groove. If otherparentage is legible via "The Little Man at Chehaw Station," applying this reading practice to Ellison's life clarifies the ambiguity of the "who" that constitutes him.

If Ellison is othermother Harrison's "baby," his otherfather must be the little man: His vernacular and syntactical wit furnishes the "idea and ideal" of the American Grammar Book. Ellison, then, is a "linguistic product of the American scene and language," suggesting that "black reality—and by extension American reality—could be embodied, literally. In whatever way the circumstances of slavery, freedom, and the vernacular expression of the blues came to be arranged in literature, these circumstances were real and part of an American literary corpus." He personifies Harrison's riddle. Yet one still tussles with this through a different lens, or "biological" push that supplies certitude at the level of DNA since the little man did not conceive Ellison alone. Harrison must also be a type of "invisible man" whose otherchild digests her idea to cathect vernacular navigation as trafficked through "him-ness"—her "advice takes on a strange, oracular quality as [her] words *flow.*"[75] She is the black feminine figuration of "the last man standing": Historically defining freedom through race, she now reaches for self-meaning when performing speech. Through enunciation, Harrison convenes "'the entanglement of the subject and the object [which] embraces the reader within the narrative as a variable 'you' who is fully dependent on, and constitutive of its corollary, the 'I.'"[76]

In this same way, the indeterminacy of *Invisible Man* constitutes the invisibility that precedes "him" due to a lacking article: definite (The) or indefinite (An). This syntax merits criticism: "as much as I admired, still admire, *Invisible Man* . . . the question for me is, invisible to whom? Not me."[77] This provocation calls attention to a latent ambiguity because the man could be, and invisibility belongs to, anyone, just as the identity of the little man is "universal." Therefore, Harrison is also a type of invisible man because of this perplexity. But Ellison further notates invisibility by mentioning those who impart vernacular to him through shadowing: "the artist may direct itself to those who are conscious of the most advanced state of his art: his *artistic peers.* But if his work has social impact, which is one gauge of its *success as symbolic communication*, it will reach unto unpredictable areas. Many of us . . . read our first Hemingway, Fitzgerald, Mann in barbershops, *heard our first opera on phonographs.* . . . Such are the circumstances that render the little man at Chehaw Station not only possible but inevitable."[78] Possibility and inevitability make visible this paternal myth. Yet this intellectual trajectory—acknowledging a space where he got follicularly "cut up" in advance of his bookish *come-up*—invites a query: Why is no one attributed "success" for the operatic, yet the unnamed barber, or his business, is a Rubicon for literacy? Who is the barber's "peer" in that heard clause?

A re-memory of when such listening occurred materializes in "That Same Pain, That Same Pleasure: *An Interview.*" Ellison divulges how his "literary situation has been special . . . vault[ing] the parochial limitations of most Negro fiction"; he invokes "sources of strength":

> . . . to the extent that one cannot ever escape what is given I suppose
> it had less to do with writing per se than with my desire, beginning at
> a very early age, to be more fully a part of that larger world which surrounded the Negro world into which I was born. . . . Then there were
> the accidents through which so much of that world beyond the Negro
> community became available to me. . . . The other accident from that
> period lay in my mother's bringing home copies of such magazines as
> *Vanity Fair* and of opera recordings which had been discarded by a

family for whom she worked. You might say that my environment was extended by these slender threads . . . These magazines and recordings and the discarded books my mother brought home to my brother and me spoke to me of a life which was broader and more interesting, and although it was not really a part of my own life, I never thought they were not for me simply because I happened to be a Negro. They were things which spoke of a world which I could [someday] make my own.[79]

Regarding that interrogative about the invisible artistic peer, the primary maternal reveals herself. Othermother Harrison's elision, vis-à-vis the little man behind the stove, marks a history of invisibility inaugurated by the obfuscation of bloodmother Ellison.

Ellison referring to his mother's actions as "accidents," regardless of being "happy" he is the product of such "mishaps," is intriguing. But that is it: Referencing these culturally educable moments of materiality as such, he proposes that she enacts these intentional appropriations of miscellany as *happenstance*, serendipity that could have been forgone if she was in another place at another time. The mother-as-"accident" epitomizes misspeaking: She is the first, as opposed to Harrison as the last, man standing, even as the first "little man at Chehaw Station" in the life of Ellison. Put differently, someone in OKC, one guesses "her," had a vernacular encounter with Ralph Waldo *Emerson*; said person thinks enough of this child to namesake him, conveying that R. W. as this R. W.'s otherfather, a second skin for the American Scholar. This naming describes how "the ideal level of sensibility to which the American artist would address himself tends to transcend the lines of class, religion, region, and race—*floating*, as it were, free in the crowd."[80] This trace obliges conversing on the (auto)biographical via ancestry and the maternal present.

Comprehensive Ellison biographies, primarily those by Lawrence Jackson and Arnold Rampersad, tie Ellison's writerliness to the agnate. Jackson declares, "[Lewis Ellison] deliberately named his son after the founder of the American Renaissance in literature and philosophy, telling family and friends that he was 'raising this boy up to be a poet.'" Rampersad explains that Mr. Ellison posthumously "left behind the well-thumbed 'thick anthology of poetry' that became one of Ralph's dearest possessions. *What did his father know of Emerson, really*? Lewis's letters to Ida—the few that have survived—suggest a poor education, though it's possible that he had started life with certain interests and tastes only to have them, and his entire sensibility, coarsened by racism."[81] These respective chapters, "Geography Is Fate: 1913–1916" and "In the Territory," point to the pragmatism of travel and chronological precision as my blood-water deployment subsequently indexes the flow/groove.

Rampersad inquiring about what Mr. Ellison knew about Emerson clears space for Mrs. Ellison. Although in these biographies, she is metaphorically absent insofar as the son's partum paternally narrates itself, she shapes Ellison more than expected. If there is a question of Father's caliber of education, is it plausible Mother names Ralph—if he *possesses* the anthology, could she *profess* it through the continuation of a name? She wrote extensively to Ellison as seen by the volume of letters between 1933 to 1937; and she herself was an "archivist," as was his second wife, Fanny McConnell Ellison, cataloguing his work to later archive with the Library of Congress.[82] All the more, this bloodmother is a "professor" because in that interview implicating his Father raising a poet, Ellison, responding to where his creative drive comes from, intuits, "[M]aybe the desire to write goes back to a Christmas gift. One Christmas my mother gave me—I must have been five—a little roll-top desk and a chair, not a swivel chair but a little straight chair, oak, and a little toy typewriter. I had forgotten that." Jackson writes on this; the account from Rampersad is brief: Intending to give him and his brother Herbert "a better chance of reaching manhood," she sold the gifts to obtain money to move to Gary, Indiana, leaving Ralph "seethed with rage." Prior to this passage, Rampersad shares, "Filial tributes from Ralph to Ida are few and far between in his writings. 'I loved her very much,' he wrote once about his mother for a publication, but he did so then to forestall any inference that he loved a certain woman . . . more." That woman is Breaux, "his mother's social superior whose wider world Ellison very much wanted to enter."[83] This presents a worthwhile juxtaposition.

Breaux co-owned the Aldridge Theater, a venue that "showed movies but also staged concerts by classical, jazz, and blues performers such as Bessie Smith and Ma Rainey, whom Ralph met. . . . Sometimes in concerts she accompanied him on the piano or lent him her own instruments, including her prized soprano saxophone."[84] Emoting *agape*, she proverbially sets the stage for his blues digestion as the in medias res othermother buttressed by Mrs. Ida and Miss Hazel. He leans into Harrison's piano when she interprets Liszt because his fingers have already contoured ivory surfaces as a teenager. One now cites Breaux as the "artistic peer" Ellison renders invisible in "Living with Music" related to Ma Rainey, Ida Cox, and Clara Smith appearing regularly in his hometown ahead of him wanting to *blow his (other)mother.*

Though Ellison forgetting his mother's yuletide gifts is telling, he presents his father as the one who lays the foundation (a "construction foreman, building buildings") and his mother as the one who makes the home. Citational wonders abound when claiming her as the impetus behind his wish to write, as well as her "encouraging my interest in reading. She had no idea that I was going to become a writer, or if she did, she had more insight into me than I had into myself. . . . And she understood that that was what was going on."[85] He states this not long before publishing "The Little Man at Chehaw Station." That he does not allude to her in that opera moment is significant though minor. If we take that filial tribute note seriously, it is apropos neither she nor Breaux obtains function there; this carries over to Harrison.

In a critical Ellison text, she receives a paragraph regarding Tuskegee. Then two pages showcase Morteza Sprague, "the most influential of all of Ellison's teachers" at the institute; he dedicates *Shadow and Act* to him: "A dedicated dreamer in a land most strange."[86] (What about Nazi Germany?) Summarily, these women lurk in the shadows, ingratiating their "son" with intellect that has "genius" outcomes. These are they who show the artist what aesthetics call for—they give him the light(n)ing. Knowing this, it is (un)surprising that Ellison dedicates *Invisible Man* "To Ida," further muddying invisibility. Ida Guggenheimer, an Ellison patron, offers him that aforementioned Vermont home to complete *Invisible Man*; "though older than Ida Bell Ellison would have been, in her maternal affection Ida Guggenheimer must have brought back memories of his mother. . . . Ellison's letters to Ida help the reader understand her ambivalence toward his dedication of *Invisible Man* to her." That this benefactor is the coincident namesake of Mrs. Ellison, and that simply writing "To Ida" assigns doubt as to whom he is referring if one knows his mother's name, highlights how even in signposting one, the other is invisible. Though Tim Parrish asserts that "Ida" is Mrs. Ellison, if this son wanted to clarify the "who," writing "To" and appending the word, or some adjective of or relating to, "mother" likely would have sufficed. After all, publicly calling a parent by her first name was, is, a cultural no-no, yes?[87] These realizations convey how the "rich literary world that Ellison came to inhabit was a man's world, but one supported by the labor of wives who nurtured, cooked, cleaned, read, typed, edited, coddled, tended to the wounds of ego and offered affirmation"; "(other)mother" is an additional laborer.[88] Yet the "absent" paternal and literary surrogacy now require attention.

The essay "The World and the Jug" is Ellison's response to Irving Howe's "Black Boys and Native Sons"; he sutures a genealogy related to the limbs of his "family tree": "[Richard] Wright himself is given a diversity of roles (all conceived by Howe): He is not only the archetypal and true-blue black boy—

the 'honesty' of his famous autobiography established this for Howe—but the spiritual father of Ellison and Baldwin and all other Negroes of literary bent to come. Further, in the platonic sense he is his own father and the cultural hero who freed Ellison and Baldwin to write more 'modulated' prose." This diction, and third-person self-referral, encompasses how Ellison does not embrace Howe's perceptual lineage. In the latter half of the essay, originally titled "A Rejoinder," he declares:

> I sought out Wright because I had read Eliot, Pound, Gertrude Stein and Hemingway, and as early as 1940 Wright viewed me as a potential rival, partially, it is true, because he feared I would allow myself to be used against him by political manipulators who were not Negro and who envied and hated him. But perhaps you will understand when I say he did not influence me if I point out that while *one can do nothing about choosing one's relatives, one can, as artist, choose one's 'ancestors.'* Wright was, in this sense, a 'relative'; Hemingway an 'ancestor.' Langston Hughes, whose work I knew in grade school and whom I knew before I knew Wright, was a 'relative'; Eliot, whom I was to meet only many years later, and Malraux and Dostoievsky [*sic*] and Faulkner, were 'ancestors'—if you please or don't please![89]

While such rhetoric is alluring, the reader too has a rejoinder.

Discounting Wright as a father, to the extent of seeming patricide, is inevitable for the purposes of masculine competition and highbrow "trash talk." Instead, Ellison inserts himself into modernism, the "classics," through an allegiance to an ilk of writers caught *playing in the dark*; he equally substitutes modernity for maternity as a writer with a penchant for invisibility— matricide is the first order, akin to maternal "death" expediting autonomy.[90] The Stein allusion supports this because her incorporation arrives as a hollow afterthought: She is only "read," not even an ostensible "relative." These genealogical nuggets may be typical of Ellison related to a "woman's thought process"; he regards "the opposite sex" as flimsily as he accounts for how their epistemic potential does not "stray afar from biological reality—even when they cloak themselves with intellectual sheep's clothing—and . . . men make a mistake to expect them to do otherwise; since men are somewhat responsible for that condition." These words—jotted down in an epistle to "Dear Dick" (read: Richard Wright) on May 11, 1940, and ahead of the two parts of "The World and the Jug" published in *The New Leader* (the irony!)— invoke the blackness of pots and kettles, nodding to diasporic gourmandizing;

or that this male wolf dons wool as witnessed in the recent metaphor. This untrained physician diagnoses the "condition" for which he is a host.[91] Maybe certain kinds of folk are never really immune.

This gendered relativism also problematizes the little man as a griot like Esu-Elegbara. Ellison reads race as the inheritance of "'group style' . . . 'bound less by blood'" in that "the 'group style' was not *genetically transmitted* but, says Ellison, was 'taught to me by Negroes, or copied by me from those among whom I lived most intimately.'" Similarly, Africa is not necessarily on his aesthetic radar when considering a material heritage, irrespective of his private art collection containing a Janus-figure of that Africanism. One might conjecture the same about black Americana(?): "if the Little Man is a *protean* trickster, he might be white, black, or both at the same time"—said Man could inhabit the persona of Eliot, Pound, Hemingway, Malraux, Dostoevsky, Faulkner, or others if a relationship with their texts constitutes a life of "intimacy."[92] The mention of "blood" also subverts kinship: Ellison's "relatives"—Wright, Hughes, Baldwin—are "family members" but only through "marriage," regardless of the symmetries and (a/e)ffects of blackness; meanwhile, disregarding chromosomal uncertainty with white-male-author "ancestors," due to their hereditary and/or cultural legacies of pillage and plunder, Ellison fortifies the bloodline. (An aside: Hemingway's official website has a section dedicated to his hunting in Africa uncannily titled "Hemingway's Africa: 1933–1954." His "trophies included a lion and other large game that roamed the African grasslands . . . [he] hunted the plains of the Serengeti, tracked animals through the bush, and recorded his experiences for later use in his work"; he "returned to the *Dark Continent* twenty years later with his fourth wife." The taxidermy, possibly contributing to species endangerment, is apparent, but no less troubling is the website, dated 2014, referring to Africa with a "god term" akin to Freud comprehending female sexuality. Moreover, these expeditions occur under colonialism in that the Democratic Republic of Congo née the Belgian Congo experiences his "wrath" in 1954; the country does not gain independence until 1960.[93]) But even this has a counterpoint.

Though Ellison distances himself from Wright, it is fascinating that years before *Invisible Man*, Wright relays motifs on Harlem, the underground, light, and Lafargue Psychiatric Clinic in "Psychiatry Comes to Harlem" (1946): "Psychologically, repressed need goes *underground*, gropes for an *unguarded outlet in the dark* and, once finding it, *sneaks out, experimentally tasting the new freedom*, then at last gushing forth in a *wild torrent*, frantic lest a new taboo deprive it of the right to exist." Ellison's "Harlem Is

Nowhere" (1948), written but unpublished, is also about the borough and Lafargue; its opening sentence: "One must descend to the basement and move along a confusing mazelike hall to reach it." This conceptual reframing also occurs when reading "Richard Wright's Blues" (1945), especially the final paragraph: "Nowhere in America today is there social or political action based upon the solid realities of Negro life depicted in *Black Boy* . . . with its refusal to offer solutions, it is like the blues. . . . Wright's most important achievement: He has converted the American Negro impulse toward self-annihilation and *'going-under-ground'* into a will to confront the world, to evaluate his experience honestly and throw his findings unashamedly into the guilty conscience of America." Ellison engenders befuddlement when denying his Wright linkage and the "tradition" in which he traffics, even as he plots rhetoric about and "borrows" from him through interpolations for his then-forthcoming novel.[94] Wright "establishes the tropes others who follow him must respond to and/or reject"; or, as argued here, rehearse and/or reconstruct. This is certainly true if they are "brothers. . . . Wright reinforced ambitions that Ellison had received from his parents."[95] That catachresis regarding "choice" of relatives and ancestors is permissible when he warns that only an artist accomplishes such subterfuge. Despite his artful dodge when "ancestors" stands in for "friends," one critiques the critique of Wright as "his own father" when Ellison, this Native Son from OKC, this Black Boy from Tuskegee, coordinates his motherless-ness, being *brought into this world* by (white) "fathers"/unto himself; or as his feminine "relatives" and "ancestors" are women made invisible.

It is not the case that the mother, these "mothers," causes an "accident" as an eggcorn, but confers *access,* the savor of "culture." When invisible man siphons that electricity, the "acts of sabotage and the art of illumination become inseparable facets of his own 'spiritual technology' and, for us as readers, the site of one more 'electrifying' Ellisonian joke—evidence that, waking or dreaming, in this thinker-tinker's theory- and concept-toting world of high fidelity and calculated distortion, the ways of invisibility remain willfully and invariably mysterious, their 'accidents' and wonders to perform."[96] This is integral to the ideation of the maternal "accident" because Ellison's "forgetfulness" may be an act of sabotage and art of illumination; the question is: of whom? That citational gap could be self-sabotage; for the mother, this trickery presumes her intellectually stimulating acts not being "thought out." One may land on the former option if Mrs. Ellison was purposeful in her motives, hence the admission that she had more insight into her son than he himself. But it is notable that the distortion of his mother's foreknowing is Ellison unconsciously showing "high fidelity" to her and her aesthetics. This is no "accident": She phenomenologically gifts him a *power surge* to which he has unlimited use, while she remains an invisible source, with others, on the grid.

This insurgent network further simulates power systems because if Mother Ellison "begets" Miss Harrison, her "artistic peer," both invested in flowin', groovin', then the phonographic recording is so large that its circularity, its tracking, its blackness, spans from OKC to Chehaw—Ellison learns the groove *in a round*. But this compels tackling the tragedy of the happy accident: If *Invisible Man* is allegory, or (auto)biography, Ellison casts the protagonist as solipsistic: "I play the invisible music of my isolation," then he almost retracts that admission by asking, "That last statement doesn't seem right, does it? But it is: you hear this music simply because music is heard and seldom seen, except by musicians."[97] Yet there is evidence that Ellison, trumpeter as possible (auto)biographical-allegorical subject, sees the music because the material itself is handed to him as records, sheet music, and periodicals that make real, phonographically and photographically, the *mater* in his midst: the missing signifier.

This psychoanalytic provocation lends insight: "The missing signifier does not reside elsewhere, on a separate plane, but rather operates within the signifying structure. . . . Because the missing signifier is *present as an absence*, it exerts a *constant pressure* . . . we would see that the missing signifier, despite appearances, does not concern those who are properly represented. It concerns the system of signification itself, *the law itself*." Like the ellipsis, this present absence, through which "the task of a psychoanalytic politics involves bringing conceptual location of the feminine—or the missing signifier—to light"(!), undoes the regulative dicta of gender semiotics when the signifier is readily apparent and almost always male. Might one ratify a new set of protocols in *her* honor: "the law of the Mother"?[98]

This "maternal legislation" would counter psychosocial modes imposed by dominant actors; the structures permitting this "legalism" would be antithetical to their predecessors:

> The missing signifier indicates the failure of any set to close itself as a whole. By emphasizing this failure through one's political activity, one works to effect a fundamental change in the relationship between inclusion and exclusion. As long as the logic of wholeness or success predominates, *inclusion within a set will provide a certain symbolic identity for those who are included, and those who are excluded will experience the absence of this identity.* The logic of the whole secures

a stable barrier that creates vastly different experiences on each of its sides, but this stable barrier is always an illusory one. The logic of the failure of any closure does not eliminate the barrier between the inside and the outside or deconstruct the difference between inclusion and exclusion. Instead, it reveals the speculative identity of inclusion and exclusion. The two positions become *visible* as the same through their very *difference*.[99]

"Political activity" toward "fundamental change"—whether reconstituting one's familial line, or viewing "the black," "him" specifically, as "a co-worker in the kingdom of culture, to escape both death and isolation, to husband and use his best powers and his latent genius"—intimates those psychoanalyzed positions of inclusion and exclusion.[100] While "the logic of wholeness or success" reads as hopeful, either tenet detracts from the power of the riddles predominating this narration. The un-visible, and their high visibility, necessarily trouble their (in)artistic peers, destabilize that "stable barrier," because the light(n)ing the unseen seek, and share, is diametric to what some crave from spotlights, especially if the obscured work best alone and/or in the dark. Another illustrative moment emerges.

Ellison has a "lifelong distaste" for sociology, seen through "grades [that] were not nearly as good" as in English, though he is deemed "much more impressive in that subject." His disciplinary disdain pronounces itself most when his sociology instructor, Howard M. Nash, does not challenge an "offensive passage" in Robert E. Park and Ernest W. Burgess's *Introduction to the Science of Sociology*: "the authors assert that while the Jew stands for idealism, the East Indian for introspection, and the Anglo-Saxon for adventure, the Negro 'is primarily an artist, loving life for its own sake. His métier is expression rather than action. He is, so to speak, the lady among the races.'" On the precipice of his May 1936 Tuskegee exit, "Ralph had already matched his dislike of sociology with an equal dislike for black racial propaganda," anticipating "aspects of his fight with Black Power separatists some thirty years later."[101] This include-exclude calculation predicates itself on the black feminine "mattering" in line with that previous ancestral retrospective. In the case of inclusion, white paternity occupies centrality, at the exclusion of maternity in toto, to convey Negro work as having reputable "standing" as *canon fodder* (see: the critique of Howe); in the case of exclusion, exerting masculinity proves the community's "art" is no longer complicated by that "lady" so that when racial gatherings, corporate or internecine, commence, blackness finds inclusion at the shindig because "a race, a people must think its way back through the *fathers*, if they will claim their rightful human place" (see: the barber-opera "peer" relationship).[102] This amounts to "[t]he protocols of recognition and exclusion or inclusion that are wordlessly, unconsciously established in reality as the type of reality itself" called "race" (or "gender," truth be told). This reifies the little man being a protean trickster, but could Harrison understand "him" as a gendered disambiguation such that she could be the *mugging of the metaphor*: the "powerful and shadowy evocation" of that "man"?[103]

In the wholesale determination to alleviate the black woman from the "kingdom of culture," inclusion becomes exclusion, and vice versa, yet the missing signifier does exert "pressure"—she is never not there. Speaking "sociologically," she is always and ever "the lady" "in waiting." The "body" in *Invisible Man* underscores this:

> The "body" of Ellison's novel is itself . . . situated in caesura . . . consider the novel and its text as a body. . . . One might say it is a body birthed from a certain womb that served as both home and reprieve from a racist onslaught: *the body of the black mother*. . . . That each of these maternal figures appears in the oneiric, multiple folds of the invisible man's Prologue, should give us some indication of the *ritual significance* of these *elided* feminine black figures . . . it is from their repressed yet mythological presence—narrative myth being one of the primary ways in which human beings seek to make sense of their existence by configuring a story of origins and roots, in short, a narrative of *originary birth and home*, and thus a narrative of *originary maternality*—that springs a metaphorics of black being.[104]

Through the spectral force of the black mother toward her child, in one's attempt to deny her, one does indeed become her—this too is identification. The novel metaphorizes a black womb. But this conjuration can be extended: The basement-under(-)ground is a womb such that invisible man's ritual departure to interact with the world connotes constant rebirth; and if a symptom of melancholia is "cessation of interest in the outside world," his ritual retreat to the underworld signals the "protection," a regenerative process to no longer consciously suppress the love object unconsciously repressed. Ascent and immersion narrativize the melancholic genius of the epic.[105] Then again, perhaps melancholy and genius are communal and not relegated to "the one."

Even if Ellison's light(n)ing quest is snuffed out due to his sophomoric actions and thinking prior to arriving at the piano studio, he graduates to "enlightenment" as a spokesperson for Lafargue, that underground mazelike Clinic. Circularity equally influences its mythos:

> To live in Harlem is to dwell in the very *bowels* of the city; it is to pass a *labyrinthine existence* among streets that explode monotonously skyward with the spires and crosses of churches and clutter under foot with garbage and decay. Harlem is a ruin . . . we are here interested in its psychological character—a character that arises from the impact between urban slum conditions and folk sensibilities. . . . This abruptness of change and the resulting clash of cultural factors within Negro personality account for some of the *extreme contrasts* found in Harlem, for both its negative and its positive characteristics. For if Harlem is the scene of the folk-Negro's *death agony*, it is also the setting of his *transcendence*.[106]

"Harlem Is Nowhere" because like Harrison's pre-Tuskegee nomadism, the Negro cannot claim, comfortably, any zip code as "home." The borough as "ruin" is concerning when imagining what Armageddon befell it such that new transplants blend in with the decay; its labyrinthine footprint encourages those who dwell there to practice mindfulness regarding their surroundings.

Apocalypse comes to Harlem.

This urban metropolis depiction has a nearly coterminous diasporic counterpart via Frantz Fanon: As Ellison confronts the South-North migratory vicissitudes of the Negro as a "death agony," could-be folk-speak for "the death drive," Fanon outlines the flight of the Negro of the Antilles circumnavigating to the *métropole*. These Negro denizens see Harlem, or Paris—stay black—and die.[107] However, the death-transcendence shift determines the work of the Clinic.

For Ellison, northbound southerners map a "cultural history" that "reads like the legend of some tragic people out of mythology," navigating Harlem despite it being ruinous. At the cost of losing "techniques of survival to which Faulkner refers as 'endurance,'" these pilgrims face "the denial of [protecting 'the citizen against the irrational, incalculable forces that hover about the edges of human life'] through segregation and discrimination that leaves the most balanced Negro open to anxiety." Badia Sahar Ahad theorizes, "The migrant's head-on collision with urbanity simultaneously expresses the promise and prevarication of the American Dream." This (false) northern hope supposes that perhaps southern folks should have stayed put as "Negroes running—but in their same old place."[108] Yet in "Richard Wright's Blues,"

Ellison opines, "In the North energies are released and given *intellectual* channelization—energies which in most Negroes in the South have been forced to take either a *physical* form or, as with potentially intellectual types like Wright, to be expressed as nervous tension, anxiety and hysteria. . . . And what is called hysteria is suppressed intellectual energy expressed physically."[109] This diagnosis forces sitting with the (auto)biographical once more.

If these upheavals invite "unwellness," is Ellison's Tuskegee-to-Harlem globetrotting, and his ensuing writing difficulty, the preexisting condition that fosters his anxiety? His hysteria?[110] Recall the joyless noise of those outside exclamations incapacitating the fluidity of his inside scribblings—it is chaos! And is it not uncanny that a "malady" irrevocably tied to the feminine manifests in the masculine through the physical, which itself elides the intellectual? Here is the performance of melancholy and genius:

> . . . female madness was put down not to melancholy, but to 'hysteria.' . . . Like melancholy, hysteria was also supposed to involve vapours rising to invade the lungs and brain. But in hysteria the source of the fumes was not the spleen, but the womb—*hystera* means 'womb' in Greek. . . . The wits of a sane woman were decreed sluggish (because of her womb); but, out of her wits, a female fared no better. She was declared hysterical: able to experience only those phantasms created by her own self, not the universal Truths of the mad male visionaries. Long before Freud, the womb was (literally) the female *sub*conscious: the vapours rising up from it were thought to interfere with her consciousness. . . . The hysterical woman was a shadowy (cold, wet and vaporous) imitation of the fiery melancholic male.[111]

Humoral theory—"The world of melancholia was humid, heavy, and cold [femininity]; that of mania was parched, dry, compounded of violence and fragility [masculinity]"—tracks with Ellison who himself traffics in (pre)-modernist thought regarding "character" via brains and brawn.[112] That said, he might have read, and riffed on, "Mourning and Melancholia" based on how Freud rehearses hysteria.[113]

If the condition creates a cathexis toward the lost object, are its "isolated actions and innervations" revealed when Ellison spends time underground, often alone; or his construction of a character who hears the maternal after smoking reefer and circles down like Dante?[114] Is this the counterintuition of the physical qua intellectual? For example, Ellison acquires an isolationist demeanor following his mother's death in 1937; he solitarily mourns her:

"February is a brook, birds, an apple tree. . . . Unemployed, tired of reading, and weary of grieving the loss of my mother, I'd gone into the woods to forget. So that now all Februarys have the aura of that early morning *coldness* . . . had survived three months off the fields and woods by my *gun.* . . . And now in this windless February instant I had crossed over into a new phase of living. Shall I say it was in those February *snows* that I first became a *man*?"[115] The humoral gestures in this short meditation register as Ellison's "coldest winter ever" in a month then dedicated to celebrating Negro History Week; February's nival frigidity unites with a parched and grieving fragility seen in a shotgun's dry violence. If melancholy, because of the lost object, psychically produces the split ego, Mrs. Ida's passing and Ellison's mourning "repair" his as he contrives himself being a "man."[116] Moreover, the hysteria-melancholy duality offers a peculiar lens for identification.

The womb, powerful in the Ellison sphere, binds hysteria; relocating catalyzes its "rising." If this affective state measures the "strong fixation to the loved object," then one not only introjects the mother, but also, and awesomely, "extrojects" her architecturally and atmospherically. The womb as "the female *sub*conscious," precursory to Freud, signifies all the *sub*terranean spaces in Ellison's oeuvre—the basement studio, under-floor apartment, Lafargue Clinic, underground lair—harnessing "her" power to enable "him." And if hysteria elicits the phantasm, might this cement maternity communing with invisibility *in the first place*? Black male South-North transplants become "hysterical" through sudden "movements"—are their emigrating black female sojourners, who have already "contracted" hysteria, infected with the contagion in a second wave? Or do they exhibit "an absence of bile, such a concentration of manlove" for their kin traveling elevated railroads with them? Is this a "genius" posture where the black feminine excretes black bile (read: melancholy)?[117]

If hysteria qualifies an identificatory mode, whether imitation or madness, Terrance Hayes may be on to something when embracing the illness through denial:

But there never was a black male hysteria
Breaking & entering wearing glee & sadness
And the light grazing my teeth with my lighter
To the night with the flame like a blade cutting
Me slack along the corridors with doors of offices
Orifices vomiting tears & fire with my two tongues

Loose & shooing under a high top of language
In a layer of mischief so traumatized trauma
Delighted me beneath the tremendous
Stupendous horrendous undiscovered stars
Burning where I didn't know how to live
My friends were all the wounded people
The black girls who held their own hands
Even the white boys who grew into assassins[118]

Where exactly is this "I"? Coordinating crime with community, glee with sadness, tears with fire, a loose tongue with a loosed tongue, the poetic subject contorts like the ampersand. Is he underground, toppled by the concrete of language or fallen stars as Chicken Little's *Homosapien* other? Is the "high top" his hair, faded, under which he faces himself, his trauma, to reckon that tongue-twisted mouth with the medulla oblongata—the control center for the lungs and heart—while rocking untied kicks? Like the undercommons, this fellowship of the people of the wound means "I" does not dress his own scars; balm is brokered through mutual aid. Yet the black girls hold their own hands—is this *social distancing* to not transmit hysteria, or has "I" not worked through his own stuff so that he, like Ellison, is the host, not the helpless? Is he traversing clinical corridors, seeking the proper office for a voluntary trial to experience "the flame like a blade cutting," the light(n)ing? Is this Lafargue on steroids?

Ellison proposes the location "both as a scientific laboratory and as an expression of forthright democratic action in its scientific willingness to dispense with preconceived notions and accept the realities of Negro, i.e., *American* life"; due to the establishment of the Clinic, "[t]he results were electric"(!): "like some Southern Negroes who consider that part of themselves best which they hide beneath their servility, [Lafargue physicians] consider their most important work that which is carried out in a Harlem basement."[119] The Clinic—this basement, this womb, this mirrored labyrinth underground—is where the light(n)ing strikes. Rethinking now the atmosphere of *Invisible Man*, one regards the lair as an offsite walk-down for palliative self-care. Though the underground can be likened to the underworld, iterative of Hell, it seems in these narrativizations, the location sublimates into (N******) Heaven—an electric space where netherworld figures saunter in the beauteous light that has broken forth.

Likewise, at the end of "The Little Man at Chehaw Station," Ellison, "circulating a petition . . . inside a tenement building in San Juan Hill" as a New

York Writers' Project member, descends to a building's basement for signatures when he hears "loud voices. They were male Afro-American voices, raised in violent argument. The language was profane, the style of speech a southern idiomatic vernacular such as was spoken by formally uneducated Afro-American workingmen." Referencing the rhetoric as "a verbal equivalent of fisticuffs," he hesitates knocking to assess the situation. Then, the confession: His assumption is "confounded" because "these foulmouthed black workingmen were locked in verbal combat over which of two celebrated Metropolitan Opera divas was the superior soprano!" These workingmen, "sprawled around a circular dining-room table," find warmth by "a fireplace with a coal fire glowing in its grate, and . . . four enormous coal scoops." The continuing conversation discloses their vocations as "coal heavers *and* Met extras." These men may have been listening to "Queen of the Night" from Act II, Scene 3 of Mozart's *Die Zauberflöte* in a room that serves as a makeshift uterus, the residential facsimile of a neonatal unit fit for a monarch to birth royalty. The behind-closed-door boisterousness, interrupted by a continuously sophomoric affect, contrives the workers as not only "huge black" men behind *and* in a San Juan Hill stove—the Brooklyn brood of Chehaw—but also light(n)ing bugs in the presence of a pesky gnat. What Ellison externally reads as "hysteria" is an internal battle of *hautes études*. We trace this aural footprint, following the tracks of men mimicking their "mothers." This may be Derridean hauntology all the way turned up; or the unorthodox prescription to quarantine in the belly of an underworld to get well soon.[120]

Having acknowledged and memorialized "the missing signifier," theoretically and practically, we subvert that moment of remembrance. Presuming performers "who ignore the judgments of the vernacular are destined for failure" seems inappropriate here: The tragedy of Mrs. Ellison and Miss Harrison, even Mrs. Breaux, is that each engages vernacular prowess, but has disengagement adjudicated upon her by her vernacular-receptive progeny. Calling them *blues people*—"the most forceful examples from the vernacular, a comprisal of the *All* of American culture"—is done with misgivings because their failure to be named, as they name, is foundational to (an) individual('s) success, someone's genius.[121] More pointedly, the little man is nameable in manners Miss Harrison and Mrs. Ellison are not: That is the blues, that is the melancholy. This disembodied riddle(r) is more visible invisibly than the women made un-visible who not only substantiate the enigma, but also secure its explanation.

If one revives Griffin's ever-important question, though the *who* of one's flowin'—the black feminine/(other)maternal—continues to exist, a more pressing issue is: Having received that insistently fluid gift, being set (up) to get down, *how* does the flow survive when the needle indeed skips?[122] On this melancholic genius journey, one bestows primacy to the phonograph by repairing the sonically affective breach. To get one's groove back, one must *write* oneself into the vernacular one has been given, as well as *right* citational errors as to whom the "who" that gave it is. In so doing, the first album on deck, specific to Ellison, should be a blues compilation with features from Mrs. Ida Ellison and Mrs. Zelia N. Page Breaux and Bessie Smith and Ma Rainey and Ida Cox and Clara Smith and Miss Hazel Harrison and the unnamed cantor upstairs and Rose Poindexter and Fanny McConnell Ellison and Shirley Jackson. The title of the project: *Say Her Name.*[123]

Another way to decree this is to take an enunciative page from the founder of Tuskegee and impose his selfsame utterance, remixed, on Ellison:

"Ralph, don't forget your mothers."

. . . How long
Since a man you called father
  Troubled the hi-fi,
smoldering
Newport in hand, and ran
  This record under a needle.
. . . Years
  Since he drifted, dreaming
Into rice fields, stammered
  Cracked Vietcong, gunboats
And helicopters swirling
  In his head. Years since
His own long walks, silent
  Returns, and Marvin's
Many voices his only salve.
. . .

Graying beard, callused hands,
  Fingernails thick as nickels,
. . . A man's
  Life is never measured
In beats, but beat-downs,
  Not line breaks, just breaks.
You hear Marvin fade down
  The avenue and it caresses
  you
Like a brick: Your father,
  Marvin, and men like them,
Have already moaned every
  Book you will ever write.
This you know, baby. This
  You know.

—JOHN MURILLO,
"Trouble Man" in *Up*
Jump the Boogie

The Hearing Eye—Do You See What I See?

When listening to Marvin Gaye's "Trouble Man," fully aware there are lyrics yet unaware what they might be, the brain fashions its own preset of REWIND.

If not for the ability to google the words or the record company publishing the liner notes, audiophiles would be left in the dark: When the tenor Gaye begins singing, it sounds like he enunciates, "I come *apart* baby / But now I'm cool / I didn't make it, sugar / Playin' by the rules." Pursuing a post-listening internet search, I learned that I performed a mondegreen because he actually confesses, "I come *up hard* baby."[1] I, searching for knowability, was haunted by these aesthetic/compositional decisions while attentive to what was seen through hearing.

This auricular puzzle-as-ambient listening situates my aims but seems amiss as if going in one ear and out the other. While "coming up hard," as opposed to "coming apart," sonically stages Gaye's lyrical jumble, such scrambling is emblematic of his in-breaking:

> "It was important that I have a male child," Mr. Gay said in the living room of the Gramercy Place home when I interviewed him ... in 1982.... Mrs. Gay appeared almost a different person from when she'd spoken to me alone ... she was remarkably reticent, saying only a few words, while her husband spoke for hours. "A namesake is what I wanted."... "The day he was born, I felt he was destined for greatness.... I thanked God for Marvin. I knew he was a special child."... "My husband never wanted Marvin," Mrs. Gay told me. "And he never liked him. He used to say that he didn't think he was really his child. I told him that was nonsense. He *knew* Marvin was his. But for some reason, he didn't love Marvin and, what's worse, he didn't want *me* to love Marvin either. Marvin wasn't very old before he understood that." The tragic triangle was established at birth—Father and Son competing for Mother's love.[2]

Juxtaposing Father's dreams with Mother's intuition reveals people who "love" each other living under one roof with different rules; these contrasting recollections of Gaye's arrival beg whether those who lack care most talk themselves into a compassionate posture for others. The parental units: Father, loquacious investor in his namesake and not paths of righteousness for His name's sake; and Mother, anxious interpreter of maladies in the paterfamilias beside whom she sits.

To say one does not behold hauntology here would misread what the page speaks. This passage portending the end, in a chapter titled "In the Beginning," suggests the ineptitude of time when conjurers speak to a biographer. Unbeknown to David Ritz, though unlikely, triangulating the parents-child bond gives pause: The presence of perichoresis supposes a competition for

"Mother's love" as a quest between Father and Son to embrace the *Holy Ghost*, The Comforter who "[w]hen [S]he comes / [S]he will guide you / Into all truth."[3] This is further demonstrable when noting the artist spells the familial surname differently than his peoples. That ghostwritten "e" makes Marvin Gay(e) as one seeks to *cherchez laghost*.

This term—"look for the ghost"—finds its translational forebear when Alexandre Dumas desired to *cherchez la femme*, "look for the woman."[4] Recognizing the sensory whims of this chapter, I appropriate the phrase to track the mantra of "communing with the dead," that being Gay(e), and the instantiation of a "shadow book" that is "Trouble Man."[5] Therefore, the record's opening sounds—to come up hard/apart then be cool—convey Gay(e) "forgetting the past and looking forward to what lies ahead . . . to reach the end of the race and receive the heavenly prize."[6] One witnesses this forgetting and looking forward when acknowledging lyrical suppression for roughly a decade: "It wasn't until 1982, when he left Motown to join CBS, that Marvin reprinted the lyrics on his album. Why? 'I respect poetry . . . and I try to write subtly, but lyrics really aren't poems. Printing them like poems can make them seem silly. Besides, I like the idea of everyone guessing at what I'm singing. I like mystery.'" The mystery, like the melody, still lingers on. This "close listening," performed heretofore and subsequently, is an act of speaking with the departed to edify the living: This is *ghostolalia*.[7]

This neologism riffs on "glossolalia," which connotes the outpouring of the Holy Ghost as tongues on Pentecost.[8] This new word discerns how "normal" communication, through word or song, manifests as a quotidian spectral act. So too, this reportage relays what happens when one is invited to partake in such a communicative endeavor, contriving "Trouble Man" as the call. This argumentation enlists two moves: Because phenomenological glossolalia biblically renders itself as "cloven tongues of fire," there is a religious air, emblematic of *heat*, paramount to the forthcoming Gay(e) plot summary. In like manner, tongues equip the community when someone interprets this "spirit speech," hence my assertion of Gay(e), among others and myself, as an interpreter. If this haunting commences a seance with the black feminine/maternal—the one we look for—Elsewhere bodies and/or flesh, as well as earthly ones, are tethered to this narration.

In this match for Mother's love, is Gay(e) endowed with "the power of 'yes' to the 'female' within"?[9] And does what we have seen, and are yet to see, about his life and his penning and performance of "Trouble Man," have an apparitional complement in a work of theory, Hortense J. Spillers's "Mama's Baby, Papa's Maybe: An American Grammar Book"; and at what reparative cost? Approaching these questions, however, requires conceding that this saga does not excuse the troubling decisions Gay(e) undertakes as an adult. Rather, the outcomes index the circumstances that account for said decisions, and divulge those who performatively comprise *Marvin's Brood* behaving in melancholically routine manners. Thus, one goes to the movies, or rather the soundtrack, to initiate "Movin' down the line."

A Gay(e) Reading of Hortense; or, Spillers's Residency in Marvin's Room—Do You Hear What I Hear?

These opening remarks highlight black flesh as channeling the wholly other to craft the "story of the tribe."[10] Gay(e)'s prenatal biography exhibits an internecine schism, confirming the gravity of "Trouble Man" and requiring a ghostolalic conjugator. His nativity reading compounds this tale when Mother is wary after marrying Father because "[o]nly later on did [she] learn about the awful violence of the Gay family back in Lexington. There were stories of shootings—Gays against Gays." And "'[t]here was tragedy in [her] younger life'": "'My father, for instance, was a violent man who once shot my mother. Mama survived, but the fear still lives inside me. My father died in a hospital for the insane.'" Gay(e)'s birth marks, shockingly, the convergence of mourning and melancholy as "some abstraction" in his bloodline. In this way, "[t]here was nothing beautiful or majestic about his appearance, nothing to attract us to him. He was despised and rejected—a man of sorrows, acquainted with the deepest grief" as his "inheritance."[11]

As the biography unfurls, Father's wants-cum-words are skinned:

Marvin Pentz Gay[e], Jr. was born at Freedman's Hospital in Washington, D.C., on April 2, 1939, a Sunday, the same day of the week he died . . . exactly one week later, the great black contralto, Marian Anderson . . . would perform at the Lincoln Memorial before seventy-five thousand spectators on Easter morning. . . . "I felt a *kinship* to Miss Anderson, just as I'd always feel a great *kinship* with Mahalia Jackson. . . . My father himself had a great voice and the capacity to become a great singer. Early on, I realized—largely through dreams—that I, too, was destined to be such a singer." Marvin had precise recollections of childhood dreams, but were these dreams engendered while awake or asleep? "Both," he replied with an inflection both regal and street.[12]

This nascence historicism projects serendipity: the extant possibility of Gay(e) being born to live a life worth singing. That a child bound to a named affiliation could be born under the shelter of a freedman's nursery and bookend that birth with the same day-of-the-week, almost birthdate, death. That what was meant for evil turned good in the person and works of Miss Anderson, the contralto progenitor of Gay(e). That Mahalia Jackson's dark soprano timbre can somehow be heard saying to him instead of King, that is Martin Luther Jr., "Tell them about the dream, Marvin!" That music is an inheritance passed down by the one who despises you, whom you also become ("You were the boy who became / That man, without meaning / To, and know now"). That what could have been an oneiric deferral does *explode*? with such force, it troubles a body to wakefulness, a somnambulist's eye-opening inversion, at times yet asleep. That a wonderful change comes over a man whose puerile visionary nostalgia enables him to code-switch, speaking the King's English and the *hoodese* of the urban dictionary in a single word.[13]

That hypothetical "dream sequence" is akin to Sigmund Freud's reading of the unconscious in "Mourning and Melancholia": "For this reason the exciting causes of melancholia have a much wider range than those of mourning, which is for the most part occasioned only by a real loss of the object, by its death . . . countless separate struggles are carried on over the object . . . these separate struggles cannot be assigned to any system but the *Ucs.*, the region of the memory-traces of *things* (as contrasted with *word*-cathexes)." Though Gay(e) engages in "*word*-cathexes" as a singer, the "memory-traces of *things*" emerge when he mimics his "lost object." Moreover, coupling these "'struggles' with loss, melancholia might be said to constitute . . . an ongoing and open relationship with the past—bringing its ghosts and specters, its flaring and fleeting images, into the present"; in turn, "[d]aring to dream is thus a double commitment to pursue the wished-for risk and revolutionary hope that by dreaming the unthinkable—namely, wanting, rather than hating, [the lost object]—[he] can . . . address and imagine another kind of *experience*, another kind of living present and future."[14] Ghostolalia indeed.

Gay(e)'s reverence for Anderson and Jackson is the "power" of the internal feminine. Yet both sound excess as examples of "When Malindy Sings." Farah Jasmine Griffin chronicles the spectacle of black women's vocality (for what it is worth, she opens her essay listing Anderson in 1939 and Jackson in 1963 as evidence!) as a proving ground that addresses momentary crises of a national order: "the black woman's voice can be called upon to heal a crisis in national unity as well as provoke one. . . . The image of the 'mother of the nation' is one that allows this construct to figure itself as reproduced. But the spectacle of the singing black woman at times of national crisis does not represent the 'mother of the nation'; instead that spectacle sometimes invokes a figure that can make no claims on the family unit, though she is 'just like one of the family.'" Gay(e) traces kinship with those women, realizing they relate to him like *ancestors* and not proxies, a relational departure from one Ralph Ellison. Though Griffin qualifies this role as "more mammy than mother," only to rebuke the former category, she discerns the black feminine espousing a power that "serves the unit . . . this figure of the singing black woman is often similar to the uses of black women's bodies as nurturing, healing, life and love giving for the majority culture . . . the black woman's singing voice can signal a crisis in the spectacle of national unity; it can even invoke a crisis by mobilizing dissent and forging a space of resistance." That vocality has ghostolalic whimsy—it haunts as it heals, endows while being eerie, provokes crisis to produce candor.[15] While those black women's aural gestures problematize the macrocosm, the sonic metaphor translates to the Gay microcosmic "unit," that is, "Trouble Man," a vocal spectacle born from the vicissitudes of kinship, structures the crisis of a "nation within a nation"—blackness, and its self-identified peoples—localized in a household. Still, these Anderson-Jackson sentiments occur concurrent to Gay(e) being his Father's child.

Anderson's Easter "sunrise surprise," cognizant of the Judeo-Christian liturgical calendar, compels sitting with Marvin Pentz Gay(e), Jr., born a week earlier on April 2, 1939, triumphantly entering the "new Jerusalem" of Washington, DC, on Palm Sunday. What would it mean now to belt "The Palms," grasping hymnody about a suffering servant-savior oddly jiving with Gay(e)'s birth? Thinking again on the chapter "In the Beginning," this divine similitude mirrors itself "At the End": Father ending his namesake with "two angry blasts of gunfire" is a tragic culmination whereby one imagines Son uttering, "'Eloi, eloi, lema sabachthani?' which means, 'My God, my God, why have you abandoned me?'" That the man who "birthed" Gay(e) eventually accomplishes his death disturbs what Martin Luther calls *the gospel in miniature* when God so loves the cosmos that said affection substantiates an only begotten Son, regardless of said child later interrogating his Parent's (in)action related to His demise, to those who merit forgiveness because they know not what they do. One is convinced "it was [their] weaknesses [Gay(e)] carried, it was [their] sorrows that weighed him down. And we thought his troubles were a punishment from God, a punishment for his own sins!"[16] His life is paraliturgical and parallactic for what it means to be wanted by the very person(s) who will lay in wait for your descent, and then voice dissent for, or even perpetrate, such a *fall.*

This religiosity is not for nothing when learning Father is a pastor. His church? The Gay homestead. He chastises the Son to strictly adhere to his "law":

It wasn't simply that my father beat me. . . . By the time I was twelve, there wasn't *an inch of my body* that hadn't been bruised and beaten by him. But Father did something else far worse. . . . He understood that if you're interested in inflicting pain, prolonging the process adds to the *excitement.* . . . The only way to *short-circuit the agony* was to provoke him even more and just get the beating over with. When he finally struck me, I knew—children know these things—that something inside him was *enjoying* the whole thing. . . . I thought I could win his love through singing, so I sang my heart out. . . . I could never *please him,* and if it wasn't for Mother, who was always there to console me and praise my singing, I think I would have been one of those *child suicide cases* you read about in the papers.[17]

Invoking and being preoccupied with death during the juvenile stage of development implies "[t]he self-tormenting in melancholia . . . a satisfaction of trends of sadism and hate which relate to an object, and which have been turned round upon the subject's own self. . . . It is this sadism alone that solves the riddle of the tendency to *suicide* which makes melancholia so interesting—and so dangerous." Though Gay(e) likely never read Freud, or Melanie Klein, he psychoanalyzes his childhood as prototypical of melancholia: "The real extent and depth of unhappiness children feel is not taken into full account . . . analytic observation has taught me that their unhappiness and depression, though not so acute as the melancholic depression of the adult, have the same causes and can be accompanied by thoughts of suicide." If his childhood suicidality is akin to adulthood melancholy, he ages prematurely; his youth is spent being treated like an elder. Moreover, this syncs with Freudian self-torment: "There seem to me to be certain points in common between the self-tormenting behavior of the masochist and the self-reproaches of the melancholiac, which, as we know, are in fact directed toward his introjected object. It would seem, therefore, that feminine masochism is directed towards the ego as well as towards the introjected objects." Considering this gendered self-castigation, does Gay(e)'s masculine outpouring mirror Klein's "'female' within"? In this conversation on "yes" and suicide, is this what Gwendolyn Brooks meant when she penned, "To say yes is to die / A lot or a little"?[18]

That strange exertion of "excitement" casts Gay(e) in comprehensive company with the likes of Richard Wright and James Baldwin—all cite parental behaviors, colored by religion and ritual, as circumventing whatever "calling" exists to mete out grace as it has been apportioned.[19] The desire to "please" Father foments this drama when reading the *Divided Soul* dedication: "*For my father, with love."* While Ritz likely nods to his patrilineage, can one remix this homage since an aspect of the biography premises troubled men who share a name? Put another way, can this vehicle expose Gay(e)'s soul division simultaneous to making him "whole" when he relives terror at the hands of the parent who caused said split, albeit psychosomatically, and strives for his unwinnable love as his "maybe"?[20]

The Gay church-home is a makeshift "plantation" where disobedience provokes the threat and action of "specifically externalized acts of torture and prostration that we imagine as the peculiar province of *male* brutality and torture inflicted by other males." This endogamous short-circuitry incites perusing systems of compulsory *impulse* that materialize in Father—"the 'overseer,' standing the length of a whip"—who "has popped [Son's] flesh open." Gay(e) is the pain receptor, and such violence bestows the capacity to translate these "hieroglyphics of the flesh."[21] The razing of his skin is the earliest musical lesson for this Son in sight-reading his bodily composition as *sheet music,* "the extended movement of a specific upheaval, an ongoing irruption that anarranges every line . . . a strain that pressures the assumption of the equivalence of personhood and subjectivity." He is a party to an "apparatus," orchestrated by a "'[man] of God,'" that "apparently colludes with a protocol of 'search and destroy.'"[22] Father's "critical distance," extended from his hand to the end of his switch, making contact with his namesake's corpus, subversively posits "intimacy." Ritz's second chapter, "Original Sin," signals Gay(e)'s natal community and his perceived defiance of/deviance in it; it also foretells what chapter three understands as "Sexual Confusion," a presumptive wink at that musical call for "Healing." Might these sonic offerings composite the resistance of the object who is Gay(e)?

Speaking about homebound discipline as "intimate" partly comes from what has been voiced as familial retribution, and a neighbor's tidbit that "Mr. Gay's violent streak . . . was especially sad and hurtful, because he'd tell me how his own father, back in Kentucky, would beat his wife, Mr. Gay's mother. He'd describe the blood and the horror he saw." Father, the quintessential product of his environment ("He came up harder than / You know, your father. / Didn't make it by the rules. / Your father came up hard, / Didn't get to make no rules"), retains a memory of abuse he installs in his house qua church—a place of praise and persecution.[23] This oppressive "love" might contemporarily be called *giving queer realness:*

A strong sexual ambiguity surrounding Mr. Gay was something I'd [Ritz] noticed the first time I met him in 1979. . . . His speech and body language were *soft and overtly feminine*. . . . "My father . . . likes to wear women's clothing . . . that doesn't mean he's a homosexual. In fact, my father was always known as a *ladies' man*. . . . There have been periods where his hair was very long and curled under, and when he seemed quite adamant in showing the world *the girlish side of himself.* That may have been to further *embarrass me*. I find the situation all the more difficult because, to tell you *the truth, I have the same fascination with women's clothes* . . . that has nothing to do with any attraction for men. Sexually, men don't interest me. But seeing myself as a woman is something that *intrigues* me. It's also something I *fear*. I indulge myself only at the most discreet and intimate moments. . . . After all, *indulgence of the flesh is wicked,* no matter what your kick. The hot stuff is lethal. I've never been able to stay away from the *hot stuff.*"[24]

This retelling fully airs the hermeneutical scope I referred to earlier: Haunting and heat have relevance. Extending the metaphor, this haint invites systems of *impulse* that visit the Gay home as a "pool of red and undulating light."[25] Freud pivots to verity when discussing melancholic diminution: "it is merely that he has a keener eye for the truth than other people who are not melancholic . . . it may be, so far as we know, that he has come pretty near to understanding himself; we only wonder why a man has to be *ill* before he can be accessible to a truth of this kind." While this "truthfulness" is provocative, the designation of one being "sick" to encounter it behooves contemplation—could Gay(e)'s truth-telling be causative of "wellness" in that these utterances ostensibly set him "free"; or, in the vein of Cameron Awkward-Rich, is Gay(e) exemplifying something like *maladjustment?* Is the object resisting in word now, and song soon enough?[26] All of this demonstrates the (dis)articulation of identity.

What is shared is complex because fascination or intrigue with something that also strikes indulgent fear or wickedness presents conceptual polysemy. Or maybe not. Robert F. Reid-Pharr theorizes that "the articulation of multiple identities was—and is—thought to be a corrective to outmoded binaristic identitarian discourses: black/white, gay/straight, man/woman . . . where one was assured that identity was not simply diffuse and diverse but constructed, unstable, and performative, as well." The latter binary sets point to what Gay(e) contends while rendering themselves murky since they hinge on his "embarrassment" of being a "ladies' man," "girlish," a "woman." Gay(e) disarticulately embodies the grammatical notation between those dueling constraints: He tells all the truth of gay and straight, man and woman, but tells it *slant*—a solidus in the flesh, "*sliding over* between two seemingly separate terms." His disavowal of a man donning women's clothing being homosexual may have deterred speculation regarding his "orientation" with respect to desire-fear-indulgence. This queer contingency "describes a constant state of uncertainty that derives from the transgression of the protocols of gender expression"—he is (in) "trouble" in flux.[27] Yet there is another articulation when Ritz incorporates Mother's confessional: "Did he believe his father was homosexual? 'I didn't know. I didn't want to know. I just drove the thought out of my mind.' I asked Mrs. Gay the same question about her husband. 'I am not certain. I do know that five of his siblings were homosexuals. And it's true that he liked soft clothing. Soft things of all kinds attracted him. He liked to wear my panties, my shoes, my gowns, even my nylon hose. Marvin would see him like that sometimes.'" Mother, the third-of-one in this Trinity, opines that sexuality has a biological basis as revealed in "behavior." Moreover, Tony Turner, "a former dresser for the Temptations and Diana Ross . . . remembers the singer asking him to make a wig . . . 'He had the cross-sex undergarments and everything. What he really liked were the bras, corsets, garter belts, and negligées that he would wear around the apartment with nothing else on top—just a wig on his head with rollers in it like any old housewife'"—this is Gay(e)'s inability to "stay away from the hot stuff." In turn, one asks: Were Father and Son *flaming?* while indwelling with the Comforter who just gave up the ghost?[28]

Inasmuch as Son disarticulates, Mother articulates how "the innate pathology of the homosexual must be revealed in order to produce the heterosexual community, but also that the homosexual works as the vehicle by which hetero-pathology itself might be negotiated." One transposes "homosexual" with "feminine," "heterosexual" with "masculine," hypothetically conflating *Keywords* as the homosexual-feminine emphasizes the torn flesh of Reid-Pharr's titular (scape)goat.[29] Sex, and sexuality, is a "dangerous force" that complicates and eventually destroys "peace of mind and the virtuous life" among the Gays. These elements confirm a diegetic arc as one shudders at the thought because, albeit critically problematic, these positions index the age-old belief, at the familial level, that *children can't be what they ain't seen.*[30] But if this is "giving queer realness," my argument syncs with the identitarian theory at play: Symbolizing the goat whose flesh is rent by the "overseer," Gay(e) implies abjection such that "we might use the figure of the abject to access 'slips' in the ideological structures of modernity, if not a complete reworking of the entire process." Thus, the Gays are "uncomfortable with 'realness' at precisely those moments when it appears to be most firmly established."[31] Said crudely, the Gay "slip" *is showing.* We access said unmentionable in the ongoing task of *cherchez laghost.*

The Gay house as "worshipful" tabernacle blueprints a threshing floor, a black bottom as unorthodox spatial category. This is holy ground where cloven tongues, divinely ordered or delivered by the unspared rod as the "firepower" to "anoint" one to do "the work," undo comprehensions about bodily affliction. This is literature on feet, whether Baldwin's *Go Tell It on the Mountain* or the hull of Toni Morrison's *Beloved* ship, in that the physicality of bodies being touched—quickened, *unctioned*—catalyzes a fever pitch.

This heat-stroke ensures the apoplexy of "hot stuff" becoming a *hot thing*.[32]

Though Yasiin Bey née Mos Def could not have foreseen his employment as a ghostolalist, this gender trouble connotes his album, *The New Danger*, whether by track list or critical framing, presenting a "Modern Marvel," even if the record interpolates *What's Going On*.[33]

In this family tree, the lateral connections with queer siblings—horizontality—and the transversal connections regarding queer offspring and parentage—verticality—map sexual crossing, and cross-dressing. Son's admission that he finds intrigue, and action, in Father's sartorial pastime christens the altar with holy water, and prepares us for the viaticum we will ingest from the transubstantiated table: In the Gay genealogical line, whether Senior or Junior (or kin numerically removed), "Sapphire" is an affective designation. Junior steps into that avatar as he "enacts [his] 'Old Man' in drag, just as [his] 'Old Man' becomes 'Sapphire' in outrageous caricature."[34] Freud would read this sequence of events through affective polarity:

> In melancholia, the occasions which give rise to the illness extend for the most part beyond the clear case of a loss by death, and include all those situations of being *slighted, neglected or disappointed*, which can *import opposed feelings of love and hate* into the relationship or reinforce an already existing ambivalence. This conflict due to ambivalence, which sometimes arises more from real experiences, sometimes more from constitutional factors, must not be overlooked among the preconditions of melancholia. . . . If the love for the object—a love which cannot be given up though the object itself is given up—takes refuge in *narcissistic identification*, then the hate comes into operation on this substitutive object, abusing it, debasing it, making it suffer and deriving sadistic satisfaction from its suffering.[35]

Returning to the biography, we envision the psychic world in which "Sapphire" resides.

Ritz asserts, "Shame and guilt *haunted* Marvin as a child. 'I wanted to beat the shit out of the guys when they teased me about Father . . . but I was afraid. I suppose I was afraid that I was *just like him*—that I was *too much of a woman* to fight back. Instead of taking blows like a man, I ran. My main memories of growing up have to do with running.'" A divided soul, having been "slighted, neglected or disappointed," Gay(e) experiences narcissistic identification, which he extends to his patrilineage, in that "he became obsessed with the idea—quite probably biblically inspired—of punishing his father for failing as a man, and punishing himself. . . . Marvin felt that the sins of one generation were being passed on to the next generation and he could not bear this. When he looked at his father he saw an addictive, sexually confused, emotionally unstable failure of a man . . . so much of what he saw in his father eventually reminded him of himself."[36] As this suffering projection happens cerebrally, he displaces that potential comeuppance for the substitutive object—Father, who he fears in and as himself—onto strangers with tongues that stammer with precision, running mouths that cause feet to behave similarly toward escape and dissimilarly toward retreat where "some people wanna run things; other things wanna run."[37] Language is the medium through which he experiences bullying such that he casts himself, through masculine parody, as a bulwark that deflects the pangs of debilitating speech acts; "[w]e might concede, at the very least, that sticks and bricks *might* break [his] bones, but words will most certainly *kill*" him, or expedite his killing possibility.[38]

Spillers, like Gay(e), observes that through a biopower that purges flesh of its "wickedness," the feminine is "ungendered" insomuch as black women are perhaps never "mothers." At this theoretical juncture, a new inquiry arrives: Does masculine ungendering occur vis-à-vis discipline as couched in *rage*—"coming up hard" previewing "coming apart"—where black men are perhaps never "fathers"? More specifically, does the Gay household thrive on, "pleasure" in, role reversals where "fathers" transmogrify to "mothers" ahead of making their "sons" "daughters" (or sadomasochistic "lovers") through intimate out-rage, dalliances in "touching" homosociality?[39] This reifies the "*specter* of black boundarylessness, the idea that there is no normal blackness to which the black subject . . . might refer," whether that breached limit maintains a pathological linkage to homosexuality or femininity.[40] To "please" one's torturer, amid active-passive expressions of "love," is a symptom of there being no boundaries unworthy of trespass—an ongoing crisis of the nation within a nation. Gay(e) would conclude "Ain't That Peculiar"; some might express, "Isn't it gay?"; others call it the queer art of failure.

This troubled man-child projects an uncanny depiction of upbringing—the coming apart of coming up hard—such that I am "invested less in the 'fact' of [the Gays'] homosexuality per se . . . as I am engaged by [their] discursive [and actual!] performance of [gender] vis-à-vis black masculinity and heterosexuality and how that performance redoubles to expose the queering of black masculinity." If these formative years posit a "queer fairy tale" inverted, there is an *unhappy ending* when Father kills Son over a dispute with Mother, the Holy Ghost. Then again, maybe this *is* the pinnacle of queer failure since Gay(e) dies April Fools' Day 1984, the day preceding the forty-fifth anniversary of his partum.[41] This provokes Spillers again.

Her statement that "before the 'body' there is the 'flesh,'" that spatiotemporal obstacle vis-à-vis the preposition, is crucial in the same way, wearing an architectural hat, vestibularity is conceptually alluring. The vestibular conundrum is that one can be *in* the space, but not be *of* the place. (Father faintly resonates on a random Sunday in his church-home—"You are in the world, but not of the world.") Transferring that prepositional formula to the Gay(e) narrative, one reimagines Marvin's birth and the ceremonial nature of his naming vestibularly—is his nascence the occasion when flesh of flesh, bone of bone, is birthed to people who are a collective embody-me(a)nt *before,* as in "to behold in front of," that newborn-and-quickly-diminishing flesh? That is, bodies in the presence of the neonatal where once the flesh *crowns,* that bundle joins the cadre of bodies in the delivery room as a new initiate, freshly ripened to undergo the "[nth] degree of social conceptualization that does not escape concealment under the brush of discourse, or the reflexes of iconography."[42] All the more, is Marvin's birth prototypical of embody-me(a)nt *after* the flesh because, striking the chiasmus, if "before the 'body' there is the 'flesh,'" then "after the 'flesh' there is the 'body'"? That being, Father namesaking Son in the presence of Mother-Holy Ghost makes real the "Word being made flesh and dwelling among" them, let alone "full of grace and truth" or bringing them "goodness and light," even if the newborn flesh's bodily maturation and degradation has a duration of roughly nine months.[43]

This is a Gay(e) reading of Hortense, or Spillers's residency in Marvin's Room.

When Marvin Meets George—Do You Know What I Know?

Marvin Gay(e) becoming his Father-Mother when he "gives up the ghost" about feminine haunting produces latent heat. Through this penchant for rhetorical prowess as combat, one understands why "[h]is debut album was the point at which Gay[e] officially added the 'e' to his name. In addition to wanting to distance himself from Father, he also thought the extra letter lent a certain class." Establishing personal space, via nomenclature and patriarchal divorce, Gay(e) "self-actualizes": With a touch of *taste* (and in homage to Sam Cooke), he becomes Gaye—neither the extrinsic muse of outrageous caricature for Father nor the intrinsic occasion of affirming Jacques Lacan when he envisions and performs a hot thing—by queering his name.[44] (The Lacanian nod refers to the mirror stage, "the watershed between the imaginary and the symbolic in the moment of capture by an historic inertia, responsibility for which is borne by everything that alleges to be psychology, even if it is by pathways that claim to release it from responsibility." This changed name flips this psychoanalytic *order of operations*: "Gay" is the symbolic by way of familial attachment, more specifically namesake-hood; "Gaye" stages the imaginary insofar as it troubles "the real" of his origin, undoing the power of speech as a signifying act because the "watershed" difference is only seen, not heard. This too may reconfigure the logic of the "ego-ideal."[45]) The trouble of masculinity distresses Gaye until becoming his own man.

He crafts a subversive persona on the recording to be acquainted with himself: "*Trouble Man* was one of only two albums where Gaye wrote every song alone. He lost himself in the mood of the movie. . . . The transitions from the lofty spirituality of *What's Going On* to the bleak pessimism of *Trouble Man* was astounding. . . . In it he identified with the hero-victim, bringing to the suite a distinctively, frighteningly *autobiographical* voice."[46] The album-as-autobiography disrupts "the history of the book," reifying anew the once-conceived naïveté of Olaudah Equiano and the foresight of Stevie Wonder: There is such a thing as a *talking book*. If, like Equiano, one puts the *Trouble Man* vinyl to the ear, when alone, in hopes it would answer, this audible living history vocalizes so pristinely, it foreshadows that tribal story.[47] Gaye sings himself into a sound that gives way to his "divided soul"—"gangster" and preacher's kid, sexual healer and shy guy, "daughter" and "son," mama's baby and papa's maybe. An album where only one track has prolonged vocality is the reading of an American Grammar Book that surpasses categorization, even if European audiences consider it "innovative."[48]

This autobiographical vocality incorporates Gaye into a literary tradition broader than my imposed kinship with Wright and Baldwin:

the project of liberation for African-Americans has found urgency in two passionate motivations that are twinned—1) to **break apart**, to rupture violently the laws of American behavior that make such *syntax* possible; 2) to introduce a new *semantic* field/fold more appropriate to his/her own historic movement. I regard this twin compulsion as distinct, though related, moments of the very same narrative process that might appear as a concentration or a dispersal. The narratives of Linda Brent, Frederick Douglass, and Malcolm El-Hajj Malik El Shabazz . . . represent both narrative ambitions as they occur under the auspices of "author."[49]

Inserting Gaye into this authorial legacy qualifies his project as telling slanted truths. Alongside Spillers's twinning, a reading of *The Song of the Andoumboulou* is apposite: "Trouble Man" is a "striving, strain, abrasion, an all but asthmatic song of aspiration. Lost ground, lost *twinness,* lost union and other losses variably inflect that aspiration, a wish, among others, to be we, that of the recurring two, the archetypal lovers who visit and revisit the poems, that of some larger collectivity an anthem would celebrate."[50] Though Gaye disbelieves lyrics are poetry, they contrive poetics, forwarding the record, and soundtrack, as an unconventional celebratory dirge.

This provocation of a talking book does not reveal an "American Grammar Book" per se, but rather an "American Songbook" when Gaye imparts what inspired *Trouble Man:* "'This is probably my favorite work,' Marvin told [Ritz], though he said the same thing about *I Want You.* 'I was listening to a great deal of Gershwin at the time, and I really wanted to do something great. I was amazed at my concentration. It had never been this intense before.'"[51] This confession propels the next inquiry regarding the examined record: To which Gershwin was he listening? Geoffrey O'Brien speaks to Gaye's musical influences: "He told *Rolling Stone* that he felt capable of everything Beethoven had been capable of, only it might take him a little longer because he lacked the technical training. *Trouble Man* was as close as he would get to the kind of seamless symphonic work he had in mind. It was the idea of movie soundtrack as object that gave him the long form he needed for a *freedom otherwise unavailable* . . . in the process becoming something like Korngold's 'opera without singing.' . . . The album itself is the movie." *Trouble Man* as opera confirms the Gershwin to which Gaye turned, in the same way sound generating capability augments my upcoming "close listening." He manipulates his deficit in "technical training" by deftly tapping into his trouble. This "private soundtrack becomes the public soundtrack, the assertion of a continuum, a republic of music"; this "sound as world-creating action" is the freedom he dreams through sonic reckoning.[52]

Gaye's previous deferment of "precise recollections of childhood dreams" fulfills itself as he shares ghostolalic *innervisions* aloud: "'Visions of myself on stage, while all the world watched and waited for me to sing something so stupendous that life as we know it would be forever altered. I was brought here to make a change.'" His psychoanalytic proclivities reify "dream work": "The dream presentations consist chiefly, if not wholly, of scenes and mainly of visual sense images. Hence a kind of transformation is not entirely absent in this class of dreams, and this may be fairly designated as the dream work. *An idea merely existing in the region of possibility is replaced by a vision of its accomplishment.*"[53] Gaye is sensate, perhaps even synesthetic, through his clairvoyance. With this vision statement, he pontificates: Do you know what I know, that being, "I don't mean to say that . . . I have already reached perfection . . . but I focus on this one thing"—to write the vision and make it plain?[54] Alongside this prognostication, there is equal recognition of the female within: If Marian Anderson's influence emerges by listening intensely to Gershwin, Mahalia Jackson's can now be legitimated.

With the operatic in tow, the record also expands the sonic canon of blaxploitation music because "this celebration/rejection friction was a by-product of a transition between *the gospel core* that underpinned soul and the secular citified attitude. . . . Soft and seductive, the song swingingly blends minor chords, scat singing, big band brass, boppish piano, and soaring flutes into a sound that defies categorization."[55] With gospel-like fervency, "Trouble Man" broadcasts Gaye's enamor with and reworking of Jackson because "the true function of her singing is not simply to entertain, but to prepare the congregation . . . to make it receptive to *the spirit* . . . to evoke a *shared community of experience* . . . she had created the spiritual and emotional climate in which *the Word is made manifest.*" The mechanics and surplus of Jackson's performativity instill that democratic listening such that she makes an aurally receptive world in her (sonic) image, her (vocal) likeness; her "power springs from [her] dedication, [her] having subjected [herself] successfully to the demanding discipline necessary to the mastery of [her] chosen art . . . a quality with which [she is] born as some are born with bright orange hair." Gaye's music is multimodal; simply by opening her mouth and nuancing the sound thrust from that organ, Jackson, like Anderson, performs *genius* in Marvin's Room.[56]

The opera-gospel communion does not make Gershwin as muse seem far afield. Rife with minor chords and soaring instrumentation, his songbook enabling the production of *Trouble Man* incites speculation: Was *Rhapsody in Blue* in heavy rotation in that small apartment on Cattaraugas Avenue in Los Angeles?[57] But if I, like Wonder conflated with bygone homileticians, tune the music of my mind's eye, I dream Gaye listening to *Porgy and Bess,* more assuredly "My Man's Gone Now," to reinterpret the character Serena's scream. If this is the medium through which ghostolalia occurs, one translates this continuum through the (un)surprising arrival of Frederick Douglass as he chronicles Hester's scream. This readies her to be the "Aunty" of Spillers's design.[58] Hearing this "translation of a translation," through risk and stress, we are privileged to taste Gaye's archive; just as someone wears a hat or sips tea, this interpretation of a phonographic paroxysm may be "eviscerated beyond utility into a synonym of culture itself."[59]

"The horror! The horror!"/The Power and the Glory—Listen to What I Say

An autobiographical linkage between Gaye and Douglass seems foolhardier than an affective correlation. Despite their birthplace proximity— Washington, DC, and Easton, Maryland—they lived in disparate times and social constructs regarding "slavery" and "freedom." Yet the violence of their childhoods, at the hands of "overseers," syncopates them as not simply blues men, but also trouble(d) ones. Having described to this point, and subsequently, melancholic horror, I further the *afterlife of genius* by examining "the power and the glory" of said affect twisted. Saidiya Hartman ushers us into the conversation.

Her discontent with rehearsing black suffering, vis-à-vis Aunt Hester's scream, portends reading her theoretical boycott when scanning the opening of *In the Break*. But what compels her inclusion here is Hartman beckoning her, a move akin to how Fred Moten discerns the discourse: "I have chosen not to reproduce Douglass's account of the beating of Aunt Hester in order to call attention to the ease with which such scenes are usually reiterated, the casualness with which they are circulated, and the consequences of this routine display of the slave's ravaged body. . . . What interests me are the ways we are called upon to participate in such scenes." Describing this scene of subjection would be difficult because we were not there, hence the reader is presumably "outside the circle, the one whose distance is supposed to allow a certain analytic objectivity, the one who exhibits mastery, the one who makes demands, the one who demands or evokes precisely that sound that he will not hear."[60] Douglass's gaze evokes the scene's theatricality, despite such drama being that of the absurd; he also offers a lens to theorize the spectacular. But that participatory "call" feels counterintuitive since that proposition conflates to be the (super)imposition of a communal clarion, an invitation.

What interests me in Hartman's calculus, *haunts* me even, is the transition from not rehearsing that primal moment in *Scenes of Subjection* to the reversal convened in *Wayward Lives, Beautiful Experiments: Intimate Histories of Social Upheaval*, namely the chapter "A Minor Figure." Inaugurated from a section break until the conclusion of the chapter, an unnamed girl, caught in the archive, soon appears nude in the odalisque pose; her image is laid behind text such that she becomes a palimpsest. Hartman's words are cartography, overlaying the girl and the couch upon which she reclines; her photograph perfectly formats at the centerfold so as to not expose her more. The image is haptic—to progress, *you must touch her*. This exploded depiction precedes a wallet-sized photo of her. Sitting with this image, I contemplate what happened to instantiate this departure from the return to that sonic scene that initiates Hartman's book. This transition shifts how one, spurred by the act of "defamiliarizing the familiar," must wrestle with the unknown—someone once "trapped" is now "pinned up."[61]

Though Hester undergoes canonization through *word-cathexes*, this unnamed girl gives us the lost-found eternal feminine through pictography. The memory-trace of a thing. This minor figure visually orates ghostolalia. Despite ambivalence—to my mind, the extant difficulty of the image is that its (pre)history, up until the reproduction, may not easily be extracted from it; such (pre)history compels writing about it in the first place. Yet, is it possible that to recuperate the image through *cloaking* the girl, to "form a circle around her," even to the extent of the prose as tattoo, repurposes the tawdry with something like tenderness?—I am invited to read Aunt Hester as an auricular ghost, in the Gaye genealogy, who troubles an unending circle of screams.[62] That is, even if one does not partake in the scene, one may eventually see what we saw, hear what they heard, know what you knew, and listen now to what I say.

Aunt Hester's case is intriguing because the topography of her screaming hinges on her getting along with a paramour, Lloyd's Ned (Roberts). Douglass hints at a peculiar ambiguity regarding his first master and whispered-about father, Captain Anthony, advising "her not to go out evenings, and warned her that she must never let him catch her in company with [the] young man." This is a seemingly "unrequited love" from Anthony for her, "a woman of noble form, and of graceful proportions, having very few equals, and fewer superiors, in personal appearance, among the colored or white women of our neighborhood." (While "Aunt" is an honorific in black sociality, I uphold Hester and Douglass having blood relation, meaning she is the sister of Douglass's mother, Harriet Bailey. If the paternity rumors are correct, Anthony whips his common-law "sister-in-law," who is also his "love interest," in front of his "son."[63]) This vocal staging meets a gender troubling methodology under the auspices of out-rage:

> I have often been awakened at the dawn of the day by the most *heart-rending shrieks* of an own aunt of mine, whom he used to tie up to a joist, and whip upon her naked back till she was literally covered with blood. . . . I remember the first time I *witnessed* this horrible exhibition. I was quite a child, but I well remember it. . . . It was the first of a long series of such *outrages,* of which I was doomed to be a *witness and participant.* . . . It was a most terrible spectacle . . . and soon the warm, red blood (amid heart rending shrieks from her, and horrid oaths from him) came dripping to the floor. I was so terrified and *horror-stricken* at the sight, that I hid myself in a *closet,* and dared not venture out till long after the bloody transaction was over. *I expected it would be my turn next.* It was all new to me. . . . I had therefore been, until now, out of the way of the bloody scenes that often occurred on the plantation.[64]

There is a sensorium here that obliges an exhaustive critical position.

Douglass ruminates on the plantation quotidian by stating that he cognizes this terror as awakening to shrieks. But the shift from present perfect tense—"have often been awakened"—to simple past—"witnessed"—connotes him possibly "viewing" the momentous whippings prior to his auditory rehearsals of those that followed. He sees what he hears. What prompts the transition from watching to hearing her, morphing from a character eyewitness to an (un)willing participant?[65] This is sensory overload as he visualizes, and later autotunes, Aunt Hester.

Douglass positivizes that Pauline epistolary recollection of the prophet Isaiah: Eyes *have* seen, ears *have* heard; he retorts YES! to the yuletide queries rehearsed here as chapter movements.[66] And what an interpretation of strife that the out-rage of the Captain—"the master, the father, the (failed) moral educator/immoral aggressor"—toward this Aunt compels Douglass's flight to a *closet* where his possible "outing" would transmogrify him from a nephew, a grandson, to being akin to his mother's sister, his grandparents' daughter![67] Though he finds himself closeted as his Aunt is "ungendered," if his participation necessitates testifying to slavery's inanity, what culpability do we have when our primal rehearsals allow us to be "familiar" but not *family,* "kith" but not *kin,* "in" but not *of?* Are we both/and?

Douglass's fear of his body being broken, to the flesh, propels his literary self-making because he "may fear that he . . . will be the next victim of his master's specifically sexual *rage*—an experience that will render his later claims to full masculine subjectivity even more problematic than they already are." A counterpoint: "Douglass narrates Hester's graphic abuse because he intimately understood it and because it was the only way that he could reference his own struggles over sex, against sexual consumption, and against the master's quest for sexual dominance over the male slave's body."[68] Either way, the Captain brutalized Aunt Hester likely knowing Douglass cohabitated with her—he performs "show and tell" in front of his "child," proving that amid the rumormongering, he could not be a "father."

This out-rage becomes legible to the Gaye saga, and his family line, because just as Douglass retreats to a closet to watch, or hear, his Aunt, Father Gay's mother traverses the "blood-stained gate" in Lexington as "the blood and the horror he saw" were simulcast in Technicolor and surround sound. If such violence "outs" the Senior namesake, preceded by the abolitionist, the Hesters of history encode as the "intermittent presence of the Mother . . . one of a chain of substitution(s) . . . in her appearances and disappearances and reappearances, fades in and out, simulates, modulates, remains, in a way the father doesn't, as the radical absence of a *problem*." Thus, "[i]n this play of paradox, only the female stands *in the flesh*, both mother and mother-dispossessed . . . it is our task to make a place for this different social subject. . . . Actually *claiming* the monstrosity (of a female with the potential to 'name') . . . . 'Sapphire' might rewrite after all a radically different text for a female empowerment"—is this an (un)intentional "invitation" to be the +1 of Hester? Is she "Miss Ebony First"? Is this ghostolalia?[69]

Douglass's closet retreat is because his Aunt shares a space with him under conditions where cruelty is nonexistent. When that structure collapses through vocal strain and eye-popping spectacle, she (un)knowingly "invites" him to the watershed (read: bloodshed) passage where she comes "apart" in conjunction with him coming "up hard." This ingratiates him with the syntactical room to constellate truth to power. Through this "invitation," one perhaps unwittingly consumes such scenes to consummate the audio co-conspiratorial: to *know* each other by making noise.

In *My Bondage and My Freedom*, Douglass asserts, "A silent slave is not liked by masters or overseers. '*Make a noise,*' '*make a noise,*' and '*bear a hand,*' are the words usually addressed to the slaves when there is silence amongst them. This may account for the almost constant singing heard in the southern states." A few pages prior to this, he recounts the story of Aunt Hester, now named Esther, but conveys, "I happened to *see* this exhibition of rage and cruelty toward Esther. The time selected was singular. It was early in the morning, when all besides was *still*, and before any of the family, in the house or kitchen, had left their beds . . . screams of his victim were most piercing . . . her piercing cries seemed only to increase his fury." Though considered the "visible institution," slavery posits itself as exceedingly *audible*.[70] This sound reading has a mirrored precedent when juxtaposing Aunt Hester's scream with Douglass's slave-songs discourse in the first autobiography. Her shrieks as "unmeaning jargon" resound beside "the songs as a powerful form of discourse after he has carefully shown that the slave owners depended upon the coercion of sound as a means of performing the regulatory power of the slave system . . . since the subversive power that they contain is one that the slave owners cannot regulate due to their own dependence upon the songs." This "analysis, self-analysis, repetition with a difference scream + one . . . is precisely that unheard, unworded sound of Hester's shriek that, though it is repressed, though Douglass resists it, returns in his narrative. It returns *in his description* as what he would describe in the slave songs, returns as the echo of these songs and what they echo."[71] We listen closely now.

If the "piercing cries" of Aunt Hester/Esther work as a public service announcement of yore, one is astonished: Through ceremonial acts of severity, the "stillness" of someone being beaten may have catalyzed "the slave system" requiring sonorous flesh to employ sound concurrent to that very brutality.[72] They made a noise, bore a hand—sang—in tandem with someone screaming.

If "constant singing" pervaded the South, floggings were set to soundtracks. Douglass portrays the potential of slaves making noise while watching and hearing violence to break the monotony of silence. Onlookers engaging in this activity, while one screams for one's life, is unconscionable in that it grounds the caveat of "This is your fate if you *disobey* me," while also convening the communal registry of I scream-you scream-we all scream to stop the (non-)noise. As a provocative countermelody, might "scream with"/"sing along" then, through parodic, perhaps even comical, inversion, equate now to "stand with/beside"? These subjected scenes instantiate an anachronistic think-tank, a microcosm in which slaves constantly analyze themselves and others—"fathers," "lawgivers"—among cacophony. Despite receiving the lash or "performing" in its midst, they scream loud and project nothing(ness) in the thingliness of flesh. Is this not troubling, man? For what it is worth, whipping being set to a soundtrack is stunningly realized in excess via *Django Unchained.*

On two separate occasions, *Jimmy Kimmel Live!* and the NAACP Image Awards, Jamie Foxx, cast as Django, narrates how Kerry Washington, who portrays Django's wife Broomhilda, "takes the lash" when filming a brutal scene. Foxx shares that Quentin Tarantino, the director (read: overseer?), often played music while shooting. The music *chosen* the day Washington is lashed is Fred Hammond's "No Weapon." To say this is chilling is an understatement, made all the more macabre when Foxx speaks with Kimmel. As he sets up the story of filming the scene, and Tarantino playing music on set, Kimmel responds, *"He was deejaying the lashings? He's a sick person.";* laughter ensues. Though Foxx says he asked for Hammond, presumably Tarantino signs off on it which leads to him crying while it plays. Similarly, recapping this filmset moment at the Image Awards is also befuddling: When Foxx begins singing "No Weapon," it urges call-and-response from the audience, on par with worship or revival—is this not Douglass's words "made flesh" in the twenty-first century?[73] But I digress.

Analyzing the enslaving snapshot, does one scream/sing as the screamer's/singer's "guest": the "scream + one"? If so, "[a] demand is placed on Douglass by the reader and all that the reader doubles in transference, in his attempt to pierce, enter, play, violate the circle" such that said reader entreats: Douglass, how did the brutalized know when to stop screaming or singing; or did the sound end once the screaming one appeared to have "escaped"?[74] That is, was the body "there," but the flesh *Elsewhere* as in "Over my head / I hear music in the air" to soothe me from the troubles of this world and those of my ungendering—the happening of music at the heralding of mutilation? If Aunt Hester speaks glossolalia in Douglass's ears, interpreting her speech act reconstitutes the body-flesh politic through ghostolalia, akin to figuring out if Gaye comes apart, up hard, or both. The slave narrative-cum-self-analysis compels participating in and witnessing decisions of sonic gravity to forgo the splitting of flesh and cease the tension of the symphonic sublime; "[w]hile perhaps heightened in the daily experiences of enslaved musicians, these qualities of transfiguration are the natural attempts at survival within a system that required minute-by-minute negotiations to preserve life."[75] Perhaps some still scream and sing now. Nonetheless, if singing and performance are on hand, let us hear *Porgy and Bess* through an invitational mode.

"My Man's Gone Now" poses a resonant performative interjection, a classical (int)irruption; the aria's premise presents a manner of purposive communalism and operatic synchronicity considering these ghostolalic conjectures. The libretto precedent to the aria is Serena loses her husband Robbins at the hands of Crown during a crap game in Catfish Row. The affect that lends a reading tantamount to our overarching thematic is the wake and funeral occur inside their home; Serena invites Row people in for Robbins's home-going. The space transforms into a mortuary. Prior to the aria, the ensemble sings "Gone, Gone, Gone"; Porgy gives Robbins his "last rites," and the community encourages itself to "fill up the saucer 'til it overflow" with a bowl atop Robbins's body to receive alms.

At these funeral proceedings, the police suddenly bust into the home and wrongfully detain Peter instead of Crown, whom Porgy calls "a killer an' for-ever gettin' into trouble":

PORGY: But there go Peter to be lock up like a thief.

ENSEMBLE MEMBER: Like a thief!

PORGY: An' here be Robbins with his wife and his fadderless chillen an' Crown done gone his ways drinkin,' gamblin,' swearin' to do the same thing over and over somewheres else.

ENSEMBLE: Gone, gone, gone!

Crown, a "trouble man," endangers Row residents; such events presage "My Man's Gone Now":

My man's gone now
Ain't no use a-listenin'
For his tired footsteps
Climbin' up de stairs

Old Man Sorrow's
Come to keep me comp'ny
Whispering beside me
When I say my prayers

Ain' dat I mind workin,'
Work an' me is travellers
Journeyin' togedder
To de promised land

But Old Man Sorrow's
Marchin' all de way wid me
Tellin' me I'm ole now
Since I lose my man

ENSEMBLE: Since she lose her man

Since I lose my man

Old Man Sorrow's
Sittin' by de fireplace
Lyin' all night long
By me in my bed

Tellin' me de same thing
Mornin,' noon, an' evenin'
That I'm all alone now
Since my man is dead

Since I lose my man[76]

What is pivotal here is the aria's antiphony.

Serena sings by herself until she faces melancholy and mourning, announcing she "lose" her man. The ensemble, unprovoked, stands beside, sits with, her and reciprocally sings, only to have her repeat it again—Since I/she lose my/her man. The remainder of the song occurs with the ensemble humming and accompanying Serena until the last lyrical line and, for lack of a better term, the vamp. The last "Since I lose my man" has an approach that belies Serena's overall sentimentality: Through multiple octave swoon and boom, she sings up the scale until she pitches a high B(5) on the lyric "Since"; "I" an A(5); "lose," a lyric polysyllable, transitions back to the B(5) then the A(5); "my" G(5); man E(5). Serena, the lyric soprano, the newfound widow, issues her operatic blues. After the sonic boom, there is a terse instrumental interlude when the orchestra mimetically plays the opening lyrical chords. Then it happens: The orchestra *loses* itself, goes quasi-silent; in that absence, the ensemble crescendoes to its own scream, concluding with Serena screaming anew an ineffable B(5). She does not enunciate—she simply screams—with an orchestral thud pronouncing the aria's finality. It is not coincidental that in my dalliances with classical training, an instructor declared singing opera is learning the proper way to scream.

This collective affect is Gershwin's doing with the aid of (Edwin) DuBose Heyward, a descendant of a signatory of the Declaration of Independence and author of *Porgy*, the novelistic basis of the opera. Langston Hughes deems him a man who saw "with his white eyes, wonderful, poetic qualities in the inhabitants of Catfish Row that [make] them come alive." But what does this (white) man know about (black) life to write "My Man's Gone

Now"? Is he summoning "second-sight in this American world . . . a peculiar sensation, this double-consciousness, this sense of always looking at one's self through the eyes of others, of measuring one's soul by the tape of a world that looks on in amused contempt and pity"?[77] When learning that Heyward spent most of his young adulthood sickly—contracting polio, typhoid fever, and pleurisy leading to a "cadaverous look"—one presumes he comprehends living under the crippling weight of circumstances out of one's control. Furthermore, proximate to where he penned *Porgy,* there is "Rainbow Row—a profusion of vibrantly colored row houses that became the inspiration for the book's Catfish Row . . . employed as a dockworker, Heyward listened to stories and observed the African Americans, basing Porgy on Sammy Small . . . many of the characters in the book are based on actual individuals he observed."[78] It seems, as one shudders again to read this forthcoming statement considering that terror in a Charleston worship space, some (black) people communicate with the (white) sick, not "dead," as well as embody the haunting. Does Heyward perform *braconnage* while working on the dock of the bay, writing himself into the novel-cum-opera as a black man disabled—is Heyward Sammy Small as Porgy? Is this "appreciation" of the worst kind; and is this work a figuration of "study," not black but self-, inasmuch as though Heyward forges "Row relations," he may twistedly forerun the character Thomas from Morrison's *Home*: The victim of a policeman's stray bullet that leads to "a bad arm," when asked by the protagonist what he wants to be when he grows up, he replies, "A man."?[79] Is masculinity the dream that forms of disability, psychic and/or somatic, defer? Affliction apparently inhibits the dominant requirement to master a compulsory *impulse* toward manhood, conferring certain persons to a masculinized Neverland. Thus, one "hears" the aria with revisions.

"My Man's Gone Now" is not Serena's love ballad to Robbins; he only has invocation as "my man" without explicit naming. The song is a conversation between her and "Old Man [of] Sorrow," his apostrophic presence: aged ("Old Man Sorrow"); languid ("Sittin' by de fireplace / Lyin' all night long / By me in my bed"); verbose ("Tellin' me de same thing / Mornin', noon, an' evenin'")—he is a "guest" overstaying his welcome. Spillers's "Old Man" makes another cameo. Though Heyward pens the aria for Serena's vocalizing, perhaps the man "lose" is his inward-outward constructed man masquerading as Robbins. It is a masculine ruse he will not encounter or resurrect, even as it peculiarly enables his "productivity," literarily and operatically, hence the need for avatars. This gender caricature has relevance too for Serena and Aunt Hester.

As sung by Porgy—"An' here be Robbins with his wife and his fadderless chillen . . ."—is Serena, through Robbins's passing, a "mother" while becoming a "father" to the "fadderless"? Does Aunt Hester's "aria" opine that with her man, Ned Roberts, "gone now," as in absent from that primal scene, the rage Anthony would save for him is exerted on her as if she were Ned, ungendering her literally and her closeted nephew psychically? If Douglass "may intentionally desexualize that rage so as to construct a gender-indifferent interpretation of the violence inflicted on both male and female slaves . . . a set of rhetorical strategies for describing sexual and sexually violent relations . . . while also preserving a writing position that is uncontaminated by those descriptions," this gender (in)difference means that unlike him, these real and fictional black women exhibit how contamination is often reducible to those juggling self-preservation amid trauma. That said, with Serena and Hester losing their significant others in disparate brutal moments, the losses expedite their status as *race men*, that is, these black women have "lives similar" to black men and become "race leaders," albeit of the racial "family," under divergent circumstances.[80] Spillers proffers a like-minded claim: "Because it was the rule, however—not the exception—that the African female, in both indigenous African cultures and in what becomes her 'home,' performed tasks of hard physical labor . . . we wonder at the seeming docility of the subject, granting her a 'feminization' that enslavement kept at bay."[81] Though her comments regard strenuous work, bestowing feminization happens *after the fact* of subjection.

Given this extant skeuomorphism, it finds equivalence in the queer impartation that *the world has made me the man of my dreams.*[82] However, in the cases of Serena and Aunt Hester, it is the man of their nightmares, their trouble; each is a "troubled man"—coming apart under affectively "hard up" conditions—left to fend for herself and those she loves, or shelters. Resonances from Hitsville, USA sound off as renditions to this theory featuring label mates: With such confusions, don't it make you wanna *scream;* or make me wanna *holler,* where the unvoiced addendum is "[t]he way they do my life / This ain't livin'"? This is the instant when we

> Picture the preacher's son   secular   sanctified
> spotlight and nightsweat   bluesmoke and silkthroat
>   Eyes closed   head tossed   knees trembling
> Trouble Man   moaning wholly   Holy
>   Love   Have mercy   Love have
>   mercy   holler   Marvin   holler[83]

The muse has stepped to the mic.

Gaye speculatively listens to "My Man's Gone Now" as the foundation for "Trouble Man" because he aesthetically samples from the aria: an orchestral arrangement that often mimics what he sings; the A-B skeleton of verses and chorus; the dynamic quality. But Gaye himself screams! He has this moment of clarity (that is pop cultural go-to)—"There's only three things that's for sure / Taxes, death, and trouble / This I know babe / This I know sugar." (Is this triad what the community decides when it "fill up the saucer 'til it overflow": the neighborhood call-and-response to aid Serena in paying for Robbins's burial to ward off financial and funereal strain [taxes and death], as well as the threat of Crown causing havoc since he is "forever gettin' into" it [trouble]?) Then Gaye sings, "I won't let it sweat me babe." A brief orchestral interlude of quasi-silence follows this lyrical line as the instruments layer themselves upon themselves, gaining in volume.[84] It is a steady procession like "[a]ntelope-horn trumpets blast[ing] and bleat[ing]" so that "when the listening ends, marking the entry of the deceased into the other life, evoking, [François] Di Dio writes, 'the wail of a new-born child, born into a terrifying world,'" Gaye screams, "Got me singin' YEAH! YEAH!"[85]

The discursive tackling of this scream reveals how such sound is the omen for a troubled man, at once signifying life (coming up hard) and death (coming apart), especially recalling Gaye's nativity. Thus, I contemplate: Is Marvin's scream, conversant with the particularities of his nascence, the (counter)intuition of the Heideggerian *Dasein* insomuch as "it is ontically distinguished by the fact that, in its very Being, that Being is an *issue* for it"? This question voices the phenomenology of the scream as an affective and fleshly category vis-à-vis resistance to Heidegger by Emmanuel Lévinas, what Peter Schwenger calls "the horror of being-there," the "'there is' . . . the *il y a*": "Is not anxiety of Being—horror of Being—just as primal as anxiety over death?"[86] In this genealogy of screams, ranging from Aunt Hester's to Gaye's, Lévinas's argument becomes intelligible as a horror that indeed determines "before the 'body' *there is* the 'flesh.'" Father namesaking Son, his words made flesh, only to snuff him out, confirms Di Dio's "new-born"- "deceased" duality and confronts this critique of presence, that is, might the matter not be Gaye being a Being, but the horror deployed on his flesh and his body, equally unprotected, simply *for* being there, for being the Being-there?

The issue here may not—simply? solely?—be *is-ness*, but *there-ness*.

Gaye's life starting with a scream at Freedman's Hospital and finishing with two bullets screaming through the air—two polarities with myriad outbursts in between—compounds how the "Trouble Man" scream is a memory and harbinger that "[w]hat you do to children matters. And they might never forget."[87] Similar to an earlier intimation, this chapter could effectively end here but alas, the forthcoming finale beckons a return to the body-flesh dichotomy: The Gaye scream, knowing vocal nuance, is stupefying because it is basically the only instance on the record when he sings from his chest (voice), often called a belt, because the rest of the song is predominantly sung in his head (voice), his falsetto.[88]

In *Bedouin Hornbook*, Mackey sits in the pocket regarding false-voice singing. His summation, by way of Flaunted Fifth, finds its rehearsal *In the Break*:

> What is it in the falsetto that thins and threatens to *abolish the voice* but the wear of so much *reaching for heaven?* At some point you'll have to follow up this excellent essay of yours with *a treatment of the familial ties between the falsetto, the moan and the shout* . . . the falsetto explores a *redemptive, unworded realm*—a meta-word, if you will—where the implied critique of momentary eclipse of the word curiously rescues, restores and renews it: *new word, new world.* . . . Flaunted Fifth was suddenly haunted by once having written that the use of the falsetto in black music, the *choked-up ascent into a problematic upper register,* had a way, as he'd put it, of "alchemizing a legacy of lynchings."[89]

Flaunted Fifth's interpretation of falsetto is scriptural—if it is a "reaching for heaven," the goal might be receiving said locality's "prize." All the more, falsetto transitioning into the "unworded realm" dialogues with the "unmeaning jargon" of that autobiographical scene as glossolalia and ghostolalia converge. The "problematic upper register" extends that sonic line of thought when the "regendering or transgendering" of the voice is brought to bear on one's falsetto, akin to Al Green or "Big Maybelle's bass." Performatively, this aural awe hints at "the quiet extremities that animate a range of social chromaticisms and, especially, in the mutations that drive mute, labored, *musicked speech* as it moves between an incapacity for reasoned or meaningful self-generated utterance that is, on the one hand, supposed and, on the other hand, imposed, and a critical predisposition to steal (away)."[90] Gaye shouting "YEAH!" transmutes Serena screaming in the fifth pianistic octave: For the male voice, he sings a high A(4), an octave and full step under the moment of her blast and blow. Apart from the time constraints between "My Man's Gone Now" and "Trouble Man," has Serena posed an imagined invitation to

Gaye—sonically, operatically—as they *scream with* each other over a lose-loose manhood? (This call-to-perform welcomes a tidbit: In a Gaye documentary, Bey ruminates on the album *Here, My Dear*, namely "Anna's Song" when Gaye screams, "A-NNA!"; mimicking him, Bey calls the yell "opera."[91]) So what of the falsetto?

Taking up Flaunted Fifth and Di Dio, if the end of the instrumental bombast evokes a thanatopic transition, how does one reconcile the vocal limit and its postmortem arrival? While the voice, anathema but often similar to the instrument, disrupts the funeral procession and announces a newborn's birth, what does this mean? Well, if one recalls Gaye's birth and the body-flesh situation, perhaps the falsetto performance is the signpost at which he, like Jackson, "step[s] out on [sonic] space / And he [looks] around and [screams]: / I'm lonely—/ I'll make me a world": new word (YEAH!), new world as ghostolalic redress.[92] Gaye and Motown songwriter/producer Lamont Dozier invigorate this logic:

> MARVIN GAYE: Motown producers pen everything as high as they could for anybody, you know. It's just, in all those records, I was just discovering my voice, and they were killing me with them, and the keys were atrocious.

> LAMONT DOZIER: Now he was going to give us a lot of mouth, a lot of lip, about "You're cutting me in these so effing eff keys, and I can't sing this stuff like this." Then he would sing and he would take the demo and then transform the relationship, and start sliding into falsetto and the parts that were too high for him to *scream* it out, and he would subtly make the song his own. [Video footage of performance of "How Sweet It Is," 1964.] He gave you a spice of life in his voice that you heard, you know. You heard the pain and the anguish, and the sweet and the love, cuz he would go to hot to cold and meek, lukewarm—you'd get all of these different feelings.[93]

Marvin patents, and patently understands the need to fashion, a new standard to compensate for the script being penned for and outside of him, even by record company bigwigs who generally do not sing. Dozier's explanation of Gaye's vocality is akin to how Donny Hathaway "possessed a technique or a gift that musicians call 'vocal crying' . . . he 'was able to make the listener "feel his heart" in his singing and playing' in a way that could make people cry."[94] While vocal cries are not explicitly associated here with Gaye's voice, these descriptors of his singing—pain, anguish, sweet, love, hot, cold, meek, lukewarm—outline a *vociferous cornucopia*, a taste of his archive on which listeners feast. This is why his "Trouble Man" approach is so intriguing.

The transition from falsetto to belting, when he screams out in his chest voice as a commingling of opera and gospel, is prototypical of Gaye's body of work, his genius, as "his mimicking of the diversity of communal voices popularizes the dominant black social paradigms, precisely at the moment when communal relations within such paradigms are increasingly fractured and disjointed both from themselves and within." Reading the song through hearing, that aural calculus is the definitive act of coming apart. His flesh authentically calls forth, and his falsetto is the willingly/willfully voiced construction of a "body" in that it is not true or false. It *is* a voice, simply, that comes up, in guttural speciousness, *hard*, "deliberately forced, deliberately 'false'": "if it is forced from us as a response to the horror of pure existence, to being trapped by existence, it belongs itself to the order of things that are wiped clean of personal being. Essentially, every scream is like every other; and no scream can reconstitute the I that emits it. And so the redoubling of the scream is not an acoustic cloning of our personal selves; what it redoubles is the horror of existence at degree zero."[95] Though Spillers is not cited here, rearranging "zero degree" confirms the fleshly underpinnings of screams.

Cognizant of the need for microphonic amplification, the voice simultaneously produces and breaks apart from the limit its "author" places on it as manifested through the scream. This necessitates understanding its innerworkings: "in our modal voice the vocal folds are seen to make contact with each other completely during each vibration. . . . This closure cuts off the escaping air. When the air pressure in the trachea rises as a result, the folds are blown *apart*. . . . In falsetto . . . when the vocal folds are *blown open* . . . a permanent oval orifice is left in the middle between the edges of the two folds through which a certain volume of air *escapes* continuously as long as phonation continues." Gaye's scream of YEAH! is the modal structure of his vocal flesh coming together as preceded by the corporeal falsity of his twin cords coming apart, "an internal pocket larger than the whole; and the outcome of [a] division and of [an] abounding [that] remains as singular as it is limitless." At this critical impasse, Griffin deploys that when Malindy, or Anderson and Jackson for our purposes, sings, the representations, and representations, of her voice "suggest that it is like a hinge, a place where things can both *come together* and *break apart*."[96] The oval orifice shapes invagination in masculine interiority.

Air taking on the personality of escapism in these infinitesimal moments of Gaye charting his melancholy, throated, signals feet not being the only "body" parts that go rogue, run, steal (away)—so too does the voice. This is auscultation:

> [Robert] Burton [*Anatomy of Melancholy* (1621)] works with the assumption of melancholy as a disorder. If we work rather with [Judith] Butler's paradigm of melancholy as an enabling condition, then a new paradigm in the history of music and musical aesthetics appears. I am filling this gap with what I am calling the anxiety of articulation—the gap between music and speech, between music and meaning, between music and the world. This is the melancholia of music itself. . . . If music wants to achieve the state of speech, it also contains in itself through its very inarticulacy an unsignifying precision that speech itself may not be able to attain. Like two desires crossing each other in the wind, music wants the status of speech while speech strives for the status of music: "What the music I love expresses to me is not thought too *indefinite* to be put in words, but, on the contrary, too *definite*."[97]

This "musicked speech" epitomizes the affective quality of music, the capacity of its melancholy to enable aesthetics—could an Aunt's unmeaning jargon inaugurate a legacy of screams in the unworded realm? Disregarding melancholy as "disorder," one infers its sensory duality to sing and hear. If one listens to the vocal cords while, somehow, watching them, and the mouth, the invitation sent to our doorsteps is that coming up hard and coming apart may be prescriptive of the potential *to be or not to be*, perhaps at the location of *there*, on the horizon. That, and the ever-present caveat of practice makes perfect. To put it in terms of the reparative, the nominality—the cost—this chapter initially sought the value of has fully appreciated so that we must put our commodity where the mouth is: Gaye's vocalization provides the constant reminder that silence is not protection, even when speech and music melancholically blur.

He comprehends this because screams are a consistently tempered troubling in the soul insofar as "'you're never really a whole person if you *remain silent*, because there's always that one little piece inside you that wants to be spoken out, and if you keep ignoring it, it gets madder and madder and *hotter and hotter*, and if you don't speak it out one day it will just up and punch you in the mouth from the inside.'" These words, shared between a daughter and mother to encourage the latter ahead of a conference paper, expound upon the cycle of boisterous declarations having widespread education. This daughter tries her tongue, although it is her mother's silence that softly breaks as the "Black Woman at the Podium."[98] YEAH! YEAH! is the Gaye vocal punch from the fantasy of a hold where a hot thing maintains primacy, even if it fantastically documents a Son coping with the childhood terror of his Father trying to "hold" him, still, as the Holy Ghost listens to and watches the horrific "disciplining." We further this ghostolalic comportment by listening ever clearer to the other ghost speaking through the pages.

The *record* of Aunt Hester, and the "hysteria" propelled onto her body, reconfigures Brooks's "The Anniad" as "an all but asthmatic song of aspiration" titled by its former name: "The Hesteriad"! This performative curation

> is built on contradictions. Locating their "answer" or meaning constitutes the [song's] puzzle and reward . . . circumlocution . . . becomes a decisive aspect of the work's style. This Song of [Hester] is a puzzle to be unraveled, and the catalogue of physical and mental traits deployed . . . becomes a set of clues . . . the [song] gathers its clues in [lyrics], and just as the questioner in the child's game withholds the solution, the [singer] here does the same thing, often to the [listener's] dismay. However, once we know the answer, the game becomes a ritual where feigned puzzlement is part of the ceremony.

The initial nomenclature, and Brooks's discarding of it, is interesting: "Well the girl's name was Annie. . . . I thought of *The Iliad* and said: 'I'll call this "The Anniad."'" At first, interestingly enough, I called her *Hester* Allen, and wanted then to say 'The Hesteriad' . . . I was fascinated by what words might do there in the poem. You can tell that it's labored, a poem that's very interested in the mysteries and magic of technique."[99] While naming "The Anniad" reads as nonchalance, does her decision prove she had Douglass's aunt in mind when penning the epic? Perhaps this is the contradiction that unravels a "reward": This "feigned puzzlement" is indulgent, playing up the continuous circumlocution in black stud(y/ies) of *the ceremony*, the event of mystery and technique that convenes a legacy of invitational happenings; or, Aunt Hester's scream, with "My Man's Gone Now" and "Trouble Man" in lockstep, as a/the precursory "listening session," with innumerable RSVPs, that later yields "think pieces." Thus, if "Aunt Hester's words, her *notes*, were bent; even the sound of the 'H,' hard aspiration/plantation peculiarity, remains in place when, in revision, Hester becomes Esther and shriek (not muted but mut[at]-ing) turns to meaningful plea," then "the dead-letter aspect" of this narration, proffered anagrammatically by Douglass, is the phoneme "H," just as it is the letter "e" for Gaye.[100]

This falsetto, "reaching for heaven" and the "heavenly prize," renders the indescribable because like Serena's scream, one notes more perplexity: The personification of "trouble man" could connote the sovereign or hegemony writ large. Although one reasons Gaye as the "trouble man," he divorces the listener from that when he calls him out. His phonating of "Trouble man, don't get in my way" elides the unsung "You" through the imperative mood. Hailing the "trouble man" remains thought provoking because of dissociation. Gaye, like Serena, converses with someone—Old Man Sorrow?—for the song's entirety. But if one parses "I come up hard/apart, baby," is he singing to his boyhood, his Manchild in the (Never) Promised Land, that sphere of dominant cultural masculinity? Or is this *fugitive planning and black study* via the falsetto?

If Son becomes the "Daughter" Father bears out—via rage, homoeroticism, sadism, and cross-dressing—when the song's dialogue names "baby" and "sugar," maybe Gaye logs his voice as an intimate soundscape tryst with/ as the feminine he earlier conceived as a site of desire-fear-indulgence. This is another instance of twinning: Gaye's "broken falsetto colored / Every hour indigo" at the same time that the listening public ponders:

what is it Marvin makes men like us holler
    and moan holler and moan why a blues
so mean she gotta come back twice[101]

This could be Gaye saying YES! to the female within as himself, twice over. This could be a cut of the regulative, governant force that obliges the generativity of the unrestrictive, liberating stitch. This could be "Trouble Man," if such vocality is the "alchemizing . . . of lynchings," hypothetically dubbing "The Hesteriad" for a forthcoming compilation of *Solid Gold Soul.* This could be Gaye espousing Édouard Glissant's "consent not to be a single being." This could be Michel Foucault (did he read Douglass's narrative, consume Gershwin's opera, listen to Gaye's soundtrack?) testifying that we "will be astonished, no doubt, that we were capable of identifying such a strange kinship between what, for a long time, was dreaded like a scream and what, for a long time, was considered a song."[102] And if we, of our spiritual (and theoretical!) strivings, keep chasing the ghosts we have been and will be looking for, we scream YEAH! with Gaye and others; and also bank on this glottal expertise, this open-mouthed-ness that once found translation as *la noche boca arriba,* this translabial ultrasound inverted, aiding us in moving (on) down the line as we fill up the saucer 'til it overflows.[103]

If this ghostolalically conjures a Gaye reading of Hortense, or Spillers's residency in Marvin's Room, despite the melancholy that *it be's that way sometime,* then what we see and hear and know is them *just saying you can do better.* Could this be the power and the glory, forever, of reversing the course, or curse, of coming up hard and apart at once? That is unclear but listen again to what I say:

If it is, we could be travailing toward that betterment and scream, in concert, AMEN!

Womanist
1. From *womanish.*
(Opp. of "girlish,"
i.e., frivolous, irresponsible, not serious.)
. . .
From the black folk expression of mothers to female children,
"You acting womanish,"
i.e., like a woman.
—ALICE WALKER, *In Search of Our Mothers' Gardens*

A Tale of Three Theorists

In the preamble of *In Search of Our Mothers' Gardens*, Alice Walker coins the term "womanist." The primary entry states it is someone engaged in "outrageous, audacious, courageous or *willful* behavior. . . . Interested in grown-up doings. Acting grown up. Being grown up. Interchangeable with another black folk expression: 'You trying to be grown.' Responsible. In charge. *Serious.*" While the four definitions communicate anecdotal, hetero- and homonormative expressions; love; and, most notably, that "Womanist is to feminist as purple is to lavender," the secondary entry's solitude nod stages quasi-"god-talk": "Not a separatist, except periodically for health. Tradition-ally universalist . . . Traditionally capable."[1] Separating from society reboots one's capacity to navigate that which inspires lethargy. While Walker does not espouse customarily "sacred" tenets, womanism's personal piety does project religiosity as its definitions read like profane beatitudes, ecclesial sacrilege. She empowers the womanist to believe one is "not free while any woman is unfree, even when her shackles are very different from [one's] own"; this translates to care of self: Regard you first before doling out such to others in surfeit. After all, self-isolation indexes being Jesus-like.[2] Nevertheless, some semblance of her formulations converge with those of Judith Butler.

Walker suggests that desiring maturity ("You trying to be grown.") could be proportionate to cultivating *gender trouble;* since her thoughts precede Butler's, the latter's own behavior has legibility:

> Contemporary feminist debates over the meanings of gender lead time and again to a certain sense of trouble. . . . Perhaps trouble need not carry such a negative valence. To make trouble was, within the reigning discourse of my childhood, something one should never do precisely because that would get one *in* trouble. The rebellion and its reprimand seemed to be caught up in the same terms . . . the prevailing law threat-ened one with trouble, even put one in trouble, all to keep one out of trouble. Hence, I concluded that trouble is inevitable and the task, how best to make it, what best way to be in it.[3]

These prefatory remarks to the 1990 edition of *Gender Trouble* align with this investigation because the confession demonstrates an act that has gained sig-nificance in public discourse: *mesearch.* The basic gist is any scholastic work, in which the scholar finds resonance, may be invalidated because one is look-ing for "me" in the (re)search.[4] Hence, academia privileges "critical distance," sterilizing a project and/or the people for whom the work accounts. Yet one contemplates whether something generates from mesearch because fully aware of its stigma, when "me" and the research collide, the impact ricochets solutions to the mysterious. Richard Wright forwards this when speculating that "'all writing is a secret form of autobiography.' . . . referring not to a de-liberate intention of concealing information but to an unconscious purpose, uniquely personal and inscribed in all language use by every individual. This secret marks the text with distinctive characteristics as much as an individual author's signature would."[5] So too, Butler's musings fall into another shunned category of rhetorical maneuvers: self-insertion into one's work. But while reading that passage, I comically envisioned Walker, as many black mothers have with their index fingers, motioning a juvenile Butler to "come real close" then whispering in her ear, "*You actin' womanish.*"

Walker being conversant with trouble recalls her own productivity regarding its curious relationship with black women and love such that a certain type of person is consistently *troublesome* or, better yet, *corpus perturbata, semper perturbanda*—a body troubled, always troubling.[6] *Homo tribulationis.* Therefore, in that stint when a thinker, trafficking in "grown-up doings," self-searches, do gendered constructs craft a new lens for melancholy and genius when one Butler dialogues with another, namely Octavia E.? Can "trouble"—how to be in and best make it—augment our understanding of blackness and affect? This three-theorist coagulation hypothesizes feminism and womanism as modes of "gender trouble" and "science fiction."

When discerning womanism's cultural import, people, from intellectuals to everyday inquisitors, posture the affect as something African Diasporic, particularly black American, women "do." This explains Walker's "standing" in seminaries and divinity schools: Womanist theology emerged when she constituted her Keyword, regardless of her elision at times in those spaces. Out of discontent with black liberation and feminist theologies' lack of acknowledging black women and their experiences, the discourse inaugurated itself in 1985 with the work of Katie Geneva Cannon and continued with that of Emilie M. Townes, Jacquelyn Grant, Delores S. Williams, and others.[7] Nonetheless, taking into account how some contrive who precisely can practice womanism, theologically and otherwise, it is interesting to consider a recent black stud(y/ies) turn that contends, "The paraontological distinction between blackness and blacks allows us no longer to be enthralled by the notion that blackness is a property that belongs to blacks (thereby placing certain formulations regarding non/relationality and non/communicability on a different footing and under a certain pressure) but also because ultimately it allows us to detach blackness from the question of (the meaning of) being"; or, said category is "ubiquitous" so that "we are fast reaching a day when black people . . . will continue to do Black Studies but also other people will do Black Studies. French people. White Americans. There are different formations of Black Studies around the world."[8] These ideas collided when I attended a womanism talk years ago.

At this meeting, someone asked, "If a running thematic in Africana/African Diasporic Studies is that blackness, and its study, is for everybody, can a white woman be a womanist?" The unequivocal response: "No, they cannot! They can access the methodology and use the tools, but they cannot be womanists, and neither can men." (Might Walker surmise *he* could be?[9]) Though the first definition states that a womanist is "a black feminist or feminist of color," the event's ensuing remarks, paraphrased here, provide further insight: "Only a human can be a woman; when you turn to the animal kingdom, the counterpart to the male/masculine [animal] is the female/feminine, but only a human can be a woman."[10] Given the semantics here, if one has missed *it*, an attempt to lay it bare: Some black feminists differentiate themselves from womanists, causing definitional dissonance and inviting speculation. (I heard a black feminist vehemently oppose womanism because she found it insufficiently capacious; similarly, one queries if a black man qualifies as a "black feminist," just as one squints when Afropessimists are white.[11]) The analogy connotes that despite "humanizing" the dehumanized, one may devolve to "animalizing" in turn. In this case, does "science"/"biology" justify who is in and out to wrestle with the theory and the event—is this (post)modern deployment something like "the law," once receiving rebuttal but now reverence? Is the trouble of womanism (not) its initial terminological stakes, perhaps, but rather, theologically speaking, the issue of *hermeneutics*, then and now?

Disregarding what "science," and its fictions, might project, I am not arguing for Butler, or her work, as womanist. Instead, juxtaposing the response at the midday chat-and-chew to mesearch, I wonder: What happens when something, or someone, is womani*sh*, a methodological assessment that reifies committing trouble as grammatically imposed in the dubious nature of the suffix? Posed paraontologically, if black people do not monopolize blackness—a question worth its own troubling—can a similar protocol apply to gender in black whereby historically, "[slavery] simultaneously—and paradoxically—disallowed distinctions in gender among black people. Enslaved black men were feminized by virtue of their subjugation as slaves, the regularity with which many were castrated, and the denial of their patriarchal and citizenship rights. Enslaved black women were masculinized by virtue of their backbreaking labor on par with black men and their being denied male protection and provision"?[12] My womanish intimation poses Octavia E. Butler as an argumentative straw *man* to address the specificities of that noonday reply as she complicates those sentiments through mesearch: "'Bloodchild' is my pregnant man story. . . . I wanted to see whether I could write a dramatic story of a man becoming pregnant as an act of love—choosing pregnancy in spite of as well as because of surrounding difficulties" such that "Gan's 'male pregnancy' is *not* an exploration of *the feminine position but a feminized position*," hence the salience of that adjectival appendage *-ish*.[13]

Could attempting to "undo" "the law" allude to how "the indeterminacy of gender might eventually culminate in the failure of feminism," and womanism, and its fortifying silos? If gender trouble necessitates *troubling* gender, can fictitious body politics be "liberated" through a case study of the law as litigated through blackness, or black letters? Is it risky, or rewarding, to detach femininity or womanliness from the question of (the meaning of) being "her" to note how "trouble sometimes euphemize[s] some fundamentally mysterious problem usually related to the alleged mystery of all things feminine?"[14] And are answers to some questions more robust when the black feminine/maternal, in the vision line of her male (filial) counterpart, has peculiar interactions with the law while subverting it? Examining "the law" through the process of hailing, and then pivoting to its vicissitudes in Butler's short story, "Bloodchild," I extend this "litigation" to read melancholy and genius in the masculine womanish. In so doing, one hopes that the worst of theoretical times catalyzes the best of creative ones.

Call the Law: Before and After the Call and the Response

"The law" as an enunciative agent seems catachrestical; though it names, conferring reflexive designations on bodies that rail against it, it can also be named: "12," "the po-po," "the man," "the penal system," "hegemony," "patriarchy." This sounds like *trouble.* Whereas it being named may be an obvious reactive position, it naming those under its purview is the paradoxical whimsy of subjectivity—this is interpellation:

> Althusser's doctrine of interpellation continues to structure contemporary debate on subject formation, offering a way to account for a subject who comes into being as a consequence of language, yet always within its terms. The theory of interpellation appears to stage a social scene in which a subject is hailed, the subject turns around, and the subject then accepts the terms by which he or she is hailed . . . a scene both punitive and reduced, for the call is made by an officer of "the Law," and this officer is cast as singular and speaking. . . . Interpellation, on this account, is not an event but a certain way of *staging the call,* where the call, as staged, becomes deliteralized in the course of its exposition or *darstellung.* The call itself is also figured as a demand to align oneself with the law, a turning around (to face the law, to find a face for the law?), and an entrance into the language of self-ascription— "Here I am"—through the appropriation of guilt.[15]

This "doctrine" rings (a)theologically when addressing the ecstatic expression of call-and-response. The simultaneity of the law enunciating and its expectant (re)capitulating signifies "understanding performativity as linguistic and casting it as theatrical" in that "[t]his ambiguity has consequences for the practice of coming out, for the insurrectionary power of the speech act, for language as a condition of both bodily seduction and the threat of injury."[16] The blocking directions for this "social scene" could (mis)construe interpellation with dramaturgy as Shakespeare teaches that this tragicomedy is *as you like it:* If "[a]ll the world's a stage . . . and one man in his time plays many parts," the law can draft a soldier for "nation-building" and eventually bar him as a purveyor of "justice."[17] While the interpellative moment is a byproduct of the time-space continuum, when the law hails bodies, does internalizing its declamation represent their subjectivity, or lack thereof? Though reiterating that "time becomes the foundation of space" may be wise, is it possible to cast time-space as disparate?[18] To be clearer, in the function of discourse, does one watch bodies in and over time but locate them as lost (and hoping to be found?) in space? This is the intellectually imm(a/i)nent tussle.

Early on in *Gender Trouble*, Butler tackles "woman" as subject. When she evokes the category with relation to the law, rhetorical calisthenics ensue: "Indeed, the question of women as the subject of feminism raises the possibility that there may not be a subject who *stands* 'before' the law, awaiting representation in or by the law. Perhaps the subject, as well as the invocation of a *temporal* 'before,' is constituted by the law as the fictive foundation of its own claim to legitimacy. . . . The performative invocation of a nonhistorical 'before' becomes the foundational premise that guarantees a presocial ontology of persons who freely consent to be governed and, thereby, constitute the legitimacy of the social contract."[19] In this stretch, she ostensibly engages the ontological and, strangely, the oxymoronic. These preliminary moves, adhering to time-space machinations, put one on the right track. The subject, who may not be, "stands 'before' the law" in a likely fictive position, presumably responding to a staged call. But something happens in the statement's predicate(d) reality and its concluding phrasticity: Subjectivity, causative to manufacturing being, is worth raising contingent on the standing one occupying the temporal category of a-waiting—for representation, recognition. The "subject" "wastes" time for the long *durée* of being a law-abiding, law-awaiting citizen.

At the turn of "Perhaps," Butler attempts to resolve the timely quandary she voices in the preceding declaration. However, thinking against Shakespeare, one signals "perhaps" as a yearning for an altogether different form of justice:

> Paradoxically, it is because of this overflowing of the performative, because of this always excessive haste of interpretation getting ahead

of itself, because of this structural urgency and precipitation of justice that [Lévinas's notion that "Truth supposes justice"] has no horizon of expectation (regulative or messianic). But for this very reason, it *may* have an *avenir,* a "to-come," which I rigorously distinguish from the future that can always reproduce the present. Justice remains, is yet, to come, *à venir,* it has an, it is *à-venir,* the very dimension of events irreducibly to come. It will always have it, this *à-venir,* and always has. . . . "Perhaps," one must always say perhaps for justice. There is an *avenir* for justice and there is no justice except to the degree that some event is possible which, as event, exceeds calculation, rules, programs, anticipations and so forth.[20]

These performative allusions scaffold a takedown of institutions which, through linguistic falsity, feign to have used bricks for "structural urgency" made without straw. Systems have an affinity for *talkin' loud and sayin' nothin'* regarding justice. Because the future betrays the kinetic potential energy to be the present's newborn, truth and justice reconcile as frenemies.[21] Yet even if the syntactical performance of justice—the "excessive haste of interpretation"—subjects the actuating of it to the haphazard erection of "time 'after' time," it does not mean justice will not happen despite unfathomability. "Perhaps" is a pivot, the striving for a just cause or effect, a desire to wait and see what "the end" will be; this occurs alongside the worry in the waiting for that (im)possible occasion as certain persons' deaths may be requirements for its accomplishment, that is, regarding the paraontological, "What will happen then if instead of demanding justice we recognize (or at least consider) that the very notion of justice—indeed the gamut of political and cognitive elements that constitute formal, multiracial democratic practices and institutions—produces or requires black exclusion and death as normative?"[22] Amid these contrasts, that "event horizon" implies the unthinkable happening as Derrida's conceit pairs with that of Hortense J. Spillers: With the *telos* of giving the "arriving company a clearer space for work," having drafted the blueprints to destroy this "regulative or messianic" tabernacle, there must be as little debris possible after the demolition; thus, one commences cleaning this house. This would-be justice "opens up for *l'avenir* the transformation, the recasting or refounding of law and politics," an absolute alterity that while unpresentable, could be fecund.[23] While this projects an oncoming fruition, wishful yet inevitably deadly, one is befuddled when rereading Butler's words because her rhetoric could format something unplanned.

If "before" is not a temporal but a spatial construction, is "the [non]subject who stands 'before' the law" an example of an entity *standing in the gap* for something or someone, the act of revelation—"the intelligible event that makes all other events intelligible"? (A gesture: "The slave bows down before the law and prays for equal rights. The slave bows down *before* the law and then there is law. *There is no law before the slave bows down.*" Here, the contranymic whims of "before" foreshadow my argument in that one wonders at the preoccupation in black thought with the spatiotemporal flip[-off] to the interpellative via the idea of prehistory.)[24] Still, she asserts that what "emerges within the matrix of power relations is not a simple replication or copy of the law itself, a uniform repetition of a masculinist economy of identity. The productions swerve from their original purposes and inadvertently mobilize possibilities of 'subjects' that do not merely exceed the bounds of cultural intelligibility, but effectively expand the boundaries of what is, in fact, culturally intelligible." If one witnesses the revelatory, what will that testimony be? And is that space, in its quintessence, temporal? As Butler invokes *darstellung,* a reading of *darstellen,* to depict, initiates "Afro-fabulation as a critical practice": "A fabulist is a teller of tales, but he or she also discloses the powers of the false to create new possibilities"; an Afro-fabulist "disrupt[s] the hostile and constraining conditions of his emergence into representation."[25] Though there will soon be a depiction of a character witness standing "'before' the law" to determine womanish possibility, I want to linger on this nonsubject.

Some years ago, regarding Richard Pryor, I wrote, "[I]t is not the father of personal prehistory he seeks, but rather the mother of personal prehistory."[26] My prehistoric invocation sidles up to Butler as she continues reading interpellation: "The narrative that seeks to account for how the subject comes into being presumes the grammatical 'subject' prior to the account of its genesis. Yet the founding submission that has not yet resolved into the subject would be precisely the *non-narrativizable prehistory of the subject . . .* this requires that the temporality not be true, for the grammar of that narrative presupposes that there is no subjection without a subject who undergoes it."[27] Reading this passage through parallelism, nonresolution engenders that nonnarrativizable prehistory; the presence of lack supplies a lacking subject, existentially, who has no past, *no there there.* Is this one of the "distinguishing mental features of melancholia . . . a profoundly painful dejection, cessation of interest in the outside world, loss of the capacity to love, inhibition of all activity, and a lowering of the self-regarding feelings to a degree that finds utterance in self-reproaches and self-revilings, and culminates in a delusional expectation of punishment"? Is no prehistory precursory to Freudian mania?[28] Is this that trouble?

If black women "in love" *stay* "in trouble," then to stay black and die is to stay *with* the trouble, especially if she is your mama. That said, the black feminine/maternal, too, may "clean house" surrounding that nonnarrativizable prehistory in that "if psychic economy 'grows,' as it were, with the historical subject, doesn't she have one long *before* she 'knows' that there is a 'white man' and certainly well in advance of her caring about him at all? . . . In other words, this 'I,' it seems, operates as the embodiment of a dialectical plot, or sufficiency, in the midst of normal/abnormal oscillations."[29] This hermeneutic, given Walker's term, converses with what Sylvia Wynter calls "a vantage point . . . towards which the diacritical term 'womanist' . . . can only be projected from a 'demonic model,'" disturbing "the 'consolidated field' of our present mode of being/feeling/knowing . . . through which alone these modes . . . can effect their respective autopeosis [*sic*] *as such* specific modes of being."[30] These (ab)normal oscillations characterize how one manipulates dominant manners of "sentience," even at the level of "the body," to (re)configure a kind of specificity no longer contingent on generalizations of the West and its Man. Though what Wynter strikes is anathema to that wholly religious underpinning of "the good," the presumptive "evil" ought to respond "as being at home in the supernatural (spirits, the devil, etc.) . . . where it designates 'a working system that cannot have a determined, or knowable outcome.'"[31] That said, a black prehistoric performance becomes significant.

In the opening scenes of Octavia E. Butler's *Fledgling*, the first utterance in the text is when the protagonist Shori encounters the character Wright Hamlin on the roadside:

> I was surprised when the car stopped alongside me. The person inside was, at first, just a face, shoulders, a pair of hands. Then I understood that I was seeing a young man, pale-skinned, brown-haired, broad and tall. . . . He lowered his window, looked out at me, and asked, "Are you all right?" . . . I opened my mouth, cleared my throat, coughed, then finally managed to say, "I . . . am. Yes, I am all right." My voice sounded strange and hoarse to my own ears. It wasn't only that I couldn't recall speaking to anyone else. I couldn't remember ever speaking at all. Yet it seemed I knew how.[32]

This language precarity raises intrigue regarding subjectivity vis-à-vis auto-pronunciation. When Shori accounts for the trucker, it is interesting that he later becomes her protector; though she is a fifty-three-year-old vampire, when Hamlin encounters her, he beholds her, and she presents, as a child—he registers as some semblance of "the law." Yet when "the law" calls Shori in a chance encounter on the side of the road, it is a psychosocial reversal of the Kafkaesque gate.[33] As important is this dialogue occurring in chapter 2, which is to say a narrative surrounding the amnesiac instantiates itself in chapter 1. Is this narrated chronology a moment when Octavia extraformally rethinks Judith's theoretical tasks as they relate to one's "calling"? It appears Butler, through Shori, positivizes the parallel and constructs the parallax—the possibility and resolution, fictionally, that there is a "before" prior to the "before" may not be contingent on subjection, but rather the existence of anamnesis, the ability to narrate one's prehistory as a form of hypermnesia. Shori enunciating, when the power of (chapter) one counterintuitively begets the consciousness of two, signals not only her *all right-ness* of being, but also the Tetragrammaton: the I AM. Blackness and "the divine" keep converging.

Divinity is not lost on Butler, Judith that is, in her theoretical wrestling: "It is important to remember that the turn toward the law is not necessitated by the hailing; it is compelling . . . because it promises identity. If the law speaks in the name of a self-identical subject (Althusser cites the utterance of the Hebrew God: 'I am that I am'), how is it that conscience might deliver or restore a self to oneness with itself, to the postulation of self-identity that becomes the precondition of the linguistic consolidation 'Here I am?'" The consequential concern with hailing as the recognition of identity is notable (despite it being "less than logical" because, as per Anthony P. Farley, the law maneuvers under the same auspice with relation to the slave's genuflection).[34] But *Fledgling* posits that there is a self-identification before an entity speaks to, or is spoken to by, some external source. That speech act reads quasi-biblical since the Tetragrammaton occurs in Exodus, the book following Genesis. One presumes that YHWH, "the Law," comprehends self-identity long *before* anything, including its very self, speaks or is hailed. Then again, an intelligible event that makes all other events intelligible: The only account of a biblical character conferring divine identity is through Hagar, that Egyptian ancestor who interpellates during her exodus in Genesis by calling God *El-roi*—"the God who sees me."

In all, this prepares us for "Bloodchild" wherein the black feminine/maternal, having equipped a child to hail himself—she who sees him as he watches her—*triggers* the son to be the pregnant boy who cried, "I am."

A Voice Cast Out to Talk Us In: The Visitation of a "Bloodchild"

While gender trouble and "the law" have been addressed in the prior sections, there is an abiding interest in science fiction and its relationship to the legal as the genre engages the philosophy of the law in practice.[35] "Bloodchild" explores that transition: "On one level, it's a love story between two very different beings. On another, it's a coming-of-age story in which a boy must absorb disturbing information and use it to make a decision that will affect the rest of his life. On a third level, 'Bloodchild' is my pregnant man story. . . . Could I write a story in which a man chose to become pregnant *not* through some sort of misplaced competitiveness to prove that a man could do anything a woman could do, not because he was forced to, not even out of curiosity?"[36] Based on these remarks, ranging from the biological, literary, or amorous, Butler *takes the law into her own hands*, whether in seclusion to or before it, as the exertion of *force*, "of positive production, the action that creates things, makes alliances, and forges interactions. . . . Desire 'experiments; it makes: it is fundamentally aleatory, inventive.'"[37] She desires to hold "the law," often the proponent of "idle threats," accountable for its reprobate mind on "civilization and its discontents," its mindless constructions; she suggests that even when "reputable" persons summon the law, there is the likelihood that lines can be still crossed. And so, "the quarrel seems also to turn on the articulation of a temporal trope . . . that flourishes *prior* to the imposition of a law, *after* its overthrow, or during its reign as a constant challenge to its authority."[38]

"Bloodchild" is fraught with troubles as Butler syncs with psychoanalysis regarding maternal potency: "If that feminine 'all-mightiness' in the survival of the species can be undermined through other technical possibilities that, or so it seems, might make *man pregnant* as well, it is likely that this latter eventuality could only attract a *small minority*, even though it fulfills the androgynous fantasies of the *majority*."[39] This all-mighty possibility lends an affective interpretation to the story's premise. Whether this pregnant boy, Gan, is womanish may be obvious due to his "biological" capacity, but the work still showcases something about feeling some womanish need, a signification of empowerment rather than inferiority.[40] Likewise, Butler's proximate "maternity," at the location of her pen, deserves attention.

In the afterword for "Bloodchild," she expounds on her impetus for the story as an "effort to ease an old fear" about encountering the botfly: it "lays its eggs in wounds left by the bites of other insects. I found the idea of a maggot living and growing under my skin, eating my flesh as it grew, to be so intolerable, so terrifying. . . . The maggot becomes literally attached to its host and leaves part of itself behind, broken off, if it's squeezed or cut out. Of course, the part left behind dies and rots, causing infection. Lovely." Insofar as she abhors incubating an insect as its "host," her abhorrence elicits awe without pursuant action. Though gender mores suggest that any opportunity for the feminine, across species, to bear life is her "lot" (while the masculine is, somehow, "free"), Butler's admission posits disgust and liberty since she overcomes her fear by writing it ("When I have to deal with something that disturbs me . . . I write about it. I sort out my problems by writing about them.").[41]

She shares in the "Bloodchild" preface, and to an extent the afterword, that she is most fulfilled when writing, creating, of her freewill, her *immaculate conception*: "I feel that what people bring to my work is at least as important to them as what I put into it. But I'm still glad to be able to talk a little about what I do put into my work, and what it means to me." She tricks psychoanalytic melancholy: Butler preoccupies herself not with being "lost" but "found," whether by readers imputing hermeneutics on her work; or an undesired agent, a botfly, that could potentiate fleshly "loss"—death, rot, infection—without her consent. She reimagines the undesired in "Bloodchild" through a character who wields (non)consensual power while disregarding her ensuing nuclear, that is familial, damage. Moreover, Butler may envision herself in Gan, her *creatio ex nihilo*, providing him with a tool she hypothetically would use on botflies without fearing "death." Does all of this encapsulate Afro-fabulation? Nevertheless, this "creationism" might confirm the minor prophet Lauryn Hill—such discourse is discomfiting if some do not "understand how *female* and *strong* work together. Or young and wise. Or *Black* and *divine*."[42] Gender trouble indeed!

This lifeworld may define what it means to "stay black and die" as the first line of "Bloodchild" calls us to literary consciousness: "My last night of childhood began with a visit home." This not only sounds like the early childhood of Judith Butler's troubling, but also presumes Gan, the character who speaks this, living "outside" "the law," even if this instantiation of legality is that of home. This confession, utilizing the first-person possessive, invests the story with "subject making," regardless of Butler's text undoing the "matrix of normative gender relations."[43] Gan elicits a melancholic reading.

As Terrans, he and his family have a precarious relationship with the alien T'Gatoi, a Tlic official in charge of their home, the Preserve; this narrative arc has its own trouble. Residence in the Preserve connotes a diasporic existence as one experiences the "outside":

T'Gatoi was hounded on the outside. Her people wanted more of us made available. Only she and her political faction stood between us and the hordes who did not understand why there was a Preserve—why any Terran could not be courted, paid, drafted, in some way made available to them. Or they did understand, but in their desperation, they did not care. She parceled us out to the desperate and sold us to the rich and powerful for their political support. Thus, we were necessities, status symbols, and an independent people. She oversaw the joining of families, putting an end to the final remnants of the earlier system of breaking up Terran families to suit impatient Tlic. . . . "And your ancestors, fleeing from their home-world, from their own kind who would have killed or enslaved them—they survived because of us. We saw them as people and gave them the Preserve when they still tried to kill us as worms."[44]

Portraying T'Gatoi as "law enforcement" harangued outside, presumably in the extraterrestrial boundaries of the Preserve, may mean that executors of the law confront certain forms of (il)legality too. She serves double duty as an "officer" and "home-visitor": a "'[friend] of the race' who policed the management of household affairs, regularly trespassing the border between the home and the world . . . the predecessor of the social worker; she dispense[s] household advice and assesse[s] the character and development" of the Terrans. This exhibits not only power, but also the complexity of a (non)subject standing "'before' the law" because the law has the self-serving need to stand "beside" you ("less than logical"). From the onset, yes—"Power, rather than the law, encompasses both juridical (prohibitive and regulatory) and the productive (inadvertently generative) functions of differential relations."[45] But if the power-starved law *has its cake and eats it too*—parceling out bodies for political gain to affirm its need for them, and interceding for those self-same bodies when existence hangs in the balance—the oppressed reify that a-waiting formulation. The law comports itself as a form of representation. However, does this reactionary protocol require the transformation of that subject, who is not one, from the status of may-not-be to yes-I-am to represent the self? These happenings in a short story-experiment on masculine pregnancy convey the experience of negative capability whereby inhabiting two dimensions at once, and possibly calmly, could reimagine the split ego.[46]

After explaining T'Gatoi's locative reality, Gan further exposes the home scene:

Now T'Gatoi used four of her limbs to push me away from her onto the floor.

"Go on, Gan," she said. "Sit down there with your sisters and enjoy not being sober. You had most of the egg. Lien, come warm me." . . .

"Nothing can buy him from me." Sober, she would not have permitted herself to refer to such things.

"Nothing," T'Gatoi agreed, humoring her.

"Did you think I would sell him for eggs? For long life? My son?"

"Not for anything," T'Gatoi said, stroking my mother's shoulders, toying with her long, graying hair.

I would like to have touched my mother, shared that moment with her. *She would take my hand if I touched her now.* Freed by the egg and the sting, she would smile and perhaps say things long held in. But tomorrow, she would remember all this as a humiliation. I did not want to be part of a remembered humiliation. Best just *be still and know* she loved me under all the duty and pride and pain.[47]

T'Gatoi performs unrestricted "soft violence" under the guise of serving and protecting the family; this alien liberty is due in part to the parental unit being intoxicated such that she airs "dirty laundry." Gan watches his mother, Lien, "unwillingly reduced from a defiant state of tension and rigidity to one of drugged tranquility as T'Gatoi strokes her shoulders, 'toys' with her hair, convinces her to ingest the liquid from a sterile egg, and finally stings her to sleep with a scorpion-like tail."[48] She figures her progeny as an exchangeable good, seemingly practicing negligence in the presence of a houseguest. Gan narrates his blues idiom, apropos of James Baldwin's "The Uses of the Blues."

Citing how "the blues" could be substituted with "anguish" or "pain" because the aesthetic tradition is itself a metaphor, Baldwin situates what the originators of the art teach practitioners and listeners alike: "The blues are rooted in the slave songs; the slave songs discovered something genuinely terrible, terrible because it sums up the universal challenge, the universal hope, the universal fear. . . . If you can live in the full knowledge that you are going to die, that you are not going to live forever, that if you live with the reality of death, you can live." Gan's death drive does not counteract that to inhabit such, he *must* live, even if such living puts touch on hiatus. This living-as-music, akin to slave songs or even Ralph Ellison's intimation, foreruns discovering something terribly generative on par with Baldwinian "joy": "The blues carries an existential mandate emanating from beneath the intellectual and cultural buttresses of the modern self . . . the method of the blues comes from a modern community that lived for many generations without the philosophical and civic consolations of modernity. . . . The lyrical slip— and the authority that comes from it—between joy and pain is the precondition, then, for *real* life and *real* learning."[49] Life in the Preserve is "real" and could constitute early onset mania, as will be discussed momentarily, just as it may engender, on the other side of this psychoanalytic economy, Baldwin's all-right-ness: "all states such as joy, exultation or triumph, which give us the normal model for mania, depend on the same economic conditions. . . . All such situations are characterized . . . by *increased readiness for all kinds of action*—in just the same way as in mania, and in complete contrast to the depression and inhibition of melancholia."[50] If this is "real life," what "real learning," what action, might Gan offer?

Although one could connote Lien as a "lost object," Gan, ever doubtful, behaves like Didymus: He desires putting his finger in her "wounds" to haptically resurrect her, wonders if noninebriation would release her from that egg-induced stupor, compelling her to reach out and touch him. He wants to be still and know that she is, indeed, his mother.[51] Encapsulating this scene, "family," then, is like a minefield "we walk and dance through . . . never knowing where or when something or someone is going to explode"; and "a living mystery, constantly changing, constantly providing us clues about who we are, and demanding that we recognize the new and challenging shapes it often takes."[52] Gan navigates explosive terrain during mesearch. Yet these plotlines are met with private shame, rendered as personal humiliation, *before* a "public servant." His homely affections purport that on the inside, he is an outsider. Culturally, mothers of yore would say Gan *smells like outside.* This incites recalling the "Bloodchild" opening: The last day of his childhood as a visit home, opining "visit" to mark relative estrangement, offers the prehistoric conjuration that Gan has been dwelling outdoors.

Such spatial survival provokes a more excellent way for interpreting this social milieu:

> Outdoors, we knew, was the real terror of life. The threat of being outdoors surfaced frequently in those days. . . . Sometimes mothers put their sons outdoors, and when that happened . . . all sympathy was with him. He was outdoors, and his own flesh had done it. . . . There is a difference between being put *out* and being put out*doors.* If you are put out, you go somewhere else; if you are outdoors, there is no place to go. The distinction was subtle but final. Outdoors was the end of something, an irrevocable physical fact, defining and complementing our

metaphysical condition. . . . But the concreteness of being outdoors was another matter—like the difference between the concept of death and being, in fact, dead. Dead doesn't change, and outdoors is here to stay.[53]

Outdoors is a site-specific poetics Gan internalizes. The italics further the "Bloodchild" narration along the lines of a subtly final distinction: When one is put *out,* there remains the chance one can still be let in; when one is put out*doors,* power rests with whomever resides behind said doors—that is where the locks are. One rehearses in rememory:

> I told you once but twice
> You wasn't very nice
> In your hands, you held my life
> I told you once but twice, my love
> Don't lock yourself out that door

Although unclear whether Lien is "heartless enough to put [her] own kin outdoors," Gan's flesh is not off the hook because he chooses to visit home, as in he may have been "slack enough to put [himself] outdoors"—a mode of being "criminal," "fugitive," yet worthy of sympathy. Is he being womanis*h,* engaging the conceit of acting as a "separatist . . . for health"?[54]

This "fugitivity" is generational since Gan and his mother were once outdoors: "I had lived outside with [T'Gatoi]. I had seen the desperate eagerness in the way some people looked at me. It was a little frightening to know that only she stood between us and that desperation that could so easily swallow us. My mother would look at her sometimes and say to me, 'Take care of her.' And I would remember that she too had been outside, had seen." The agonism of "Bloodchild" differentiating death and the outdoors marks home as "not just the manifest geographic place that we're born to, grow up in, and in many ways want to return to. It's something else. It's a sense of arrival. . . . It's the getting home that strikes so deeply . . . that sense of having gotten home. But there's also a sense that home gets up and leaves after you've gotten there that propels the agitation and unrest . . . and you have to go chase it. It keeps moving on."[55] Ruing home; returning home as a visitor; reconciling home as that which runs away from you as you run back to it, hoping to evade detonations; regarding home as a burden and blessing carried when first vacating its premises—this is mourning and melancholy.

Being othered out(-side/-doors) registers as familiar, alluding to this family's prehistory, because "it *was* an honor to have T'Gatoi in the family, but it was hardly a novelty. T'Gatoi and my mother had been friends all my mother's life, and T'Gatoi was not interested in being honored in the house she considered a second home." Likewise, she "introduced my mother to the man who became my father. My parents . . . married as T'Gatoi was going into her family business—politics . . . my mother promised T'Gatoi one of her children. She would have to give one of us to someone, and she preferred T'Gatoi to some stranger."[56] She is the invited friend who troubles her comrades in their own house, actions typical of "the stranger / we always thot it wd be." These complexities prove that "[f]amilial relationships are quasi-incestuous. The narrator, Gan, and the Tlic whose children he will carry, T'Gatoi, are both children of the same father, whose sperm produced Gan and whose belly carried T'Gatoi." The hitch of the story reveals itself before our arrival: "She had been taken from my father's flesh when he was my age."[57] Is this a prehistory we know all too well?

T'Gatoi is not a contextual home-visitor, but rather a common-law *other-mother* of a different sort. A matchmaker with political proclivities. "A sister and aunt to her future spouse . . . a second mother to him as well." T'Gatoi needs the Terrans because the Tlic invented them: "The circumstances that oppress the narrator do not stem from any metaphysical imperative; they are not historically inevitable, and therefore can be altered . . . they are *constructed* out of social and material conditions that result in the appalling crisis at the start of the story—the Tlic have *changed themselves and the humans before,* and can do so again."[58] Sameness abounds between these instances of gender trouble-science fiction and the law. These symptoms point to not only a potential intergenerational "curse"—pregnant men incubating oppressors—but also a parent who rebuts what nonfiction "law" overdetermines as an impenetrable gender role: Gan's father is "motherly," performing surrogacy due to his people's "creation" ("He has done it three times in his long life. . . . How had he done it? How did anyone do it?").[59] This is the mimicry of children to be their "fathers" or "mothers" who historicize otherness through subversion. This is a moment of literary intelligibility: Not discounting Butler's misgivings of reading "Bloodchild" as a slave narrative, it parallels the genre despite effacing "blackness," or calling Gan "an Asian boy."[60]

(An educated guess about this racial categorization is its linkage to his siblings' names, Qui and Xuan Hoa, and his mother's, all being ostensibly "Asian." However, this presumption hints at the nature of the unspecific, nomenclatural dubiousness as race-ing cosplay. Working knowledge of Asian languages attests to "Xuan" being sourced to at least Mandarin Chinese and Vietnamese—does Gan embody "all" of Asia? Could he not be Asian? Such characterizations recall the ongoing racial "need-to-know" of Toni

Morrison's "Recitatif." One ponders what the social would look like if the ease of name etymology could trace one's ethnogeographic "identity," that is, where "home" is: Every [black] woman named Antoinette would be "French"; and every [white] man named Leroy would be . . . but I digress.)

Formally, "Bloodchild" is a metaslavery.[61] Glimpses emerge in the plot when Gan confesses, "[Lien] lay down now against T'Gatoi, and the whole left row of T'Gatoi's limbs closed around her, holding her loosely, but securely. I had always found it comfortable to lie that way, but except for my older sister, no one else in the family liked it. They said it made them feel caged." This "comfort" metaphor posits Gan as a singing bird caged at home, simultaneous to connoting himself as Preserve prey when he leaves. (Qui undoes this: "Then he began running away until he realized there was no 'away.' Not in the Preserve. Certainly not outside. . . . 'Yeah. Stupid. Running inside the Preserve. Running in a cage.'" Ironically, Elyce Rae Helford claims "caging" as the Terrans becoming *species*. Perhaps Qui too is a bird, uncomfortable, in a larger maniacal contraption. Moreover, this elicits my pushback that "Gan must decide whether hosting the eggs in exchange for a new start on another planet is mutually symbiotic" because Butler narrates *nowhere to go*. Thus, Gan's visit home when "Bloodchild" begins might mean he too is "stuck," just not under the strictures of his childhood abode.)[62] Gan's camaraderie with an outsider indoors—or his proximity to her as protection because "T'Gatoi certainly coerces Gan into carrying her children by threatening to impregnate" his sister, Xuan Hoa—internalizes "oppressive" frameworks, even exoskeletally; and to such a degree that he starts *looking* like T'Gatoi ("'Don't give me one of *her* looks,' [Qui] said. 'You're not her. You're just her property.' One of her looks. Had I picked up even an ability to imitate her expressions?").[63]

The Preserve is an (un)safe space for "the human dwelling on the Tlic planet (an animal farm, ghetto, Native American resettlement, and Nazi concentration camp all at once)"; there is no need to list "plantation" because we *get it*. Either way, "[a] close reading of 'Bloodchild' demonstrates several of the general themes attributed to slave narratives, especially the first-person narration by a captive minority."[64] That may-not-be to yes-I-am paradigm resurfaces as a structural signifier through Butler's narrativizing. Yet with this melancholy being reducible to "environmental influences" of the Preserve— "The correlation of melancholia and mourning seems justified by the general picture of the two conditions. Moreover, the exciting causes due to environmental influences are, so far as we can discern them at all, the same for both conditions"—does genius emerge?[65] The answer is threefold.

To begin, metaslavery in science fiction likely has its earliest manifestation via Olaudah Equiano who utters, "Indeed such were the horrors of my views and fears at the moment, that, if ten thousand worlds had been my own, I would have freely parted with them all to have exchanged my condition with that of the meanest slave in my own country." Similarly, Hagar is a sociopolitical complement to these Terrans: "Hagar's position was not much different from those of the brother and sister who could carry the alien egg in Butler's 'Bloodchild.' They could no more control their own reproductive potentials in the confines of the ruling aliens than could Hagar in the confines of slavery."[66] "Bloodchild" inserts itself into a broad canon of diasporic black stud(y/ies) that has at its center the act of being *held.* Through metaphor or first-person account, black (auto)biography welcomes a fantastical addition with this work; Butler, like Hagar, names the power by speaking directly to it since her "success at remaking history and our relation to it demonstrates that slavery is an established part of [science fiction], even with its long-standing record of critical neglect."[67] Equally deft is the narrative intent of "Bloodchild."

Butler contends, "[S]ome people assume I'm talking about slavery when what I'm really talking about is *symbiosis.*" This line of thinking mirrors the afterword: "I tried to write a story about paying the rent—a story about an isolated colony of human beings on an inhabited, extrasolar world . . . the humans would have to make some kind of accommodation with their um . . . their hosts. Chances are this would be an unusual accommodation. Who knows what we humans have that others might be willing to take in trade for a livable space on a world not our own?"[68] That "um" hints at a nomenclatural grasping: Is "hosts" subterfuge for "masters"? Embedded in this caveat is the gravity that while Gan has already lost his innocence, hence returning home, and T'Gatoi perpetuates timeworn subjugating maneuvers, Butler troubles the quest not for home necessarily, but for "livable space," even if said space is a womb. Though home can up and leave, the "real terror of life" is (home/space)lessness, the outdoors. This may be why Butler offers her spatiotemporal term: Who cathects to chase an entity that is transient, static, and problematic singularly and/or all at once? Thus, in that scene of reckoning—when the ovipositor implantation catalyzes ontological destabilization; when the sonic doubling to "take care of" haunts because the original admonition toward the alien othermother has her declaring it to the "son" she impregnates to ensure communal continuation; when bloodchild is bloodsurrogate—we picture them: two home-less beings, alien and human, finding space in each other's survival. Beside the defeat and the terror, there would be this too: the glimpse of symbiosis, the instant of possibility.[69] The risk in dealing with a partner.[70]

Second, T'Gatoi has a moment of awakening when she asks Gan, "Would you really rather die than bear my young?"; he does not answer. Having maintained silence when the law questions him, he takes on a critical posture, even as the prelude to his eventual disrobing ("Yet I undressed and lay down beside her. I knew what to do, what to expect. I had been told all my life.").[71] Her inquiry plays on a spiritual in that given the interrogative, a Preserve retort could be that *before* being a slave, one prefers burial in one's grave then going *home* to one's Lord and being "free." But if one conjectures what Gan might have said, despite his actions foreshadowing the upcoming hypothetical remonstration, it would sound a little something like this—you, Tlic, who do this thing, who practice this oppression, are bereft; there is something distorted about the psyche: a huge waste, a corruption, a distortion. It's like a profound neurosis that nobody examines for what it is: It feels crazy, it *is* crazy. And it has just as much of a deleterious effect on you, and possibly equal, as it does the Terrans. An example:

> "They don't take women," [Qui] said with contempt.
>
> "They do sometimes," [Gan] glanced at him. "Actually, they prefer women. You should be around them when they talk among themselves. They say women have more body fat to protect grubs. But they usually take men to leave the women free to bear their own young."
>
> "To provide the next generation of host animals," he said, switching from contempt to bitterness."
>
> "It's more than that!" I countered. Was it?

Etymologically, then, Gan lives *utopia* in these symbiotic snapshots: He has no place, no home, he is literally off center, off the track, unlocatable, when he enacts antiphony ineffably. Hence, "Butler's insistence on maintaining a closed family structure . . . serves as her means of emphasizing the vital need for collaboration underlying both the Tlic-human and the male-female relationships of the story . . . to structure an imperfect but *just* society."[72] This mutual aid is, sensibly, raggedy.

Notwithstanding these Butler instigations, the last bit of genius occurs unassumingly, as if one's eyes walk past it in the expanse of black lines and white spaces, not unlike an inability to notice the color purple in a field somewhere and piss God off in turn. This profoundly mundane act poses what I consider the crux of the story, bridging and expediting Preserve machinations to an act of preservation conducted near the story's conclusion: Gan wields a rifle placed among other tools from his mother's garden.

"Leave room in your garden for angels to dance.": In Search of Our Mothers' Gardens (and Our Fathers' Toolsheds)—A Redux

In her eponymous essay, "In Search of Our Mothers' Gardens," Walker extends her poiesis regarding mothers not being "Saints, but Artists; driven to a numb and bleeding madness by the springs of creativity in them for which there was no release."[73] This intervention seems apt for discerning Lien's melancholy; while one is careful claiming T'Gatoi either as "ignorant and depraved" or the wielder of the "lash," the complexity of a lifelong friend possessing the flesh, the wombs, of children that are not hers re-presents that frenemy status.[74] The overseer's weapon transmogrifies to be her tail sting, which "drew only a single drop of blood from my mother's bare leg."[75] New tool, same difference. If one sympathizes with a child put out*doors*, is there sympathy for a mother put *out* of "maternity"? Judging Lien seems austere if submitting to T'Gatoi is an extraterrestrial life insurance policy for her children. Her affinity for self-medication, performed through Tlic-ian puncture, is temporary surrender for an assurance of filial permanence. Hence, "Gan's mother knows that humans have no control over their lives, yet she still resists in whatever form possible (without risking further her children's lives). Although Gan longs for the motherly affection that only submission to T'Gatoi will enable, he at least intellectually comprehends his mother's resistance and is, perhaps, inspired by it later in the story."[76] I dwell momentarily on this comprehension as inspiration.

Free associating on the maternal Artist-cum-creator, Walker performs her own mesearch:

> my mother adorned with flowers whatever shabby house we were forced to live in. . . . Whatever she planted grew as if by *magic* . . . even my memories of poverty are seen through a screen of blooms . . . because whatever rocky soil she landed on, she turned into a garden. . . . I notice that it is only when my mother is working in her flowers that she is radiant, almost to the point of being invisible—except as Creator: hand and eye. . . . Ordering the universe in the image of her personal conception of Beauty.
>
> Her face, as she prepares the Art that is her gift, is a *legacy* of respect she leaves for me, for all that illuminates and cherishes life. She

has handed down respect for the possibilities—and the will to grasp them . . . the woman who literally covered the holes in our walls with sunflowers. . . . Guided by my *heritage* of a love of beauty and a respect for strength—in search of my mother's garden, I found my own.[77]

This is a reply vis-à-vis readerly nosiness when Walker preconceives, "But when, you will ask, did my overworked mother have time to know or care about feeding the creative spirit?" This homage, she suggests, "is so simple that many of us have spent years discovering it. We have constantly looked high, when we should have looked high—and low."[78] So low that it was right under the nose. Underfoot. Walker's passage riffs on the parable of the sower *undone.*

This mother, landing on rocky soil yet sowing seeds nonetheless to reap a garden, defies the parabolic gesture that seeds on rocky soil represent children who hear their mother's messages and immediately receive them with joy; but since they do not have deep roots, they do not last long, falling away as soon as they have problems or are persecuted for believing (in) her. This subversion occurs precisely because to be poor in spirit is to survive off the haul a mother cultivates, the kingdom come on soil as it is in Elsewhere. These are "activities black [children] have watched their mothers and grandmothers engaged in for years without knowing that true artists were at work." This mother, meek, "inherits the earth" as it bequeaths to her Beauty as a method. She, and her children, shall be called *blessed.*[79] Is this Derridean "inheritance"—"The critical choice called for by a reaffirmation of the inheritance is also, like memory itself, the condition of finitude. . . . The injunction itself (it always says 'choose and decide from among what you inherit') can only be one by dividing itself, tearing itself apart, differing/deferring itself, by speaking at the same time several times—and in several voices"—a legacy generative of sunflowers as wall-hanging portraiture in the twinkle of a mother's eyes and manipulation of her hands?[80] These presumptive blessings from outdoors, from a garden bed where the commingling of tending to seedlings mixed with patience may not always yield buds but blasted possibility, puts into relief what happens inside of the indoors in "Bloodchild" as Gan makes a choice, a decision, among what he "inherits" from Lien.

Pressured to help T'Gatoi while envisioning his future *partum,* Gan reveals, "I went to the corner cabinet where my mother kept her large house and garden tools . . . there was a pipe that carried off waste water from the kitchen—except that it didn't anymore. My father had rerouted the waste water below before I was born. Now the pipe could be turned so that one half slid around the other and a rifle could be stored inside. This wasn't our only gun, but it was our most easily accessible one. . . . Firearms were illegal in the Preserve."[81] Here is the determinacy of what is known about Lien, the artist, and the indeterminacy of what is known about Lien, the artist. Keeping large house and garden tools signifies an existing garden, meaning amid Tlic-ian mandates, she maintains reverence for, believes in, Beauty: the revelatory, the intelligible, event that will soon contrive Venus as a Boy named Gan. Was the gun a tool of the garden, even in its occlusion? Maybe she, in tandem with her husband, sought added security to safeguard the lives she cherished. On the inside of the inside of the indoors is an instrument useful to Gan outside in the outside in the outdoors, its instrumentality warning outdoor boundary breakers who come indoors looking for "home."

With more than one residential gun, the parents likely purchased artillery for each child. Both believe in arms, proving that in the search for her garden, and his toolshed, their children, informed of and outfitted with equipment to "stand their ground," are the beneficiaries of a radical act called *safety*. This resonates in miniature: A noted historian once shared that as a child, her grandmother had a shotgun and once a week, went outside and fired a round in the air. One day, the historian questioned why her grandmother did so; her reply: "I want the white men out there to know I'm here"—is this a nonfictional occasion that mirrors the fictional threat Gan poses to T'Gatoi as conditioned by his parents? Is this the theory of stay black and die, of melancholy and genius, as quotidian performance—though you seek to impose the loss of my singular abstraction, my liberty, on me and those I love, it will not be met without consequence?

I am not saying guns are the answer, perhaps, but they can elicit a response.

If the rejoinders to the queries about the occluded weapon are in the affirmative, perhaps the rifle concretizes aesthetic kinship with an ex-colored man who experiences his mother's garden: "I can see in this half vision a little house. . . . I can remember that flowers grew in the front yard, and that around each bed of flowers was a hedge of vari-colored glass bottles stuck in the ground neck down. I remember that once, while playing around in the sand, I became curious to know whether or not the bottles grew as the flowers did, and I proceeded to dig them up to find out"; he also recalls that behind the little house, there was a shed. Apparently, "African Americans who kept subsistence gardens used bottles to protect crops and flowers from rabbits and moles, because the sound of wind blowing against the glass frightened such pests away. . . . The sounds created by this arrangement were thought to ward off evil spirits and thieves."[82] If an analogy beckons, neck-down bottles are to the flowers and crops what rifles are to Gan and his siblings—each entity grows like a tender green shoot in a mother's presence. Regarding T'Gatoi's rifle sentiments, Gan comments, "It occurred to me that she was afraid. She was old enough to have seen what guns could do to people. Now her young and this gun would be together in the same house. She did not know about the other guns. In this dispute, they did not matter."[83] The Tlic—kin of rabbits and moles, pests, evil spirits, thieves—fear the wind blowing against a whizzing bullet. That minefield sublimates to a spatiotemporal scene of blastoff.

Gan wields protection to diminish T'Gatoi's power; this intellectual calculation by his mother, due to her oppression, materializes with arms seen and unseen. ("It was an honor, my mother said, that such a person had chosen to come into the family. My mother was at her most formal and severe when she was lying. I had no idea why she was lying, or even what she was lying about.")[84] Perhaps one need not show "the law" all of one's armamentaria to obscure something like Wright's "mystery," while searching for the self, in the cause of future insurrection. That Kongo tradition is an Africanism in America that correlates with a continued maternal-internal search and seizure Walker completes: "And perhaps in Africa over two hundred years ago, there was just such a mother" like hers who loved Beauty.[85] "Bloodchild" remixes this declaration: And perhaps in the Preserve, that extrasolar world, some two hundred years from now, there will be just such a mother . . . who guides her son, through a love of Beauty and a respect for strength, to search for her garden, and his father's toolshed, to sprout rebellion. This is what Janelle Monáe concedes is a chance to "Dance or Die": Gan, this bird, "is chirping and he's singing a song / He's shaking 'em and waking 'em and giving 'em *mas* / As the clock tick tocks and the bodies drop," with the addendum "A long, long way to find the one / [He'll] keep on dancing 'til [it] comes / These dreams are forever." Oh freedom! (Coincidentally, or maybe not, an article on the exhibition of Butler's ephemera at the Huntington Library states, "In several interviews Butler said she wrote because she had two choices: *write, or die.* 'If I hadn't written, I probably would have done something stupid that would have led to my death,' she said cheerfully." Writing and/or dancing are accomplices to "staying black," prolegomena to the epilogue death. That said, I remain haunted that considering genius by way of the garden here, reports suggest Butler's death was brought about by a head injury sustained from a stroke; said injury occurred from a fall outside on her walkway.)[86]

Gan choreographs a disruption to T'Gatoi's gestational forever, a rehearsal for which his parents lay the groundwork. Becoming his mother through instrumentation and his father through fertilization, he admonishes T'Gatoi to *get this dance:* "Before he agrees to the implantation, however, Gan demands one thing more: that T'Gatoi treat him with the respect he deserves by allowing his family to keep the (forbidden) rifle which T'Gatoi knows he has. . . . He will have some measure of power to defend himself."[87] The rifle compels Gan's outside voice to pronounce itself while indoors; he weaponizes words without discharging ammo. His maternal figure(s) disobey/s perceived expectations to (re)produce after the initial productive act: They fashion their child with a weapon of minor destruction to do himself in as an act of protest, *hara-kiri* gunned down, if his othermother acts out of pocket, if T'Gatoi gets it—her tail, or Gan for that matter—twisted. This is to say, "Operating under a vivid fiction of the 'powers of presence,' these [rifles] *make it all right.* [!] But isn't *that* the trouble, that [Gan] must come reconciled to death?"[88] That these parents produce a radical, etymologically speaking, in Gan, a salient query returns: Is he woman*ish*?

A fine place to begin answering this would be approaching what it means "to accept a metaphorization, a semiosis of woman":

> . . . while examinations of cultural constructions of "woman" and "femininity" are proving extremely useful for feminist theorists and activists, and while it may not be possible to transcend the gender implications of language, the limitations inherent in reliance on a "metaphorization of woman" must be acknowledged. Perhaps the most promising rhetorical response involves overt acknowledgment—in the form of critical theory such as [Alice] Jardine's, and fiction such as Butler's, which foregrounds and problematizes this process. When "woman" emerges through the metaphor of an impregnated young boy, as it does in "Bloodchild," we are invited to examine and challenge our understanding of the construction of gender.[89]

Like someone put outdoors, this critique presumes gender hurdles as exemplary of one's flesh *doing it,* that one provokes certain theoretical leaps. However, I indulge the argument that Butler deploys critical theory: Though her medium is "atypical," "Bloodchild" predates what almost six years later will be her surname namesake's *Gender Trouble.*[90] Judith diagrams how "[t]he difference between the materialist and Lacanian (and post-Lacanian) positions emerge in a normative quarrel over whether there is a retrievable sexuality either 'before' or 'outside' the law in the mode of the unconscious or 'after' the law as postgenital sexuality" since it "became the object of significant criticism from feminist theorists of sexuality."[91] Contrastingly, Octavia E. critiques the law when crafting Tlic-human interactions: Gan unconsciously (?) retrieves his "sexuality" "before the law" through justifiable suicidality when arming himself, brandishing the rifle *before* T'Gatoi; and he retrieves his "sexuality" "after the law" by no longer supplementing business as usual vis-à-vis his impregnation. And if melancholy pervades this story, Butler equally predates the proposition that "[t]he lesser or greater violence of matricidal drive . . . entails, when it is hindered, its inversion on the self . . . the depressive or melancholic *putting to death of the self* is what follows, instead of matricide" as Gan works through a psychoanalytic frame in this self-life-narration. One Butler troubles the challenge of gender before the other, and others, "receives" it.

Moreover, if one applies sexuality to Preserve events, it is inclusive of "normative" (Lien and her husband, or T'Gatoi and the sons) and "non-normative" (Lien and T'Gatoi, or T'Gatoi and Xuan Hoa) expressions, similar to how being "stung" by T'Gatoi is itself postgenital because said "biology," performed by "law enforcement," is not "intelligible" (for that matter, neither is the genitalia of the "normal"). Admittedly, Butler practices flipped opacity: While I agree that "it is too reductive to transpose our subjectivities and identity categories onto the nonhuman," namely T'Gatoi, the Tlic themselves choreograph normative gender, seen in the aforementioned Qui-Gan conversation about male and female host animals; or when Gan, having desired to "find a girl and share a waking dream with her," explains, "Back when Tlic saw us as not much more than convenient, big, warm-blooded animals, they would pen several of us together, male and female, and feed us only eggs. That way they could be sure of getting another generation of us no matter how we tried to hold out." Is sharing a waking dream code for consensual erotica; and were the Tlic "grooming" Terrans, thus the need to "tailor" that pipe with a rifle?[92] Nonetheless, and what is said here is rife with linguistic limits but we press on, what constitutes "man" and "woman" is debatable since Gan "learns" "womanliness" from his mother *and* father, just as T'Gatoi's "manliness" extends from "her" body. So, while the secondary and tertiary definitions of "womanist" may further the semiosis and metaphorization of the black feminine, "Bloodchild" symbiotics proffer that Gan, this pregnant boy, "[a]ppreciates and prefers . . . women's emotional flexibility . . . and women's strength," that Gan "loves dance."[93]

Butler, toying with time-space and gender trouble-science fiction, intends to resolve being "before" the law, and the repercussions of "after," as if there is an "outside" to the "inside," an outdoors to the indoors, presuming that what one wants is that livable space, a tabernacle exploded, even for working out one's theory salvation with fear and trembling. Hence, whether of (black) science fiction or "Bloodchild," Butler is an Artist, a genius, and "black art, like any others, is innovative, demanding and/or outside to the extent that it addresses the wings and resistances indigenous to its medium qua medium, address ranging from amorous touch to agonistic embrace, angelic rub. To don such wings and engage such resistances as though they were the stuff of identity and community is to have taken a step toward making them so."[94] Butler takes that step and coopts a page from her own short story as a womanish ethic:

She is Responsible enough to "take care of" you, reader. Perhaps.

Go on and up! Our souls and eyes
Shall follow thy continuous rise;
Our ears shall list thy story
From bards who from thy root shall spring,
And proudly tune their lyres to sing
Of Ethiopia's glory.
—PAUL LAURENCE DUNBAR,
"Ode to Ethiopia"

A Trick-Turning Cocoon; or, an Ecology of Terms

The decision to "pimp" anything, or anyone, is an overdetermined masculinist gesture. That is, "in a warped and unhealthy way the pimp's ability to control his environment (i.e., his stable of women) has always been viewed as a rare example of black male authority over his domain." This "badman" regulates his specific ecosystem based on the societal perception he cannot complete such "management" elsewhere.[1] His female retinue peopling a "stable" offers its own rhetorical oppression, a subtlety confirming Zora Neale Hurston that "de nigger woman is de mule uh de world" because she is "not a woman with power, not a liberated woman (if liberation means the freedom to make choices about one's life), but a mule, picking up the burdens everyone else has thrown down and refused to carry."[2] If these gendering endeavors are valid, this pimp might intrude upon the freedom of another being: the butterfly.

Whether the female-layered vocalizations of Sounds of Blackness who vibe, "Awakening / A *genius* has been asleep to long / A people with a beauty rich and strong / A heritage that rates second to none / . . . . / Spread your wings and fly"; or Deniece Williams who imparts, "You've survived / Now your moment has arrived / Now your dream has finally been *born* / Black butterfly / Sail across the waters / Tell your sons and daughters / What the struggle brings"—the butterfly in the black lifeworld elicits femininity. This creature codes as genius, trespassing its slumber toward liberation, and metaphorizes the ancestral mother. The survivor's dream being "born" provides her children to collectively "Let [their] rejoicing rise / High as the listening skies, / Let it resound loud as the rolling sea."[3] Likewise, this insect circumnavigating the aquatic "pregnant" engenders discerning the Maafa whimsically. What was comprehended as a ship's hold, populated by the enslaved, may have been a lepidopterarium, also given tongue as a conservatory, a kaleidoscope—a butterfly sanctuary.[4]

Such ruminations clarify the (post-)black imagination being preoccupied with slavery as its deadly residue posthumously coats the living: "If slavery persists as an issue in the political life of black America, it is not because of an antiquarian obsession with bygone days or the burden of a too-long memory, but because black lives are still imperiled and devalued by a racial calculus and a political arithmetic that were entrenched centuries ago."[5] These are quotidian mathematics of enslavement. Satisfying a ledger balance or tabulating manifests' equations where unnamed persons contrive demographic data—"eyes beaten out, arms, backs, skulls branded, a left jaw, a right ankle, punctured; teeth missing, as the *calculated* work of iron, whips, chains, knives, the canine patrol, the bullet"—presupposes a plentiful "harvest," in word and deed, despite the (unpaid) laborers not being few.[6] While these sums, differences, products, and quotients abound, they somehow herald a work by Kendrick Lamar.

With its surprise, spring 2015 release, his album *To Pimp a Butterfly* aims to love blackness amid terror.[7] It collapses genres, moving from jazz to hip-hop, even incorporating skits. One album interpretation characterizes Lamar as

coming to terms with material success, contemplating his relationship with his hood, reconnecting with his values, reaccepting himself with love, and assuming a leadership role. . . . The concept is encapsulated

in a story Lamar reads to legendary deceased rapper Tupac Shakur . . .
he outlines the metaphors central to the album:

- The *caterpillar*, "a prisoner to the streets that conceived it / Its only
  job is to eat or consume everything around it." . . .
- The *butterfly*, "the talent, the thoughtfulness / And beauty within the
  caterpillar"—e.g., the artist in Lamar. . . .
- The *pimp*, in which the caterpillar sells out the butterfly to its own
  benefit; and
- The *cocoon*, an encasing that "institutionalizes him" and traps him
  so that "He can no longer see past his own thoughts"—i.e., insti-
  tutionalized racism, the structures that support it, and social and
  psychological pressures that prevent one from breaking free.

The concepts behind these metaphors . . . appear in varying degrees
across all songs on *Butterfly*.[8]

To Pimp a Butterfly is scalar, critiquing the institutional and the interior.
Lamar occupies multiple worlds—caterpillar, butterfly, pimp—within a
world—the cocoon—as his project, too, supplies *sounds of blackness*. However, the acclaimed work has been pinged for its gendered overtures. Notwithstanding features from rapper Rapsody on "Complexion (A Zulu Love),"
and vocals from Anna Wise and Lalah Hathaway, it convenes confusion
for its overt manliness and the absence of embodied others. Yet listeners
hear an altogether different Lamar during what I deem the project's "middle
passage"—"u," "Alright," "For Sale? (Interlude)," and "Momma." With fans citing his time in South Africa as the impetus for this audioconceptual shift,
that epochal provocation seems apropos.[9]

During these successive tracks, Lamar invokes a being called "Lucy," announcing his encounters with its "evils" and often miming said being in *evil-
voice*. This notion riffs on the recently named-yet-borrowed album section
because while those four tracks basically constitute the middle of *To Pimp a
Butterfly*, the shift in voice could be discerned, operatically and otherwise,
as Lamar flirting with his *passaggio*. But if this diasporic stint creatively augments his sound study, though "Lucy" could be Lucifer, the generally understood characterization from "Alright" or "For Sale? (Interlude)," might "Lucy"
also be the oldest known human skeleton excavated in Ethiopia in 1974, or
"Momma"?[10] Concatenated, these titles inquire, "u alright for sale, momma?",
analogously staging the album's premise: The seller is to the maternal what
the pimp is to the butterfly.

Channeling my speculation through Ethiopia contrives Lamar activating neoteric Pan-Africanism: "new underground political expressions that are marked by fantastic modes of transnational Black social relations outside of normative politics . . . to signify newness in thought or to describe those who speculate about contemporary Black politics innovatively. . . . Neoteric Pan-Africanism is not synonymous with or even contingent upon literal returns. It is about determining how to live more freely in the present and how to *fly* resolutely into the future." Expanding on Richard Iton's "black fantastic," Michelle D. Commander deploys neoteric Pan-Africanism to question "[w]hat can emerge from homelessness" and "[w]hat new worlds are imagined out of *thin air.*"[11] This flight/air trope—sketching a through line to a past erecting no home, simultaneous to claiming a nebulous home in the present and (Afro)future—interests me in this continental linkage. Subsequently, Toni Morrison, vis-à-vis *Song of Solomon,* has something to say, even to Lamar: "If you surrender to the air, you could *ride* it" is precursory to the neoteric in that "the sustained metaphor of flight . . . unfolds in a taut pattern of images like the suspended strings of a parachute, holding the reader absolutely breathless." With this novel in tow, one aspires when consuming *To Pimp a Butterfly,* in congress with others who soar up close and afar; at the same time, one also aspires to be "quite satisfied in knowing *what* happened and has little interest in reexamining the technique of describing '*how.*'"[12]

Implicated as a listener-reader, I submit not only that this chapter is a byproduct of Hartman's "afterlife of slavery," but also that I am one of "many men" who maintains a "fascination, certain awe, and suppressed respect" for the potential indexed by transformed pimps and unorthodox butterflies.[13] I am also clear in not characterizing Lamar as a black feminist; rather, speculating through that episteme and practices of abstraction to (re)unite him with the black feminine/maternal, I theorize the metamorphosis innate to a cocoon and surmise that what unleashes itself is more than meets the ear.

The Obvious Not

Previously invoking "(post-)black" compels numerous interlocutory permutations. Margo Natalie Crawford poses an apt interpretation through her phrase *black post-black.* Relaying a conversation between Thelma Golden and Glenn Ligon about being "post–Black Arts (Movement)" (BAM), she discerns black post-blackness as the simplicity of the nod or wink, then links her idea with William Pope.L's reply when asked if he was "still black": "Obviously. Of course not." Jiving with eschatology—the already-not yet—

Crawford suggests, "In the definitive space (marked by the period), the wink makes it 'obvious' that people can feel both black and post-black."[14] In total, black post-blackness is a dialogue on blackness's surplus, staged as an "inside joke," and published in *Freestyle* catalog; and a query of blackness's immanence with the teleology of cultural singularity. Such critical gazes describe a "dual investment in articulating a coherent black identity and aesthetic while also resisting limiting notions of either. This divergent aesthetic also describes twenty-first-century cultural approaches to black racial identity. An embracing of blackness paired with a questioning of that exact category unites the past and the present."[15] A prototype of this occurs through the visual arts collective African Commune of Bad Relevant Artists (AfriCOBRA).

During the BAM, the commune "produced some of the most vivid images of the tension between the representational and the abstract." A tenet of this tensile relationship is "mimesis at midpoint": "design that marks the spot where the real and the unreal, the objective and the nonobjective, the plus and the minus meet. A point exactly between absolute abstractions and absolute naturalism . . . the spot where the real and the overreal, the plus and the minus, the abstract and the concrete—the real and the replete meet. *Mimesis*." Conflating the representative and abstract, these artists "paused and anticipated what was at stake in making art that could have a message and remain as free as any abstract or experimental art." Contending with the black post-black imagination, this "midpoint" is a ruse for that other Middle Passage because said dualities constituted *the new world*. Moreover, AfriCOBRA principles that join "mimesis at midpoint" as the collective's philosophy produce a "sankofic corrective."[16]

Commune cofounder Wadsworth A. Jarrell shares that "COBRA's ideology regarding art representing our people was congruent with and advocated what" Aimé Césaire uttered in a 1956 Paris speech: Surrounded by "'cultural chaos,'" black people should "organize a new synthesis which will be the reconciliation . . . of the old and the new." A Martinican orating in the metropole, Césaire radicalizes these artists in their American context. Under various protocols—cool ade color, frontal images, open color, positive images, arbitrary use of light and line, written statements, visibility, free symmetry, the programmatic, shine, expressive awesomeness, mimesis at midpoint, and horror vacui—AfriCOBRA proverbially *worries the line*, artistically and otherwise, in the ongoing battle of to whom should the art belong: "The importance of creating a new aesthetic lies in its ownership— Black ownership, where in the past only whites . . . claimed ownership of inventive artistic endeavors. . . . African Americans create their own artistic language so that generations of young African American artists have a storehouse of knowledge, a library, of new visual information to be proud of and relate to as influential in their progress and growth. It is important to create something that is our own, that hasn't been copied, reinterpreted, and co-opted by mainstream American society."[17] Projecting that old-new dichotomy, commune practitioners are "owned" by the art, and what it structures regarding "uplift"; and "own" it, laying the groundwork for that Afrofuture. Yet this "ownership" language reads as the mimesis of Morrison when Macon Dead (Jr.), father of the protagonist in *Song of Solomon*, imparts to his namesake, "'Let me tell you right now the one important thing you'll ever need to know: *Own things*. And let the things you own own other things. Then you'll own yourself and other people too.'"[18] Although AfriCOBRA did not "own" creators through aesthetic pimping, the commune's sentiments reveal that wholesale ownership of "the self" and what it produces. And if owned things own things, that legacy runs in perpetuity, qualifying that "storehouse of knowledge, a library, of new visual information" for generations of black artists. The AfriCOBRA-Morrison commingle cyclically establishes mimesis at midpoint. Hence, blackness, and its art, is neoteric and possibly *neutronic*: Nuclear, so to speak, either-or and neither-nor, it is "history's mocking double."

In her eponymous essay to "call forth" this dueling categorization, Haley Konitshek stages a hypothetical conversation between Karen Barad's "Post-humanist Performativity" and Hortense J. Spillers's "Mama's Baby, Papa's Maybe: An American Grammar Book." Given the opening sentence of the former piece, "Language has been granted too much power," Konitshek argues that "reading Barad alongside Spillers enables us to understand the indistinguishable co-formation of materiality and meaning" in that "[Spillers's] intervention from 1987 necessarily reframes how the field of feminist studies can and should respond to Barad's 2003 charge that theorists and scientists alike have yet to, and *must*, 'make matter matter.'" These proclivities for naming, and how they intersect with pimped butterflies, spark attention:

> the difference between a name and its "name," in quotation marks, does not manifest in misrepresentation but in the *event of misaddress*. . . . Spillers's meditation on the name as enclosed in quotation marks disrupts the signification material binary. "Names"—"these social and cultural subjects"—*"make doubles"* . . . to **swarm** a particular figure with quotation marks performs an agentive act of *disownership*. . . . Where the interpellative effects of naming, on the part of the captor (signi-

fier), dispossess the named subject of her sovereignty, Spillers's use of naming stylizes this dispossession *strategically*. She reformulates this American grammatical function—the power to name, the power to cite, the power to address and dispossess—in service of rendering extant a new symbolic space, that of the *"mocking presence."*[19]

The pervasion of quotation marks performs what Kevin Young explains as using a hypocorism to (re)act in the place of one's true name because it "is never told to strangers [as] a means of survival, of coding not just behavior, or art forms."[20] Spillers captivates the reader from the start of her essay because marking does not imply knowledge. These punctuation marks-as-*scare quotes* shock the "signifier" insofar as what resides within the brackets might shield "the one" from recursive incursions that historically foreshadow linguistic and other demises.[21] A contemporary example, albeit problematic, is Dave Chappelle's special, *Sticks & Stones*, when he chronicles writing a sketch that uses the word "faggot." When executives advise that he would never be able to air the sketch, he retorts, "Why is it that I can say the word 'nigger' with impunity, but I can't say the word 'faggot'?" When told it is because he is not gay, he responds, "I'm not a 'nigger' either." Punctuating the pejorative by yelling it during his stand-up, he hints at what quotation marks might do. Still, bracketed terms are debatable based on the proverbial eye of the beholder: Chappelle may not view himself as a "nigger," but others, presumably, could. The conversation, then, becomes complex when distinguishing a "nigger" and a "nigga"—the issue is "authenticity."[22] Like a pimp's environmental "mastery," these warped speech acts install social codes whereby people are behooved to *govern themselves accordingly*.

However, the signified replicates itself because while one has a name to which one answers, one also has a "call" to which one "responds" because "quotation marks are as queer as they are quotidian. . . . The art of quotation triggers and produces our understanding of mnemonic traces—a double discourse that moves in two directions at once. . . . The re-circulation and recycling that is a hallmark of the discourse of quotation links it to a performance of memory or, to use Toni Morrison's more active term, 're-memory' . . . the 'queer' interactions among performance, memory, the quotidian, and the quotation." Assigning nomenclature to someone, who replies "in turn," does not necessarily cohere "guilt," but a relative contingency that the declaration "Here I am" is better understood as "Here is the thing you improperly named."[23] Through dissociation, this interpellative undercut subverts the name for the name*d*, (dis)owning the latter in service to the former.

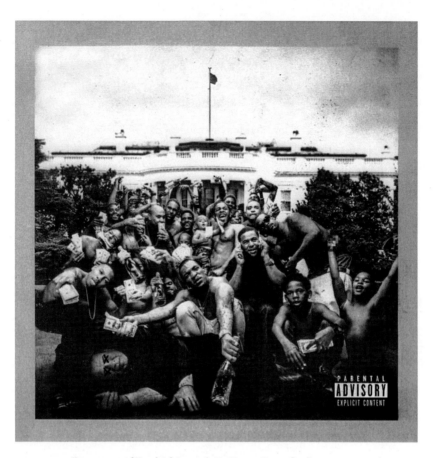

FIGURE 5.1. Front cover of Kendrick Lamar's *To Pimp a Butterfly*, 2015.
(Courtesy of Top Dawg Entertainment.)

The marked term tricks the eye as inverted commas display like furnished shackles. But reasoning alongside Thadious M. Davis, the open space within the coffle—the torus, where one cocoons another's (")name(")—"offers possibilities. This small space, to break through adversity, becomes the central metaphor" to wrestle with "Lucy."[24] Yet if this persona is the album's historic mocking double, does its creator have a doppelgänger, a tether à la *Us?* I assert that like the AfriCOBRA-Morrison amalgam, Lamar mocks Macon Dead (III), Milkman, as his double. Examining the album cover inaugurates this kinship (fig. 5.1).

Debuting during the second term of the first black president of the United States, Barack Hussein Obama, *To Pimp a Butterfly* criticizes the nation-state with a visual provocation that is an ostensible kickback, a brethren convention, on the White House lawn. Foregrounded by bodies—boys to men; covered and topless; preparing to pop bottles or make a call; moneyed and flipping a pixelated bird—the location takes a backseat to blackness under greyscale. Meanwhile, a white judge, perhaps a presumptive Supreme Court Justice, clasps a gavel in the bottom lefthand corner while being "put down," his eyes lettered with X. Ogling black male flesh, across all manner of difference, one *listens to this image*, "a radical visual archive of the African Diaspora that grapples with the recalcitrant and the disaffected, the unruly and the dispossessed."[25] What noise do they make in stillness? Though unclear whether the image takes down Obama as figurehead, let alone one empowered to appoint arbiters of judgment, its black-and-white-ness inscribes the very polarity between his office and the statuses of the men occupying his yard. Yet what lingers is the primacy of the flag in the visual, acting as both vanishing point and literal vision line which, if extended, bisects Lamar and the held child.

The quasi-uncolored effacement of "Old Glory" seemingly mimics the optics of the only black resident of a white house. But when the cloth has its color fully restored through fragmentation in *Song of Solomon*, one imagines the aping at length:

> When the dead doctor's daughter saw Mr. Smith emerge as promptly as he had promised from behind the cupola, his wide blue silk wings curved forward around his chest, she dropped her covered peck basket, spilling red velvet rose petals. . . . The singing woman wore a knitted navy cap pulled far down her forehead . . . [the hospital people] ventured outside into the cold: white-coated surgeons, dark jacketed business and personnel clerks. . . . Downtown the firemen pulled on their greatcoats, but when they arrived at Mercy [Hospital], Mr. Smith had seen the rose petals, heard the music, and leaped on into the air.
>
> The next day a colored baby was born inside Mercy for the first time. Mr. Smith's blue silk wings must have left their mark, because when the little boy discovered, at four, the same thing Mr. Smith had learned earlier—that only birds and airplanes could fly—he lost all interest in himself. . . . When the baby was born the day after she stood in the snow, with cloth roses at her feet and a man with blue wings above her head, she regarded him as a beautiful toy, a respite, a distraction, a physical pleasure as she nursed him . . . then he was no longer her velveteened toy. He became a plain on which, like cowboys and Indians in the movies, she and her husband fought. Each one befuddled by the

values of the other. Each one convinced of his own purity and outraged by the idiocy he saw in the other.

Blue silk wings. Red velvet rose petals. The singing woman in a navy cap. White coats. Dark jackets. Firemen, likely in red, steering a red truck. Black and white onlookers. Snow. Cowboys ("white"). Indians ("red"). This chromaticism unfurls that star-spangled banner as a tapestry in tatters among a raced citizenry, "the national canvas/flag upon which the narrative works and against which the lives of these black people must be seen, but which must not overwhelm the enterprise the novel is engaged in."[26] Striated across a colorful landscape, this flag mosaic contrives a schismatic discourse-as-backdrop for a localized *national tragedy*, whether this mourning happens in a hamlet on (Not) Doctor Street and then within a household; or on the cover of a CD booklet composed of liner notes and kinfolk.

Robert Smith, the North Carolina Mutual Life Insurance agent donning blue silk wings, hastens Milkman's birth; his flight delay induces contractions that catalyze the delivery of the newborn. Smith and Milkman synchronize because "the loss of some abstraction," the desire to fly, transitions to the loss of self, whether from suicide or interest; both are melancholy—men with clipped wings, visible and invisible, shaded blue.[27] Though Milkman's mother, Ruth, exists in this opening scene, as do other women, Morrison subsumes her for the patrifocal: "Writing *Song of Solomon* destroyed all that ['artists' chatter about muses']. I had no access to what I planned to write until my father died. . . . The challenge of *Song of Solomon* was to manage what was for me a radical shift in imagination from a female locus to a male one."[28] Is this what that cover envisions—does the femicide/matricide of the image report the child Lamar holds as born of his own gut? Does the flag's ghostwritten line scored downward declare that a black parent can bear a child only ever dispossessed, a pupil's severance from his patriarch through the abusive power of the fatherland? Or have we mistaken Lamar for a pimp, due to this masculinist scene, when he may be a butterfly? (That is, the album cover, and booklet, has feminine-presenting figures: a person directly to the right of Lamar whose face is visible over his shoulder; and two people to the left of the image, "stacked" on each other, with a hand and a bottle obfuscating their faces.) Such a tragedy further illumines how Smith and Lamar converge.

In the 2004 foreword to *Song of Solomon*, Morrison explicates Mercy's plight: "[Smith] hopes his flight . . . toward asylum . . . or home, is interpreted as a radical gesture demanding change, an alternative way, a cessation of things as they are . . . a deep commitment to his people. And in their response to his decision there is a tenderness, some contrition, and mounting respect . . . an awareness that his suicide enclosed, rather than repudiated them." If Mercy "pimps" its black citizens, with this flight disrupting the status quo, that cover conveys the nation as such—a pimp of black butterflies, of black genius. Posing in front of "the people's house," this flesh (re)defines "the abstract and the concrete": Their presence pressures who comprises "the people," and that the whimsy of flight for some incites complication in others who prefer fashioning their wings for cages. The image's excess is precisely black congregation being a radical flip-off to white structures that prefer that it get off their lawns. Lamar, similar to Smith, may tarry for mercy, "the grace note," in a place where none exists.[29]

These aesthetic moves outline an AfriCOBRA affect, even if the respective epochal creators are not speaking directly to each other. Ready now to ponder the album's "middle passage," one forges ahead to Morrison and Lamar vocalizing like the navy-capped woman:

> *O Sugarman done fly*
> *O Sugarman done gone.*[30]

Mimesis and the Nemesis

Though this chapter focuses on *To Pimp a Butterfly*, a "radical shift in imagination" provokes the black feminine/maternal. The pimp-butterfly dyad presences her, in interlocution with *Song of Solomon*, so that a (re)turn to 2012's *good kid, m.A.A.d city* affirms for ears what eyes vocalize.

On "Sing about Me, I'm Dying of Thirst," Lamar raps:

> Tired of running
> Tired of tumbling
> Tired of running
> Tired of tumbling
> Back once my momma say,
> "See a pastor,
> Give me a promise
> What if today was the rapture,
> And you completely tarnished." . . .
> You dying of thirst
> You dying of thirst
> So hop in that water
> And pray that it works

Then a woman intercedes for his soul, leading him, and other men, in "The Sinner's Prayer." This mediator, Maya Angelou, performs this before her death in 2014; unnamed yet omniscient, ushering Lamar into holiness, she haunts *To Pimp a Butterfly* along with these closing lyrics.[31]

That the mother spurs baptism ("'What if today was the rapture / And you completely tarnished'"), and Angelou "loves the sinner" into salvation, portends the black feminine/maternal being "born again" in 2015 in that what is unfinished on *good kid, m.A.A.d city* carries over to its follow-up whereby she which hath begun a good work in you will perform *it* until three years later, instilling confidence in that very thing.[32] No wonder the found thing on "Sing About Me, I'm Dying of Thirst"—the salvific black feminine/maternal—catalyzes success that initiates a lost-and-found mission that implicates "u" and "i," records and not, on *To Pimp a Butterfly*, a mirroring of Ruth and Pilate in *Song of Solomon* who live at the beginning of the novel and drop out during Milkman's "maturity," only to be integral to his saga in the end. Similarly, this "Water, water, everywhere / Nor any drop to drink" ("You dying of thirst") symbolizes that bygone Passage and the one I conceive because while the past event incapacitates imbibing, mine invites immersion. Yet if Lamar "thirsts," is this a mocking double reversed when instead of Father watching Son be crucified, Mother encourages Son to die unto Himself as one of the seven last words is set to a beat?[33] Therefore, "u alright for sale, momma" is predated by "u alright to *save*, momma," and fosters this close listening.

A meditative posture sustains the mood throughout *To Pimp a Butterfly*; Lamar sounds the running monologue right before the track "These Walls":

I remember you was conflicted
Misusing your influence
Sometimes I did the same
Abusing my power, full of resentment
Resentment that turned into a deep depression
Found myself screaming in a hotel room

Through this transition, "u" emerges. The record begins with screams that move into repeating "loving u is complicated" ten times in the chorus; "complicated" is a paroxysm on the first, fifth, and eighth iterations. Verse 1 speaks of a parental figure on whom Lamar places blame and shame as "anonymous strangers" tell him he belongs to this "father" (:42-:53); he is absent. As a brother, he abandons his young pregnant sister who he purports to protect—he is a self-professed leader the world does not need. Lamar announces that this persona is ashamed of him; he hates him back (:58–1:24). Following the chorus, verse 2 opens with "u" being the reason "momma n'em leavin'"; he is unlovable, irresponsible, selfish, a liar, a denier. Drunk, Lamar states, "A friend never leave Compton for profit"; this fleeing decision, entertaining "on the road, bottles and bitches," leads to a FaceTime session by "u" with a dying friend (2:25–3:18). This Compton sentiment is telling because "'Black Boy Fly,' a bonus track on *good kid, m.A.A.d city*, is a backward-gazing confession regarding Lamar's previous jealousy (and admiration) toward those who have escaped." This "backward-gazing" is sankofic, akin to Milkman riding in his father's Packard: "So it was only by kneeling on the dove gray seat and looking out the back window that he could see anything. . . . But *riding backward* made him uneasy. It was like *flying blind*, and not knowing where he was going—just where he had been—troubled him."[34] Verse 3 implies the mental health of "u" ("I know depression is restin' on your heart for two reasons, nigga"). This affection solidifies the resentment Lamar has toward "u." The record culminates with him declaring money does not counter "suicidal weakness" (3:31–4:26), which syncs with Sigmund Freud's "overcoming of the instinct which compels every living thing to cling to life."[35]

In the truncated visual album "God Is Gangsta," which combines "u" with "For Sale? (Interlude)," the identity of "u" is problematized.[36] Lamar is alone in a room with alcohol, "100 proof"; a table rife with scratches (by someone's nails?); and a mirror. As the blurring and shaky camera lens conveys intoxication, the mirror has a prominent role in this tête-à-tête with "u." Meanwhile, locked in this room he calls "confinement," Lamar peculiarly exits and returns to the room (2:14)—did he escape? Is this a funhouse that is not one? As he breaks the fourth wall, rapping verse 2 to the camera, the mirror beside him exhibits an empty chair and soon his reflection. However, it is and is not Lamar as the mirrored bodies are incongruent; he reflects his double, but the bodies are contorted in completely different manners. The treatment ends with the extrojected man in the mirror breaking its façade from within the glass (fig. 5.2).

Laura Mulvey, deconstructing the Lacanian mirror, deduces:

The mirror phase occurs at a time when the child's physical ambitions outstrip his motor capacity, with the result that his recognition of himself is joyous in that he imagines his mirror image to be more complete, more perfect than he experiences his own body. Recognition is thus overlaid with mis-recognition: the image recognised is conceived at the reflected body of the self, but its misrecognition as superior projects this body outside itself as an ideal ego, the alienated subject,

FIGURE 5.2. Still from "God Is Gangsta" video, 2016. (Courtesy of Top Dawg Entertainment.)

which, re-introjected as an ideal ego, gives rise to the future generation of identification with others . . . an image that constitutes the matrix of the imaginary, of recognition/misrecognition and identification, and hence of the first articulation of the "I," of subjectivity.[37]

Reading the video against Mulvey, Lamar exits this makeshift psych ward, nonstraitjacketed, as he who breaks a *reflection eternal*, projecting his "body outside itself as an ideal ego." But if this portrayal articulates the ideal, the "I," which will be salient soon, the "father," "u," is Lamar as his melancholy self. He "displays something else besides which is lacking in mourning—an extraordinary diminution in his self-regard, an impoverishment of his ego on a grand scale. . . . represents his ego to us as worthless . . . reproaches himself, vilifies himself and expects to be cast out and punished. He abases himself before everyone and commiserates with his own relatives for being connected with anyone so unworthy . . . incapable of love and achievement as he says." The verses accomplish that diminution and self-incapability; Lamar juxtaposes the "picture of a delusion of (mainly moral) inferiority" as an illusion in the first half of "God Is Gangsta."[38] He exposes a deperfected image; "under the influence," he is not "joyous" about this selfie. Gazing upon himself, and forcing the spectator to do the same, he turns physical inability psychical; he envisions himself, divorced from himself, as an alien who fractures his community for a price. This is reproach, vilification, abasement.

The "u" reference to abandoning a sister resonates with Milkman, particularly events linked to the childhood "wetting" of his sibling Magdalene called

Lena—"A large colorful bouquet of [purple violets and wild jonquil] was in her hand, but her face was crumpled in anger. Over her pale-blue dress dark wet stains spread like fingers." In adulthood, when Lena confronts him about this *soiling*, as urine splatter performed touch, she invokes phallogocentrism, among other assessments, against Milkman: "'I picked them and took some twigs from a tree. When I got home I stuck them in the ground right down there.... The flowers... the ones you peed on—well they died, of course, but not the twig. It lived. It's that maple.... But it's dying now Macon.... I'll tell you where [Macon gets 'the *right* to decide our lives']. From that hog's gut that hangs down between your legs.... You are to blame. You are a sad, pitiful, stupid, selfish, hateful man.'" Prior to this dressing-down, he ruins the romance between his other sister, First Corinthians, and a local man, Porter; and before being bailed out of jail for stealing "gold," that being his grandfather's bones, he readies himself "to knock down an old black lady who had cooked him his first perfect egg, who had shown him the sky, the blue of it," if caught red-handed.[39] Recalling the pimp and butterfly, one reductively parallels the tree and flowers in this masculine-feminine pairing. Put crudely, stains from pee simulate the stamina of pesticide—they wield haptic destruction, ranging from violets and jonquil to a maple tree, regardless of prior "growth." Ironically, Lamar mouths, almost verbatim, Lena's grievances when discussing "u."

The perplexity of loving "u," in line with the novel plot, is the very muscle, metaphoric or real, that (re)produces "life" can expedite "death," most assuredly when the organ centers itself in the lives of others to whom the "instrument" is "unattached." These storylines, not explicitly similar, posit intramurals of familial *waste*, of neglect, and require hearing Morrison more to pivot to Lamar. Said differently, as part 1 of *Song of Solomon* ends, Milkman's confrontation with Lena is the paradigmatic event that speeds up his encounter with the black feminine/maternal to gain his wings in part 2, no different than how undermining "u" has generative consequence in its mediated phase as chrysalis.[40]

Throughout the novel, while most of the men are *Dead*, per se, many of the women have a lofty or aerial perspective at the level of naming—Milkman's paternal great-grandmothers Ryna, possibly derived from *reina*, royalty in another tongue, and Heddy, which is to say heady; his grandmother Sing, daughter of Heddy, shorthand for Singing Bird/Byrd; and his aunt Pilate, the "old black lady" he robs, "a positive, full, aggressively alive character who recalls the name's near homonym, pilot: one who guides the flight, directs it, takes charge." (An aside: Morrison describes Heddy as "[a]n Indian woman," attesting to black and native peoples' liaisons. When discussing Milkman's tension with his parents, she further metaphorizes indigineity: "[Ruth] was the Indian, of course, and lost her land, her customs, her integrity to the cowboy [Macon] and became a spread-eagled footstool resigned to her fate and holding fast to tiny irrelevant defiances." Ruth sources "Indianness" through *experience*. With Tiffany Lethabo King's "shoal" being "simultaneously land [native] and sea [black]," another element ostensibly arrives via the footstool "spread-eagled": air.)[41] Lena's verbal altercation, coupled with "one hand out of the pocket of her robe and smashed . . . across his mouth," drives her brother, this son, not one of Farah Jasmine Griffin's "Daughters," on a quest to know the names of his "Mothers," that is, if all the men are Dead and all the women soar, Milkman may be "brave" for this journey.[42]

As the novel concludes, Milkman asks who would save his life and who would take it. The narrator proffers his friend-turned-foe, Guitar, among others, as the latter response; the former is the women he consistently treats conveniently: "With two exceptions, everybody he was close to seemed to prefer him out of this life. And the two exceptions were both women, both black, both old. From the beginning, his mother and Pilate had fought for his life, and he never so much as made either of them a cup of tea."[43] While this is Morrison's *shade*, stirring the prosaic pot, she also foments the psychoanalytic theory of maternal origin.

In *Beyond the Pleasure Principle*, namely Freud's "theory of the death instinct, the male child's renunciation of the mother and mastery of subjectivity belies a regressive longing for quiescence and the peace of death as a substitute experience for the maternal origin . . . and yet the negative valuation attached to Freud's notion of progression as regression is itself 'undone' in Morrison's novel." Milkman performs "asked and answered" in that self-reflexive moment; he does not renounce the maternal, wherein Ruth and Pilate pose as a composite figure, but he does *pronounce* them as his "lifeline." This is concurrent with his "death instinct," knowing Guitar is on his heels for the "treasure" having almost decapitated him in the Blue Ridge Mountains.[44] Undoing Freud is evident, even with the imminence of maternal loss (Pilate) and the uncertainty of Milkman and Guitar flying or being fatalities. Nonetheless, while the B(i/y)rd-Dead clan's matrifocality proves salvific, Milkman's penchant for escape signifies some acts of departure having devastating ramifications, especially for those who remain, or are reduced to being, grounded.

Solomon, Milkman's "great-granddaddy," is "that motherfucker [who] could fly! . . . Lifted his beautiful black ass up in the sky and flew on home" to Africa as Morrison rehearses the Flying Africans myth. Tired of work and being worked over ("'He just took off; got fed up. *All the way up!* No more cotton! No more bales! No more orders! No more shit! He flew, baby."), he vacates his responsibility to his wife Ryna "and twenty children. Twenty-one, since he dropped the one [Macon Dead, Sr. née Jake] he tried to take with him. And Ryna had thrown herself *all over the ground, lost her mind,* and was still *crying in a ditch.* Who looked after those twenty children? Jesus Christ, he left twenty-one children!"[45] Though Milkman never meets Solomon, despite the boundaries of life and death, like great-granddaddy, like great-grandson. This ancestor, pissed (off) about his condition, foretells the future of his "seed" who will "piss" on the women he "loves," resulting in their weeping and gnashing of teeth as preceded by cornstarch.[46] This is why Lena confronts him: You cannot care for someone whose unprotection you facilitate. Yet the biblical allusions, via nomenclature, to the women in this immediate family—mother Ruth, and sisters Magdalene called Lena and First Corinthians—imply surrogacy, respectively enabling the "wellness" of the melancholic, whether as the catalyst of the *marriage contract,* clinging to her grieving mother-in-law who prefers no longer to be called "pleasant" but "bitter"; the nard spiller who anoints her soon-crucified savior and later resounds, "He lives!" as the originary preacher of the Easter sermon; or an epistolary canvas that broadcasts to its specified church that "the greatest of these is love."[47] The women under this roof are the resurrection and the life—*the living Deads.* Still, Ruth, whose deliberate actions route the genealogy of the Redeemer in the Good Book, concretizes mimesis at midpoint.

As a character of antiquity who grasps the attention of her future husband, Boaz, by lying beside his feet (which she uncovers while he sleeps to "warm" them), old Ruth stares at her new mime in the *Song of Solomon* mirror: "Ruth turned toward her son. She lifted her head and looked deep into his eyes. 'And I also prayed for you. Every single night and every single day. *On my knees.* Now you tell me. *What harm did I do you on my knees?*'"[48] This Midrash exposes black feminine/maternal *grounded*-ness as those who comprise the office perpetually elevate the ungrateful. But the lesson of "u," the same one Milkman catches as the novel ends, is humility too is born of grounding, of (en)forced self-isolation.[49] That mirror room as an asylum-cum-cocoon obliges Lamar confronting whom he has abandoned and abandoning all self-possessive pretense. If "[i]n a world ordered by sexual imbalance, pleasure in looking has been split between active/male and passive/female," Mulvey might discern him occupying a nonbinary crossroad in "u" as he passively and actively strives for *pleasure,* notwithstanding him being "morally despicable." This visuality is equally an omen—does "Lucy" as Lucifer ventriloquize Lamar to inhabit "u"? Or does "Lucy" as "Momma" evolve from lost object to found subject, the maternal origin, by shattering Narcissus to rehabilitate her self-medicating child?[50]

This first passage rest stop is a mimetic whirlwind. Yet this occasion further allows (re)consideration of the split ego when "one part of the ego sets itself over against the other, judges it critically, and, as it were, takes it as its object," just as Milkman "resembles the Freudian 'split subject,' 'torn precariously' . . . between conscious and unconscious memory of . . . sustaining maternal presence."[51] Perhaps Lamar, and Dead III, undoes this egoic logic because born on June 17, he has a history of splitting: "To express a bout of delirium, Kendrick often taps into this panic driven voice [his Gemini alterego]." And "u" invoking "antennas" refutes earlier butterfly gendering to confirm female-male twoness. Such body parts instruct migration—Kendrick Lamar, grounded, transforms into "Kendrick Lamar," the mocking presence ready for liftoff.[52] This may be why after such strife, our next destination assures us we gon' be "Alright."

The first "Alright" utterance enjoins Lamar to Sofia from *The Color Purple*: "Alls my life I has to fight, nigga!"[53] In the music video, he adds more texture to the continued meditation:

> Lucifer was all around me
> So I kept runnin'
> Until I found my safe haven
> I was tryna convince myself the stripes I got
> Making myself realize what my foundation was
> But while my loved ones was fighting a continuous war back in the city
> I was entering a new one
> A war that was based on apartheid and discrimination

Like Milkman and Guitar, "[b]reathing the air that could have come straight from a marketplace in Accra" as they enact that bone heist, Lamar referencing "apartheid" plays up the neoteric. Still, the "Alright" visuals, set against LA- and Bay-area cityscapes, track with Michael Boyce Gillespie: if "the unstable and textual nature of the city coupled with . . . mobility of rhythms of place and placelessness . . . bonds a subject," and it is the "intersections of these traces that produce the city as an affective phenomenon," the record is *medicine for melancholy* (even as, [ethno]musicologically/linguistically speaking, Noriko Manabe ponders whether Pharrell Williams's chorus intonation—"We gon' be alright"—is him "posing a question, asking if we would really be alright? Was he betraying a feeling of uncertainty, repeating the phrase as if to reassure his audience against the odds? Or was he making a statement?").[54] Lamar the apothecary measures an elixir while "driving" the prelude to the track visually:

Aye on my mama nigga
Imma be the greatest to ever do this shit
On my mama doe like
On the dead homies
Hey Sounwave, turn this shit up nigga! Turn this shit up! Sounwave, turn
 this shit up!

Tell me who the bitch nigga hatin' on me
Jumpin' on my dick but this dick ain't free
To Pimp a Butterfly another classic CD
Ghetto lullaby for every one-day emcee
Nigga, now RIP
My diligence is only meant to write your eulogy

This unreleased work, referred to as the "Frontseat Freestyle," extols "mama" and superimposes Lamar with her. If *To Pimp a Butterfly* is a "ghetto lullaby," he steps into the maternal avatar, performing the "classic CD" as he puts a one-day emcee to bed. (And is he signifying when repeating, "Turn this shit up!" as a cypher of Jordan Davis with his passenger pouring libation for the "dead homies"?[55]) This "fun" exceeds the frame when the camera pans out and the car Lamar "steers" with Black Hippy—Schoolboy Q, Ab-Soul, and Jay Rock—inside is carried by policemen (fig. 5.3). This "big reveal" is "Kendrick and the guys being held up by cops like a carriage or something"; though Manabe reads the police as "pallbearers carrying a coffin, symbolizing the disproportionate impact on black lives," I, like video director Colin Tilley and Yoh Phillips ("this is a play on King Kunta/Kendrick, and how in ancient times royalty was carried on litters, a wheelless form of transportation"), construe this as Shakespearean—the car is a "barge [they] sat in, like a burnish'd throne" à la Cleopatra.[56]

The "Alright" background vocals, mimicking Take 6, skip like a needle on vinyl until they resolve on unresolved chords with saxophone accompaniment. Locating Nazareth and everyone being "fucked up," but "If God got us / Then we gon' be alright," is prototypical of hip-hop's religiosity. Defined by Rick Rubin as "our generation's protest song," "Alright" is a would-be anthem with various people populating the video scenes and reciting lyrics with Lamar.[57] Through an abstracted body, he takes flight for the first time, emergent from the cocoon crafted by "u"; he floats while people on the ground bone-break, dancing and clowning around as peers of sound systems (fig. 5.4). This masquerade abuts three moments. He raps:

> What you want, you a house, you a car?
> 40 acres and a mule, a piano, a guitar?
> Anything, see my name is Lucy, I'm your dog
> Motherfucker, you can live at the mall
> I can see the evil, I can tell it, I know it's illegal
> I don't think about it, I deposit every little zero

Lamar naming "Lucy" like so enlists the imagination: Has he doubled himself insomuch as one is unsure which side of his Gemini is blessing track 6, verse 2; or is he speaking through "Lucy" the maternal about "Lucy" the evil? This material-possessions rundown foresees the "Interlude" as the listing occurs while standing on a streetlight at the intersection of 11th Street and Chick Hearn Court. That Lamar "can see the evil" and tell its criminality means a conversation soon ensues, and that the recent "Lucy" intimation could be correct. All of this converges at the Outro:

> I keep my head up high
> I cross my heart and hope to die
> Lovin' me is complicated
> Too afraid, a lot of changes
> I'm alright, and you're a favorite
> Dark nights in my prayers

The "me" who is "u" endows that loving complication. This precedes the pervading meditation with these words after "screaming in the hotel room": "I didn't wanna self-destruct / The evils of Lucy was all around me / So I went running for answers."

This running desire is notable since Lamar's soaring is "like a fantasy, a dream world . . . him being like a superhero to these kids, him being something these kids can aspire towards. So, when they look up, it's almost like it's Superman." It is as if "[p]art of his flight was over the dark sea, but it didn't frighten him because he knew he could not fall. He was alone in the sky, but somebody was applauding him, watching him and applauding. He couldn't see who it was." He runs the sky, a Flying African(-American) who

FIGURE 5.3. Still from "Alright" video, 2015. (Courtesy of Top Dawg Entertainment.)

FIGURE 5.4. Still from "Alright" video, 2015. (Courtesy of Top Dawg Entertainment.)

"testifies to the complexity of the hyphenated subject-formation."[58] Interestingly, Lamar, almost a year before "Alright," features on "Never Catch Me" from Flying Lotus's album, *You're Dead*. (The irony! Is Kendrick Dead?) The video treatment projects the funeral of two children who revivify themselves and dance out the church into a hearse, driving to a better unknown. Lamar's opening bars vocalize:

> I can see the darkness in me, and it's quite amazing
> Life and death is no mystery and I wanna taste it
> Step inside of my mind and you'll find curiosity, animosity
> High philosophy, hyperprophesied meditation[59]

These open-casket departures present the final resting places as cocoons, riffing on seeing a darkness quite amazing. Lamar flying so soon after this video gives pause because maybe he can never be caught, maybe he floats like a butterfly. Considering Shintaro Kago's artwork for "Never Catch Me," this self-disemboweled, psychedelic woman may be "Lucy" (fig. 5.5).

Transported to "For Sale? (Interlude)," we meet the alter ego. The album's midpoint, this record, and its mimetic engagement, traffics in the religious because the music video shows Lamar's baptism—the mark of that "monstrosity" named "mama" is fulfilled from *good kid, m.A.A.d city*.[60] Bilal layers his voice in an SATB construction. An ominous being speaks:

> What's wrong nigga?
> I thought you was keeping it gangsta
> I thought this what you wanted
> They say if you scared, go to church
> But remember he knows the Bible too

Followed by heavy breathing, this dream sequence with instrumentation floats over the track. God is speaking based on the line "keeping it gangsta" and the video's title; as well, the "he" who knows the Bible is Lucifer. Lamar sings the chorus as Bilal responds, "WANT YOU." In the verses, he uses *evil-voice*, evoking a "feminized" timbre or that of a soothsayer making a pitch. (This is paramount because on the self-explanatory track "You Ain't Gotta Lie [Momma Said]," he raps in the same vocal pitch as in "For Sale? [Interlude]"—is "Lucy" "typically" gendered or something more?) This befuddles the narrative: Assigning a "feminine" name to a "masculine" being, and then performing that assignment as said "feminine" character, Lamar convenes "the event of misaddress."

FT.KENDRICK LAMAR

NEVER CATCH ME

FIGURE 5.5. "Never Catch Me" manga from Flying Lotus's *You're Dead*, 2014. (Courtesy of Shintaro Kago.)

In verse 1, Kendrick-as-Lucy, speaking to Kendrick, raps, "You said Sherane ain't got nothing on Lucy / I said, 'You crazy?'" Mentioning Sherane, a *good kid, m.A.A.d city* love interest, projects this "Lucy" "romance" as unrequited. Yet one troubles the gender binary because whether "Lucy" is Lucifer, a dialogue between the nemesis and Lamar gives pause:

You said to me
You said your name was Lucy
I said, "Where's Ricardo?"
You said, "Oh no, not the show!"

. . .

You said, "My name is Lucy, Kendrick
You introduce me, Kendrick
Usually I don't do this
But I see you want me, Kendrick"

How queer: "Lucy," perhaps transgender or nonbinary, cajoles Lamar that she/he/they/it stand in for his paramour, just as the artist's vocal performance not only regenders his voice, but also pays homage to Prince, the androgynous incarnation of the color purple.[61] This trans* ethic riffs on Christina Sharpe who determines, "[Trans*] speaks . . . to a range of embodied experiences called gender and to Euro-Western gender's dismantling, its inability to hold in/on Black flesh. . . . We might say that slavery trans* all desire as it made some people into things, some into buyers, sellers, owners, fuckers, and breeders of that Black flesh."[62] "Lucy" is a being whose talk has turned cold, telling this butterfly he can gain the whole world for the price of his soul.[63] One confirms this when "Lucy" propositions Lamar to "sign this contract if that's possible."

Some consternation exudes this unpacking because juxtaposed to the music, the butterfly, entranced, visually navigates a strip club with seminude women: Is the monarch pimping again? Is this what he means by "I'm Lucy"? Interspersed throughout the second half of "God Is Gangsta," Lamar flashes quasi-subliminal messages as he meanders the bargain hunt:

CLEARANCE SALE 100% OFF

LIFE IS LIKE A BOX OF CHICKEN

INSTAGRAM 2016 = DUSSY UNLIMITED

IF I BLAME YOU FOR A LOSS, ILL BE GIVING YOU ALL THE CREDIT

GOOD DUSSY CAN MAKE YOU MELT

ALWAYS TRUST A NIGGA WITH CORNROLLS

NEVER TRUST A NIGGA WITH TOO MANY HAIR CUTS

TRACY ELLIS ROSS IS VIBRANT

I MADE MONEY. I LOST MONEY. I DID IT AGAIN

DUSSY SALARY CAP

WATERDAWG

I FOLLOWED YOUR RULES FOR WAY TOO LONG

NIGHTS LIKE THIS I WISH. THAT BOMB HEAD WOULD FALL

MY TASTE BLOODS IS EXPENSIVE

YOU'LL BUY THE MALL IF LUST INVOLVED. THE EVILS OF IT ALL

YOU PLAYED THE GAME. I PIMPED IT

GOD IS GANGSTA

FIN.

These streams of consciousness, leading to the penultimate one, are reducible to him being dipped in the water, dying to the past, and emerging anew to endear himself to the gangsta Zulus call *uNkulunkulu*. THE END. This solidifies the last addition to the long-form meditation as we taxi into this final disembarkation: "So I went runnin' for answers / Until I came home."

Lalah Hathaway, in a rather oneiric manner, opens "Momma" sampling her song, "On Your Own": "living that dream / So it seems."[64] Each lyric, separated by the slash, bookends the repetitive hook "We've been waiting for you." Verse 1 is a tribute to hip-hop and creativity:

Thank God for rap
I would say it got me a plaque
But what's better than that?
The fact it brought me home

Verse 2 is Lamar telling us everything he knows, prototypical of intellectual rigor:

I know everything
I know everything, I know myself
. . .
I know the price of life
I know how much it's worth
I know what I know
And I know it well not to ever forget
Until I realized I didn't know shit
The day I came home

Verse 3 reveals him viewing himself as a little boy and the potential yet to come:

I met a little boy that resembled my features
Nappy afro, gap in his smile
Hand-me-down sneakers
Bounced through the crowd
. . .
He looked at me and said,
"Kendrick, you do know my language,
You just forgot because of what public schools had painted"
. . .
It's just a new trip
Take a glimpse at your family's ancestor

Melismatic of Mulvey, this recognition/misrecognition extends the "perfect"; it is not mirroring alone, but also what home dignifies. Lamar viewing the child as a distant relative, bloodless, foretells his Afrofuture. The Outro transforms into a frenzy that aphoristically *takes you there:*

> I've been looking for you my whole life
> An appetite
> For the feeling I can barely describe—
> Where you reside?
> Is it in a woman, is it in money or mankind?
> Tell me something, got me losing my mind—AH!
> You make me wanna jump
> Jump, jump, jump, jump
> Let's talk about love

Love and home are what Lamar has been looking for, but the track title is "Momma." Africa as motherland can certainly demonstrate "home" or "love," especially if the album is neoteric.

The drumming and frantic nature of the record, specifically verse 3 through the Outro (3:30–4:43), mimics the soundscape at the opening and close of "Playa Playa" and the ending of "Africa" on D'Angelo's *Voodoo*—this is a channeling of the sacred that is equally profane.[65] Moreover, when Lamar intimates, "Maybe I'm paranoid—HA! / Maybe I don't need you anyway / Don't lie to me / I'm suicidal any day," his "middle passage," a liberatory striving, stands beside Robert Hayden's:

> "Tenth April Eighteen Hundred:
> Blacks rebellious. Crew uneasy. Our linguist says
> their staunchless moaning is a prayer for death,
> ours and their own. Some try to starve themselves.
> Lost three this morning *leaped with crazy laughter*
> to the waiting sharks; *sang as they went under.*"[66]

Lamar's AH!-ing and HA!-ing epitomizes "crazy laughter"; his "jump" is like the leaping coincident to the outbursts of the "Blacks rebellious." Is he suggesting that despite Lucifer's evil capture of free bodies, jumping-as-suicide makes him akin to those who chose wading in the water or soaring in the air? Is "Lucy" home in the deep where living (in) that dream (state), she and the ancestors await Lamar *so it seems?* Does this reify the baptism? Is that protection, lost toward his sister, found when returning to "Momma" because although he does not "know shit" in the world, when he arrives home, he knows "everything"? Is this genius? Contemplating black Christian rhetoric, one recalls the profession of faith before baptism when the newly saved is encouraged to give the preacher your hand and God your heart. Perhaps he gives both to "Lucy" by immersing himself in the substance that is her home; he says "'yes' to the 'female' within," a mode of Sapphiric empowerment.[67] We learn something about Lamar and perhaps ourselves.

If he is Milkman's mocking double, does the narrative of masculine waste as spillage seep into Lamar's appearance as the butterflies' pimp while traversing the strip club, wherein he can find what he is looking for through the monetary objectification of pole women, the capitalist control of a "stable"? Or is this the metamorphosis of "The Anthropocene (*anthropo*, or man, and *cene*, or new)" in black, a telltale tall tale when a butterfly transitions out of the buyer-seller's market and instead comes back to "Momma" and his lepidopterarium?[68] Milkman's grandfather may inculcate us with what Kendrick is up to by the end of his "middle passage": "Sing. Sing." This is the directive Macon called Jake reveals to his daughter Pilate amid "some dark lonely hours"; however, it is not necessarily just the repetition of a verb doubling and mocking itself in the imperative mood. No, the Dead grandfather may be imploring his Afrofuture to Sing Her. Sing Ryna. Sing Heddy. Sing Pilate. Sing Ruth. Sing "Song of Solomon" who "left his" children, your ancestors, who "sang about it and kept the story of his leaving alive," all while surviving with the Dead, your mothers, who made a life in the aftermath of that selfish loss. Sing Bird, Singing Bird who, in this case, is a Butterfly. Kendrick, Sing "Lucy." Kendrick, Sing Butterfly. Kendrick, Sing Me, Dying of Thirst. Kendrick, Sing the eternal feminine you so "love" because "[w]ithout ever leaving the ground, she could fly."[69]

To Pimp a Butterfly portrays Lamar as Cio-Cio-san in "outrageous caricature."[70]

Genius surfaces for Lamar because channeling "Momma," and retrospectively accounting for wrongdoings and temptations, not only affords him "knowledge of self," but also augments his performances on the ground and in the air. He imparts through an epistle as prose-praise poem, "Dear Lucy, sometimes there are bodies that slip between us, as in not where I was, but what I left, how I got so loose—*practice*—so where I pivot from is how in this body you are in where I leave, this pose, our set, redone." Claiming the monstrosity, Kago's never-caught being, by exorcising "Lucy," the mocking presence, Lamar may project that what "Momma" was name*d* has no standing when knowing what her name really is.[71]

"A token of love from me, to thee"; or, What Happens When a Streetlight Becomes a Tree

If "[b]lack post-blackness is the inseparability of *what is* and *what could be*," the tonal shift between *To Pimp a Butterfly* and DAMN., not forgetting *good kid, m.A.A.d city*, marks a return and an exit to the racialized wheelhouse.[72] What I mean is with the overt race talk Lamar does on the former project, on the latter's "YAH," he shares:

> I'm not a politician
> I'm not 'bout a religion
> I'm a Israelite
> Don't call me black no mo'
> That word is only a color
> It ain't facts no mo'[73]

Lamar syncopates with Raymond Saunders's 1967 BAM pamphlet *Black Is a Color*: "Saunders insisted that color is too abstract to be contained by racial and political discourse."[74] Nonetheless, a redux of *To Pimp a Butterfly* reroutes us home.

In an MTV News interview, Lamar confesses that the album is about "leadership. How can I use it, for better or for worse? With money and with my celebrity, how can I use it? How can I pimp it? Can I pimp it negatively or pimp it in a positive way? Positive for me is showing what I go through, showing what I've been through with 'u,' and coming all the way back to 'i' and saying I still love myself at the end of the day." Invoking "i" is intriguing if his search for "Momma" is legitimate. As the record nears its end, he is already home cerebrally:

> Retraced my steps on what they never taught me
> Did my homework fast before government caught me
>
> . . .
>
> On how the infamous, sensitive N-word control us
> So many artists gave [Oprah] an explanation to hold us
> Well this is my explanation, straight from Ethiopia
> N-E-G-U-S, definition:
> Royalty, king, royalty, wait listen—
> N-E-G-U-S
> Description: black emperor, king, ruler, now let me finish. . . .
> Kendrick Lamar, by far, realest negus alive[75]

FIGURE 5.6. Still from "Alright" video, 2015. (Courtesy of Top Dawg Entertainment.)

While this royalty is not out of Egypt, Ethiopia psalmodically stretches out her hands—"not mere hands of helplessness and supplication, but rather are they hands of pain and promise; hard, gnarled, and muscled for the world's real work; they are hands of fellowship for the *half-submerged* masses of a distempered world; they are hands of helpfulness for an agonized God!"—to Lamar; he invites others to this embrace as she whispers, "We gon' be alright" (fig. 5.6).[76] Ethiopia imposes rhetorical weight, imbuing him with the reclamation of a name, slurred or otherwise, for doubling himself as he runs home. Furthermore, "i" samples the Isley Brothers' "That Lady." With the chorus's rehearsed inquiry—Who's that lady?—the answer is obvious (of course not!): "i" am, and i am She, loving myself. These are the makings of "u," Ethiopian Israelite. Kendrick Lamar—not the child of "Lucy," but rather Dinkinesh. By the end of *To Pimp a Butterfly*, he has *flown home* because "'[u] ndoubtedly ... Afro-Americans are a branch of the wonderful and mysterious Ethiopians who had a prehistoric existence of magnificence, the full record of which is lost in obscurity.'"[77]

This language, from Pauline Hopkins's *Of One Blood. Or, the Hidden Self*, serialized from 1902 to 1903, is interesting because Ethiopia as "lost" converges with psychoanalysis regarding the object, predating "Mourning and Melancholia"; "[w]hether invoked as a temporally distant primal nation, as an abstract nation of the black race or synecdoche for Africa in general, or as an imaginary locus of biblical or antique nostalgia, the figure of Ethiopia resonates throughout the African American literary tradition." Marcellus Blount, agreeing with this theorization, also discerns Ethiopia, vis-à-vis Paul Laurence Dunbar's poem "Frederick Douglass," as a "gendered space, one that suggests both African origins and a kind of nascent Pan-Africanism." Ethiopia, emblematizing the neoteric, straddles multiple worlds: the macro- and microcosmic, the mythic and mundane, the old and new. While Blount anchors his criticism in the "Douglass" elegy, he also applies his move to Dunbar's "Ode to Ethiopia": "Ethiopia . . . is gendered as the mother. . . . The figure of the mother in the poem depends a great deal on historical gender assignments and relations . . . it is important that the figure of the mother be assigned a certain degree of authority, albeit constrained by 19th-century es- sentialist thinking . . . the poem posits the figure of the mother as a vehicle of inheritance."[78] This merits perusal.

As an elegy, "Ode" is expansive, documenting through history and rever- ence the bond blackness has to this ancestral home. This may be why the first three lines read like an anthem: "O Mother Race! to thee I bring / This pledge of faith unwavering, / This tribute to thy glory." Nadia Nurhussein conceives the opening exclamatory apostrophe as a "pledge [that] would ap- pear to counter the pledge of allegiance to the flag of the United States, which had been written a year prior to Dunbar's publication." Yet the musicality suf- fusing this chapter proposes these lyrics as the reimagining of "My country tis of thee / Sweet land of liberty / Of thee I sing"—the incorporated diction itself ("thee I"), the assonant consonance of "bring" and "unwavering" rhym- ing with "sing," and the sestina structure AABCCB.[79] Moreover, the poem also mimes the running premise regarding natal kinship, melancholy, genius, and nationalist relation: knowing "the pangs" the Mother "didst feel / When Slav- ery crushed [her] with its heel," a re-reading of Solomon's or Lamar's escape and its affective residue; "Sad days" that complement her "fruitful seed . . . growing . . . blossoming" as the violets and the jonquil and the maple tree sprout in spite of tumult, or the hope of a cocoon meeting its purposive end; "High 'mid the clouds of Fame's bright sky / Thy banner blazoned folds now fly" as the vanishing point of Old Glory materializes; "And labour's painful sweat-beads made / A consecrating chrism" when (re)birth alchemizes sac- ramental salve; "No other race, or white or black / . . . . / So seldom stooped to grieving" as the ground spatializes an altar or a final resting place; "Go on and up! Our souls and eyes / Shall follow thy continuous rise; / . . . . / From bards who from thy root shall spring, / And proudly tune their lyres to sing /

Of Ethiopia's glory" whereby "[t]he historic men of the Race (there is no mention of women, other than Ethiopia herself) sing 'hymns' but they are also the subjects of the bards' song, a national epic."[80] What comes into focus through the poetry is the affinity for flight in the black post-black imagination.

Yusef Komunyakaa, sitting with flying in "songs and poems rooted in the tenets of early African American Christianity," understands this motif investment:

> The desire for flight takes many forms. The impulse to throw off the bonds of slavery by fleeing from one's worldly master is sometimes overshadowed by a fascination with transcendence, with psychological and spiritual leave-taking that constitutes a second uprooting and is transformed into the hope for ascension to heaven. Because of the depth of belief and the vagaries associated with historical circumstance, it appears that many of the earlier black believers embraced a flight motif that attempted to defy physics and logic, and that the reality of this belief could be viewed as a desperate covenant with the unknowable and indefinable.[81]

As per Claudia Tate, the forebears were "satisfied" with the "what" and not "the technique" of the "how," defying the apparent to desire the aerial.[82] Is oppression *a* reason for escape but not always *the* one, like when a child says, "'Mama, I'm walking to Canada and I'm taking you and a bunch of other slaves with me.' Reply: 'It wouldn't be the first time.'"?[83] Is flight a 360 deal, a boomerang that repeats in its comings and goings, repeats despite one's (purchased) freedom because it ain't no fun if the homies can't have none?[84] Is it covenantal, a promise (dis)regarding the real and the overreal, the plus and the minus? If these questions have plausible answers, one could surmise that the ancestors were *Ego Tripping*—born in Africa, some in the Congo, they turned themselves into themselves and were Jesus; we intone their loving names. They cannot be comprehended except by their permission. They are avian: I mean they can fly like birds in the sky.[85]

This is the *Song of Negus*.

Yasiin Bey curated a rendition of this Song in 2019 at the Brooklyn Art Museum under the title, *Negus*. In "A Note on Language," one learns, "*Negus* (pronounced *nuh-goose*) takes its name from *nəguś*, the word for 'king' or 'ruler' in Ge'ez, an ancient South Semitic language now used primarily in religious ceremonies in Eritrea and Ethiopia." Furthermore, "In the last five years, the word has been appropriated by several U.S. rappers," such as "Bronx rapper Ye the Cynic and the late Brooklyn rapper Capital Steez of the Pro Era collective"; nearby wall script supports this: "*Negus* is a collaborative listening installation that reimagines the possibilities of hip-hop as an art form." A "time-limited listening experience" with art, *Negus* has a tracklist:

0. Dream study
1. Negus zero
2. Hemp
3. PGK—A
4. waves
5. Pomo
6. Day Trippers
7. BINGWA

While *negus* reads heavily masculinist, trafficking in the flawed myth that once, somehow, we all were "kings," another curated statement puts my argument in distress.

On an adjacent wall, one learns, "This installation refers to a constellation of historical and contemporary figures who, from the artist's point of view, have led noble lives": Prince 'Alämayyähu Tewodros (1861–1879) ("a nineteenth-century Ethiopian prince and son of Emperor Tewodros II and Empress Təru Wärq Wəbe"); Nipsey Hussle (1985–2019) ("a Grammy nominated rapper, community organizer, and entrepreneur from Los Angeles"); and Emahoy Tsegué-Maryam Guèbrou (1923–) ("a pianist, composer, and Ethiopian Orthodox nun"). The fourth person is particularly captivating: Henrietta Lacks (1920–1951), "(born Loretta Pleasant) . . . a tobacco farmer whose cancer cells became the source of the first *immortalized* human cell line, widely regarded as one of the most important cell lines in medical research." This immortality—flesh, without consent, being offered for medical utility ad infinitum and assigned a "new name"—evokes Dinkinesh and her unsolicited renaming. The exhibit has an installation called "shakur the beloved. Eastern band," no doubt gesturing to Tupac like Lamar's "Mortal Man." Akin to the AfriCOBRA tenet of "written statements"—"direct, unequivocal statements written on the picture plane and incorporated in the composition to clarify the concept; art is imbued with a specificity of sophistication that speaks to African people and carries messages with the visual impact of a billboard—poster art"—this piece holds a quote: "'Remember? Gratitude is shattering darkness.' There was silence and it was understood."[86]

In this curation, where a specified stable of persons receives headphones to listen to *Negus* in silence while meandering the exhibition space, to read the "noble life" of Lacks as aesthetic muse silences the noisiest gong, the most clanging cymbal. But it also lays bare "the unknowable and indefinable"—is this "the beauty of love and what can be challenging about it": "undefinability, which, further, is to pose the questions of what might it mean to orient ourselves around indeterminacy, to locate ourselves more with the urgent, unstable, and risky unknown? Understanding that love is not something to be wielded, owned or possessed, but is an intimate, incessant embrace of failure—realizing that failure isn't a singular moment, but a constancy that commits to the queerness inherent in failure, disorientation, multiplicity, nonnormativity."?[87] Undefinably, I surmise Henrietta *née* Loretta as the mimesis at midpoint of Dinkinesh.

Amharic for "you are marvelous," Dinkinesh is given that *other name* after The Beatles' "Lucy in the Sky with Diamonds," which played during her excavation: Did science "pimp" the foremother? "Born again" through sediment unsettling—a baptism of dirt, not water—Dinkinesh compels similitude with Lamar through how she supposedly died. Scientists attribute the death of Dinkinesh to injuries likely sustained by a fall from a tree; this was based on CT scans that divulged "a series of sharp, clean breaks [of the right humerus] with bone fragments and slivers still in place . . . consistent with a long fall in which the victim tries to break the impact by extending an arm before landing." One scientist emotes, "'When the extent of [Dinkinesh]'s multiple injuries first came into focus, her image popped into my mind's eye, and I felt a jump of empathy across time and space. [Dinkinesh] was no longer simply a box of bones, but in death became a real individual: a small, broken body lying helpless at the bottom of a tree.'"[88] At the end of the "Alright" video, a police officer, with "[j]ust the wave of a finger," shoots Lamar standing atop a streetlight. Unlike Dinkinesh, he falls backward, colliding with the dirt. This symbolizes, supposedly, that "at the end of the day, we're all human and nobody's untouchable," even if Lamar superhumanly awakes after his *grounding*, that black post-black wink as a blink.[89]

In my estimation, this streetlight reimagines the tree because both victims, of either apparatus, exposit black death engendering "empathy" *after* final respiration. Dinkinesh becomes "real" at the tree's bottom, just as broken flesh became "real" strung up. This might be that "vicious pantomime of unvarying reification and compulsive fascination, of whites taking a look at themselves through images of black desolation, of blacks intimately dispossessed by that selfsame looking . . . the disfiguring impact of those imagoes . . . and their effects of our unconscious beliefs and desires." But, somehow, amid this (un)consciousness, an oppositional provocation imprints itself: Why was she up a tree and out on a limb? Was she harvesting food for herself, a hunter-gatherer who made ends meet as a single black female; or for her family as the daughter who insured her parents maintained a hearty diet in their twilight years? Did she launch herself up there to secure a *snack* for her lover ahead of being one herself? Was she climbing to see if someone, something, was on the horizon, a foretaste of Zacchaeus witnessing the Messiah then welcoming him as an unannounced but embraced *umvakashi*?[90] Was she, like Solomon, *pissed* with the world, retreating for momentary flight?

Did she fall so Lamar, so we, the people, *could fly*? Could Sing She?

Yet simultaneously, in advance of *Alice in Wonderland*, or John Lennon's son painting Lucy, a "school friend," Dinkinesh is "the image of the female who would someday come *save* me—a 'girl with *kaleidoscope* eyes' who would come *out of the sky* . . . this secret love that was going to come one day."[91] Said day is here, Butterfly, and all that is left to say, winking, is: thanks for coming.

P.S. IWEDISHALEW.

The African-American male, has been touched, therefore, by the mother, handed by her in ways that he cannot escape, and in ways that the white American male is allowed to temporize by a fatherly reprieve.
—HORTENSE J. SPILLERS, "Mama's Baby, Papa's Maybe: An American Grammar Book"

The Promise of Blackness?; or, She Touched Me

As someone overly attentive to details, I have experienced discursive convergence related to this epigraph concluding *Stay Black and Die: On Melancholy and Genius.* The first instance occurred while watching ESPN when a sportscaster referred to a basketball player having a PhD: proper hand development. The phrase resonates with the quotation because to "hand"—or, in that case, "palm"—something or someone registers as a laborious act of grace and dexterity, to grasp, sometimes with care, that which wants to "escape." Synchronicity also occurred reading this:

> when I first took up what I have already spoken of as the problem of the black masculine, I wrote in my very first published piece, "if there is to be an enduring theory of black male identity construction in the West,

it will be significantly indebted to a careful synthesis of post-Freudian psychoanalysis and the epistemological work of black feminism." ... [Spillers] wrote in that astounding essay which, like so much of Claudia Tate's work, we all dig so profoundly, "Mama's Baby, Papa's Maybe: An American Grammar Book" that "the African American male has been touched by the mother, *handled* by her in ways that he cannot escape."

And this:

> Impossible, substitutive motherhood is the location of Aunt Hester, a location discovered, if not produced, in Hortense Spillers's improvisational audition of sighting, not-sight, seen; of the heretofore unheard and overlooked (overseen) at the heart of the spectacle. Spillers explains what Douglass brings in his prefigurative disruption of and irruption into a fraternal science of value that emerges in a "social climate" in which motherhood is not perceived "as a legitimate procedure of cultural inheritance":
>
> The African American male has been touched, therefore, by the *mother*, handled by her in ways that he cannot escape.[1]

Beneficiaries of Spillers, as witnessed in their citations, Maurice Wallace and Fred Moten respectively showcase why they, and others, "dig" the essay: They are implicated as the *touched*. Yet what interests me is not the jiving with Spillers, but the constancy of the typographical error. Transcribed here as it is in print, their repetition of her—"sighting, not-sight, seen"—generates something in this ending, or beginning, for what it means to stay black and die:

Is there a difference between being handed and hand*l*ed by the mother?

What compels this attention is that whenever my eye reads those works, I hear the original author incorrectly, bringing me back to how her writing sounds. Ruminating on Nathaniel Mackey, one could assert that the "l" characterizes "the dead-letter aspect" of these citations, surfacing as an (un)conscious insertion in the aftermath of the 1987 publication; another could return to his creationist proclivities and testify to a similar erasure-insertion with word and wor*l*d.[2] This misprint-as-human fallibility is obvious, even if spellcheck supports such incorrection. But what if this mistake elicits contemplating black stud(y/ies) as that which induces a "vibe" from what has been abstracted?

On par with *Stay Black and Die* taking up psychoanalysis and affect theory, Kevin Young offers a heuristic that encapsulates the textual arguments:

"*storying* is both a tradition and a form; it is what links artfulness . . . with any of the number of stories (or tall tales or 'lies' or literature) black folks tell among and about themselves . . . the fabric of black life has often meant its very fabrication, making a way out of no way, and making it up as you go along. . . . Each good solo tells a story, one that while collective in nature—a calling out—must also be unique, your own. Otherwise, you yourself can be called out." This sounds like the blues whereby it "seeks an empathetic though not sympathetic audience . . . the blues functions best with a (silently) implicit audience because no matter the problem the blues is not a call for help but rather an itemization of the problem itself."[3] The blues calls one out. The blues *stories*. And if such a calculation enlists a solo now, here is an unabashed *blow*.

To "hand" or "handle" exemplifies storying because "theorists" and "practitioners" have been handed blackness, in all its multiplicity, to handle its stud(y/ies) and reckon with its staying and dying—the development of proper hands. The movement, the touch, of the mother:

> That mothers can alter the experience of their young by touching them is not something I dispute. What I counter is the notion that the senses are controlled by one body and given to another or withheld. This attitude posits as its point of departure a stable body that exists in a pre-given space-time which contains an active giver and a passive receptor. . . . Whereas in the active-passive commonsense model, time and space are located as stable signifiers into which the body enters, within a relational model, space and time are qualitatively transformed by the movements of the body. The body does not move *into* space and time, it *creates* space and time: there is no space and time before movement.[4]

This reciprocity fosters consideration for "stay black and die," whether phrase or text, as a critical position. That being, if the mother *handed* the black man, or black persons for that matter, what duty does she bestow to her brood to *handle* something like stud(y/ies) as a postlude to that (in)alterable creation? In this way, Spillers heralds Ranjana Khanna, and her reading of affect, and its theory, insomuch as "the space between the one who touches and the one who is touched is the trace of alterity making even the most intimate caress on oneself into hiatus. Affect, then, becomes the porous form of the parergon, a relationality, an opening of the singular onto the other . . . the interface of ontology and the ontic—an epistemological task that understands affect as the anxious spectral form of the interface." Maternal handing necessarily embellishes "proper hand development" toward something like a "radically different text for . . . empowerment."[5] The active-passive duality collapsing stability seems apt, concretizing "stay black and die" as an expression of melancholic genius. Not conflating Spillers as "parental," I believe something can be said for how black people manage what is handed to them, that they themselves handle, then hand off to others in this "relational model." The acts of "study" and "storying" triangulate with the "situation" perpetually occurring vis-à-vis blackness.

Interactions involving others constitute learning alternate forms of *lived experience* where some, within community and without, have not only not been about the work of study, but also have a steady and abiding interest in "dialing it in" when asked to account for the material. To be even more pointed, perhaps a "conviction" of blackness, and its stud(y/ies), is this: Even if it is the case that said critical position is not the monopoly of black people, when "we," however that formulation manifests, have that primal encounter with the other, our eyes should not glaze over in a kind of deep yearning.[6] That is, should one forgo strategizing how to *keep up* because "aspiring after the white world creates antagonisms among the black community" through the (re)inscription of those worldly "standards," whether they allude to "celebrity" or what some call "rigor"?[7] Is the "call out" that "strangers," who "study" "us," are given high regard over those who "touched" in the first place but remain disengaged? This too may carry over to nationalism.

I contend that before claiming any allegiance to nationality, in this case Americanity—a contestation that persists under the rocket's red glare (read: [para]military insurgency while protesting as a "citizen" in your natal country) / the bombs bursting in air (read: the concession that "[f]or Fanon, it is the policeman and the soldier [not the discursive, or hegemonic, agents] of colonialism that make one town white and the other Black. For Martinot and Sexton, this Manichean delirium manifests itself by way of the U.S. paradigm of policing that [re]produces, repetitively, the inside/outside, the civil society/Black world, by virtue of the difference between those bodies that do not magnetize bullets and those that do")—one inaugurates *singing* "home."[8] To be sure, "sing" can occur in variegated ways when working under an aleatory aegis, whether it be actual musicality (Gaye, Lamar) or delegitimizing the sanctity of property since it has historically taken precedence over personhood (Douglass, Ellison) or arming oneself as a furtherance of one's "constitutional right" (Butler). A song in real time: Margaret Bradley was "convicted of trying to poison two white people" in York, Pennsylvania in 1803; "black inhabitants of the area revolted en masse" by aiming to "destroy the town by fire and succeeded, within a period of three weeks, in burning eleven buildings."[9] These black Pennsylvanians "are the ones who cultivate the philoso-phy of right. It is [their] calling to create the rule of law. And that is what they will burn to free themselves from the Promised Land. It only takes a single spark." This improvisational mode may expose "how the ethical is mediated by the promise and actuality of such 'invention' by becoming actively creative at the level of history . . . this constant risk and sojourn is conceived in orphic terms." This engenders, peculiarly, Lucille Clifton because "born in babylon / . . . / what did i see to be except mysef? / i made it up."[10] To stay black and die may be, in and in excess of itself, inventive.

Performing in this way recollects that before being invited to the table, we were *made*—through social construction or, for some, "divine providence"—"to eat in the kitchen / When company comes." This happened regardless of how "beautiful" we are and how ashamed the host *ought* to be. And yet, such a moment is supposedly regenerative because in that solitude, "[we] laugh / And eat well / And grow strong."[11] Though this may ring in some ears as an isolationist move, does the admonition fortify what Billy Preston sounds: "Nothing from nothing leaves nothing / You've gotta have something / If you want to be with me," even as I recall that of the things one could be by now, anything-as-nothing could epitomize Charles Mingus's "All"?[12] So maybe this paradigmatic singing hears like those women of Sweet Home who "assem-bled outside 124. . . . When the music entered the window . . . as though the Clearing had come to [Sethe] with all its heat and simmering leaves, where the voices of women searched for the right combination, the key, the code, the sound that broke the back of words. Building voice upon voice until they found it . . . a wave of sound wide enough to sound deep water and knock the pods off chestnut trees. . . . It broke over Sethe . . . like the baptized in its wash." This sound wave exorcises the spiteful as this antelope gesticulates like a sanctified fish. This auricular event prepares Sethe's hand to double as an ice pick, an evolutionary transmogrification to slay the miraged white-haired phantom in black riding his mare past 124.[13] These women voice commence-ment as double entendre. That said, if one poses and professes, "What can I do? / One must begin somewhere. / Begin what? / The only thing in the world worth beginning: / The End of the world of course," then the requisite *doing* would be to "sing" this world into oblivion because in its current version, a small few have made it totally unsustainable for all. One should not request world 2.0, but a radical vocabulary that discerns that even if the "world" is "new," framing it like so will likely oblige its inhabitants to revert to old pat-terns. If this singing metaphor is apt, one may call the new thing, à la India. Arie, *Beautiful*. Or, having survived such destruction, one may phonate like

Luther Vandross: "I who have nothing / I who have no one."[14] Or one may just stay black and then die. Full stop. Is this the promise of blackness?

Might the promise be blackness holding within it the potential of the eschaton, the Parousia—the Second Coming: "In a sense, if there is no black culture, or no longer black culture (because it has 'succeeded'), then we need it now; and if that is true, then perhaps black culture—as the reclamation of the critical edge, as one of those vantages from which it might be spied, and no longer predicated on 'race'—has yet to come"? Can it "come again," even if the people who attempt to thrive with/in it imbibe its "successful" aperitif? If this is so, would the Second Coming be reminiscent of *l'avenir* in that one never arrives at it but is always in a posture of arrival to it?.[15] When Jacques Derrida summons the specter, an intriguing literary device could become a force of *habit* as read through *Timon of Athens*:

> Timon curses corruption, he casts down anathema, he swears against prostitution . . . [he] also begs [*conjure*] the other. . . . In truth, he *conjures by feigning the truth*. . . . But if he feigns to make the other promise, it is in truth to make the other promise not to keep his promise, that is, not to promise, even as he pretends to promise: to perjure or to abjure in the very moment of the oath; then following from this same logic, he begs him to spare all oaths. As if he were saying in effect: I beg you [*je vous en conjure*], do not swear, abjure your right to swear, renounce your capacity to swear, moreover no one is asking you to swear . . . you who confuse in equivalency the proper and the improper, credit and discredit, faith and the lie, the "true and the false," oath, perjury, abjuration and so forth. . . . And it is the fidelity to infidelity, the constancy in perjury . . . nature . . . enslaves itself to what is betrayal itself, perjury, abjuration, lie and simulacrum. Which are never far from the specter.[16]

Does this impress upon the reader that one can no longer be enthralled by the notion of storying as "black property"? Does Shakespeare *make a way out of no way* "on the fly"? Is this an "improvisatory exteriority that can occasion something very much like sadness and something very much like devilish enjoyment"? Is the theoretical bard composing his music on cloth? If one scores this rhetoric as musical, is it "[Derrida's jazz] as a mode and a model for expressing the experiences of performing among multiple aesthetic impulses, multiple emotional states, and multiple psychological selves simultaneously"?[17] Is this the power, the truth, of perjury?

For spectral proximity, one would have to become like Timon; "keeping them honest," he negates the descriptive promise, the oath, the swear. He stages a polemic against the constitution of the "subject," constructed as having a certain *value* with regard to how and what it can "produce." Taking this critical position, one would object to subject-ion; or, if remaining a "subject," somehow, one would be bound by death and attempt retrieving the lost, encouraging the accompaniment of others for the death drive.[18] If this is what the political project of psychoanalysis, the embrace of the political deadlock, suggests, acknowledging the death drive may be bound up in a twisted "joy," one counter to that suffering-*jouissance* pathway:

> The enjoyment that the death drive produces also achieves its infinitude through self-limitation. It revolves around a lost object that exists only insofar as it is lost, and it relates to this object as the vehicle for the infinite unfurling of its movement. The lost object operates as the self-limitation of the death drive through which the drive produces an infinite enjoyment. Rather than acting as a mark of the drive's finitude, the limitation that the lost object introduces provides access to infinity. A society founded on a recognition of the death drive would be one that viewed its limitations as the source of its infinite enjoyment rather than the obstacle to that enjoyment.[19]

Although this rationalization may sound subverted, should certain attuned ears believe in possibility? By sussing out the limit of emancipation at the limits of who we are, is the "death drive" catachresis for the stealth of a "joy ride," an absconded existential scavenger hunt to scour for the unknowable thing? Is it freedom? If lost-love-objectivity and death-bound-subjectivity instantiate that quest, would blackness be that prolific encounter with the haint?

Regarding the twinship of mourning and melancholia, and the theory that melancholia can transform into mania, if blackness contains any maniacal vestiges, is it, perhaps, *mourning sickness*?[20] Maybe blackness has perpetually wandered in wonderment, attempting to emboss a permanent address having once known or lost that abstraction called home.[21] This might be why its "unthought position," for psychoanalysis or affect theory, offers disappointment yet lacks surprise. If Freud was himself homeless—"Freud's uneasy relationship with the orthodoxy of his own community is very much a part of the complex of ideas so well described by [Isaac] Deutscher, who forgets to mention what I think is an essential component of it: its irremediably diasporic, unhoused character"—the analyst *and* analysand have likely contracted nostomania.[22] The "thinking" one, in a seat of power, writes long-form "prescriptions" for the "unthinking" other free-associating supine, regardless of both needing "help." One extends the boundaries of separation, that splitting of egos, to encompass the definitional legacy of diaspora.

Such repression, even by the "father of psychoanalysis," would run in line with rac(e)ing from death: "While we might forget or repress the darker, more painful conditions of individual development and collective history . . . the opacity and trauma remain an essential part of our drives, interactions, and identities. Even our desires for liberation are animated by experiences marked by agony and fear." This un-remembrance mirrors a suspicion in response to Freud's homelessness, as per Jacqueline Rose, that "*Israel represses Freud*."[23] This forgetfulness is not an attempt to counter those recent "drives," whether they relate to death and/or other "ends," but a willful decision to ignore them wholesale. So it is that by embracing loss as finite, as an agony and fear that arrests desires for liberation due to the belief that the lost thing is capturable, attaining "enjoyment" may be ephemeral but unfulfilling, or held in indefinite abeyance. Yet the one experiencing the loss might intrude upon the self, and the other, and declare:

Speak the dead letter—tell the lie.

Recalling what my mother imparted to me, it is *ground zero* for this argument in that the phrase, shared as a finite gesture to mitigate my whining, might be best understood as potentially ongoing: To need, or want, something immediately, yet receive word that the only necessary thing is to "stay black and die" means that in hindsight, momentary "agony" may metastasize into elongated "enjoyment," even in its currently bittersweet pill as *Stay Black and Die: On Melancholy and Genius*. She told the lie, storied, even if referring to her statement as an untruth now would have been the *death* of me then! Her genius, as a part of that long critical tradition, in telling me to stay black and die resides in the fact that it was, and is, not all I "needed" to do, but somehow was, and still is, all I needed to "do."

She interpreted the truth—handed it in advance of me handling it—to evidence her prognosticating, working from a history of being uprooted to putting down roots:

Inter-ethnic wars . . . are proliferating, driven by an *archaic* phantasm and concept, by a *primitive conceptual phantasm* of community, the nation-State, sovereignty, borders, native soil and blood . . . the process of dislocation is no less arch-originary, that is, just as "archaic" as the archaism that it has always dislodged. . . . All stability in a place being but a stabilization or a sedenterization, it will have to have been necessary that the local differance, the spacing of a displacement gives the movement its start. And gives place and gives rise [*donne lieu*]. All national rootedness, for example, is rooted first of all in the memory or the anxiety of a displaced—or displaceable—population. It is not only time that is "out of joint," but space in time, spacing.[24]

Is blackness Derrida's phantasm? Because this unrootedness does not permit the aggrieved or the lost the time and space to convene a proper voicing of its perpetual misgivings, has blackness tried to theoretically limn the severed bridge that accounts for the locative gravity of the lost-loved-object—Africa, the mother(land)—and the site at which those who were death-driven because of that loss became death-bound-subjects—diaspora, the father(lands)? Time and space as out of joint. (While one may read this reductively, I consider the gendered aphorisms aligned with continental characterization and nation-building, respectively: Africa as the "cradle of civilization" runs alongside the notion that "the hand that rocks the cradle is the hand that rules the world," an overt maternal gesture; meanwhile in diaspora, national lore is often birthed through "founding fathers."[25]) Hence, is "the source or 'root' of our turmoil . . . the all too human need to attach ourselves to practices, rituals, symbols, and collective projects (nation, race) that are both life-forming and death-producing . . . the shared condition of being *death-bound subjects* . . . this shared predicament should not merely be an occasion for *melancholy;* it should also be an occasion for joy, passion, and the experience of life's mysteries."?[26]

If blackness is a critical predicament wherein one locates oneself to better view the world through the lens of and in preparation for "life's mysteries," would one wish "neither of his older selves to be *lost*. He would not *Africanize America*, for America has too much to teach the world and Africa. He would not bleach his Negro soul in a flood of *white Americanism*, for he knows that Negro blood has a message for the world. He simply wishes to make it possible for a man to be *both Negro and an American* . . . without having the doors of Opportunity closed roughly in his face"?[27] Before "Mourning and Melancholia" bursts onto "the scene," is the split mind already "covered," dare we say *veiled*? The melancholy in the desire to not lose the older self later arrives for Du Bois as "latent genius," a power concomitant to that of his coworkers. Predated by Anna Julia Cooper and her "genius of young Africa in America," were these sentiments meant to "avoid despair at the very nadir of black life and development" as "the tremor throughout every fiber and to feel it [every day] is not the usual circumstance, but within these respective biographical outlines, it was the gadfly that dispatched . . . black men and women to *write* and *think* as though their very lives depended on it" (even as one questions Du Bois's sentential masculinism and what those two-way lessons might be)?[28] Does life, yet and still, depend on "it," that being staying black and dying; in fact, may life, or lives, hang in the balance because of and at the limits of "it"? That in mind, the iterative term "black or Afro-[insert nationality/ethnicity]" "hyphenates" an existence at the level of *parentage*, an "identity divided in the first instance both from its new situation and severed from the old one," which limns that bridge via imaginative conjuring—a nomenclatural move toward some semblance of "home." But could that formulation alone constitute a lie told to the self?[29]

Yet in an instant of psychoanalytic inversion, Lauryn Hill proffers, "I had to lose myself / Had to lose myself / So I could love you better."[30] Is the promise of blackness that in choosing to lose oneself, over and against one's judgment, that DuBoisian "Opportunity" surfaces? Is that the lie to be told? This may be what one grapples with when unpacking Langston Hughes's "I, Too":

> The verb here ["sing"] is important because it suggests the implicit if unrecognized creative work that African-Americans provided to make America. African-Americans helped sing America into existence and for that work deserve a seat at the table, dining as coequals with their fellows and in the company of the world. At the end of the poem, the line is changed because the transformation has occurred.
> "I, too, am America."
> Presence has been established and recognized. The house divided is reconciled into a whole in which the various parts sing sweetly in their separate harmonies. The problem for the politics of all this, if not for the poem itself, is that the simple assertion of presence—"They'll see how beautiful I am."—may not be enough.[31]

Apropos to that "second-sight . . . a peculiar sensation," the ostensible "problem" of the poem emerges because the "I," having been viewed through another's eye, "self-actualizes" an innate beauty in word and deed despite such action not being "enough." Said differently, is the lie that one feels one "deserves" a seat at the table when "making a way out of no way" surfaces as the community having craftspeople who could build tables themselves? Might the lie be that the house under which this gathering convenes is "reconciliatory," even as the singing remains inharmonious while partygoers sniff the embers of the house's singeing curtains?[32] All the more, the gravest question may be: enough for whom? Who is Hill's "you"?

Is blackness enough for itself—"black consciousness claims to be an absolute density, *full of itself,* a stage preexistent to any opening, to any abolition of the self by desire.... I *needed to lose myself* totally in negritude ... black consciousness is immanent in itself; I am not a potentiality of something; I am fully what I am. I do not have to look for the universal. There's no room for probability inside me. My black consciousness does not claim to be a loss. It *is.* It merges with itself"—such that sight and song are sensorial approaches to this melancholic genius because a promise of blackness may be while seeing is *sometimes* believing, hearing may be the surer sense? Is this the reification of the phantasm, just as the chapters of *Stay Black and Die* showcase the matrilineal gift of literacy rendered through rumor; the certain sound of women, often in/through the under(-)world, compelling vernacular; the "screaming" at a Monument and a church-home being (re)interpreted in a recording booth; the fear of a whistling rifle cultivating retribution; and a prehistoric "flight" stirring one's creative nest?[33]

Maybe this is the ongoing arrival, while still in motion, of what genius can be in relation to what it has been: Rewinding the black cinematic archive, if something one should never forget is that *success is nothing without someone you love to share it with,* then the hurdle of genius is the idea that success is the prize of only and ever being "self-made." Thus, this search for, this hearing of, the black feminine/maternal may be an opportunity to "share the love" with the very one who made you look and sound "good," or blackly "bad." Though it may not materialize tangibly, this intangible presence seemingly enables, just as "hearing, listening, waiting, meditating give way to a deep height, if we could say so, of activity omnipresent in its 'everywhereness.' But it becomes ... the Pauline situation of 'faith'—the 'substance of things *hoped for*,' the evidence of things *not* seen." In this manner, "[t]he recent return to melancholy in black studies should make us *rehear* [Hughes's "Harlem"] as meditating on the implosions that are unrecognizable forms of explosion."[34] Blackness, the phantasm, would be the remainder, then, that force which causes the rehearsal of the combustible as its own accelerant. Is this the haunting of "stay black and die": If one (properly?) performs the first act of the imperative, then the second act of the phrase—to die—may accomplish itself "nobly. ... / So that our precious blood may not be shed / In vain; then even the monsters we defy / Shall be constrained to honor us though dead!"? Does Claude McKay's "If We Must Die" "lie," that is, the verbiage "stories" dying as not readily apparent: "If" is not "When"? (Perhaps we do not, must not, die but *multiply*?)[35] Is this the limit, or excess, of blackness; and what of the "whom," which may be whiteness, in that "enough" query?

If "singing" hastens the end times, might the sonic move toward the other mime Roberta Flack and Donny Hathaway as they urge one to "Be Real Black for Me"; or Nina Simone, in homage to Lorraine Hansberry, cajoling that "To Be Young, Gifted and Black. . . . That's where it's at!"? Or instead of storying "them," after the blues were taken and gone, may one realize that

> someday somebody'll
> Stand up and talk about me,
> And write about me—
> Black and beautiful—
> And sing about me,
> And put on plays about me!
> I reckon it'll be me
> Me myself!
> Yes, it'll be me. [?][36]

Then again, if the goal is to "embrace the deadlock as a political position," can whiteness witness to itself—*lose itself*, clean its home for an eventual departure, "accept the fact that what [it] thinks [it] is, [it] is not. [It] has to give up, [it] has to surrender [its] image of [itself]."?[37] Does this mean that as one has been admonished to "stay black and die," another should *leave white and live*? That is unclear and could be a good lie. But if, vis-à-vis that presumptive "joy ride," this conclusion recalls exegesis and eisegesis, recalls playing the dozens, recalls "lies" and "truths," recalls the slippage of sight and sound, what may now be obvious—of course not!—is that *the* promise of blackness is it has always and ever been, in no uncertain terms, the project of wight folk. . . .

ECHO | I

1 Razinsky, *Freud, Psychoanalysis and Death*, 134; and Holloway, *Passed On*, 58.
   See also Perry, *More Beautiful and More Terrible*, 23; and Freud, *Beyond the
   Pleasure Principle*.

2 Though this term seems self-explanatory, it combines the categories Black-
   Fem and captive maternal—see Frazier, "Thinking Red, Wounds, and Fungi
   in Wangechi Mutu's EcoArt"; and James, "The Womb of Western Theory,"
   255–56.

3 "melancholy, n.1," OED *Online*.

4 Gillespie, *Film Blackness*, 54. For more on "race-ing," see Myrsiades and
   Myrsiades, eds., *Race-ing Representation*.

5 Eng and Kazanjian, "Introduction: Mourning Remains," 7–8; and Sharpe, *In
   the Wake*, 111–12. For more on humoral theory, see Battersby, "*Gender and
   Genius*," 566–67.

6 Aristotle, *Problems*, XXX.1, 10–13, 1498; and Varga, "From Melancholia to
   Depression, 144. See also Foucault, *Madness and Civilization*, 118.

7 Hughes, "Necessity," 392 (emphasis in original); and Derrida, *The Animal That
   Therefore I Am*.

8 Wallace, *Improvisation and the Making of American Literary Modernism*, 91.

9 A scene from *Love Jones* captivates this melancholy-sad sentiment: Darius
   (Larenz Tate) encounters Nina (Nia Long) in a record store and asks if he

can play her something; he puts on Charlie Parker's "Parker's Mood." Having listened, Nina says, "It's kinda sad," to which Darius replies, "Melancholy maybe, but not sad—there's a difference I think." And for a reading of "black art" vis-à-vis Frantz Fanon, whereby "it accustoms us to a form of libidinal economy that, at the level of psyche and culture, both 'protects and permits,'" perhaps one vantage for reading "black aesthetics" in this text, see Marriott, "Judging Fanon."

10 "Exegesis is an honest task. Eisegesis is often deceptive and shaped by our own desires." See Richardson, *Walking Together*, 30.

11 Dunne, *Reading Theory Now*, 19 (emphasis in original).

12 New, *Imaginative Preaching*, 86.

13 West, *Biblical Hermeneutics of Liberation*, 131–73; and Dunne, *Reading Theory Now*, 20 (my emphasis).

14 Schappell and Lacour, "Toni Morrison, The Art of Fiction No. 134."

15 Ross, *Manning the Race*, 182, 222. While I focus on "race men" in the United States, the category is not particular to said location; a conversant work is Macharia, *Frottage*. And speaking of diaspora, I want to acknowledge a one-woman play about a black girl growing up in mid-twentieth-century Winnipeg that shares the name of this book. See Sumter-Freitag, *Stay Black and Die*.

16 Equiano, *The Interesting Narrative of the Life of Olaudah Equiano. . . .*, 24, 31; and Baldwin, "Here Be Dragons," 675, 689–90 (my emphasis). This essay was originally titled "Freaks and the American Ideal of Manhood." Also, inasmuch as I presence Equiano's mother here, Habiba Ibrahim offers a similar gesture regarding his sister; that is, as she provokes "Equiano Girl," I render "Equiano Woman." See Ibrahim, *Black Age*, 165–202.

17 Trilling, "Introduction," 13. Ironically, this quote is in a paragraph that begins, "Overtly and without apology, Freud hoped to be a genius, having before that avowed his intention of being a hero."

18 An example: Baldwin penned a screenplay that projected Malcolm X's queerness; Spike Lee "borrowed" and rethought it, cutting the scene in his update—see Norman, "Reading a 'Closet Screenplay,'" 103–16. For more on Malcolm X in this vein, see Marable, *Malcolm X*; and Ball and Burroughs, eds., *A Lie of Reinvention*. Likewise, "funking" the "race man" riffs on Stallings, *Funk the Erotic*.

19 Terrefe, "Speaking the Hierogylph," 133–37.

20 Spivak, "Echo," 17.

21 Spillers, "Moving on Down the Line," 93; and Durham, email message to Kevin Quashie (paraphrase), July 12, 2020.

COLOR | BLACKNESS

1 "The living-dead" references Sharon Patricia Holland who, citing bell hooks, rehearses, "'Reduced to the machinery of bodily physical labor, black people learned to appear before whites as though they were zombies. . . . Safety resided in the pretense of invisibility.'" See Holland, *Raising the Dead*, 14–15; and hooks, "Representations of Whiteness," in *Black Looks*, 168.

2   Hinson, *The Pianist's Dictionary*, 104; and Allen, "Everything You Want to Know About Poetic Apostrophe."

3   JanMohamed, *The Death-Bound-Subject*, 4.

4   Gordon, "Theory in Black," 206; and Morrison, "Unspeakable Things Unspoken, 32; hereafter, "Unspeakable."

5   Morrison, *Beloved*, 210–11, 149. On the Maafa, see Akinyela, "In the Wake of Destruction," 250.

6   Morrison, *Beloved*, 211–13, 215; Brown, *The Repeating Body*, 102–6; and Gordon, "Theory in Black," 207.

7   JanMohamed, *The Death-Bound-Subject*, 10 (emphasis in original).

8   Spillers, "Mama's Baby, Papa's Maybe," 67; hereafter, "MB"; and Morrison, *Beloved*, 213; 1.

9   Spillers, "The Idea of Black Culture," 10; hereafter, "Idea"; and "Unspeakable," 32 (my emphases).

10 "Idea," 17.

11 JanMohamed, *The Death-Bound-Subject*, 10; and Nash, "Black Maternal Aesthetics," 551. In line with the spectral black feminine/maternal, although Nash contextualizes this haunting in the contemporary, to my mind it constitutes itself through the first African being removed from her home and brought "low" elsewhere, the originary moment of flesh traversing toward meat.

12 Freud, "Mourning and Melancholia," 243–45.

13 Freud, "Mourning and Melancholia," 245–46; and Foucault, *Madness and Civilization*, 11.

14 Tettenborn, "Melancholia as Resistance in Contemporary African American Literature," 104.

15 Kristeva, *Black Sun*, 43; 27–28 (my emphasis). See also Lechte, *Julia Kristeva*, 186–87.

16 Baucom, *Specters of the Atlantic*, 132; and Kristeva, *Black Sun*, 29.

17 Moynihan, "The Negro Family"; and Freud, "Mourning and Melancholia," 251. Tiffany Lethabo King deftly interprets Moynihan's "Report" as a reduction of the "black family" through comparison to the Western "family": "The Black matriarch—female flesh ungendered—becomes a threat to the social order" (81). See King, "Black 'Feminisms' and Pessimism," 68–82.

18 Freud, "Mourning and Melancholia," 249–50 (my emphasis).

19 First Corinthians 11: 24–26, New International Version; Hughes, "Necessity," in *The Collected Poems of Langston Hughes*, 392; and Freud, "Mourning and Melancholia," 246; 245.

20 Philip, *Zong!* For more on the formulation of "ditto," see also Sharpe, *In the Wake*, 52.

21 Freud, "Mourning and Melancholia," 257–58.

22 Spillers, "Moving on Down the Line," 106. On the politics of "normal" amid blackness's regulation, see Brand, "On Narrative, Reckoning and the Calculus of Living and Dying."

23 JanMohamed, *The Death-Bound-Subject*, 2; and Freud, "Mourning and Melancholia," 250, 257. Here, JanMohamed seems to channel Richard Wright: "Negro writers must have in their consciousness the foreshortened picture of the *whole*, nourishing culture from which they were torn in Africa, and of the long, complex (and for the most part, unconscious) struggle to regain in some form and under alien conditions of life a *whole* culture again." See Wright, "Blueprint for Negro Writing," 203.

24 Du Bois, *Souls of Black Folk*, 3–12; and Joseph R. Winters, iMessage, November 28, 2020. Some foundational sources, though not exhaustive, for Afro(-)pessimism and black optimism in North America and abroad are Hartman and Wilderson, "The Position of the Unthought," 183–201; Moten, "Black Op," 1743–47; Wilderson, *Red, White and Black*; and *Afro-Pessimism*. For criticisms, see Sexton, "The Social Life of Social Death, 1–47; Marriott, "Judging Fanon"; Gordon, "Afro pessimism," 105–37; Thomas, "Afro-Blue Notes, 282–317; and "Hortence [*sic*] Spillers and Gail Lewis at the Institute of Contemporary Arts."

25 Tony Scherman, "The Omni-american"; hereafter, "Omni-american." See also Wallace, "Richard Wright's Black Medusa," 72–74. Though I date Murray's "blues idiom" to 1996, he used it throughout his career. See Maguire, *Conversations with Albert Murray*, 8–11, 15–18, 19–24, 57–65.

26 Holloway, *Passed On*, 60–61; "MB," 77; Winters, *Hope Draped in Black*, 6; and Norman Mailer, "The White Negro." And for aesthetics (in)expressing loss, see Tettenborn, 106–13; and on the black fantastic, see Iton, *In Search of the Black Fantastic*.

27 "MB," 67 (emphasis in original). Cannibalism was a relevant threat during slavery—see Woodard, *The Delectable Negro*, 127–70; and for eating as a race-power act, see Tompkins, *Racial Indigestion*.

28 "Thingification" may have entered the lexicon in a sermon preached by Martin Luther King, Jr. See King, "Levels of Love" 438–39; and Spillers, "The Permanent Obliquity of an In(pha)llibly Straight," in *Black, White, and in Color*, 240.

29 "MB," 70, 72–73, 80. In the Romantic period, effeminacy coded as monstrous: "Nor does Effeminacy, wherever it governs the Monster, who possesses a plentiful Fortune, stop at the most absurd and inconsistent Actions." Though effeminacy here may reference sodomy, could Spillers be critiquing the Romantic feminine by "queering" and/or (re)claiming monstrosity for black feminist theory since Her gendering has historically been undone? Does She become a site of "plentiful Fortune"? See "A Well-Wisher to Great Britain," 10–14; and Elfenbein, *Romantic Genius*, 9–12, 21.

30 Sharpe, *Monstrous Intimacies*; and Moten, *In the Break*, 18.

31 Spillers posits that, "the replication of ideology is never simple in the case of female subject-positions, and it appears to acquire a thickened layer of motives in the case of African-American females" ("MB," 79). See also Walcott, "Moving Toward Black Freedom," in *The Long Emancipation*, 7; and Wilderson, "The Prison Slave as Hegemony's (Silent) Scandal," 21–26.

32 Cooper, *A Voice from the South*, 144–45 (my emphasis). For more on Cooper as foundational to "modern intersectionality theory," see Nash, *Black Feminism Reimagined*, 6–7; and for more on the Cooper-Du Bois relationship, see Washington, "Anna Julia Cooper," 9–10. Likewise, Daphne A. Brooks contends another "race woman" is lodged between Cooper and Du Bois who espouses double consciousness: Pauline Hopkins. See Brooks, *Liner Notes for the Revolution*, 65–66, 86.

33 Du Bois, *The Souls of Black Folk*, 8 (my emphasis); see also Reich, "B. B. King Teaches NU Crowd a Thing or Two about the Blues"; and Cooper, *A Voice from the South* 177 (my emphasis).

34 Murray, *Stomping the Blues*, 64; and Cole, "The Blues," 160. For more on the terminological origin of "the blues," see Bolden, *Afro-blue*, 39.

35 NPR Staff, "Indigo"; hereafter, "Indigo"; Murray, *Stomping the Blues*, 64; and Bolden, *Afro-blue*, 39. Oliphant also references "the blues" and "blue devils" in Henry David Thoreau's *Walden*. See Oliphant, *Texan Jazz*, 368n2.

36 McKinley, *Indigo*, ix. See also "Indigo."

37 Cole, "The Blues," 160. The metaphor of people craving the sky is linguistically self-determinative: In South Africa, the word "Zulu" means "sky" or "heaven," that is, Zulus translate to "the people of the sky."

38 Robinson, *Black Marxism*, 404–5n6, 405–6n10; Equiano, *The Interesting Narrative of the Life of Olaudah Equiano . . .* , 47; and Alexander, "Absence," in "The Negro Digs Up Her Past," 467. For Freud, identification is interchangeable with "introjection" ("Mourning and Melancholia," 240n1); and related to what was brought to the New World, Fatima El Shibli argues that the blues may have been influenced by Islam since West African Muslims were Transatlantic cargo. See El Shibli, "Islam and the Blues," 162–70.

39 Taylor, *Black Is Beautiful*, 1; and Lehman, "Blue History." For more on the affective toll of the slave ship, see Bruce, *How to Go Mad Without Losing Your Mind*, 1–5.

40 LeRoi Jones/Imamu Amiri Baraka, *Blues People*, 2; and Alexander, "Absence," 467. For more on indigo and new-world blackness, see King, "The Labor of (Re)reading Plantation Landscapes Fungible(ly)," 1022–39.

41 Robinson, *Black Marxism*, 5, 121–71. Clyde Woods equally converses with Taylor: He "originally intended to call [the blues epistemology] 'the blues ontology'" because "what ontology might have done is draw on Robinson's insights about the entire worlds that also travelled in slave ships—via captives' consciousness and culture—and the subsequent forms of being made palpable in otherwise unendurable situations." See Woods, *Development Arrested*, xii. And regarding national fabric, in her interview with Catherine McKinley, Michel Martin states, "[T]he sails that powered Columbus' journey to the so-called New World . . . were, in fact, indigo"; McKinley replies that the indigo-dyed sails were "denim . . . and the original American flag was made from indigo textile." Martin exclaims, "So it's literally woven into the fabric of the country." This is the "blueness" of blackness—a stolen African good, and an affective posture.

42 Taylor, *Black Is Beautiful*, 2; Mackey, *From a Broken Bottle Traces of Perfume Still Emanate*; and Spillers, "'All the Things You Could Be By Now If Sigmund Freud's Wife Was Your Mother,'"140; hereafter, "Things."

43 See "Omni-american"; and Du Bois, *Souls of Black Folk*, 3.

44 Wright, "Blueprint for Negro Writing," 196–97. See also Wright, "Introduction," xxxi–xxxiv.

45 Hughes, "Mother to Son," *The Collected Poems*, 30. See also Miller, *The Art and Imagination of Langston Hughes*, 35–37. Hughes's corpus is rife with the maternal, and maternal adjacent, imparting affect to the "son." Another example is "Aunt Sue's Stories":

Aunt Sue cuddles a brown-faced child to her bosom
And tells him stories.

. . .

And black slaves
Singing sorrow songs on the banks of a mighty river
Mingle themselves softly
In the flow of old Aunt Sue's voice,

. . .

And the dark-faced child, listening,
Knows that Aunt Sue's stories are real stories.
He knows that Aunt Sue never got her stories
Out of any book at all,
But they came
Right out of her own life.

. . .

The dark-faced child is quiet
Of a summer night
Listening to Aunt Sue's stories.

Embracing the child as if to rock him to sleep, Aunt Sue's stories are lullabies. Her vocal flow parallels a "mighty river," providing the rhythm for melancholy-tinged mellifluousness. The child's attentive listening, "quiet," marks how the replay of sorrow signposts the emergence of the "real." See Hughes, "Aunt Sue's Stories," *The Collected Poems*, 23–24.

46 Davis, *Blues Legacies and Black Feminism*, 4–6, 77 (my emphasis); and Lordi, *Black Resonance*, 18.

47 Wall, *Worrying the Line*, 7–8; and Spillers, "Fabrics of History," 71. Wall refers to "worrying the line" as "a blues trope . . . the blueswoman is a symbol of female creativity and autonomy whose art informs and empowers . . . worrying the line may be used for purposes of emphasis, clarification, or subversion." I similarly foreground the black feminine/maternal and her ability to be and create genius, despite melancholy, through subversion.

48 For more on blackness and the human, see Walcott, "2. Black Life-Forms," *The Long Emancipation*, 9–10.

49 "Things," 97–99.

50 McGowan, *Enjoying What We Don't Have*, 263–64 (my emphasis); and Terrefe, "Speaking the Hieroglyph," 142.

51 Cheng, *The Melancholy of Race*, 8; and Freud, "Mourning and Melancholia," 246.

52 My "elemental" turn can be interpreted multiply, whether it is "in life, you live and lose" or to "stay black and die" is necessary for the continuity of "the world" à la Calvin L. Warren. Thus, the phrase is psychoanalytic. See Warren, *Ontological Terror*, 7.

53 Though not exhaustive, a list of recent works regarding black maternity, aside from what has been cited heretofore, includes Gumbs, China, and Williams, *Revolutionary Mothering*, 101–36; Celeste, "'What Now?,'" 110–31; and Owens, "Still, Nothing," 70–84.

54 Wright, "Blueprint," 198; and Crawford, "The Twenty-First-Century Black Studies Turn to Melancholy," 799.

55 Singleton, *Cultural Melancholy*, 10. He tracks with Diana Taylor's "performance ghosting," which "makes visible (for an instant, live, now) that which is always already there: the ghosts, the tropes, the scenarios that structure over individual and collective life . . . alter future phantoms, future fantasies." See Taylor, *The Archive and the Repertoire*, 142. For Singleton, "embodied practice is a site where the living and the dead [commingle], organizing our scenarios of interaction and infusing our sense of self and community with the memories that belong to some other body, place, and time" (13).

56 Etoke, *Melancholia Africana*, 10.

57 Derrida, *Geneses, Genealogies, Genres, and Genius*, 1. Additional historicizations of genius include Elfenbein, *Romantic Genius*; Stadler, *Troubling Minds*; Battersby, "*Gender and Genius*," 559–70; Korsmeyer, "Genius," in *Gender and Aesthetics*, 29–31; and Williams, "Genius," 143–44. Likewise, for the section heading, see West, "Monster," *My Beautiful Dark Twisted Fantasy*; and the Moten quote occurred during a lecture Q&A in his capacity as the Visiting Distinguished Professor in the Program for the Study of Women, Gender, and Sexuality at Johns Hopkins University, February 18, 2021.

58 Derrida, 91; and "genius, n. and adj.," OED *Online*. Battersby discusses how "the English term 'genius' was as associated with male sexual and generative powers as the Latin *genius* . . . the Roman *genius* involved the divine aspects of male procreativity which insured the continuance of property belonging to the *gens* or male clan . . . the fertility of the land, as well as the fertility of the man." See Battersby, "*Gender and Genius*," 563.

59 Immanuel Kant, *The Critique of Judgment*, 188. Expanding this reading of "Art," specifically craft guilds, Battersby writes that while women were active in them, they were soon removed when "artists" and "craftsmen" became distinct offices; men eventually hoarded all artistic wealth. See Battersby, "*Gender and Genius*," 561.

60 Battersby, "*Gender and Genius*," 564; and Eng and Kazanjian, "Introduction," 7–8. Foucault also explicates the humors' affection: "The world of melancholia

was humid, heavy, and cold; that of mania was parched, dry, compounded of violence and fragility; a world which heat—unfelt but everywhere manifested—made arid, friable, and always ready to relax under the effect of a moist coolness." See Foucault, *Madness and Civilization*, 129.

61 James, "The Womb of Western Theory," 260.

62 "genius," OED, def. 1a and 2.

63 Winnicott, *Playing and Reality*, 13–14, 16; and "genius," OED, def. 8a. Regarding the maternal as composite, "When Winnicott uses the term 'mother' he usually means it to signify the person who is in the mothering role—the mother might therefore be a person other than the natural mother, and may even be father." See Jacobs, *D. W. Winnicott*, 47.

64 "genius," OED, def. 1b; and Winnicott, *Playing and Reality*, 108–9.

65 Battersby, "*Gender and Genius*," 564–65.

66 Elfenbein, *Romantic Genius* 5, 17. See also Eng, *Racial Castration*, 4–5.

67 "MB," 68; and Morrison, *Beloved*, 16–17. This also extends to wet nursing. See Dunaway, *The African-American Family in Slavery and Emancipation*, 134–41.

68 Siddhartha Mitter, "Kara Walker Takes a Monumental Jab at Brittania"; and Grandy, *Narrative of the Life of Moses Grandy*, 17. Regarding Queen Vicky, she "is alive, joyful and caught mid-laughter. At her feet is a crouching personification of *Melancholy*, a human representation of deep sadness. His bowed head and crouched demeanour contrasts with the lively *Queen Vicky* who also holds a coconut at her breasts, a symbol of life and sustenance." The woman Melancholy is beneath could be his lost object—does this uncannily render "stay black and die"? See "Look Closer—Kara Walker's *Fons Americanus*."

69 Tate, *Psychoanalysis and Black Novels*, 18 (my emphasis).

70 King offers a similar subordination when "[Sylvia] Wynter and Frank Wilderson meet," namely Wilderson posits "a more extreme—or less orthodox—end of Fanon's notion of the zone of nonbeing that the Black is nonhuman. In fact, the Black must be rendered nonhuman for White subjects to know their own humanity." See King, *The Black Shoals*, 17–18.

71 Phillips, *Winnicott*, 93; and Winnicott, *Playing and Reality*, 16. Winnicott arrived at "suspended animation" by taking "the ordinary development born of good-enough mothering as the norm and then set out to understand whatever interfered with it." Slavery is an obvious interference, and Winnicott's aporia.

72 Winters, *Hope Draped in Black*, 6.

73 Snorton, *Black on Both Sides*, 104.

74 Hughes, *The Negro Mother and Other Dramatic Recitations*, 156.

75 "Things," 140.

76 Hughes, *Ask Your Mama*.

77 Freud, "Mourning and Melancholia," 243.

78 Seigworth and Gregg, "An Inventory of Shimmers," 1. Regarding the absence of race in affect theory, see Palmer, "What Feels More Than Feeling?," 35.

79 Seigworth and Gregg, "An Inventory of Shimmers," 2 (my emphasis).

80 Khanna, "Touching, Unbelonging, and the Absence of Affect," 230; and Brooks, "Primer for Blacks," 119.

81 Harper, *Abstractionist Aesthetics*, 4. Palmer aligns with Harper when describing abstraction: "This very malleability [of being], or 'fungibility,' as an ontological fact of blackness, positions the Black body as an abstraction upon and through which the desires, feelings, and ideas of others are projected" (37). To my mind, these sentiments sync with Darby English regarding Black art production: "My issue with generalization is that it feels an irresponsible way to respond to art's diversity and specificity. . . . Accounts of art that suppress variation, that are nonchalant about those precious opportunities, need to be resisted." See Ologundudu, "Art Historian Darby English on Why the New Black Renaissance Might Actually Represent a Step Backwards."

82 Seigworth and Gregg, "An Inventory of Shimmers," 11 (my emphasis). See also Latour, "How to Talk about the Body?," 205.

83 Spillers, "Interstices," in *Black, White, and in Color*, 155 (emphasis in original); Jackson, *Becoming Human*, 3, 219n2; Hartman, *Scenes of Subjection*, 119; and "Becoming Human." See also Griffin, "That the Mothers May Soar and the Daughters May Know Their Names," 497; and Holland, *Raising the Dead*, 43.

84 Khanna, "Touching, Unbelonging, and the Absence of Affect," 216; and "Things," 84. See also Griffin, "That the Mothers May Soar," 495–96; and Terrefe, "Speaking the Hieroglyph," 130, 137.

85 Spillers, "Mama's Baby, Papa's, Too," 3; "Things," 125; and Stadler, *Troubling Minds*, xv. In like manner, Kevin Quashie, also thinking with Spillers, contrives my "individual" as his "one" and vice versa; despite our semantic differentiation, some similarity holds. See Quashie, *Black Aliveness, or A Poetics of Being*, 31–32, 38–39.

86 A linguistic convention regarding the multiplied individual: The general Zulu greeting is "Sawubona"/"Sanibona." "-wu-" and "-ni-" respectively mark the second-person singular and plural as the phrase translates to "I see you," that is, even if one person greets one person, uttering "Sanibona" conveys, "I see [all of] you"—an acknowledgment of the ancestral plane surrounding the singularly greeted. And for blackness and pathology, see Sexton, "The Social Life of Social Death," 26–28; and Sharpe, "Response to 'Ante-Anti-Blackness.'"

87 "Things," 105, 108; 87; 111; 127–40; and 115.

88 Morrison, 88–89. Bile is a trope throughout her work; for example, Sula's grandmother, Eva, has an "absence of bile." For more, see Schreiber, *Race, Trauma, and Home in the Novels of Toni Morrison*, 65–106; and Akhtar, *Dismemberment in the Fiction of Toni Morrison*, 79–105.

89 "Things," 140.

90 King, Jr., "Where Do We Go from Here" (1967), 246 (my emphasis).

91 Fanon, *Black Skin, White Masks*, 206; and Marriott, *On Black Men*, x.

92 Morrison, "It Is Like Growing Up Black One More Time." To my mind, a counterpoint to Morrison is the Last Poets' "Black Is Chant" and "Black Is," two records on an album ironically called *This Is Madness* (Douglas, 1971). For more on Morrison's *Book*, see Crawford, *What Is African American Literature?*, 14–15. By extension, regarding *The Bluest Eye*, Morrison writes about penning the novel, "the struggle was for writing that was indisputably black.

I don't know yet quite what that is, but neither that nor attempts to disqualify an effort to find out keeps me from trying to pursue it." This is what I am up to here. See Morrison, "Foreword," in *The Bluest Eye*, xii.

93 "Things," 140 (my emphasis); and Brand, *The Blue Clerk*, 8.

94 Harper, *Abstractionist Aesthetics*, 2; and Snorton, *Black on Both Sides*, 106–7. For more on abstraction, see Quashie, *Black Aliveness, or A Poetics of Being*, 43–55.

95 Freud, "Mourning and Melancholia," 247, 253; and Battersby, "*Gender and Genius*," 560. Insanity, especially regarding blackness, is perhaps best seen in the diagnosis of drapetomania. See Metzl, *The Protest Psychosis*, ix.

96 Freud, "Mourning and Melancholia," 254.

97 Jacobs, *Incidents in the Life of a Slave Girl*, 173–78. See also Wright, *Black Girlhood in the Nineteenth Century*, 15.

98 Tate, *Psychoanalysis and Black Novels*, 10 (my emphasis); and Griffin, *In Search of Billie Holiday*, 14.

99 "MB," 80.

100 Leonard, *Fettered Genius*, 4; and James, "The Womb of Western Theory," 264–66.

101 Harper, "Crazy," 25.

102 Harper, "Crazy," 27 (my emphasis). Ironically, men performing maternity to birth cool is a trope found in a series of letters between Alain Locke and Hughes as Locke metaphorizes his body as parental and a midwife in the cause of poetry. See Marriott, *Haunted Life*, 134–50.

103 Ecclesiastes 9:11a; and Matthew 24:13.

104 Musser, *Sensual Excess*, 3–4.

105 Musser, *Sensual Excess*, 5.

106 Musser, *Sensual Excess*, 170.

107 Mark Kernan, "In Praise of Melancholia." For more on the blue note/the blues having "a slower, more melancholy feeling . . . that allowed for freedom and improvisation," see Oliphant, *Texan Jazz*, 36.

108 Palmer, "'What Feels More Than Feeling?'" 33.

109 Jordan, "Nobody Mean More to Me Than You and the Future Life of Willie Jordan," 164 (my emphasis); and Tate, *Psychoanalysis and Black Novels*, 7.

110 Ramlochan, "Dionne Brand."

READ | FREDERICK

1 "Editor's Preface," in Douglass, *My Bondage and My Freedom*, v; hereafter, MBMF. Likewise, the notion of "lived experience" nods to "the lived experience of the black man" insofar as regardless of the gender component, these words by Frantz Fanon have also been translated as "the fact of blackness." See Fanon, "The Fact of Blackness," in *Theories of Race and Racism*, 257–66; and Fanon, "The Lived Experience of the Black Man," in *Black Skin, White Masks*, 89–119.

2　*MBMF*, xvii, xxi–xxii, xxix (my emphasis). Regarding the "man of genius" designation, see also Stadler, *Troubling Minds*, 12–13.

3　Huggins, *Slave and Citizen*, 3. There are multiple spellings of Douglass's
grandmother's name; I will use "Betsey" and "Betsy" interchangeably.

4　*MBMF*, 51–52; 58 (emphasis in original).

5　*MBMF*, 53.

6　*MBMF*, 53, 60 (my emphasis).

7　Blumenthal, "Canonicity, Genre, and the Politics of Editing," 178–79.

8　Eng, *Racial Castration*, 4–5. See also Singleton, *Cultural Melancholy*, 6–7;
Tate, "Freud and His 'Negro,'" 58–61; and Rocchi, "Literature and the Meta-
Psychoanalysis of Race," 52–67. Jacques Lacan also makes this claim: "our
discipline—which, justifying its field in terms of sexuality, seemed to promise
to bring the whole secret of sexuality to light." See Lacan, *Écrits*, 612.

9　Klein, *The Psychoanalysis of Children*, 218. See also Klein, "Mourning and
Its Relation to Manic-Depressive States," 125–53. For criticism of this essay,
which concludes Klein is analyst and analysand in her work, see Steiner, "The
Conflict between Mourning and Melancholia," 98–99.

10　Walker, *David Walker's Appeal . . .* , 1 (my emphasis); and Fanon, *The Wretched
of the Earth*. Moreover, the "wretched" respectively prefigure and exceed Walker.
See Equiano, *The Interesting Narrative of the Life of Olaudah Equiano . . .* , 41;
and Jacobs, *Incidents in the Life of a Slave Girl, . . .* , 173.

11　*MBMF*, 88. For more on this, see Sharpe, *Monstrous Intimacies*, 1–9.

12　Freud, "Mourning and Melancholia," 243. Some recent work addresses
whether there is continuity between melancholia and depression; though I am
careful claiming that, the work is noteworthy. See Varga, "From Melancholia
to Depression," 141–55; and Tettenborn, "Melancholia as Resistance in Contemporary African American Literature," 103–6.

13　Foucault, *The History of Sexuality*, 1; hereafter, *HS*. For photography of black
Victorians, see O'Hagan, "The Black Victorians."

14　Stauffer, "Frederick Douglass and the Aesthetics of Freedom," 122–23; hereafter, "FDAF"; and Freud, "Mourning and Melancholia," 250.

15　Eliot, *Daniel Deronda*, 3; 214; 57; Douglass, *The Narrative of the Life of
Frederick Douglass, An American Slave*, 22; hereafter, *Narrative*; and Giles,
"Douglass's Black Atlantic," 134, 141; hereafter, "DBA." For more on Douglass's
transatlanticism, see Giles, *Virtual Americas*, 22–46; and Gilroy, *The Black
Atlantic*, 58–71.

16　Freud, "Mourning and Melancholia," 250–51.

17　*HS*, 3 (my emphasis).

18　Haraway, *Simians, Cyborgs, and Women*, 170.

19　Foucault, *Madness and Civilization*, 16; and Freud, "Mourning and Melancholia," 253. I also borrow from Holloway, *Private Bodies, Public Texts*.

20　McLennan, *Studies in Ancient History. . . .*

21　*MBMF*, 64; and Hartman, "The Belly of the World," 168. See also Sexton, *Black
Men, Black Feminism*, 86–89. The plantation-as-"little nation" persists in the

Narrative: Colonel Lloyd's "plantation . . . was the seat of government for the whole twenty farms. . . . If a slave was convicted of any high misdemeanor, became unmanageable, or evinced a determination to run away, he was brought immediately here, severely whipped, put on board the sloop, and sold . . . as a warning to the slaves remaining" (26–27).

22 Davis, "Reflections on the Black Woman's Role in the Community of Slaves," 5.

23 Hartman, "The Belly of the World," 169. Tiffany Lethabo King tracks with this when unpacking the illegibility of the "Black family" in the West via Kay Lindsey: "The family as a social formation can be reconceived as an amalgamation of land, slaves, property, conquest and the state. The family could be constructed as a geopolitical unit or assemblage (family-land-slaves-property-state-empire) that creates the American frontier, or the time-space coordinates of the human. The family as the geopolitical unit of women-children-land-slaves is a form of property that can be accumulated." See King, "Black 'Feminisms' and Pessimism," 74; and Lindsey, "The Black Woman as a Woman," 103–8.

24 "Left of Black with Hortense Spillers and Alexis Pauline Gumbs"; and *HS*, 3–4. Davis too opines animality regarding these liaisons: "Aspiring with his sexual assaults to establish her as a female animal, [the white master] would be striving to destroy her proclivities toward resistance" ("Reflections on the Black Woman's Role in the Community of Slaves," 13). That said, these sentiments sync with Fanon and James H. Cone: "when the colonist speaks of the colonized he uses zoological terms"; therefore, "[a]nd certainly the history of the black-white relations in this country from the Civil War to the present unmistakably shows that as a people, America has never intended for blacks to be free . . . the black man remains subhuman." See Fanon, *The Wretched of the Earth*, 7; and Cone, *Black Theology and Black Power*, 10.

25 *MBMF*, 59. See also Jacobs, *Incidents in the Life of a Slave Girl*, 85.

26 Weheliye, *Habeas Viscus*, 11. See also Sexton, *Black Men, Black Feminism*, 78-86.

27 R. L., "Inextinguishable Fire."

28 Wallace, *Constructing the Black Masculine*, 84; and Kristeva, *Black Sun*, 27.

29 For the Hagar-Ishmael narrative, see Genesis 16; 21:1–21; on Douglass and religion, see Huggins, *Slave and Citizen*, 8, 18–19; and regarding "[t]he whisper" of Douglass's paternity, see *Narrative*, 22; and *MBMF*, 58.

30 *MBMF*, 47 (my emphasis). For more on Douglass's grandmother in the autobiographies, see Riss, "Sentimental Douglass," 103–10. Leigh Fought also outlines this series of losses when Douglass refers to the rotating departures of "children living with Betsey in the cabin as 'not her own, but her grandchildren—the children of her daughters,'" even though this was not entirely accurate: Having birthed children well into her forties, she was raising, and losing, her children as well. See Fought, *Women in the World of Frederick Douglass*, 13–19.

31 Tettenborn, "Melancholia as Resistance in Contemporary African American Literature," 114.

32 Freud, "Mourning and Melancholia," 249–51 (emphasis in original, my boldface).

33 Kristeva, *Black Sun*, 26; and Marriott, *On Black Men*, xiv (my emphasis). I also rhetorically borrow from Washington, "Zora Neale Hurston," 1–19.

34 Baraka, "Poetry and Karma," 23. Being "loved to death" tracks with Aliyyah I. Abdur-Rahman quoting Elisabeth Young-Bruehl: "'as domestic or slaves or as a fantasized part of the prejudiced persons household, [they] are love and hate objects. . . . They are needed alive, so they can be loved like mammies, prostituted or raped like whores, sexually mutilated, beaten, deprived of their power, crippled, emasculated—and in all instances kept in their place.'" See Abdur-Rahman, *Against the Closet*, 34. See also Jacobs, *Incidents in the Life of a Slave Girl*, 58–66; and Wright, *Black Girlhood in the Nineteenth Century*, 11–12. Also, regarding wickedness in the flesh, see Johnson, *Wicked Flesh*.

35 Kristeva, *Black Sun*, 26 (my boldface).

36 Scherman, "The Omni-american"; *Narrative*, 30; and *MBMF*, 217 (my emphasis). Though not an exhaustive list, I think particularly about Hughes, "Note on Commercial Theatre," in *The Collected Poems of Langston Hughes*, 216; hereafter, *CP*; Ellison, *Invisible Man*, 3–14; Jones/Baraka, *Blues People*; Cone, *The Spirituals and the Blues*; Davis, *Blues Legacies and Black Feminism*; and Brooks, *Liner Notes for the Revolution*. See also Cruz, *Culture on the Margins*, 1–6, 15–16; and Griffin, "When Malindy Sings," 109–10.

37 *Narrative*, 29–30.

38 Stadler, *Troubling Minds*, 10 (my emphasis); and Freud, "Mourning and Melancholia," 253. Jennifer Lynn Stoever argues, "the slave songs Douglass exhumes refuse to remain in the past, creating a dissonant aural effect." See Stoever, *The Sonic Color Line*, 48–51.

39 "A demand is placed on Douglass by the reader and all that the reader doubles in transference, in his attempt to pierce, enter, play, violate the circle." See Moten, "Bridge and the One," in *Performing Hybridity*, 240.

40 Spillers, "Mama's Baby, Papa's Maybe," 72.

41 *Narrative*, 30; Freud, "Mourning and Melancholia," 254; and George, *Trauma and Race*, 3. See also Lacan, "On Jouissance," 1–13. While Lacan's lecture primarily takes up sexual *jouissance* between men and women, "jouissance of the Other's body" (4), his discussion of phallic *jouissance* ("Jouissance, qua sexual, is phallic—in other words, it is not related to the Other as such" [9]) interests me, and how it synchronizes with his conversation on "the One [which] is based only on (*tenir de*) the essence of the signifier" (5): Is phallic singularity what Douglass confers on the man singing in desolation, only to conflate him, through "contentment and happiness," with the singing slave?

42 Glissant, *Poetics of Relation*, 203.

43 Glissant, *Poetics of Relation*, 203.

44 Woods, *Development Arrested*, 25, 26, 29, 39.

45 *MBMF*, xxix–xxxi. The Ralph Ellison nod is serendipitous: Douglass is present in *Invisible Man* through portraiture, no different than pharaoh's bust. Moreover,

McCune Smith's "roll call" of the black aesthetic canon is how Ellison situates himself within the broader American literary canon such that he wonders why he is the namesake of Ralph Waldo Emerson and not Douglass. See Ellison, *Invisible Man*, 378–81, 428, 442; Ellison, *Shadow and Act*, 45–59, 151; Magee, *Emancipating Pragmatism*, 102; and Cook and Tatum, *African American Writers and Classical Tradition*, 89–91.

46 Haley, *The Autobiography of Malcolm X*, 167–71; and Levine, "Identity in the Autobiographies," 36; hereafter, "Identity." Like the Nation, Douglass also mythologizes whiteness: "It is only about six centuries since the blue-eyed and fair-haired Anglo-Saxons were considered inferior by the haughty Normans . . . you will find that this proud Anglo-Saxon was once looked upon as of coarser clay than his Norman master, and might be found in the highways and byways of Old England laboring with a brass collar on his neck, and the name of his master marked upon it." See Douglass, "What the Black Man Wants (1865)," 55.

47 Levine, "Road to Africa," 220, 226; hereafter, "RtA"; "DBA," 143; and "FDAF," 124–26.

48 For this term's origin, see Schuessler, "Use of 'African-American' Dates to Nation's Early Days"; and "The Term 'African-American' Appears Earlier Than Thought: Reporter's Notebook."

49 *Narrative*, 22.

50 I will call Douglass "Frederick Bailey" throughout this chapter section because I am interested in the self-naming surrounding his "death" and "resurrection."

51 *Narrative*, 67–70; Mackey, *Discrepant Engagement*, 245–46; and Bruce, "James Corrothers Reads a Book," 667. For Jenkins as conjurer, see Huggins, *Slave and Citizen*, 10.

52 *Narrative*, 70; Huggins, *Slave and Citizen*, 10; and MBMF, 244–45.

53 Yothers, *Reading Abolition*, 129; and McFeely, *Frederick Douglass*, 46–48.

54 MBMF, 241–44 (my emphasis). Figure 1.3 recounts the fight using *Narrative* (70–71). That said, "Read | Frederick" engenders my interest in the artistic liberties taken to depict those in his orbit. For example, outside of the image in Prichard's text, Douglass superficially explains the appearance of his matrilineage: "My grandmother . . . was marvelously straight in figure, elastic, and muscular"; and "My knowledge of my mother is very scanty, but very distinct. Her personal appearance and bearing are ineffaceably stamped upon my memory. She was tall, and finely proportioned; of deep black, glossy complexion, had regular features, and, among the other slaves, was remarkably sedate in her manners" (MBMF, 46, 52). Yet in David F. Walker and Damon Smyth's *The Life of Frederick Douglass*, both women are illustrated counter to these conjectures; yet first wife Anna Murray and Abraham Lincoln keep their veracity as transmitted through photographic evidence (vii, ix). Similarly, though Stauffer shares Covey's demographic data, in the comic strip and graphic novel, neither rendering syncs. Inasmuch as matrilineal literacy catalyzes Douglass's imagination, he apparently catalyzes it in others—the interplay of ART and FACTS.

55 Hughes, "Dream Variations," CP, 40.

56 Hughes, "Frederick Douglass: 1817–1895," in *The Panther and the Lash*, 31. Regarding Douglass elegies, their transmission and fame compel others to write about him, in particular Dudley Randall's "Frederick Douglass and the Slave Breaker": "I knew that two other poets, Robert Hayden and Langston Hughes, had already written two famous poems about Douglass, so I was treading on hallowed ground." See Boyd, *Wrestling with the Muse*, 228; and Randall, "Frederick Douglass and the Slave Breaker," in *Roses and Revolutions*, 109.

57 Goldstone, "Hughes, Langston (1902–1967)," 85. R. Baxter Miller views the poem as "optimistic. In "Frederick Douglass," his narrator anticipates the return of good, despite a period of regression, like that which began in 1895, the year of Douglass's death, with the Atlanta Compromise speech in which Booker T. Washington spoke of the races as being "separate as the five fingers." See Miller, "Langston Hughes, 1902–1967," 58.

58 Stauffer, *Giants*, 32; hereafter, *Giants*. Cynthia R. Nielsen also picks up on these Covey narrations, arguing his plantation mastery as an ante-Foucauldian instantiation of the panopticon. See Nielsen, "Resistance Is Not Futile," 254–55; and Foucault, *Discipline and Punish*, 195–228. See also *MBMF*, 210–16; and Jay, "American Literature and the New Historicism," 232.

59 Wexler, "A More Perfect Likeness," 19.

60 Genesis 32; and Butler, *The Psychic Life of Power*, 4 (my emphasis).

61 Walcott, "Moving Toward Black Freedom," in *The Long Emancipation*, 2–3; *Narrative*, 71 (my emphasis); and Huggins, *Slave and Citizen*, 9–15. This "triumph" from the Covey fight again projects Freud as Douglassonian: "all states such as . . . triumph, which give us the normal model for mania, depend on the same economic conditions. . . . when a long and arduous struggle is finally crowned with success" (254). As well, Sharpe concedes the fight indexing Douglass's "making and unmaking in the same moment"; see Sharpe, *Monstrous Intimacies*, 9. For more on the name change, see Fishkin, *Writing America*, 75–76.

62 Boissoneault, "The Hidden History of Anna Murray Douglass."

63 Fought, *Women in the World of Frederick Douglass*, 15. In the Bible, Jacob's father's name is Isaac.

64 *Narrative*, 48 (my emphasis); "Moses Hogan Chorale—Elijah Rock"; Hughes, "Dream Variations," *CP*, 40; and Farley, "Perfecting Slavery," 254.

65 Velde, "The Cat as Sacred Animal of the Goddess Mut," 127–37.

66 "FDAF," 116–17 (my emphasis). See also Douglass, "Pictures and Progress," 452–73; hereafter, "Pictures."

67 Stauffer poses Kant and Edmund Burke as Douglass's interlocutors ("FDAF," 117). To read the similarities, see Kant, *The Critique of Judgment*. Furthermore, regardless of whom he read, if Douglass engages in philosophical thought, his characterization of dogs, let alone Covey as such, joins a genealogy, as far back as "ninth-century Arabic literatus . . . al-Jāḥiz," of construing the animal as lacking "the capacity for deliberative reason." Does this confirm Douglass's Pan-African linkage? See Judy, *Sentient Flesh*, 440–46.

68 Bennett, *Being Property Once Myself*, 2; and Jackson, *Becoming Human*, 56.

69 Wexler, "A More Perfect Likeness," 23 (my emphasis). See also "Pictures," 465.

70 Derrida, *Specters of Marx*, 1–61.

71 Jacobs, *Incidents in the Life of a Slave Girl*, 16; Redmond, "Tip Toes and River Rolls," 151; and Walker, "Foreword," xi. Nick Nesbitt's Marxist account of the enslaved-as-machine also converges, through different means, with mine. See Nesbitt, "The Slave-Machine."

72 Sharpe, "Black Studies," 63.

73 Sean Ross Meehan reads this clock metaphor as a cypher for photography, affirming my eye preoccupation. See Meehan, *Mediating American Autobiography*, 157–59; and for another reading of Douglass as "king," see *MBMF*, 54–56.

74 Biblical passages abound regarding the right hand as a sign of power: Matthew 22:44; Acts 2:33; 7:55–56; Romans 8:34; Ephesians 1:20; Colossians 3:1; Hebrews 1:3, 8:1, 10:12, 12:2; 1 Peter 3:22; and Revelation 3:21.

75 *MBMF*, 247 (emphasis in original).

76 Huggins, *Slave and Citizen*, 1–3 (my emphasis). Ralph Waldo Emerson offers an (in)direct take on Douglass's genius, though it is couched in a peculiar display of homoeroticism/-sociality, reducing Douglass to a commodity based on his appearance and how he pervaded space; this may be another way to say jealousy(?). See Stadler, *Troubling Minds*, 13–20.

77 Hudson, "Frederick Douglass and American Empire in Haiti." And regarding Douglass's physical appearance, namely his hair, see Cobb, *New Growth*, 25–27; 48–55.

78 Goldstone, "Hughes, Langston (1902–1967)," 85.

79 Phillips, *When Blackness Rhymes with Blackness*, 79–80.

80 *MBMF*, 249; and Byron, *Childe Harold's Pilgrimage*, 102. For what it is worth, Hughes may misquote Douglass insofar as I have not found evidence, and it could exist, of him inserting "first" when quoting Byron; that insertion in the phrase presumably happens via Henry Highland Garnet in 1843. Though Phillips riffs on the added word in relation to Douglass (81–82), I want to stay true to Douglass's rewriting. See Levine, "Part One. Pittsburgh, the *Mystery*, Freemasonry," in *Martin R. Delany*, 27.

81 Burke, *The Works of the Right Honourable Edmund Burke. . . .*

82 Douglass, *Men of Color, to Arms!* For more on Byron's phrase in abolitionist rhetoric, see Rediker, *The Amistad Rebellion*, 233–34; and Phillips, *When Blackness Rhymes with Blackness*, 78–79.

83 Gray, *The Confessions of Nat Turner*, 4; and Spillers, "Moving on Down the Line," 96, 102. Bowen, quoted by Spillers, states: "On the other hand, a people 'that would be free must strike the first blow: and this race, if it is to be counted, must resolutely set itself to the answering of the question, What shall *we* do for ourselves? It must give up the unreasonable and unhistorical basis of expecting to have its future made for it, and begin with might and main to write its own history and make its own future'" (102). Saying this in Washington, DC, highlights that (regional) spirit of revolt.

84 JanMohamed, *The Death-Bound-Subject*, 285.

85 Haraway, *Simians, Cyborgs, and Women*, 174–77 (my emphasis). Soyica Diggs Colbert parallels Haraway: Through dance, she surmises the black body "as ubiquitously cyborgian and therefore mutable, self-generative, transformative, and innovative." See Colbert, *Black Movements*, 54.

86 Lorde, *Zami*; and Haraway, *Simians, Cyborgs, and Women*, 174, who furthers Lorde's logic by contriving the cyborg as *Sister Outsider*, the title of Lorde's essay collection.

87 Haraway, *Simians, Cyborgs, and Women*, 1.

88 Chaney, "Picturing the Mother, Claiming Egypt," 400.

89 Prichard, *The Natural History of Man*, 159. The picture of Ramses II is on page 157. Vincent Woodard tracks with this sentiment too in *The Delectable Negro*, 123–25.

90 Vargas and James, "Refusing Blackness-as-Victimization," 201. For a problematizing of the cyborg as "an assemblage yoked to anti-Blackness and ableism," see Pickens, *Black Madness :: Mad Blackness*, 19–20. With Pickens in mind, I want to say something, possibly counterintuitive, so here it goes: In the same way that calling Douglass a "cyborg" is "backdated," that being anachronistic, so too would calling him "ableist" in that both terms emerge in contemporary parlance, the latter more recent than the former. At the same time, Pickens's valid critique of Donna Haraway is not lost on me, though I cite her solely on the premise of the cyborg being linked to "US black women" and their capacity for literacy, a capacity Douglass predatively imbues to his mother, Harriet Bailey. Nevertheless, given the recent Pickens quotation, she completes her thought by saying, "What the cyborg ushers in . . . is . . . a method of becoming that requires theoretical overcoming since the theories rely on but refuse disabled and Black embodiment." I want to complicate this: Whether "humanity" is accessible to the slave, the fact that Douglass, as well as Harriet Jacobs, makes a machinic gesture in print—let alone in an abolitionist speech for him, or an autobiography for her—suggests something about his understanding of becoming *and* "Black embodiment" precisely because said language work invites his conception of becoming, embodying, the *exceptional*. That is why this chapter opens and refers to Douglass encountering his "I" between art and fact because his understanding of self-as-subject arrives on the page, ranging from chimera (slave-man-cat-Jesus) to the "Black Man at the Podium." Writing such works, then, may traffic in "ableism" because the genres mark "theoretical overcoming," most especially for someone formerly enslaved: The author of such a speech, or autobiography, pens it with the presumption of "freedom," itself a "human" invention, under which one proverbially lives, moves, and has one's being. Thus, referring to Douglass as a "cyborg" is to say that no different than my argument of him preceding psychoanalytic thought, he, as well as Jacobs, equally precedes the notion of a *cyb*ernetic *org*anism at its most originary level—the person-cum-machine; Douglass heralds Freud just as he heralds Haraway, regardless of the theorists' own critical limits, and the problematic excesses that compound such constructions up to, during, and

after the nineteenth and twentieth centuries. But some questions become all the more salient (again): Are the disabled and "the human"/"the subject" (in)compatible? Does the act of writing, and furthermore publication, whether under the abolitionist or autobiographical guise, put said (in)compatibility under pressure? If slavery renders the slave disabled—I am thinking here of the work of Jenifer L. Barclay—are slave narratives some of the earliest work in "disability studies"? This is all to say, I do not know; and perhaps I agree with Pickens, hence the allusion to counterintuition. But what I do know, I guess, is I am still, and will continue, wrestling with how to "Read | Frederick."

91 *MBMF*, 58 (my boldface, emphasis in original). For the black race as "exemplary," over and against "degrading portraits" from various sciences, see Rusert, "Delany's Comet," 806. Although Stadler approaches Douglass's genius differently—"genius is a concept increasingly given shape through particular bodies able to navigate ideal *and* particular spaces" (xxvi)—his "geography" preoccupation elides Douglass referring to his genius mother being in Tuckahoe, "the last place in the world where she would be apt to find facilities for learning" (*MBMF*, 58). While the *Narrative* is Stadler's focus, this tidbit highlights a germane opportunity to sit with the "geography of genius" as intersectional to Harriet's gender *and* race—all social signposts reducible to Douglass's intellectual reception.

92 *MBMF*, xxix; and McFeely, 18 (my emphasis). Regarding birthdate, McFeely suggests that Betsey was born in 1772 (*Frederick Douglass*, 5), while Fought cites May 1774 (*Women in the World of Frederick Douglass*, 12); as well, Fought expands on Betsey's intellectualism when discussing that she was also a farmer, fisher, maker of nets, and midwife/nurse (12–13). In these ways, she provides nourishment for, as well as births, said republic. That said, the nod to "republican formation" refers to an ongoing project by Spillers, "Toward an Ontology: Women and Republican Formation"; and Linda Brent /Harriet Jacobs also renders republican formation in *Incidents in the Life of a Slave Girl* as she "traces the family history back before the Revolutionary War, establishing her own rightful placement within the national polis by putting her family at the pivotal scene of the country's formation." See Abdur-Rahman, *Against the Closet*, 43.

93 Clewell, "Mourning Beyond Melancholia," 49 (my emphasis). For what it is worth, while elegy is a genre of poetry, Kimberly Juanita Brown exemplifies my contention that it can break with form and become multimodal, whether through the autobiography or the curated website. See Brown, "Black Elegies in Sight and Sound."

94 Clewell, "Mourning Beyond Melancholia," 48–49.

95 *Narrative*, 22 (my emphasis).

96 Blumenthal, "Canonicity, Genre, and the Politics of Editing," 184–85. See also McDowell, "In the First Place," 192–214.

97 "RtA," 225–26. For an alternate reading of McDowell and this image, see Meehan, *Mediating American Autobiography*, 170–80.

98 Spillers, "Mama's Baby, Papa's Maybe," 68. For the Franklin-Douglass duality, see Zafar, *We Wear the Mask*, 89–116; and Morgan, *Benjamin Franklin*, 50.

99 Wallace, *Constructing the Black Masculine*, 84.

100 *Giants*, 312–13 (my emphasis).

101 "FDAF," 134–35.

102 Marriott, *On Black Men*, 58 (my emphasis); and Diedrich, *Love Across Color Lines*, 331–75.

103 Martin, *The Mind of Frederick Douglass*, 136; and Washington, "Anna Julia Cooper," 7–8. See also Boissoneault, "The Hidden History of Anna Murray Douglass."

104 Clewell, "Mourning Beyond Melancholia," 47–48 (my emphasis).

105 McCluskey, "The Poet and His Art," 185; and Chrisman, "Robert Hayden," 133–34.

106 Fetrow, "Minority Reporting and Psychic Distancing in the Poetry of Robert Hayden," 118–22; and for an elegy about Hayden regarding these circumstances, see Lux, "Ode to Asa Bundy Sheffey," in *To the Left of Time*, 51.

107 Hayden, "Frederick Douglass."

108 Chrisman, "Robert Hayden," 135–36; and Fetrow, "Reading the Man," 195; hereafter, "Reading." Fetrow also reads the repetition of "when," and "this," in the sonnet: The former marks "the tone of yearning for that freedom. . . . The instinctive longing"; the latter provides "an historical portrait of Douglass, and the increasing emotional intensity of the content gathers momentum." See Fetrow, "Robert Hayden's 'Frederick Douglass,'" 82–83; hereafter, "FaM." As an aside, Fetrow further exhibits the similitude of Douglass's and Hayden's lives: He includes a "Pen and Ink Drawing" of Hayden, dated October 21, 1973, by James E. Lewis in his article—portraiture!

109 "Reading," 189–91; and McCluskey, "The Poet and His Art," 187 (my emphasis). See also *MBMF*, 160.

110 Hayden, "Frederick Douglass."

111 Hayden, "Frederick Douglass"; and "FaM," 84.

112 Alexander, "The Negro Digs Up Her Past," 465. I refer here to Isaac Julien's *Lessons of the Hour*; and an Afro Sheen commercial that played during portions of *Soul Train*. In this latter treatment, Douglass materializes at a black student's bedroom door as he leaves home with an unkept natural hairdo. What intrigues me about the commercial are the subtle hints displayed that allude to much of what I have argued in this chapter: a poster of Jesse Jackson (visuality), an African mask (Pan-Africanity), university wall banners for Iowa, Illinois, and two other institutions, and a typewriter (life of the mind/ literacy), and such. Espousing pride in oneself, Douglass emerges as a ghost who has been watching "the progress of our people." I read this moment as nostalgia for this "hero" and an opportunity for *Soul Train* viewers, some perhaps unlearned about him, to get *hip* to his *trip*. See Julien, *Lessons of the Hour*; and "Afro Sheen Commercial (Featuring Frederick Douglass)." For more on Douglass influencing poets, see Komunyakaa, "A Needful Thing,"

11–12; and for his incorporation on *Soul Train*, see Cobb, *New Growth*, 57–60; and Neal, "Soul Train and the Desire for Black Power."

113 "FaM," 83.

114 Hughes, "The Negro Mother," in *The Negro Mother and Other Dramatic Recitations*, 1. See also Miller, *The Art and Imagination of Langston Hughes*, 37–41.

115 Exodus 1:15–22–2:1–10. Regarding liberty, it is perhaps no coincidence that Hayden becomes a sonneteer in the legacy of John Keats and Gerard Manley Hopkins in that "Keats urged poets to unfetter the sonnet from traditional rigidity to allow it to [find] its own organic form"; and Hopkins, "with his 'sprung rhythm' and syntactical innovation, adapted the traditional form to his 'modern' impulse" ("FaM," 79). Hayden apparently forwards the task of setting this "bound" genre free. For understanding his insertion into this generic conversation, see McCluskey, "The Poet and His Art," 185–86.

116 Dunbar, "Frederick Douglass" in *Majors and Minors*, 17, 19.

117 Dunbar, "Frederick Douglass" in *Majors and Minors*, 3.

118 Braxton, "Introduction," xiii; and Blount, "Paul Laurence Dunbar and the African American Elegy," 242–43. Braxton also alludes to Douglass expressing "a kind, fatherly role toward the young poet" when he "arranged for Dunbar to read his poems at the Colored American Day celebration . . . and he introduced him to other black writers and artists. . . . Douglass's introduction on this occasion provided Dunbar with a wider audience, especially among black writers with whom he shared certain spiritual and aesthetic affinities. Douglass's interest also gave Dunbar increased confidence in his abilities" (xiii).

119 Psalm 68:31b (King James Version); and for the black nature nod, see Dungy, *Black Nature*.

120 Vargas and James, "Refusing Blackness-as-Victimization," 201.

121 Blount, "Paul Laurence Dunbar and the African American Elegy," 242.

122 Patten and Fredrickson Hemy, "Faith of Our Mothers," 193 (my emphasis).

123 Blount, "Paul Laurence Dunbar and the African American Elegy," 245; and Johnson, "Lift Every Voice and Sing," in *Lift Every Voice and Sing*, 101–2. See also Nurhussein, *Black Land*, 48–49. Douglass having a "thunderous" voice comes from a second Dunbar elegy for him, simply titled "Douglass":

Now, when the waves of swift dissension swarm,
And Honor, the strong pilot, lieth stark,
Oh, for thy voice high-sounding o'er the storm,
For thy strong arm to guide the shivering bark,
The blast-defying power of thy form,
To give us comfort through the lonely dark.

See Dunbar, *Lyrics of Love and Laughter*, 127–28; and Blount, "Paul Laurence Dunbar and the African American Elegy," 243–44. Likewise, for the intersections of Dunbar with the black national anthem, namely its performances at a school in Washington, DC, named in his honor, Dunbar High, "a superior segregated school par excellence" that "became a feeder to elite northern colleges," see Perry, *May We Forever Stand*, 72–109; and for the song soundtracking social movements, see Redmond, *Anthem*, 63–98.

124 Spillers, "Interstices," in *Black, White, and in Color*, 163. When referring to the subject who sees, Spillers, like Wallace, probably points to Hagar who, after fleeing Abram/Abraham and receiving help from God for her and her son Ishmael, names God *El-roi*—"the God who sees me"—because she too has seen God (Genesis 16).

125 Fought traces Douglass's family tree to his great-grandmother Jenny (*Women in the World of Frederick Douglass*, 11–12, 306).

126 Riss, "Sentimental Douglass," 113.

127 Wallace, "Form, Facticity, and the Struggle for Symmetry." For more art-fact comparisons in the autobiographies, see "Identity," 37; and "DBA," 136–37.

128 Chaney, "Picturing the Mother, Claiming Egypt," 393–98.

129 *Narrative*, 21.

130 Vargas and James, "Refusing Blackness-as-Victimization," 201.

TRAVEL | RALPH

1 Ellison, "The Little Man at Chehaw Station," 25–26 (emphasis in original); hereafter, "LM."

2 I recall here my father talking about him and his twin ploughing the family acreage before "daily life" began. They sounded "gee" and "haw" so loudly that my grandmother said that quite far away from the house, you could hear them as they made tracks in fields of growth taller than they were. To me, this memory embodies the riddle.

3 "LM," 26, 33, 37; and Spillers, "'The Little Man at Chehaw Station' Today," 7–8; hereafter, "Today."

4 "LM," 26.

5 "LM," 27; and Bosher, et al., "Introduction," 11 (my emphasis).

6 Bosher, et al., 11; Warren, *So Black and Blue*, 96–98; and Spillers, "Peter's Pans" in *Black, White and in Color*, 2; hereafter, "PP."

7 Wall, *On Freedom and the Will to Adorn*, 169. Gerald Early times Ellison's Tuskegee tenure lasting from June 1933 to the end of his junior year in 1936, so my premonition of when this conversation occurs is apt. Arnold Rampersad also speculates it occurred "[o]ne day, probably at the time of the annual music school recital in the spring of 1934," which would have been the end of Ellison's freshman year. See Early, *Ralph Ellison*, 23–27; Rampersad, *Ralph Ellison*, 71–72, 78–80; and "Today," 9–10.

8 Moten, *In the Break*, 17–18 (my emphasis); Moten, *In the Break*, 16 (emphasis in original).

9 Regarding the groove, especially in the work of Ellison, see Weheliye, *Phonographies*, 1–17, 46–144.

10 Freud, "A Note Upon the 'Mystic Writing-Pad,'" 226–30 (my emphasis).

11 Freud, "A Note Upon the 'Mystic Writing-Pad,'" 230.

12 Freud, "Mourning and Melancholia," 256–57.

13 Ellison, "To Fanny Ellison . . . September 14, 1947," in *The Selected Letters of Ralph Ellison*, 234; hereafter, *TSL*. See also Young, "Ralph Ellison's Slow-Burning Art"; hereafter, "Slow-Burning."

14 The Notorious B.I.G. (featuring Sadat X), "Come On."

15 Posing these questions heralds my argument: The black feminine/maternal is the very person(s) to whom the questioner finds the answer. See Ellison, *Invisible Man*, 11; hereafter, *IM*.

16 Lawrence Jackson calls the failure a "humiliating dressing-down," thus the need of Harrison's "dressing(-up)." See Jackson, *Ralph Ellison*, 114–15; hereafter, *REEG*. Ironically, the first iteration of "The Little Man at Chehaw Station" was as a commencement address at the Curtis Institute of Music in Philadelphia in May 1975 (Rampersad, *Ralph Ellison*, 501), so Ellison ostensibly steps into the assistive office Harrison held. See also Wall, *On Freedom and the Will to Adorn*, 169.

17 "LM," 25; and *REEG*, 99.

18 Spillers, "The Idea of Black Culture," 7–28; Gilroy, *The Black Atlantic*, 111–45; and Bromell, *The Time Is Always Now*, 98–100. Though these sources regard W. E. B. Du Bois, multiple perspectives on the "black experience" in Germany during the early twentieth century exist, especially those contemporaneous to Harrison's tenure there. See Campt, *Other Germans*; Niven, "Cornelius Johnson and a Forgotten Protest Against Hitler at the 1936 Olympics"; and Mims, "The Very Unlikely Story of Mohamed Husen—a Black Actor of Nazi Germany."

19 "LM," 30.

20 Hartman, "Ralph Ellison's Letters Reveal a Complex Philosopher of Black Expression"; hereafter, "Letters"; and "LM," 27.

21 *IM*, viii; Baraka, "So the King Sold the Farmer #39," 274; and The Angry Architect, "The Perfect Drawing." Section drawings are intriguing because they expose nonspace, or negative space, as revealed through a hypothetical "cut" of the solid form. Hence, if one were to cut into the spaces in which Ellison writes the novel, one realizes the negative spaces produced across various heights.

22 Bosher, et al., "Introduction," 12 (my emphasis).

23 *IM*, viii, xi.

24 *IM*, xi. Regarding the undercommons, particularly "a kind of comportment or ongoing experiment with and as the *general antagonism*, a kind of way of being with others" for Ellison, see Harney and Moten, *The Undercommons*, 105, 112.

25 *IM*, xi–xii; and "Today," 6. For more on Ellison's construction of "Americanness," see Posnock, *Color and Culture*, 184–219.

26 *IM*, xiii.

27 Brody, "The Blackness of Blackness . . . Reading the Typography of *Invisible Man*," 96.

28 Macharia, "black . . . gay"; and Kazanjian, "Scenes of Speculation," 80–81.

29 *IM*, xii.

30 "LM," 36; and *IM*, xii.

31 *IM*, xii, xv. The criticism I find most appealing to Ellison's spatial theory of "Nowhere," apposite to Harrison's precarity at this moment in her performa-

tive life, comes from Badia Sahar Ahad. All this to say, it is interesting that she flees fascism only to return to deeper, and perhaps more entrenched, oppression. See Ellison, "Harlem Is Nowhere," in *Shadow and Act*, 294–302; hereafter, SA; and Ahad, *Freud Upside Down*, 97.

32 Freud, "Mourning and Melancholia," 243; and "LM," 30. I use "griot" based on Henry Louis Gates, Jr.'s "Esu[-Elegbara], the little man whose earthly dwelling place is the crossroads" in a Yoruba poem. The little man at Chehaw is this Africanism in America in that Ellison too wants "to live at the intersection of these crossroads." See Gates, *The Signifying Monkey*, 65.

33 Collins, *Black Feminist Thought*, 119, 132, 136 (my emphasis). See also O'Reilly, *Toni Morrison and Motherhood*, 1–9; and Bailey, *African American Mystery Writers*, 81.

34 Rampersad, *Ralph Ellison*, 18, 26 (my emphasis).

35 REEG, 99–100; Wall, *On Freedom and the Will to Adorn*, 165; and Freud, "Mourning and Melancholia," 257. Similarly, in a letter to Miss Hester Holloway, the best friend of Ellison's mother and "a loyal, dedicated, and grateful member of the 'tribe' as he playfully called African Americans in his 1964 rejoinder to Irving Howe," Ellison regards her like a maternal proxy who "lift[s his] spirits" after "feeling depressed"; this exemplifies how, according to Freud, the same economic conditions through which melancholy devolves into mania can transform instead to "joy, exultation or triumph" ("Mourning and Melancholia," 254). See Callahan, "John F. Callahan on Ralph Ellison's Two Inviolable Identities"; hereafter, "TII"; and TSL, 619–20.

36 Weheliye, *Phonographies*, 112–23. See also "Living with Music," in SA, 187–98; hereafter, "Living."

37 "Living," 189; 187 (my emphasis).

38 "Living," 189–90.

39 "Letters."

40 "Living," 192; Davis, *Miles*, 28–29; and Griffin, "When Malindy Sings," 116–18; hereafter, "Malindy." See also Brooks, *Liner Notes for the Revolution*, 43.

41 A byproduct of melancholy, "identification is a preliminary stage of object-choice, that it is the first way—and one that is expressed in an ambivalent fashion—in which the ego picks out an object. The ego wants to incorporate this object into itself, and . . . it wants to do so by devouring it" (Freud, "Mourning and Melancholia," 250). Via Ellison's eating, I mark a form of identification that becomes more explicit as this chapter continues. Identifying ambivalently with the (lost) object is how Ellison relates to most of the women in his life. Likewise, C. Riley Snorton offers a similar culinary fabulation when reading *Up from Slavery*: Booker T. Washington conflates his mother with molasses. See Snorton, *Black on Both Sides*, 130–31.

42 "Malindy," 113; and "Living," 190–91, 192–93.

43 Freud, "Mourning and Melancholia," 249. For more on braconnage—"'an art of using' that is like poaching in 'its clandestine nature, its tireless but quiet activity.' . . . A full analysis of a cultural artifact involves interpreting not only

the code of the artifact's intended message . . . but also the oppositional decoding, the ripping of code that has been done through the guerilla operations of various consumers." See Cobb, *The Blackwell Guide to Theology and Popular Culture*, 59–62.

44 Lee, *Mo' Better Blues*.

45 "Living," 192.

46 "Living," 193–94 (my emphasis).

47 Wright, "Blueprint for Negro Writing," 196; and "Living," 190, 195–96.

48 Freud, "Mourning and Melancholia," 250 (my emphasis).

49 O'Meally, "Living with Music," 3. See also "Living," 195–96.

50 Weheliye, *Phonographies*, 119–22; and "Living," 195.

51 Wright, *Shadowing Ralph Ellison*, 146–47; hereafter, *Shadowing*; and Weheliye, *Phonographies*, 120–21.

52 "Living," 187, 198. In the fifties, Ellison corresponds with pen pals, like Albert Murray and Saul Bellow, who "we now think of as contenders for producing" such a work ("Slow-Burning").

53 Furlonge, "'To Hear the Silence of Sound.'"

54 "Living," 196.

55 Fisher, *Habitations of the Veil*, 337–38.

56 Rampersad, *Ralph Ellison*, 224–36. See also Spillers, "Ellison's 'Usable Past,'"53–69; hereafter, "EUP." Rampersad argues *IM* is "not an autobiographical work." However, after being asked, "You weren't thrown out of school like the boy in your novel?," Ellison confesses, "No. Though, like him, I went from one job to another" (Chester and Howard, "The Art of Fiction"). Likewise, (auto)biographical gestures abound throughout Ellison's oeuvre, that is, the short stories, "Boy on a Train," "Hymie's Bull," and "I Did Not Know Their Names" (Rampersad, *Ralph Ellison*, 99–100; and *REEG*, 195). For more on (auto)biography in Ellison's writing, see Parrish, *Ralph Ellison and the Genius of America*, 104–6; hereafter, *REGA*; and Jackson, "Ralph Ellison's Invented Life," 11–34. Lastly, Ellison discusses whether the novel is autobiographical in a letter to Harrison; see *TSL*, 304–5.

57 "EUP," 62–63; *IM*, 123; and Rice, "The Invisible Man in Ralph Ellison's *Invisible Man*," 120. See also Early, *Ralph Ellison*, 27.

58 Armstrong, "(What Did I Do to Be So) Black and Blue" on *Satch Plays Fats*; and *IM*, 8. Ironically, regarding this record in the prologue, Ellison tells Langston Hughes that the novel is "the blues, but nobody understands what I mean." See *TSL*, 301; and "Slow-Burning." Moreover, Armstrong's aesthetic interrogation has contemporary heft. See Sheets, "How Glenn Ligon Is Using Black and Blue to Begin a Dialogue"; and Cotter, "Glenn Ligon Rethinks the Color Line in the Show 'Blue Black.'"

59 "EUP," 60–61 (my emphasis). Spillers, borrowing from Maud Bodkin, further explains the "archetype": "Psychic residual inherited 'in the structure of the brain, a priori, determinants of individual experience.' The specific application of Jungian theory to literary types, Bodkin's study implies the valorization of a 'Collective Unconscious' which makes it possible to ascribe psychological

motives of filiation and kinship to widely dispersed ancestral groups." These moves, even juxtaposed to disciplinary interventions regarding the psychic life, are apposite to my (other)maternal/kinship contentions.

60 "EUP," 60; and Freud, "Mourning and Melancholia," 244 (my emphasis).

61 "EUP," 60.

62 Freud, "Mourning and Melancholia," 245.

63 "EUP," 60; 53.

64 *IM*, 13. Adam Bradley considers the oddity of the number of bulbs in the basement as Ellison "playing the dozens," especially since the 3–6–9 trio is "a numeric combination with its roots in Southern hoodoo." See Bradley, *Ralph Ellison in Progress*, 1–3.

65 Collins, *Black Feminist Thought*, 132; Young, *The Grey Album*, 28–29; and *IM*, 13. Tim Parrish counteracts the idea of *Invisible Man* as not (auto)biographical; how one views Ellison, postrecital, jives with how he reads invisible man's quest to understand power. See Parrish, *Walking Blues*, 125.

66 Beckford, *Jesus Dub*, 25.

67 Griffin, "*Who Set You Flowin'?*," 134; and *IM*, 8–9 (my emphasis). For more on Dante and the novel, see Foley, *Wrestling with the Left*, 69; and "EUP," 59–60. And for the sensorial and spatiotemporal in the lair, see Mackey, *Discrepant Engagement*, 245.

68 Freud, "Mourning and Melancholia," 244 (my emphasis).

69 Beckford, *Jesus Dub*, 25.

70 Moten, *In the Break*, 192–211; and *IM*, 10. The formulation "black mo'nin'," and my provocation, extends from Elizabeth Alexander, "'Can you be BLACK and Look at This?,'" 77–94.

71 *IM*, 9 (my emphasis).

72 Snorton, *Black on Both Sides*, 108 (my emphasis).

73 "Today," 9.

74 Spillers, "Mama's Baby, Papa's Maybe," 65; hereafter, "MB"; and "LM," 28 (my emphasis).

75 "LM," 28; and Rankine, *Ulysses in Black*, 184–85 (my emphasis). See also Kuryla, "A Few Thoughts on Ellison's 'Little Man at Chehaw Station' with Special Thanks to an Outlaw Philosopher."

76 Spillers, "Women and Republican Formation"; and Brody, "The Blackness of Blackness . . . Reading the Typography of *Invisible Man*," 96. Though Harrison is a "'sphinx-like' presence . . . the core interventionist figure who, through musical proverb, teaches her student a lesson not only about heterogeneous Black subjectivity in American culture but also about the critical meaning of Black womanhood in relation to that culture" (Brooks, *Liner Notes for the Revolution*, 33–34), this logic is applicable to many, if not all, of the Black women in Ellison's life.

77 Morrison and West, "We Better Do Something." Ellison cuts "The" from the title in "the homestretch" of the novel's publication (*TSL*, 995). Also, speculatively speaking, Morrison may "feel some type of way" about Ellison due to an intriguing moment in a letter to James Allen McPherson about a "young

black woman whose fiction McPherson has asked [Ellison] to read." Based on context clues, I believe the fiction is *Tar Baby*. See TSL, 960–61; and "TII." See also "Slow-Burning."

78 "LM," 30 (my emphasis).

79 SA, 3–5. For another example of a mother imparting knowledge to her son, see Neal, "Oddities of the Family."

80 "LM," 30 (my emphasis).

81 REEG, 1; and Rampersad, *Ralph Ellison*, 7, 11 (my emphasis). For more on this namesake convergence, see "Hidden Name and Complex Fate" in SA, 144–66; and Magee, *Emancipating Pragmatism*, 97–103.

82 TSL, 12–13, 26–91.

83 Hersey, "A Completion of Personality," 276; REEG, 26; Rampersad, *Ralph Ellison*, 20–21; 18; and Wall, *On Freedom and the Will to Adorn*, 168.

84 Rampersad, *Ralph Ellison*, 26.

85 Hersey, "A Completion of Personality," 276; 273.

86 Early, *Ralph Ellison*, 24–26. For more on Ellison "tracing his schooling" to make the SA dedication possible, see *Shadowing*, 14–15.

87 TSL, 119; and REGA, 106.

88 "Letters." Another figure like this for Ellison is Shirley Jackson: "five years before [publishing IM] Ralph seized on Shirley Jackson's effective, matter-of-fact transitions to escape the narrative jams he had gotten himself into with successive drafts of *Invisible Man*" (TSL, 996).

89 SA, 108, 140 (my emphasis).

90 Kristeva, *Black Sun*, 43. Since Ellison mentions Hemingway, it behooves examining his and others' relationship to blackness in the literary canon. See Morrison, *Playing in the Dark*, 61–91. For more on Eliot, see Young, *The Grey Album*, 46, 142; and North, *The Dialect of Modernism*, 77–99. North reads Stein similarly (59–76).

91 TSL, 134. This "condition" metastasizes when Hartman shares that Ellison "was reluctant to leave his first marriage, to Rose Poindexter, an actress, despite the intensity of his feelings for [Sanora] Babb," with whom he "had a brief but passionate affair in the early 1940s." When he marries his second wife, Fanny McConnell—"pretty, extremely competent, and bright and ambitious enough to sustain Ellison as he made his long climb to the top of the literary mountain and social ladder"—he refers to her as "'manor born—only it took a hell of a time to get her there.'" After having a "very public affair at the American Academy in Rome that nearly ended their marriage," he encourages McConnell "'to be calm and avoid depression'" because he has "'enough of it . . . for both of'" them. In a letter about her "depression," Ellison refutes calling what he has put McConnell through "simple sadism"; he also puts in quotation marks the word "hunting." One surmises that perhaps she used the term in her "letter of the 5th" to which he replies, "I wasn't hunting for anybody and I'm not the kind of man who would marry for money and you shouldn't imply that I am, even in a joke." See "Letters"; TSL, 513–15; and "Slow-Burning."

92   Posnock, *Color and Culture*, 201 (my emphasis); Gates, *The Signifying Monkey*, 34; and Rankine, *Ulysses in Black*, 184–85. See also Wall, *On Freedom and the Will to Adorn*, 171–72.

93   "Ernest Hemingway in Africa" (my emphasis); and Freud, *The Question of Lay Analysis*, 38. See also Bennett, "Whenever Hemingway Hums Nigger," 141; and Tate, "Freud and His 'Negro,'" 55–56, 59–60.

94   Wright, "Psychiatry Comes to Harlem," 49 (my emphasis); and *SA*, 294–302; 94 (my emphasis). See also "Slow-Burning"; and for more on the Wright-Ellison confluence and psychoanalysis, especially their Lafargue conceptions, see Ahad, *Freud Upside Down*, 82–109.

95   Griffin, "*Who Set You Flowin'?*," 124, and *REGA*, 104.

96   *Shadowing*, 159.

97   *IM*, 13.

98   McGowan, *Enjoying What We Don't Have*, 276–77, 79 (my emphasis); and "*MB*," 80.

99   McGowan, *Enjoying What We Don't Have*, 276–77 (my emphasis).

100 McGowan, *Enjoying What We Don't Have*, 279 (my emphasis); and Du Bois, *The Souls of Black Folk*, 5.

101 Rampersad, *Ralph Ellison*, 77–78. See also Wall, *On Freedom and the Will to Adorn*, 173; and "Slow-Burning."

102 Spillers, "Moving on Down the Line," 97. For another reading of "the lady among the races," through "racialization, feminization, and nonheteronormativity," see Ferguson, *Aberrations in Black*, 54–81. Likewise, Nicholas Boggs queers Ellison's "Little Man" to give "a name to those black queer figures that occupy the margins of Ellison's oeuvre, even as his essay paradoxically mobilizes them to represent and exemplify the heterogeneous American social, literary, and cultural landscape." See Boggs, "A Grammar of Little Manhood," 245–66.

103 "*PP*," 29; and "*MB*," 80. I rhetorically borrow from Wahneema Lubiano, "Like Being Mugged by a Metaphor," 64–75.

104 Fisher, *Habitations of the Veil*, 336, 340 (my emphasis). An apt reading of this, routed through *Invisible Man* and the character Mary's "cast-iron figure of a very black, red-lipped and wide-mouthed Negro," is the Jolly Nigger Bank in Spike Lee's *Bamboozled*. See DeLue, "Envisioning Race in Spike Lee's *Bamboozled*," 76–77, 79; and Lee, *Bamboozled*.

105 Freud, "Mourning and Melancholia," 244; and Stepto, *From Behind the Veil*, 163–94. Though this ascension-immersion move is appealing, my intervention fortifies the foundation Stepto lays. I would then ask, since his criticism leans heavily on the novel's masculinism: What about the women?

106 *SA*, 295–96 (my emphasis).

107 Fanon, *Black Skin, White Masks*, 7; 3. See also Marriott, "Judging Fanon."

108 *SA*, 298–99; Ahad, *Freud Upside Down*, 99; and *IM*, xv.

109 *SA*, 88.

110 David Marriott aligns with this diagnosis: "[Alain] Locke will, over time, pursue the idea of race as a changing respite, as the last refuge of America.

It is a balancing intention: to bring out into the public life the spectral life of race; to show racism is the result of history and temperament; to expose the hysteria and violence behind America's ethnic character, a reaction brought on by crises of immigration and assimilation in the first decades of the century, crises which required the land and people of America to change." Marriott highlights not only black emigres' northbound "illness," but also their haunted moving patterns. See Marriott, *Haunted Life*, xxii.

111 Battersby, "*Gender and Genius*," 568.

112 Battersby, "*Gender and Genius*," 568; and Foucault, *Madness and Civilization*, 129. Carolyn Korsmeyer argues, "Hysterics represent a kind of biological disturbance in psychological form, not the profound depth of spirit that artistic madness supposedly taps in the course of artistic creation. Although this version of the imaginative genius is founded on an understanding of creativity that is anti-rationalist, it still describes a male domain." See Korsmeyer, "Genius," in *Gender and Aesthetics*, 30.

113 Ellison apparently read Freud. Jackson narrates two encounters with *The Interpretation of Dreams*: In 1924, roughly at age 10, Ellison happens upon a copy at dentist William L. Haywood's home, a moment characterized as "unsupervised, heavyweight intellectual exercises"; and in "Introduction to Psychology" at Tuskegee wherein "the class stressed the 'application' of psychology to solve problems, and probably made Ellison and his classmates familiar with the terms of Freudian psychoanalysis" (*REEG*, 48; 120). This supports my notion of him reading "Mourning and Melancholia." For a speculative conflation of *IM* and Freud's essay, see Cheng, "Ralph Ellison and the Politics of Melancholia," 121–36.

114 Freud, "Mourning and Melancholia," 250.

115 Ellison, "February," in *The Collected Essays of Ralph Ellison*, 3–4 (my emphasis).

116 Freud, "Mourning and Melancholia," 247; and "Slow-Burning." See also *TSL*, 92; Ellison pens this letter the day after his mother passes.

117 Morrison, *Sula*, 42.

118 Hayes, "But There Never Was a Black Male Hysteria," 55.

119 *SA*, 301–2.

120 "*LM*," 45–48 (emphasis in original); and Wall, *On Freedom and the Will to Adorn*, 171. See also Derrida, *Specters of Marx*, 10.

121 Baker, *Blues, Ideology, and Afro-American Literature*, 13.

122 Snorton makes a similar adverbial pivot regarding black maternity when he flips the "question of 'who' but . . . in an anagrammatical rearrangement as the problem of 'how'" (*Black on Both Sides*, 108).

123 For Wall, the work of the invisible, namely black women writers, is like Ellison's model and one he could acknowledge: "Nowhere in Ellison's essays do the names Alice Walker or June Jordan appear . . . black women artists are mainly invisible in his writing, even though by the time that 'The Little Man at Chehaw Station' was published, a renaissance among African American

women writers was rounding out its first decade. In crucial revisions to the tradition that Ellison bequeathed, Walker and Jordan reinsert their black female precursors into a literary history that excluded them. They make their own gendered as well as racialized experiences central to their writing . . . a mode of fusing high and low styles, which he might have recognized" (*On Freedom and the Will to Adorn*, 175). See also Sexton who argues, "Though #SayHerName is framed as a compliment to #BlackLivesMatter, it also bears the trace of a corrective" (*Black Men, Black Feminism*, 89–97).

MAN | MARVIN

1   Gaye, "Trouble Man."
2   Ritz, *Divided Soul*, 6–7 (emphasis in original).
3   Hawkins, "The Comforter."
4   Alexandre Dumas used this phrase in *Les Mohicans de Paris;* it has since had iterative qualities, including records by Ghostface Killah and Dr. Buzzard's Original Savannah Band. See Shapiro, ed., *The Yale Book of Quotations*, 219; Killah, "Cherchez LaGhost"; and Dr. Buzzard's Original Savannah Band, "Whispering/Cherchez La Femme/Se Si Bon."
5   Young, *The Grey Album*, 11–19.
6   Philippians 3:13b–14a (New Living Translation). All references will be from this version unless otherwise noted.
7   Ritz, *Divided Soul*, 163–64. I borrow mystery-cum-melody from Chaka Khan, "And the Melody Still Lingers On—Night in Tunisia." Likewise, I first used "ghostolalia"—a call to the spirits to come sit in the lushness—in a review of D'Angelo and the Vanguard's *Black Messiah*. Early criticism of the project regarded listeners being unable to understand what D'Angelo sang; he, in the office of interpreter, published the lyrics on the album's website. My word places D'Angelo's move in a ghostolalic genealogy with "Trouble Man"/ Gaye as an ancestor. See Murphy, "A Guide to Understanding D'Angelo's 'Black Messiah'"; Durham, "The D'Angelo Cycle"; and D'Angelo and The Vanguard, *Black Messiah*.
8   Acts 2:1–4.
9   Spillers, "Mama's Baby, Papa's Maybe," 80; hereafter "MB."
10 Donahue, "Epic World."
11 Ritz, *Divided Soul*, 6; Freud, "Mourning and Melancholia," 243; and Isaiah 53:2b-3.
12 Ritz, *Divided Soul*, 9 (my emphasis). This kinship with Mahalia Jackson reminisces on Dagmawi Woubshet's sentiments on Jessye Norman, which he reads through his melancholy, his being "[i]n *trouble*." See Woubshet, "Tizita," 510.
13 Hansen, "Mahalia Jackson, and King's Improvisation"; Murillo, "Trouble Man," in *Up Jump the Boogie*, 48–49; and Hughes, "Harlem [2]," in *The Collected Poems of Langston Hughes*, 426.

14 Freud, "Mourning and Melancholia," 256–57; Eng and Kazanjian, "Introduction—Mourning Remains," in *Loss*, 4; and Marriott, *On Black Men*, vii.

15 Griffin, "When Malindy Sings," 102, 104, 105–6. For Ralph Ellison's black women erasure, see "The World and the Jug," in *Shadow and Act*, 107–43; hereafter, *SA;* and for a contemporary example of a black woman, René Marie, singing national crisis, see Brooks, *Liner Notes for the Revolution*, 24–26.

16 Gabriel, "The Palms," 72; Ritz, *Divided Soul*, 7; Mark 15:34b; John 3:16; Luke 23:34 (King James Version); and Isaiah 53:4. For Luther on John 3:16, see Hamilton, *Christianity and World Religions*, 128.

17 Ritz, *Divided Soul*, 10, 11–13 (my emphasis). See also Phillips, "Marvin Gaye," 38–39.

18 Freud, "Mourning and Melancholia," 251–52 (my emphasis); Klein, *The Psychoanalysis of Children*, 218, 279; and Brooks, "'Do Not Be Afraid of No,'" in *The Essential Gwendolyn Brooks*, 34. Though conjecturing that Gaye did not read Freud, I may be wrong since he does make intertextual moves: He quotes T. S. Eliot's "Sweeney Agonistes" for the *Let's Get It On* liner notes, which is "strikingly reminiscent" of the "Trouble Man" lyrics. See Neal, "Trouble Man," 258; hereafter, "Trouble."

19 Wright, *Black Boy*, 11–16; and Baldwin, *Go Tell It on the Mountain*.

20 Freud writes, "[L]et us dwell for a moment on the view which the melancholic's disorder affords of the constitution of the human ego. We see how in him one part of the ego sets itself over against the other, judges it critically, and, as it were, takes it as its object. Our suspicion that the critical agency which is here split off from the ego might also show its independence in other circumstances will be confirmed by every further observation" ("Mourning and Melancholia," 247). If Father is the origin of Son's melancholy, he constitutes this ego split.

21 "MB," 68; 67.

22 Moten, *In the Break*, 1; hereafter, *ItB;* and "MB," 67.

23 Ritz, *Divided Soul*, 13; and Murillo, "Trouble Man," in *Up Jump the Boogie*, 48.

24 Ritz, *Divided Soul*, 17–18 (my emphasis). See also Phillips, "Marvin Gaye," 39–40.

25 Morrison, *Beloved*, 15.

26 Freud, "Mourning and Melancholia," 246 (my emphasis); and Awkward-Rich, *The Terrible We*, 1–9.

27 Reid-Pharr, *Black Gay Man*, 1–2; Dickinson, "1129," in *Essential Dickinson*, 65; Palumbo-Liu, *Asian/American*, 1; and Avilez, "Uncertain Freedom," 50.

28 Phillips, "Marvin Gaye," 52; and Jones, *Flaming?*, 1–13, particularly her approach of "setting the atmosphere," as I too engage in the "atmospherics" of the Gay church-home.

29 Reid-Pharr, "Tearing the Goat's Flesh," 353; hereafter, "Tearing."

30 Ritz, *Divided Soul*, 18–19; 17.

31 "Tearing," 355.

32 The most pertinent words for our consideration are from this passage in *Beloved:* "she wants her earrings   she wants her round basket   I want her face

a hot thing in the beginning the women are away from the men and the men are away from the women storms rock us and mix the men into the women and the women into the men." This is "fantasy in the hold." See Morrison, 210–13.

33 On *The New Danger*, there is a track called "Modern Marvel," an homage to Gaye that sonically references "Flyin' High (In the Friendly Sky)" and "Mercy Mercy Me (The Ecology)," all records from the album *What's Going On*. See Mos Def, "Modern Marvel," in *The New Danger*.

34 Spillers, "MB," 66.

35 Freud, "Mourning and Melancholia," 251 (my emphasis).

36 Ritz, *Divided Soul*, 18 (my emphasis); and Phillips, "Marvin Gaye," 57. Ritz also shares, "[Marvin] was unable to lose the feeling that the world revolved around him; a spiritual, childlike egocentricity would be one of Marvin's life-long characteristics. His father shared the same quality of self-centeredness" (10). Again, he epitomizes psychoanalytic poetics, even if he is not trafficking in its "language."

37 Moten, 46:25–29, "Black Kant (Pronounced Chant)."

38 Spillers, "MB," 68.

39 Moten, "Bridge and the One," 245; hereafter, "Bridge." Endnote 16 is particularly interesting. Triangulating Frederick Douglass with Sandy Jenkins and Mr. Covey, while contemplating Aunt Hester's scream, Moten writes, "The animation of the object/fetish by a woman's resistant scream, its derivation of its character from that scream, and its being exchanged between men is a double operation. . . . What remains, and what this essay can only weakly preface and call for is a much fuller understanding of how utopian resistance actually emerges from the connection and disconnection of acoustical mirroring and male homosociality." I surmise the object/fetish animates itself through feminine haunting in the Gay family too. Nonetheless, Douglass will be important momentarily, as will "Trouble Man," as acoustical mirroring.

40 "Tearing," 353–54 (my emphasis).

41 Johnson, *Appropriating Blackness*, 60; and Ritz, *Divided Soul*, 331–34. Johnson and I also align because he opens his chapter thinking through, and giving complementary readings of, "Mourning and Melancholia" (48–51).

42 Spillers, "MB," 67 (my strikethrough). Gaye's "crowning" resonates with Ritz: "Confusion about manhood would become another great theme in Marvin Gaye's life. His search for strong male role models led him into boxing rings and onto football fields while he fought to prove, fought to deny, fought to win his self-respect—gallant attempts which proved futile. . . . If Marvin saw Father as a king, he quickly began perceiving himself as a prince" (19–20). Regarding football, he tried out for the Detroit Lions; see Tinsley, "How Marvin Gaye's NFL Tryout Changed His Career."

43 Using "Do You Hear What I Hear?" as section headings is pivotal: If Gaye's life vibes with that of Jesus, their nativities hold similitude. The lyrics "'The child, the child, sleeping in the night / He will bring us goodness and light'" conclude the verse, "Said the king to the people everywhere / 'Listen to what I say.'" The

culminating phrases are what the king says: This is the Word being made flesh, even if that flesh is "the least of these," the one for whom there is "nothing beautiful or majestic." See Regney, "Do You Hear What I Hear?"

44 Ritz, *Divided Soul*, 74.

45 Lacan, *Écrits*, 54–55.

46 Ritz, *Divided Soul*, 163.

47 Equiano, *The Interesting Narrative of the Life of Olaudah Equiano . . . ,*" 50; and Wonder, *Talking Book*.

48 Ritz, *Divided Soul*, 163. These characteristics mirror an account from Marvin's second wife, Janis (Jan) Gaye, of attending his concert: "Soon he was singing 'Trouble Man.' He *was* Trouble Man—sexy and dangerous, gentle and sweet . . . this was well-mannered and mellow Marvin. But when the romantic Marvin emerged . . . pandemonium broke out. Women lost their minds. The piercing screams shattered the night." See Gaye, *After the Dance*, 84; hereafter, *AtD*.

49 "MB," 79 (my boldface; emphasis in original).

50 Mackey, *Splay Anthem*, xi (my emphasis); hereafter, *Splay*.

51 Ritz, *Divided Soul*, 163; 164. Moten equally does a close reading of the record "Since I Had You" from *I Want You*—see *ItB*, 224–29.

52 O'Brien, "Interrupted Symphony," 101 (my emphasis).

53 Ritz, *Divided Soul*, 9–10; and Freud, *On Dreams*, 13 (emphasis in original).

54 Philippians 3:12–14a (New Living Translation); and Habakkuk 2:2 (King James Version).

55 Nelson George, reading "Trouble Man" as a complex hybrid of musical traditions, sets the tone for what I consider its melancholic execution; see *Buppies, B-boys, Baps, and Bohos*, 71 (my emphasis). For a musicological history of *Trouble Man* among other blaxploitation-era soundtracks, see Flory, *I Hear a Symphony*, 150–53.

56 "As the Spirit Moves Mahalia," *SA*, 219; 213–4. Ironically, Ellison asserts Jackson is Anderson's performative kin: "They are the sincere ones whose humanity dominates the artifices of the art with which they stir us, and when they sing we have some notion of our better selves" (214). For more on the Ellison-Jackson relation, see Lordi, *Black Resonance*, 66–98.

57 Ritz, *Divided Soul*, 173. For more on Cattaraugus Avenue, see Gaye, *Marvin Gaye, My Brother*, 93–94; and *AtD*, 45–57.

58 Spillers, "MB," 65.

59 Edwards, "The Taste of the Archive," 952.

60 Hartman, *Scenes of Subjection*, 3; hereafter, *Scenes*; and "Bridge," 241.

61 Hartman, *Wayward Lives*, 24–28; and *Scenes*, 4.

62 Kevin Quashie mirrors my ambivalence:

> I want to know more about the choice to publish—and the manner of reprinting—that image of the young Black girl on the horsehair sofa in "A Minor Figure," especially since Hartman has declined from such presentations before. Is it that the world of the book could sustain this and other tender moments, that the whole of it is a cushion of regard so

that the visual and the narrative apparatuses would not conjure only the pornotropic? Is there a praxis of elision, or something else at work in this moment and other moments? Is elision not even necessary, and if so, why or how? One longs to hear from this master writer on this thinking/doing.

Hartman responds:

> In *Wayward Lives*, the look is in service of an intramural labor that yearns to produce a different account of the document. In looking at the girl, we must bear the burden of the gaze with her, be situated by its violence, defeat its logic, look so that she might be covered, no longer captured in the frame. . . . I believe we can look at the girl, see her, yet not reproduce the violence of the compelled image, but instead cloak her in the collective utterance, take on the labor of care, form a circle around her. Of course, this depends on a huge *if* or *might be*: Might a look be capable of holding her, capable of gathering us, allowing us to care for one other, and in the process make something else of the photograph, if not destroy the compelled image?

See Quashie, "A Flash of Light and Life"; and Hartman, "Intimate History, Radical Narrative."

63 Douglass, *The Narrative of the Life of Frederick Douglass*, 21–24; hereafter, *Narrative*. For more on the Bailey family tree, see Fought, *Women in the World of Frederick Douglass*, 9–40.

64 *Narrative*, 24–25 (my emphasis).

65 Brewton, "'Bold Defiance Took Its Place,'" 707–8. For Douglass as "ethical listener" in this scene, see Stoever, *The Sonic Color Line*, 42–48.

66 Isaiah 64:9.

67 "Bridge," 241.

68 Burgett, *Sentimental Bodies*, 202 (my emphasis); and Woodard, *The Delectable Negro*, 101–4. Likewise, "the slave was not simply the product of sexual criminality [Hester's whipping and Douglass's birth through rape] but its very *incarnation*." See Abdur-Rahman, *Against the Closet*, 35–38.

69 "Bridge," 237; and "MB," 80; 65.

70 Douglass, *My Bondage and My Freedom*, 97 (emphasis in original); 87–88 (emphasis mine). This aurality reifies and counters Abdur-Rahman who analyzes "the trope of silence" under slavery (28–33): It is a total sonic enterprise.

71 Messmer, "'If Not In the Word, In the Sound,'" 15–16; and "Bridge," 239–40 (emphasis in original). See also Stoever, *The Sonic Color Line*, 45; 49; and *Narrative*, 24–25; 29–30.

72 Cone, *The Cross and the Lynching Tree*, 31.

73 "JAMIE FOXX SINGS—FRED HAMMOND—NO WEAPON"; and "Carlton Hall Video Blog-Jamie Foxx NAACP Image Award Speech."

74 "Bridge," 240.

75 Redmond, "Tip Toes and River Rolls," 151.

76 Gershwin, "Gone, Gone, Gone"; and "My Man's Gone Now." See also "Gershwin: Porgy and Bess—Gone Gone Gone"; and "My Man's Gone Now (Old Man Sorrow)."

77 Hutchinson, *Dubose Heyward*, 4; Foxwell, *A Visitor's Guide to the Literary South*, 148; and Du Bois, *The Souls of Black Folk*, 5.

78 Hutchinson, *Dubose Heyward*, 11; and Foxwell, *A Visitor's Guide to the Literary South*, 148.

79 Morrison, *Home*, 30–33. Daphne Brooks addresses the appropriative history of Heyward, initiated through his mother Janie (the irony!), in a recent lecture—"'One of the These Mornings, You're Gonna Rise Up Singing': Black Women Performers and the Art of (Un)Doing Gershwin Time"—and her forthcoming book in a trilogy on black women's sonic practices. See "Daphne Brooks, 'Lemonade from Lemons.'"

80 Burgett, *Sentimental Bodies*, 202; and Carby, *Race Men*, 9–10.

81 Spillers, "MB," 72–73.

82 Ndegeocello, *The World Has Made Me the Man of My Dreams*. Francesca T. Royster extends the concept of Ndegeocello's album in *Sounding Like a No-No*, 167–85.

83 Jackson, "Scream (featuring Janet Jackson)," in *HIStory*; Gaye, "Inner City Blues (Make Me Wanna Holler)," in *What's Going On*; and Murillo, "Soon I'll Be Loving You Again," in *Up Jump the Boogie*, 77.

84 Neal, *What the Music Said*, 67–68. For a further reading of Gaye's project, see Dyson, *Mercy, Mercy Me*, 86–92.

85 Mackey, *Splay*, ix.

86 Heidegger, *Being and Time*, 32; Schwenger, "Phenomenology of the Scream," 389; and Lévinas, *Existence and Existents*, 5. As an aside, insomnia as one of Lévinas's world-interrupting, world-suspending, repercussions of "the horror that accompanies [existence] . . . the continual play of our relations with the world" (Schwenger, 389) syncs with the Freudian symptom of melancholia being sleeplessness ("Mourning and Melancholia," 246).

87 Morrison, *God Help the Child*, 43.

88 There is ongoing debate over what constitutes the head voice and falsetto. To an extent, what Gaye achieves is probably a mixed voice, an aesthetic quality that could peculiarly affirm with what this chapter argues. However, the falsetto designation is more appropriate based on Gaye's generally understood performativity. For more on (black) male falsetto, see Ravens, *The Supernatural Voice*, 203; and on the slight differentiation between the head voice and falsetto, see "Ep. 21 'Falsetto Vs. Head Voice'-Voice Lessons to the World." See also Eidsheim, *The Race of Sound*, 91–113.

89 Mackey, *Bedouin Hornbook*, (hereafter BH), 51–52; 201 (my emphasis); and *ItB*, 193–94.

90 Harney and Moten, *The Undercommons*, 50 (my emphasis).

91 Pollard, "Marvin's Divorce from Anna—Exclusive Scene"; and Gazaway, "Anna's Love Song."

92 Johnson, "The Creation," in *God's Trombones*, 17.

93 Marre, *What's Going On* (my emphasis). This ploy of placing music in keys higher than the singer could comfortably accomplish was commonplace by Dozier through his songwriting team Holland Dozier Holland: The same compositional effect often happened to the lead singer of The Four Tops, Levi Stubbs. See Flory, *I Hear a Symphony*, 56.

94 Lordi, *Donny Hathaway's* Donny Hathaway Live, 13.

95 "Trouble," 254; *BH*, 51; and Schwenger, "Phenomenology of the Scream," 395. For additional readings of Mackey theorizing falsetto, see Lock, *Blutopia*, 172; and Okiji, *Jazz and Critique*, 83–86.

96 Ravens, *The Supernatural Voice*, 7–8 (my emphasis); Derrida, "The Law of Genre," 7; and Griffin, "When Malindy Sings," 104.

97 Steinberg, "Music and Melancholy," 310 (emphasis in original).

98 Audre Lorde's daughter imparted these words to her ahead of a December 28, 1977 Modern Language Association paper. See "The Transformation of Silence into Language and Action," in *Sister Outsider*, 42 (my emphasis); Philip, "She Tries Her Tongue, Her Silence Softly Breaks," 69–86; and "MB," 65. What is serendipitous about Philip's poem is that she equally understands glossolalia/ghostolalia in trying the tongue: She quotes Acts 2:1–6 (77)!

99 Spillers, "Gwendolyn the Terrible," in *Black, White and in Color*, 121–22; and Brooks, *Report from Part One*, 158 (my emphasis). For more on "The Anniad," see Gyarkye, "The Importance of Being Ordinary."

100 "Bridge," 240 (my emphasis); *BH*, 201; Sharpe, *In the Wake*, 75–77; and Douglass, *The Life and Times of Frederick Douglass*, 24–34. See also Rowe, *At Emerson's Tomb*, 115–18. Fought also states that Hester was sometimes called, ironically, "Easter" (*Women in the World of Frederick Douglass*, 14).

101 Murillo, "Trouble Man"; "Soon I'll Be Loving You Again," in *Up Jump the Boogie*, 48; 78.

102 Harney and Moten, *The Undercommons*, 50; Glissant, "One World in Relation," 5; and Foucault, "Madness, the Absence of Work," 104.

103 Julio Cortázar, "*La noche boca arriba*." Likewise, this last phrase uttered in "Trouble Man" resonates with Spillers's "Moving on Down the Line," 83–109.

WOMAN | GAN

1 Walker, *In Search of Our Mothers' Gardens*, xi–xii; hereafter, *Search*.

2 Lorde, "The Uses of Anger," in *Sister Outsider*, 132–33. For Jesus as "a model for balance between being alone and being in community," see Arnold and Fohl, *When You Are Alone*, 68–69.

3 Butler, *Gender Trouble*, xxix (emphasis in original); hereafter, *GT*.

4 For the racial implications of mesearch, see Ray, "The Unbearable Whiteness of Mesearch."

5 Tate, *Psychoanalysis and Black Novels*, 94. See also Wright, "On Literature."

6 I refer here to Walker, *In Love and Trouble*. See also Christian, "A Study of 'In Love and Trouble,'" 21–30, 70–71. Likewise, I borrow from a credo

heard during seminary: *ecclesia reformata, semper reformanda*—the church reformed, always reforming.

7 For a primer on womanist theology and its foundational texts, see Townes, "Womanist Theology," 159–76. See also Cannon, *Black Womanist Ethics* and *Katie's Canon*; Grant, *White Women's Christ and Black Women's Jesus*; and Williams, *Sisters in the Wilderness*. While this is not exhaustive, these sources install womanism at its inception and early years in the academy. Likewise, regarding Walker's general elision, "a number of Afrocentric black women critics chose to call their practice 'Africana Womanism' . . . even though the black nationalist politics of their project differed greatly from Walker's own." See Griffin, "That the Mothers May Soar and the Daughters May Know Their Names," 487–88.

8 Moten, "Blackness and Nothingness," 749–50; and Leonard, "First Questions," 1056.

9 Walker's feelings on Richard Wright's *Black Boy* exemplify my contention: "I realized sometime after graduation [from Sarah Lawrence], that when I had studied contemporary writers and the South at this college . . . the writings of Richard Wright had not been studied and that instead I had studied the South from Faulkner's point of view. . . . It was only after trying to conduct the same kind of course myself—with black students—that I realized that such a course simply cannot *be* taught if *Black Boy* is not assigned and read, or if 'The Ethics of Living Jim Crow' is absent from the reading list." Although Walker's words are from 1970, roughly a decade before positing "womanism," her canon formation interests me. That is, texts coded as deeply masculinist, to the point of misogynoir (Cheryl A. Wall says Wright engages in sexism that Walker "abhors"), are "required reading." All the more, this move counteracts a review of Wright's work by the person Walker resurrects: Zora Neale Hurston ("'Stories of Conflict,' Review of *Uncle Tom's Children* by Richard Wright," 32). In all, I am not saying Wright is a womanist, but rather people change their minds, regardless of later consciousness seeming antithetical to the initial charge; and perhaps definitions are more inclusive than expected in that one can "honor" people despite them not "honoring" one back. See "The Unglamorous but Worthwhile Duties of the Black Revolutionary Artist, or of the Black Writer Who Simply Works and Writes," in *Search,* 130–31; and Wall, *Worrying the Line,* 210. Also, regarding who can be womanist, Layli Phillips suggests "a consensus among the main progenitors of womanism, namely, Walker, [Chikwenye Okonjo] Ogunyemi, and [Clenora] Hudson-Weems, that people other than Black women or women of color can be womanists." See Phillips, "Introduction—Womanism," xxxvi–xxxviii.

10 Walker, xi. This human-animal rhetoric syncs with Hudson-Weems. See Masenya, "African Womanist Hermeneutics," 152n11. Also note, via Masenya's title, the locative yet specific differentiation of womanism; she furthers this in an eponymous section of the article (153–55).

11 Traci C. West extends this through social and theological thought. See "Is a Womanist a Black Feminist," 291–95. Monica A. Coleman offers "third-wave" womanism as a critical posture and intervention in "Must I Be a Womanist?,"

85–96. A roundtable of responses to her range from Cannon to Irene Monroe, "an African American Christian lesbian ordained minister, theologian, and activist"; Debra Mubashshir Majeed, a Muslim womanist, to Lee Miena Skye, "an Australian Christian womanist" of the Tasmanian Palawa people (96–134). Regarding black men as feminists, see Awkward, *Scenes of Instruction*; Neal, *New Black Man*; and Sexton, *Black Men, Black Feminism*, 41–74.

12 Abdur-Rahman, *Against the Closet*, 40.

13 Butler, "Afterword," in *Bloodchild and Other Stories*, 30; hereafter *Bloodchild*; and Jackson, *Becoming Human*, 148.

14 *GT*, xxix.

15 Butler, *The Psychic Life of Power*, 106–7 (emphasis in original); hereafter, *PLP*.

16 *GT*, xxvi–xxvii.

17 Shakespeare, *As You Like It*, act 2, scene 7.

18 Foucault, *The Order of Things*, 340.

19 *GT*, 4 (my emphasis).

20 Derrida, "Force of Law," 969, 971.

21 Hesse, "Marked Unmarked," 980–83. For more on "justice" as ambivalence, see Panaram, "SayHerName."

22 Vargas and James, "Refusing Blackness-as-Victimization," 193. For an additional reading on the paraontological, see Karera, "Paraontology."

23 Spillers, "The Crisis of the Negro Intellectual," 116; and Derrida, "Force of Law," 971.

24 Niebuhr, *The Meaning of Revelation*, 50; and Farley, "Perfecting Slavery," 228 (emphasis in original). Another example of the prehistoric in black thought, possibly germane to this chapter's argument about Terran-Tlic interactions, is Oyěwùmí, *The Invention of Women*.

25 *GT*, 40; and Nyong'o, "Unburdening Representation," 71–72.

26 Durham, "Richard Pryor," 143.

27 *PLP*, 111–12 (my emphasis).

28 Freud, "Mourning and Melancholia," 244, 253. For what it is worth, W. E. B. Du Bois rhetorically predates these Freudian lines when discussing the results of "disdain for everything black": "But the facing of so vast a prejudice could not but bring the inevitable self-questioning, self-disparagement, and lowering of ideals which ever accompany repression and breed in an atmosphere of contempt and hate." See Du Bois, *The Souls of Black Folk*, 10.

29 Spillers, "'All the Things You Could Be by Now If Sigmund Freud's Wife Was Your Mother,'" 96–97 (my emphasis).

30 Wynter, "Beyond Miranda's Meanings," 364 (emphasis in original). See also Weheliye, *Habeas Viscus*, 21–22.

31 Weheliye, *Habeas Viscus*, 144n13. See also McKittrick, *Demonic Grounds*, xxiv.

32 Butler, *Fledgling*, 7–8.

33 Kafka, "Before the Law."

34 *PLP*, 108.

35 This chapter heading relays itself from Ed Roberson, *Voices Cast Out to Talk Us In*.

36 "Afterword," *Bloodchild*, 30.

37 Tate, *Psychoanalysis and Black Novels*, 10.

38 *GT*, 40.

39 Kristeva, *Black Sun*, 29 (my emphasis).

40 Toni Morrison refers to Paul D feeling some "womanish need," akin to Lot's wife, ahead of having sex with Beloved. See Morrison, *Beloved*, 117. Moreover, Marlon Riggs, thinking about *In Living Color*'s "Men on" skit, speaks of "[a] notion that black gay men are sissies, ineffectual, ineffective, womanish in a way that signifies inferiority rather than empowerment." Though I depart from reading Gan's sexual orientation, Riggs's "womanish" invocation benefits my cause even as I flip it. See Hemphill, "'In Living Color,'" 393.

41 "Afterword," *Bloodchild*, 30.

42 Morgan, "They Call Me Ms. Hill." Alice Walker also traffics in divinity when Shug Avery, carried over from *The Color Purple*, publishes a pamphlet called *The Gospel According to Shug*: "Helped are those who learn that the deliberate invocation of suffering is as much a boomerang as the deliberate invocation of joy." A profane beatitude, ecclesial sacrilege. See Walker, *The Temple of My Familiar*, 144.

43 *Bloodchild*, 3; and *GT*, 39–40.

44 *Bloodchild*, 5; 25. Gan also narrates, "There had been incidents right after the Preserve was established—Terrans shooting Tlic, shooting N'Tlic. This was before the joining of the families began, before everyone had a personal stake in keeping the peace . . . for our protection, we were told. There were stories of whole Terran families wiped out in reprisal back during the assassinations" (12). The interjection "we were told" indicates a "master narrative" about "life together," which T'Gatoi extends when discussing Terran history. These complex, and questionable prehistories, connote hidden truths.

45 Hartman, *Scenes of Subjection*, 160; and *GT*, 40.

46 McEntyre, *Caring for Words in a Culture of Lies*, 54; and Freud, "Mourning and Melancholia," 247.

47 *Bloodchild*, 5; 7 (my emphasis).

48 Helford, "'Would You Really Rather Die Than Bear My Young?,'" 267.

49 Baldwin, "The Uses of the Blues," 57, 65; and Pavlić, *Who Can Afford to Improvise?*, 153–55 (emphasis in original).

50 Freud, "Mourning and Melancholia," 254 (my emphasis).

51 John 20:24–29. Butler's phrase "be still and know" allows me to consider whether she maneuvers through the biblical text like Judith Butler, that is, such wording is psalmodic—see Psalm 46:10.

52 Washington, "Introduction," 1.

53 Morrison, *The Bluest Eye*, 17–18 (emphasis in original).

54 D'Angelo and The Vanguard, "The Door"; and Morrison, *The Bluest Eye*, 17; and *Search*, xi.

55 *Bloodchild*, 5; and Donahue, "Epic World."

56 *Bloodchild*, 4; 8.

57 Shange, *For Colored Girls Who Have Considered Suicide/When the Rainbow Is Enuf*, 34–35; Green, "'There Goes the Neighborhood,'" 172; and *Bloodchild*, 29.

58 Green, "'There Goes the Neighborhood,'" 172 (my emphasis).

59 *Bloodchild*, 22.

60 Lavender, *Race in American Science Fiction*, 70. Regarding "Bloodchild" as slave narrative, Butler writes, "it amazes me that some people have seen 'Bloodchild' as a story of slavery. It isn't. It's a number of other things, though" (*Bloodchild*, 30). As well, Helford opines, "we are exposed to no literal human race relations in the story. . . . Race relations become central to the story only in the metaphoric representation of alien-human conflict and the master-slave quality of the relationship between T'Gatoi and Gan" ("Would You Really Rather Die Than Bear My Young?," 266). For more on the "Bloodchild"-slavery trope, see McCaffery, "An Interview with Octavia E. Butler," 56–57; Holloway, *Private Bodies, Public Texts*, 33; and Jackson, *Becoming Human*, 129.

61 Helford, "Would You Really Rather Die Than Bear My Young?," 266–67; and Lavender, *Race in American Science Fiction*, 54–55.

62 *Bloodchild*, 6, 19–20; Helford, "'Would You Really Rather Die Than Bear My Young?,'" 269, 271; and Jackson, *Becoming Human*, 133.

63 Lavender, *Race in American Science Fiction*, 70; and *Bloodchild*, 18.

64 Green, "'There Goes the Neighborhood,'" 171; and Lavender, *Race in American Science Fiction*, 70.

65 Freud, "Mourning and Melancholia," 243.

66 Lavender, *Race in American Science Fiction*, 54; Equiano, *The Interesting Narrative of the Life of Olaudah Equiano . . .* , 39; and Holloway, *Private Bodies, Public Texts*, 66. Equiano's "exchange" is similar to Frederick Douglass who preferred to be "the meanest reptile" instead of acquiring literacy. See Douglass, *The Narrative of the Life of Frederick Douglass*, 48.

67 Lavender, *Race in American Science Fiction*, 70. Like my canonical insertion, Jackson views "Bloodchild" as "thematically linked to the African American literary tradition" (123–25).

68 McCaffery, "An Interview with Octavia E. Butler," 56; and "Afterword," *Bloodchild*, 31–32.

69 Helford, "'Would You Really Rather Die Than Bear My Young?,'" 267–68; and *Bloodchild*, 29. Here, I also reimagine and borrow from Hartman; see "Venus in Two Acts," 8.

70 *Bloodchild*, 26.

71 *Bloodchild*, 25; 27.

72 "Toni Morrison Interview on 'Jazz' (1993)"; *Bloodchild*, 21; and Green, "'There Goes the Neighborhood,'" 172–73 (my emphasis).

73 This section heading correlates with Wall's chapter title, "In Search of Our Mother's Gardens and Our Fathers' (Real) Estates: Alice Walker, Essayist," from *Worrying the Line*, 209–33.

74 Walker, *Search*, 233.

75 *Bloodchild*, 6.

76 Helford, "'Would You Really Rather Die Than Bear My Young?,'" 267.

77 Walker, *Search*, 241–43 (my emphasis).

78 Walker, *Search*, 239.

79 Washington, "Introduction," xi; and Sharpe, "Beauty Is a Method." This is my undoing of Matthew 13:20–21 (New Living Translation), or the Parable of the Sower; and Matthew 5:3, 5.

80 Derrida, *Specters of Marx*, 18.

81 *Bloodchild*, 12.

82 Johnson, *The Autobiography of an Ex-Colored Man*, 5; and Johnson, *The Autobiography of an Ex-Colored Man*, ed. by Jacqueline Goldsby, 5.

83 *Bloodchild*, 26.

84 *Bloodchild*, 4.

85 Walker, *Search*, 243.

86 Monáe "Dance or Die"; Bates, "Octavia Butler"; and Aguirre, "Octavia Butler's Prescient Vision of a Zealot Elected to 'Make America Great Again.'"

87 Helford, "'Would You Really Rather Die Than Bear My Young?,'" 268.

88 Spillers, "Moving on Down the Line," 96.

89 Jardine, *Gynesis*, 37; and Helford, "'Would You Really Rather Die Than Bear My Young?,'" 261.

90 "Bloodchild" was first published in 1984. See "Bloodchild," 34–54. This also predates Kristeva's "pregnant man."

91 *GT*, 38–39.

92 Jackson, *Becoming Human*, 149; and *Bloodchild*, 9. I also make this claim because what Gan narrates about the Tlic is verbatim what Angela Davis argues about the plantation: "master forcibly coupled men and women with the aim of producing the maximum number of healthy child-slaves." See Davis, "Reflections on the Black Woman's Role in the Community of Slaves," 5.

93 Walker, *Search*, xi–xii.

94 Mackey, "Destination Out," in *Paracritical Hinge*, 239.

LOVE | KENDRICK

1 George, *Hip Hop America*, 36. For more on the badman, see also Perry, *Prophets of the Hood*, 129; and Sexton, *Black Men, Black Feminism*, 1–3.

2 Hurston, *Their Eyes Were Watching God*, 14; and Washington, "Introduction," xi.

3 Sounds of Blackness, "Black Butterfly," in *Africa to America*; Williams, "Black Butterfly," in *Let's Hear It for the Boy*; and Johnson, "Lift Every Voice and Sing," in *Lift Every Voice and Sing*, 101 (emphases mine). Jasmine Nichole Cobb and Britt Rusert also theorize the black butterfly symbolizing freedom in Sarah Mapps Douglass's 1833 illustration "A Token of Love from Me, to Thee." See Cobb, *Picture Freedom*, 24; and Rusert, *Fugitive Science*, 203–15. Likewise, black butterfly is a spatial category as rendered in Baltimore, "a reference to the fact that Baltimore's majority-Black population spreads out on both sides of the coveted strip of real estate running down the center of the city like a butterfly's wings. Lawrence T. Brown reveals that ongoing historical trauma caused by a combination of policies, practices, systems, and budgets is at the

root of uprisings and crises in hypersegregated cities around the country." See Brown, *The Black Butterfly*.

4   This fantasy plays on in scene 1, episode 2 of the STARZ series *American Gods*: the god Anansi, a spider who cosplays as a black man (Orlando Brown), shape-shifts onto a 1697 slave ship and incites the cargo to revolt; they proceed to burn the ship and Anansi washes up on shore in his arachnid form. Ironically, the cargo all appear to be men.

5   Hartman, *Lose Your Mother*, 6.

6   Spillers, "Mama's Baby, Papa's Maybe," 67 (my emphasis); hereafter "MB."

7   Lamar, *To Pimp a Butterfly*; hereafter, TPAB.

8   Manabe, "We Gon' Be Alright?"

9   Willis, "To Pimp the Black Woman"; and Killakam, "South Africa's Influence on Kendrick Lamar's 'To Pimp a Butterfly.'" See also Maner, *Kendrick Lamar's To Pimp a Butterfly*, 6; 90–96.

10 Russell McLendon, "8 Interesting Facts about Lucy the Ancient Ape"; hereafter, "Lucy."

11 Commander, *Afro-Atlantic Flight*, 18–19; 15 (my emphasis). See also Iton, *In Search of the Black Fantastic*.

12 Morrison, *Song of Solomon*, 337; hereafter, *SoS*; Dixon, "Review: 'If You Surrender to the Air. . . . ,'" 172; and Tate, "Review: *The Song of Solomon* by Toni Morrison," 329 (my emphasis).

13 George, *Hip Hop America*, 35.

14 Crawford, *Black Post-Blackness*, 11–12.

15 Golden, *Freestyle*; and Avilez, "Review: Margo Natalie Crawford, *Black Post-Blackness*," 457. As well, Francesca T. Royster extends the genealogy of the post-black conversation in *Sounding Like a No-No*, 202.

16 Crawford, *Black Post-Blackness*, 49, 51; and Commander, *Afro-Atlantic Flight*, 35–43. I would be remiss, invoking sankofa and "the new world," not mentioning Haile Gerima's *Sankofa*, which might, too, embody neoteric Pan-Africanism. Apropos to the current theme, when the character Joe kills his mother, Nunu, the immediate corrective is to kill the priest who initially told Joe she was "kill-able," further inciting the other slaves to revolt then "fly" back to Africa. More-over, Gerima being Ethiopian is serendipitous for what this chapter later argues.

17 Jarell, AFRICOBRA, xvii–xix; 6; 3.

18 *SoS*, 55 (my emphasis).

19 Barad, "Posthumanist Performativity," 801; and Konitshek, "Calling Forth History's Mocking Doubles," 660–61; 665–68 (my boldface, emphasis in original).

20 Young, *The Grey Album*, 235.

21 I reference Spillers's first two sentences of "Mama's Baby" when she states, "Let's face it. I am a marked woman, but not everybody knows my name," then lists historicized appellations of black women in quotation marks (65).

22 Lathan, *Sticks & Stones*; and Judy, "On the Question of Nigga Authenticity," 211–30.

23 Brody, *Punctuation*, 108, 110; and Butler, *The Psychic Life of Power*, 106–7.

24 "Thadious Davis, NDIAS Fellow."

25 Campt, *Listening to Images*, 3. For an example of Campt's concept, see Winters, "Beyond Flight and Containment," 219–20.

26 *SoS*, 5–9, 132; and Morrison, "Unspeakable Things Unspoken," 29; hereafter, "Unspeakable."

27 Freud, "Mourning and Melancholia," 243; hereafter, "Melancholia"; and *SoS*, 9.

28 Morrison, "Foreword," *Song of Solomon*, xi–xii.

29 In the 2004 foreword, Morrison also explains tragedy based on the novel's opening sentence—"The North Carolina Mutual Life Insurance agent promised to fly from Mercy to the other side of Lake Superior at 3:00": "Two other words of significance are 'fly' and 'mercy'. . . . flight as escape of confrontation; mercy the unspoken wish of the novel's population. . . . Mercy is . . . what the townsfolk believe can never come from the white world, as is signified by the inversion of the name of the hospital from Mercy to 'No-Mercy'" (xiii). Again, Lamar, and his album cover, converses with the novel. See also "Unspeakable," 27–28.

30 *SoS*, 9.

31 Lamar, "Sing About Me, I'm Dying of Thirst," in *good kid, m.A.A.d city*; and O'Connor, "How Maya Angelou Influenced Tupac and Hip-Hop." For more on this record, see Neal, *Black Ephemera*, 89–91.

32 Philippians 1:6, King James Version (emphasis in original).

33 Coleridge, *The Rime of the Ancient Mariner*, 31; and John 19:28.

34 Winters, "Beyond Flight and Containment," 212; and *SoS*, 32.

35 Freud, "Melancholia," 246.

36 "Kendrick Lamar—God Is Gangsta."

37 Mulvey, "Visual Pleasure and Narrative Cinema," 836.

38 Freud, "Melancholia," 246. Winters picks up on Lamar's affect: "after the wide acclaim of *good kid, m.A.A.d city*, Kendrick revealed that he experienced severe depression when faced with the fissure between his newfound freedom and 'things going on back home'"; this was right before *TPAB*. Thus, in verse 3 of "u," when referencing depression "restin' on" the heart of the record's subject, he engages in displacement, even though he is speaking of/to himself as an "object of ridicule in order to voice self-anger, insecurity, and failure" ("Beyond Flight and Containment," 212; 225). This may confirm why Spencer Kornhaber calls "u" a "horror-show of a song." See Kornhaber, "The Power in Kendrick Lamar's Complexity," and "Breakfast Club Classic—Kendrick Lamar Talks Overcoming Depression, Responsibility to the Culture"; and for an additional reading of "u" in this vein, see Maner, *Kendrick Lamar's To Pimp a Butterfly*, 3.

39 *SoS*, 35; 213, 215–16; 209. These narrative plotlines occur from 185 to 216.

40 Ashley Tidey writes, "The moment at the end of Part I, when Milkman initially reacts cynically to Pilate's notion of keeping the dead 'right there with you,' [referring to the bones] is also the moment when he begins to register, on some level, her central importance to him. And yet, embarking on his crucial journey to Pennsylvania and Virginia in Part II, he is not able to acknowledge, until the latter part of the trip, the full extent to which Pilate inspires his devel-

opment toward selfhood and community." The same happens to Lamar: In his "middle passage," self-possession at the beginning of the four-track journey is subsumed for his dependence on the black feminine/maternal by the end. See Tidey, "Limping or Flying?," 63.

41 Dixon, "Review," 172; *SoS*, 321, 132; and King, *The Black Shoals*, 4.

42 Griffin, "That the Mothers May Soar and the Daughters May Know Their Names," 483–507. Griffin remixes the *SoS* epigraph: "The fathers may soar / And the children may know their names." Also, I rhetorically borrow from Hull, Scott, and Smith, *All the Women Are White, All the Blacks Are Men, But Some of Us Are Brave.*

43 *SoS*, 331.

44 Tidey, "Limping or Flying?," 50; and *SoS*, 278–79. See also Freud, *Beyond the Pleasure Principle.*

45 *SoS*, 328; 332 (my emphasis). For more, respectively, on the myth in general and in the novel, see Commander, *Afro-Atlantic Flight*, 3; and Colbert, *Black Movements*, 41–47. Moreover, "[o]f the flights in the novel, Solomon's is the most magical, the most theatrical and, for Milkman, the most satisfying. . . . Solomon's escape from slavery is also the abandonment of his family. . . . These flights, these erstwhile heroics, are viewed rather differently by the women left behind. Both the quotation and the song of the title fairly shout that different understanding"; see Morrison, "Foreword"; and *SoS* (2004), xiv.

46 When Ruth carried Milkman, Macon tried to abort the pregnancy; Pilate had Ruth "[g]nashing the cornstarch" (131–32), among other protective measures, to deter him. This moment also requires acknowledging Milkman messing over his cousin-lover Hagar, a saga that compels an altogether different chapter (305–19).

47 Ruth 1–4; Mark 14:3–9 or John 12:1–8, and John 20:1–18; and I Corinthians 13:13b. Naomi, Ruth's mother-in-law, means "pleasant"; after becoming widowed and losing her sons, one being Ruth's husband, she asks to be called Mara meaning "bitter" (Ruth 1:19–21). For more on naming in the novel, see LeClair, "The Language Must Not Sweat."

48 Ruth 3:1–18; and *SoS*, 126 (my emphasis). Morrison reimagines this biblical story insofar as when Naomi tells Ruth to uncover sleeping Boaz's feet, she tells her to prepare by taking a bath, putting on perfume, and wearing the nicest clothes (Ruth 3:1–4). Pilate is Naomi-like when she gives Ruth, having been threatened with death by Macon and remaining untouched by him after First Corinthians' birth, "'funny things to do. And some greenish-gray grassy-looking stuff to put in [Macon's] food. . . . I felt like a doctor, like a chemist doing some big important scientific experiment. It worked too. Macon came to me for four days. . . . And two months later I was pregnant'" with Milkman; the narrator calls Pilate's conjuring "sexual hypnosis"; see Morrison, *SoS*, 125, 131.

49 Morrison on isolation: "Milkman's flight binds these two elements of loyalty (Mr. Smith's) and abandon and self-interest (Solomon's) into a third thing: a

merging of fealty and risk that suggests the 'agency' for 'mutual' 'life,' which he offers at the end and which is echoed in the hills behind him, and is the marriage of surrender and domination, acceptance and rule, commitment to group *through* ultimate isolation"; see "Unspeakable," 28.

50 Mulvey, "Visual Pleasure and Narrative Cinema," 837; and Freud, "Melancholia," 246.

51 Freud, "Melancholia," 247; and Tidey, "Limping or Flying?," 63.

52 Mench, "Tracking the Many Voices of Kendrick Lamar"; and Leggett, "Butterflies Use Antenna GPS to Guide Migration." The Gemini "split" is also intriguing when learning what "m.A.A.d." means in the title of the previous album, with emphasis on the first definition: "In an interview with *Los Angeles Leakers*, the Compton's rising rap savior broke it down: 'It's two meanings. The first one is, "my angry adolescence divided," and the basic standout meaning is "my angel's on angel dust"'" (Martins, "Kendrick Lamar.") Of course, the splitting is also doubling as seen with the "A" in duplicate. Moreover, La Marr Jurelle Bruce also highlights ma(a)dness, perhaps of a different sort, when reading "The Blacker the Berry" on *TPAB* as "Lamar's representation of a malevolent person under the sign of 'schizophrenia' [that] lends itself to the stigmatization of people living with the condition" (*How to Go Mad Without Losing Your Mind*, 221–23).

53 Walker, *The Color Purple*, 40.

54 *SoS*, 185; Gillespie, *Film Blackness*, 120; and Manabe, "We Gon' Be Alright?" This medicine reading may vibe with Colin Tilley, the video's director: "For this particular video, I really wanted to tell this story of Kendrick bringing positivity to the world that we created, the m.A.A.d city we created." See Tardio, "Exclusive"; hereafter, "Exclusive." Likewise, Lamar displays the neoteric during his 2016 Grammy performance when he produces a "black-and-white image of Africa . . . The single word 'Compton' is typed in calligraphic letters across the expanse of the continents northern hemisphere" such that Maner contrives, "All of Africa is Compton or Compton is all of Africa"; see Maner, *Kendrick Lamar's* To Pimp a Butterfly, 96–104.

55 Phillips, "The Definitive Breakdown of Kendrick Lamar's 'Alright' Video"; and Dubler and Lloyd, *Break Every Yoke*, 197. See also George, *Trauma and Race*, 1–10.

56 "Exclusive"; Manabe, "We Gon' Be Alright?"; Phillips, "The Definitive Breakdown of Kendrick Lamar's 'Alright' Video"; and Shakespeare, *Antony and Cleopatra*, act 2, scene 2.

57 "Kendrick Lamar Meets Rick Rubin and They Have an Epic Conversation"; hereafter, "EC"; and Manabe, "We Gon' Be Alright?".

58 "Exclusive"; *SoS*, 298; and Tidey, "Limping or Flying?," 52.

59 Flying Lotus, "Never Catch Me" and "Flying Lotus—Never Catch Me ft. Kendrick Lamar." For more on this video, see Neal, *Black Ephemera*, 91–95.

60 Spillers, "MB," 80.

61 Harney and Moten, *The Undercommons*, 50; and "EC," 13:47–16:08.

62 Sharpe, *In the Wake*, 31–32.

63 Hill, "Lost Ones," in *The Miseducation of Lauryn Hill*.

64 Hathaway, in "On Your Own" in *Self Portrait*.

65 D'Angelo, "Playa Playa" and "Africa," in *Voodoo*.

66 Hayden, "Middle Passage," 248 (my emphasis).

67 Spillers, "MB," 80.

68 Ellsworth and Kruse, "Evidence," 20.

69 Morrison, *SoS*, 147, 208, 304, 322, 332, 336.

70 Spillers, "MB," 66. Cio-Cio-san refers to Giacomo Puccini's *Madama Butterfly* (1904), an opera that ironically enough interpolates "The Star-Spangled Banner" in its score. This winks at the nationally tragic, as well as this tidbit: The one-act play the opera derives from by David Belasco is called *Madame Butterfly: A Tragedy in Japan*. See also Honey and Cole, *Madame Butterfly*.

71 Wilson, "Lucy and All of Us," 56; and Spillers, "MB," 80.

72 Crawford, *Black Post-Blackness*, 72.

73 Lamar, "YAH."

74 Crawford, *Black Post-Blackness*, 43–44.

75 "Kendrick Lamar Talks 'u,' His Depression and Suicidal Thoughts (Pt. 2)"; and "i," *TPAB*.

76 Psalm 68:31; and Du Bois, "The Hands of Ethiopia," in *Darkwater*, 94 (my emphasis). See also Maner, *Kendrick Lamar's To Pimp a Butterfly*, 112–16.

77 The Isley Brothers, "That Lady," in *3 + 3*; and Hopkins, *Of One Blood: Or, the Hidden Self*, in *The Magazine Novels of Pauline Hopkins*, 532. For a further reading of "i," see Maner, *Kendrick Lamar's To Pimp a Butterfly*, 108–12; and under the guise of the Black feminine enabling Black male genius in Hopkins's text, see Brooks, *Liner Notes for the Revolution*, 88–90. Likewise, regardless of whether he is a pimp or butterfly, does Lamar, and his apparent Ethiopianism, elicit his (self-)contrivance as a "Black Messiah"? For more on this neoteric history, see Price, "The Cultural Production of a Black Messiah," 418–33.

78 Nurhussein, *Black Land*, 6; and Blount, "Paul Laurence Dunbar and the African American Elegy," 242–43.

79 Nurhussein, *Black Land*, 46.

80 Dunbar, "Ode to Ethiopia," in *Lyrics of Lowly Life*, 30–32; and Nurhussein, *Black Land*, 48.

81 Komunyakaa, "Sorrow Songs and Flying Away," 23.

82 Tate, "Review," 329.

83 Walker, *In Search of Our Mothers' Gardens*, xi.

84 Snoop Doggy Dogg (featuring Nate Dogg, Warren G, and Kurupt), "Ain't No Fun," in *Doggystyle*.

85 Giovanni, "Ego Tripping," in *The Reason I Like Chocolate*. For this poem exemplifying "black female relationality, self-regard," see Quashie, *Black Aliveness, or A Poetics of Being*, 37–39.

86 Jarell, *AFRICOBRA*, xviii. The information about *Negus* is firsthand: I attended the exhibition. See Bey, *yasiin bey*. For exhibition criticism, see Jackson,

"'There Was Silence. It Was Understood'"; and Sundaresan, "The Paradox of Yasiin Bey's 'Negus,' A Rap Album Trapped in An Art Museum." Regarding Lacks's name, Rebecca Skloot writes, "No one knows how she became Henrietta"; either way, that is the name she used and to which she responded. This suggests her nomenclatural agency which devolves into the coinage "HeLa." See Skloot, *The Immortal Life of Henrietta Lacks*, 18. Likewise, Fahamu Pecou has two exhibits that incorporate "negus" in their titles; see *Real Negus Don't Die*; and NEGUS *in Paris*.

87 Moore, "A Meditation on Love."

88 "Lucy."

89 "Exclusive."

90 Marriott, *On Black Men*, xiv; and Luke 19:1–10.

91 Sheff, *All We Are Saying*, 207 (my emphasis).

STUDY | US

1 Wallace, "Richard Wright's Black Medusa," 72; and Moten, *In the Break*, 15; hereafter, *ItB* (emphases in originals). See also Spillers, "Mama's Baby, Papa's Maybe, 65–81; hereafter, "MB."

2 Mackey, *Bedouin Hornbook*, 201; 52.

3 Young, *The Grey Album*, 17–18; and Phillips, *When Blackness Rhymes with Blackness*, 88. Another storying tradition example can be found in the introduction of Muyumba, *The Shadow and the Act*, 1–23.

4 Manning, *Politics of Touch*, xii–xiii.

5 Khanna, "Touching, Unbelonging, and the Absence of Affect," 230–31; and "MB," 80.

6 Moten, "Blackness and Nothingness (Mysticism in the Flesh)," 749–50. Here, I am thinking about Stephen Best's problematizing of the "we"/"our" in *None Like Us*, and especially his turn to melancholy. In brief, he quotes Bryan Wagner who argues, "Africa and its diaspora are older than blackness" such that "Blackness is an indelibly modern condition that cannot be conceptualized apart from epochal changes" (21). I agree with this. But it is how Best spins out Wagner's theorization that gives pause. In other words, if the "issue" with black study is the construction of "we," then how "we" come to be "black" is on the table and thus, a definition of what the "black" in "black study" signifies. If Wagner suggests that blackness is younger than Africa, then what bore blackness such that "we" could even be a legitimating category? Furthermore, if one presumes that the "modern condition" that creates blackness is the Transatlantic slave trade, which itself divided many of "us" because of "them," might Best's formulation be the making of "us" versus "them" where one can never be sure who's who? In all, I am not suggesting that slavery should inhibit one's ability to function, most certainly being "far removed" from it (?). And, for what it is worth, I am not even saying that "we" does not pose its own problems, especially when some decide that "we" does not exist or when others feel

that to exist, "we" must be given up or the cultural fare of "rooting for every-body" who ostensibly constitutes "we." But if an indelible epochal change is that which makes "the black" "black," then should "we" not acknowledge that such a catastrophe is always and ever with "us"? See Best, *None Like Us*, 1–26; and for a review of his text, see Rinehart, "Shadow Acts."

7   Washington, "Introduction," xxx.

8   Wilderson, "The Prison Slave as Hegemony's (Silent) Scandal," 20.

9   Davis, "Reflections on the Black Woman's Role in the Community of Slaves," 10.

10 Farley, "Perfecting Slavery," 251; Marriott, *Haunted Life*, 237, 241; and Clifton, "won't you celebrate with me," 25. Toni Morrison too chronicles invention, almost verbatim to Clifton, regarding Nel Wright and Sula Peace: "Because each had discovered years before that they were neither white nor male, and that all freedom and triumph was forbidden to them, they had to set about creating something else to be." See Morrison, *Sula*, 52. For more on Clifton and Morrison as inventive, see Quashie, *Black Aliveness, or A Poetics of Being*, 23–26, 39–43.

11 Hughes, "I, Too," in *The Collected Poems of Langston Hughes*, 46.

12 Preston, "Nothing from Nothing," in *The Kids & Me*. An aside: This nod to music in black thought always brings to mind how, for example, Spillers's work on psychoanalysis and race is named after Charles Mingus's "All the Things You Could Be by Now If Sigmund Freud's Wife Was Your Mother," 75–141; or how each chapter in Kara Keeling's *The Witch's Flight* "corresponds with a song on the book's soundtrack" (6). Richard Wright would call this the "blue-print for Negro writing."

13 Morrison, *Beloved*, 257–62; 29–31. For more on the antelope scene, see Sharpe, *In the Wake*, 103–4.

14 Césaire, *Notebook of a Return to the Native Land*, 22; India.Arie, "Beautiful"; and Vandross, "I (Who Have Nothing)," in *Power of Love*. For more on ending "the world," see Palmer, "Otherwise Than Blackness," 247–83.

15 Spillers, "The Idea of Black Culture," 26; hereafter, "Idea"; and Derrida, "Force of Law," 969–71. As well, Rinaldo Walcott, in line with Derrida, asserts, "Black free-dom has been denied despite juridical emancipation, and that denial produces the conditions of a future-oriented Black expressivity—a Black freedom to come." See Walcott, "Moving Toward Black Freedom," in *The Long Emancipation*, 5.

16 Derrida, *Specters of Marx*, 52–55.

17 *ItB*, 255; and Muyumba, *The Shadow and the Act*, 21. Apropos to Derrida's jazz, see also Lesinrocks, "Quand Ornette Coleman improvisait avec Jacques Der-rida"; and Murphy, "The Other's Language," 319–29.

18 Marriott, *Haunted Life*, 237–38, 240.

19 McGowan, *Enjoying What We Don't Have*, 284.

20 Freud, "Mourning and Melancholia," 243, 253.

21 For more on black wandering over and against Western philosophical ideals, see Cervenak, *Wandering*.

22 Hartman and Wilderson, "The Position of the Unthought," 183–201; and Said, *Freud and the Non-European*, 53. See also Tate, "Freud and His 'Negro,'" 54–55.

23 Winters, "Rac(e)ing from Death, 383; and Said, *Freud and the Non-European*, 66 (emphasis in original).

24 Derrida, *Specters of Marx*, 103 (emphasis in original).

25 Wallace, "The Hand that Rocks the Cradle Is the Hand that Rules the World," 248.

26 Winters, "Rac(e)ing from Death," 386 (my emphasis).

27 McEntyre, *Caring for Words in a Culture of Lies*, 54; and Du Bois, *The Souls of Black Folk*, 5 (my emphasis). For what it is worth, Du Bois's "Negro and an American" formulation foreruns Stuart Hall who, thinking with Paul Gilroy, intuits that one "can be black *and* British." See Hall, "What Is This 'Black' in Black Popular Culture?," 111.

28 Du Bois, *The Souls of Black Folk*, 5; Cooper, *A Voice from the South*, 144–45; and "Idea," 15 (emphasis in original).

29 Spillers, "Moving on Down the Line," 89; hereafter, "MDL." She also states, "And the whole cluster of contrary, contradistinctive, and contradictory movements, reposing in complex figures of paradox—irony, double entendre, catachresis, oxymoron, ambiguity, ambivalence—answered for me a conceptual theme whose resources would be worked and elaborated across a wide swath of cultural phenomena; through Ellison and Brooks, it appeared that I had arrived at a provisional reading of [Du Bois's] 'double consciousness,' except that the outcome would conduce to the eternal play of oppositions and not their closure. The logic of the hyphen, if we could say so, rests in the movement *between* punctualities so that its elements are always coming and going in the 'contact zone' of mutually incommensurable contents." See Spillers, "Peter's Pans" in *Black, White and in Color*, 10–11. In a similar vein, see also Pinsker, "The Financial Consequences of Saying 'Black,' vs. 'African American'"; and Sigelman, Tuch, and Martin, "What's in a Name?," 429–38.

30 Hill, "Lose Myself."

31 Ward, "What Langston Hughes' Powerful Poem 'I, Too' Tells Us About America's Past and Present."

32 I am contemplating Martin Luther King, Jr. and the notion of integrating black people into a burning house. See Autodidact 17, "Dr. Martin Luther King Jr.: 'I Fear I Am Integrating My People into a Burning House.'"

33 Fanon, *Black Skin, White Masks*, 113–14 (my emphasis).

34 "MDL," 105 (emphasis in original); and Crawford, "The Twenty-First-Century Black Studies Turn to Melancholy," 806–7 (my emphasis).

35 McKay, "If We Must Die," in *Harlem Shadows*, 53; and Lamar, "untitled" in *untitled unmastered*.

36 Hughes, "Note on Commercial Theatre," in *The Collected Poems*, 216.

37 Baldwin, "The Uses of the Blues," 61.

Abdur-Rahman, Aliyyah I. *Against the Closet: Black Political Longing and the Erotics of Race.* Durham, NC: Duke University Press, 2012.

Afro-Pessimism: An Introduction. Accessed April 1, 2022. https://ia601609.us .archive.org/33/items/AfroPessimismread/Afro-pessimism-AnIntroduction.pdf.

"Afro Sheen Commercial (Featuring Frederick Douglass)." *YouTube*, last modified May 28, 2010. https://youtu.be/g8ffzI2czHs.

Aguirre, Abby. "Octavia Butler's Prescient Vision of a Zealot Elected to 'Make America Great Again.'" *The New Yorker*, last modified July 26, 2017. http:// www.newyorker.com/books/second-read/octavia-butlers-prescient-vision-of -a-zealot-elected-to-make-america-great-again/amp.

Ahad, Badia Sahar. *Freud Upside Down: African American Literature and Psychoanalytic Culture.* Urbana: University of Illinois Press, 2010.

Akhtar, Jaleel. *Dismemberment in the Fiction of Toni Morrison.* Newcastle upon Tyne: Cambridge Scholars, 2014.

Akinyela, Makungu M. "In the Wake of Destruction: Ujamaa Circle Process Therapy and Black Family Healing." In *Out of the Revolution: The Development of Africana Studies*, edited by Delores P. Aldridge and Carlene Young, 247–66. Lanham, MD: Lexington Books, 2000.

Alexander, Elizabeth. "'Can You Be BLACK and Look at This?': Reading the Rodney King Video(s)." *Public Culture* 7, no. 1 (1994): 77–94.

Alexander, Elizabeth. "The Negro Digs Up Her Past: 'Amistad.'" *South Atlantic Quarterly* 104, no. 3 (Summer 2005): 463–80.

Allen, Shundalyn. "Everything You Want to Know About Poetic Apostrophe." *grammarly* (blog), July 24, 2016. https://www.grammarly.com/blog/apostrophe-poetry/.

Angelou, Maya. *I Know Why the Caged Bird Sings*. New York: Ballantine Books, 2009 (1997, 1969).

The Angry Architect. "The Perfect Drawing: 8 Sensational Sections That Raise the Bar for Architectural Representation." *Architizer* (blog), May 6, 2014. http://architizer.com/blog/cross-sections/.

Aristotle. *Problems*. In *The Complete Works of Aristotle*, vol. 2, edited by Jonathan Barnes, 1319–1527. Princeton, NJ: Princeton University Press, 1995 (1991, 1985, 1984).

Armstrong, Louis. *Satch Plays Fats: A Tribute to the Immortal Fats Waller*. Columbia, 2000 (1955).

Arnold, William V., and Margaret Ann Fohl. *When You Are Alone*. Louisville, KY: Westminster/John Knox, 1990.

Autodidact 17. "Dr. Martin Luther King Jr.: 'I Fear I Am Integrating My People into a Burning House.'" *New York Amsterdam News*, last modified January 12, 2017. http://amsterdamnews.com/news/2017/jan/12/dr-martin-luther-king-jr-i-fear-i-am-integrating-m/.

Avilez, GerShun. "Review: Margo Natalie Crawford, *Black Post-Blackness: The Black Arts Movement and Twenty-First-Century Aesthetics*." *Journal of American Studies* 54, no. 2 (2020): 456–58.

Avilez, GerShun. "Uncertain Freedom: RuPaul, Sylvester, and Black Queer Contingency." *The Black Scholar* 49, no. 2 (2019): 50–64.

"A Well-Wisher to Great Britain." *The Ten Plagues of England, of Worse Consequence Than Those of Egypt*. London: R. Withy, 1757.

Awkward, Michael. *Scenes of Instruction: A Memoir*. Durham, NC: Duke University Press, 1999.

Awkward-Rich, Cameron. *The Terrible We: Thinking with Trans Maladjustment*. Durham, NC: Duke University Press, 2022.

Bailey, Frankie Y. *African American Mystery Writers: A Historical and Thematic Study*. Jefferson, NC: McFarland, 2008.

Baker, Houston A, Jr. *Blues, Ideology, and Afro-American Literature: A Vernacular Theory*. Chicago: University of Chicago Press, 1984.

Baldwin, James. "Freaks and the American Ideal of Manhood." *Playboy* 32, no. 1 (1985): 150–51, 192, 256–60.

Baldwin, James. *Go Tell It on the Mountain*. New York: Bantam Dell, 1981 (1952).

Baldwin, James. *The Price of the Ticket: Collected Nonfiction, 1948–1985*. New York: Saint Martin's Press, 1985.

Baldwin, James. "The Uses of the Blues." In *The Cross of Redemption: Uncollected Writings*, edited by Randall Kenan, 57–66. New York: Pantheon Books, 2010 (1964).

Ball, Jared A., and Todd Steven Burroughs, eds. *A Lie of Reinvention: Correcting Manning Marable's Malcolm X*. Baltimore: Black Classic Press, 2012.

Barad, Karen "Posthumanist Performativity: Toward an Understanding of How Matter Comes to Matter." *Signs: A Journal of Women in Culture and Society* 28, no. 3 (2003): 801–31.

Baraka, Imamu Amiri (LeRoi Jones). *Blues People: Negro Music in White America.* New York: William Morrow, 1999, (1963).

Baraka, Imamu Amiri. (LeRoi Jones). "Poetry and Karma." In *Raise, Race, Rays, Raze: Essays Since 1965*, 17–26. New York: Random House, 1971.

Baraka, Imamu Amiri (LeRoi Jones). "So the King Sold the Farmer #39." In *S O S: Poems 1961–2013*, 273–76. New York: Grove Press, 2014.

Barclay, Jenifer L. *The Mark of Slavery: Disability, Race, and Gender in Antebellum America.* Urbana: University of Illinois Press, 2021.

Bates, Karen Grigsby. "Octavia Butler: Writing Herself into the Story." *NPR*, last modified July 10, 2017. http://www.npr.org/sections/codeswitch/2017/07/10/535879364/octavia-butler-writing-herself-into-the-story.

Battersby, Christine. *"Gender and Genius (The Clouded Mirror)."* In *The Bloomsbury Anthology of Aesthetics*, edited by Joseph Tanke and Colin McQuillan, 559–70. New York: Bloomsbury Academic, 2012.

Baucom, Ian. *Specters of the Atlantic: Finance Capital, Slavery, and the Philosophy of History.* Durham, NC: Duke University Press, 2005.

Beckford, Robert. *Jesus Dub: Theology, Music and Social Change.* New York: Routledge, 2006.

"Becoming Human: Matter and Meaning in an Antiblack World." The Center for Religion & the Human Presents Zakiyyah Iman Jackson in Conversation with J. Kameron Carter." March 24, 2021. https://crh.indiana.edu/news-events/past-events/zakiyyah-iman-jackson.html.

Belasco, David. *Madame Butterfly: A Tragedy in Japan.* In *Six Plays.* Boston: Little, Brown, 1929 (1900).

Bennett, Joshua. *Being Property Once Myself: Blackness and the End of Man.* Cambridge, MA: Harvard University Press, 2020.

Bennett, Joshua. "Whenever Hemingway Hums Nigger." *Obsidian* 40, nos. 1–2 (Spring 2015): 141.

Best, Stephen. *None Like Us: Blackness, Belonging, Aesthetic Life.* Durham, NC: Duke University Press, 2018.

Bey, Yasiin. *yasiin bey: Negus.* Brooklyn Museum. Brooklyn, NY, November 15, 2019–January 26, 2020. https://www.brooklynmuseum.org/exhibitions/yasiin_bey_negus.

Björk. *Debut.* Elektra, 1993.

"Black Elegies in Sight & Sound." caresyllabus.org. Accessed April 1, 2022. https://www.caresyllabus.org/black-elegies-in-sight-and-sound.

Blount, Marcellus. "Paul Laurence Dunbar and the African American Elegy." *African American Review* 41, no. 2 (Summer 2007): 239–46.

Blumenthal, Rachel A. "Canonicity, Genre, and the Politics of Editing: How We Read Frederick Douglass." *Callaloo: A Journal of African Diaspora Arts and Letters* 36, no. 1 (Winter 2013): 178–90.

Boggs, Nicholas. "A Grammar of Little Manhood: Ralph Ellison and the Queer Little Man at Chehaw Station." *Callaloo: A Journal of African Diaspora Arts and Letters* 35, no. 1 (Winter 2012): 245–66.

Boissoneault, Lorraine. "The Hidden History of Anna Murray Douglass." *Smithsonian Magazine,* last modified March 5, 2018. https://www.smithsonianmag .com/history/hidden-history-anna-murray-douglass-180968324/.

Bolden, Tony. *Afro-blue: Improvisations in African American Poetry and Culture.* Urbana: University of Illinois Press, 2004.

Bosher, Kathryn, Fiona Macintosh, Justine McConnell, and Patrice D. Rankine. "Introduction." In *The Oxford Handbook of Greek Drama in the Americas,* edited by Kathryn Bosher, Fiona Macintosh, Justine McConnell, and Patrice D. Rankine, 1–14. New York: Oxford University Press, 2015.

Boyd, Melba Joyce. *Wrestling with the Muse: Dudley Randall and the Broadside Press.* New York: Columbia University Press, 2003.

Bradley, Adam. *Ralph Ellison in Progress: From* Invisible Man *to* Three Days Before the Shooting. New Haven, CT: Yale University Press, 2010.

Brand, Dionne. "On Narrative, Reckoning and the Calculus of Living and Dying." *The Toronto Star,* July 4, 2020. https://www.thestar.com/entertainment/books /2020/07/04/dionne-brand-on-narrative-reckoning-and-the-calculus-of -living-and-dying.html.

Brand, Dionne. *The Blue Clerk: Ars Poetica in 59 Versos.* Durham, NC: Duke University Press, 2018.

Braxton, Joanne M. "Introduction: The Poetry of Paul Laurence Dunbar." In *The Collected Poetry of Paul Laurence Dunbar,* edited by Joanne M. Braxton, ix–xxxvi. Charlottesville: University Press of Virginia, 1993 (1913).

"Breakfast Club Classic—Kendrick Lamar Talks Overcoming Depression, Responsibility to the Culture." *YouTube,* last modified April 11, 2017. https:// youtu.be/nVtH55HizPM.

Brewton, Vince. "'Bold Defiance Took Its Place'—'Respect' and Self-Making in *Narrative of the Life of Frederick Douglass, an American Slave.*" *The Mississippi Quarterly* 58, no. 3–4 (Summer–Fall 2005): 703–17.

Brody, Jennifer DeVere. "The Blackness of Blackness . . . Reading the Typography of *Invisible Man.*" In *Ralph Ellison's* Invisible Man, edited by Harold Bloom, 85–110. New York: Infobase, 2009.

Brody, Jennifer DeVere. *Punctuation: Art, Politics, and Play.* Durham, NC: Duke University Press, 2008.

Bromell, Nick. *The Time Is Always Now: Black Thought and the Transformation of US Democracy.* New York: Oxford University Press, 2017 (2013).

Brooks, Daphne A. *Liner Notes for the Revolution: The Intellectual Life of Black Feminist Sound.* Cambridge, MA: Harvard University Press, 2021.

Brooks, Gwendolyn. "Primer for Blacks." In *The Essential Gwendolyn Brooks,* edited by Elizabeth Alexander, 118–20. New York: Library of America, 2005.

Brooks, Gwendolyn. *Report from Part One.* Detroit, MI: Broadside Press, 1972.

Brown, Kimberly Juanita. *The Repeating Body: Slavery's Visual Resonance in the Contemporary.* Durham, NC: Duke University Press, 2015.

Brown, Lawrence T. *The Black Butterfly: The Harmful Politics of Race and Space in America*. Baltimore: Johns Hopkins University Press, 2021. Accessed April 1, 2022. https://jhupbooks.press.jhu.edu/title/black-butterfly.

Bruce, La Marr Jurelle. *How to Go Mad Without Losing Your Mind: Madness and Black Radical Creativity*. Durham, NC: Duke University Press, 2021.

Bruce, Dickson D, Jr. "James Corrothers Reads a Book; Or, the Lives of Sandy Jenkins." *African American Review* 26, no. 4 (Winter, 1992): 665–73.

Burgett, Bruce. *Sentimental Bodies: Sex, Gender, and Citizenship in the Early Republic*. Princeton, NJ: Princeton University Press, 1998.

Burke, Edmund. *The Works of the Right Honourable Edmund Burke in Twelve Volumes, Volume the First*. Project Gutenberg Ebook, 2005; London: John C. Nimmo, 1887 (1757, 1756). http://www.gutenberg.org/files/15043/15043-h/15043-h.htm.

Butler, Judith. *Gender Trouble: Feminism and the Subversion of Identity*. New York: Routledge, 2008 (2006, 1999, 1990).

Butler, Judith. *The Psychic Life of Power*. Stanford, CA: Stanford University Press. 1997.

Butler, Octavia E. "Bloodchild." In *Bloodchild and Other Stories*, 3–29. New York: Seven Stories Press, 2005.

Butler, Octavia E. "Bloodchild." *Isaac Asimov's Science Fiction Magazine* (June 1984): 34–54.

Butler, Octavia E. *Fledgling*. New York: Grand Central, 2007.

Byron, Lord. *Childe Harold's Pilgrimage: A Romaunt*. London: John Murray, 1812.

Callahan, John F. "John F. Callahan on Ralph Ellison's Two Inviolable Identities." *Literary Hub*, last modified January 16, 2020. https://lithub.com/john-f-callahan-on-ralph-ellisons-two-inviolable-identities/.

Campt, Tina M. *Listening to Images*. Durham, NC: Duke University Press, 2017.

Campt, Tina M. *Other Germans: Black Germans and the Politics of Race, Gender, and Memory in the Third Reich*. Ann Arbor: University of Michigan Press, 2004.

Cannon, Katie Geneva. *Black Womanist Ethics*. Eugene, OR: Wipf and Stock, 2006 (1988).

Cannon, Katie Geneva. "The Emergence of Black Feminist Consciousness." In *Feminist Interpretation of the Bible*, edited by Letty M. Russell, 30–40. Louisville, KY: Westminster John Knox, 1985.

Cannon, Katie Geneva. *Katie's Canon: Womanism and the Soul of the Black Community*. New York: Continuum, 1995.

Carby, Hazel V. *Race Men*. Cambridge, MA: Harvard University Press, 1998.

"Carlton Hall Video Blog-Jamie Foxx NAACP Image Award Speech." *YouTube*, last modified February 27, 2013. https://youtu.be/iBs1vPjXDac.

Celeste, Manoucheka. "'What Now?': The Wailing Black Woman, Grief, and Difference." *Black Camera: An International Film Journal* 9, no. 2 (Spring 2018): 110–31.

Cervenak, Sarah Jane. *Wandering: Philosophical Performances of Racial and Sexual Freedom*. Durham, NC: Duke University Press, 2014.

Césaire, Aimé. *Notebook of a Return to the Native Land,* translated and edited by Clayton Eshleman and Annette Smith. Middletown, CT: Wesleyan University Press, 2001 (1947).

Chaney, Michael A. "Picturing the Mother, Claiming Egypt: *My Bondage and My Freedom* as Auto(bio)ethnography." *African American Review* 35, no. 3 (2001): 391–408.

Cheng, Anne Anlin. *The Melancholy of Race: Psychoanalysis, Assimilation, and Hidden Grief.* New York: Oxford University Press, 2000.

Cheng, Anne Anlin. "Ralph Ellison and the Politics of Melancholia." In *The Cambridge Companion to Ralph Ellison,* edited by Ross Posnock, 121–36. New York: Cambridge University Press, 2005.

Chester, Alfred, and Vilma Howard. "The Art of Fiction: An Interview." *The Paris Review* 8 (Spring 1955): 55–71. http://www.theparisreview.org/interviews/5053 /the-art-of-fiction-no-8-ralph-ellison.

Chrisman, Robert. "Robert Hayden: The Transition Years, 1946–1948." In *Robert Hayden: Essays on the Poetry,* edited by Laurence Goldstein and Robert Chrisman, 129–54. Ann Arbor: University of Michigan Press, 2013 (2001).

Christian, Barbara. "A Study of 'In Love and Trouble': The Contrary Women of Alice Walker." *The Black Scholar* 12, no. 2 (March/April 1981): 21–30, 70–71.

Clarke, Shirley, dir. *Portrait of Jason.* Film-Makers' Distribution Center, 1967.

Clewell, Tammy. "Mourning Beyond Melancholia: Freud's Psychoanalysis of Loss." *Journal of the American Psychoanalytic Association* 52, no. 1 (March 2004): 43–67.

Clifton, Lucille. "won't you celebrate with me." In *Book of Light,* 25. Port Townsend, WA: Copper Canyon Press, 1993.

Cobb, Jasmine Nichole. *New Growth: The Art and Texture of Black Hair.* Durham, NC: Duke University Press, 2023.

Cobb, Jasmine Nichole. *Picture Freedom: Remaking Black Visuality in the Early Nineteenth Century.* New York: New York University Press, 2015.

Cobb, Kelton. *The Blackwell Guide to Theology and Popular Culture.* Malden, MA: Blackwell, 2005.

Colbert, Soyica Diggs. *Black Movements: Performance and Cultural Politics.* New Brunswick, NJ: Rutgers University Press, 2017.

Cole, Caroline. "The Blues." In *Blue: Cobalt to Cerulean in Art and Culture,* 158–73. San Francisco: Chronicle Books, 2015.

Coleman, Monica A. "Roundtable Discussion: Must I Be a Womanist? [with Response]." *Journal of Feminist Studies in Religion* 22, no. 1 (Spring 2006): 85–134.

Coleridge, Samuel Taylor. *The Rime of the Ancient Mariner,* edited by M. A. Eaton. Boston: Educational Publishing, 1906.

Collins, Patricia Hill. *Black Feminist Thought: Knowledge, Consciousness, and the Politics of Empowerment.* New York: Routledge, 1991.

Commander, Michelle D. *Afro-Atlantic Flight: Speculative Returns and the Black Fantastic.* Durham, NC: Duke University Press, 2017.

Cone, James H. *Black Theology and Black Power.* New York: Orbis Books, 2008 (1997, 1989, 1969).

Cone, James H. *The Cross and the Lynching Tree*. New York: Orbis Books, 2011.

Cone, James H. *The Spirituals and the Blues*. New York: Orbis Books, 1991 (1972).

Cook, William W., and James Tatum. *African American Writers and Classical Tradition*. Chicago: University of Chicago Press, 2010.

Cooper, Anna Julia. *A Voice from the South*. New York: Oxford University Press, 1988 (1892).

Cortázar, Julio. "La noche boca arriba." *Ciudad Seva*. Accessed April 1, 2022. http://www.ciudadseva.com/textos/cuentos/esp/cortazar/la_noche_boca _arriba.htm.

Cotter, Holland. "Glenn Ligon Rethinks the Color Line in the Show 'Blue Black.'" *The New York Times*, last modified August 10, 2017. https://www.nytimes.com /2017/08/10/arts/design/glenn-ligon-rethinks-the-color-line-in-the-show -blue-black.html.

Crawford, Margo Natalie. *Black Post-Blackness: The Black Arts Movement and Twenty-First-Century Aesthetics*. Urbana: University of Illinois Press, 2017.

Crawford, Margo Natalie. "The Twenty-First-Century Black Studies Turn to Melancholy." *American Literary History* 29, no. 4 (Winter 2017): 799–807.

Crawford, Margo Natalie. *What Is African American Literature?* Hoboken, NJ: John Wiley, 2021.

Cruz, Jon. *Culture on the Margins: The Black Spiritual and the Rise of American Cultural Interpretation*. Princeton, NJ: Princeton University Press, 1999.

D'Angelo. *Voodoo*. Cheeba Sound/Virgin, 2000.

D'Angelo and The Vanguard. *Black Messiah*. RCA Records, 2014.

"Daphne Brooks, 'Lemonade from Lemons: Black Women Artists and the Gershwin Problem, 1935–2020' Pt. 2." *YouTube*, last modified October 29, 2020. https://youtu.be/Kyv8hJvKxYU.

Davis, Angela Y. *Blues Legacies and Black Feminism: Gertrude "Ma" Rainey, Bessie Smith, and Billie Holiday*. New York: Vintage, 1999.

Davis, Angela Y. "Reflections on the Black Woman's Role in the Community of Slaves." *The Black Scholar* 3, no. 4 (December 1971): 2–15.

Davis, Miles. *Miles*. New York: Simon and Schuster, 1989.

DeLue, Rachel Ziady. "Envisioning Race in Spike Lee's *Bamboozled*." In *Fight the Power!: The Spike Lee Reader*, edited by Janice D. Hamlet and Robin R. Means Coleman, 61–88. New York: Peter Lang, 2009.

Derrida, Jacques. *The Animal That Therefore I Am*, edited by Marie-Louise Mallet and translated by David Wills. New York: Fordham University Press, 2008 (2006).

Derrida, Jacques. "Force of Law: The 'Mystical Foundation' of Authority," translated by Mary Quaintance. *Cardozo Law Review* 11, nos. 5–6 (1990): 919–1046.

Derrida, Jacques. *Geneses, Genealogies, Genres, and Genius: The Secrets of the Archive*, translated by Beverley Bie Brahic. New York: Columbia University Press, 2006 (2003).

Derrida, Jacques. "The Law of Genre." In *Signature Derrida*, translated by Avital Ronell, 3–32. Chicago: University of Chicago Press, 2013.

Derrida, Jacques. *Specters of Marx: The State of the Debt, the Work of Mourning and the New International*, translated by Peggy Kamuf. New York: Routledge, 2006 (1994, 1993).

Dickinson, Emily. *Essential Dickinson*. New York: HarperCollins, 1996.

Diedrich, Maria. *Love across Color Lines: Ottilie Assing and Frederick Douglass*. New York: Hill and Wang, 1999.

Dixon, Melvin. "Review: 'If You Surrender to the Air . . .'" *Callaloo: A Journal of African Diaspora Arts and Letters* 4 (October, 1978): 170–73.

Donahue, Joseph. "Epic World." *poetryfoundation.org*, last modified May 6, 2014. https://www.poetryfoundation.org/features/articles/detail/70116.

Douglass, Frederick. *Men of Color, to Arms! A call* (broadside). Rochester, 1863. https://cdm.bostonathenaeum.org/digital/collection/p16057coll37/id/1336.

Douglass, Frederick. *My Bondage and My Freedom*. New York: Dover, 1969 (1855).

Douglass, Frederick. "Pictures and Progress: An Address Delivered in Boston, Massachusetts, on 3 December 1861." In *The Frederick Douglass Papers: Series One, Speeches, Debates, and Interviews*, vol. 3, edited by John W. Blassingame, 452–73. New Haven, CT: Yale University Press, 1985.

Douglass, Frederick. *The Life and Times of Frederick Douglass*. New York: Dover, 2003 (1892).

Douglass, Frederick. *The Narrative of the Life of Frederick Douglass, An American Slave*. LaVergne, TN: Anti-Slavery Office, 2009 (1845).

Douglass, Frederick. "What the Black Man Wants (1865)." In *Great Speeches by Frederick Douglass*, edited by James Daley, 51–58. New York: Dover, 2013.

Drake. *Take Care*. Young Money, 2011.

Dr. Buzzard's Original Savannah Band. *Dr. Buzzard's Original "Savannah" Band*. RCA, 1976.

Du Bois, W. E. B. *Darkwater: Voices from Within the Veil*. New York: Humanity Books, 2003 (1920).

Du Bois, W. E. B. *The Souls of Black Folk*. New York: Penguin, 1996 (1989, 1903).

Dubler, Joshua, and Vincent W. Lloyd. *Break Every Yoke: Religion, Justice, and the Abolition of Prisons*. New York: Oxford University Press, 2020.

Dunaway, Wilma A. *The African-American Family in Slavery and Emancipation*. New York: Cambridge University Press, 2003.

Dunbar, Paul Laurence. *Lyrics of Love and Laughter*. New York: Dodd, Mead, 1908 (1903).

Dunbar, Paul Laurence. *Lyrics of Lowly Life*. New York: Dodd, Mead, 1898 (1896).

Dunbar, Paul Laurence. *Majors and Minors: Poems*. Toledo, OH: Hadley and Hadley, 1895.

Dungy, Camille T., ed. *Black Nature: Four Centuries of African American Nature Poetry*. Athens: University of Georgia Press, 2009.

Dunne, Éamonn. *Reading Theory Now: An ABC of Good Reading with J. Hillis Miller*. New York: Bloomsbury Academic, 2013.

Durham, I. A. "Richard Pryor: Melancholy and the Religion of Tragicomedy." *Journal of Religion and Health* 50, no. 1 (2011): 132–44.

Durham, I. Augustus. "The D'Angelo Cycle." *NewBlackMan (in Exile)* (blog), December 19, 2014. http://www.newblackmaninexile.net/2014/12/the-dangelo -cycle.html.

Dyson, Michael Eric. *Mercy, Mercy Me: The Art, Loves and Demons of Marvin Gaye.* New York: Basic Civitas Books, 2004.

Early, Gerald. *Ralph Ellison: Invisible Man.* New York: Marshall Cavendish Benchmark, 2010.

Edwards, Brent Hayes. "The Taste of the Archive." *Callaloo: A Journal of African Diaspora Arts and Letters* 35, no. 4 (2012): 944–72.

Edwin Hawkins and the Edwin Hawkins Singers. *The Comforter.* Birthright Records, 1977.

Eidsheim, Nina Sun. *The Race of Sound: Listening, Timbre, and Vocality in African American Music.* Durham, NC: Duke University Press, 2019.

Elfenbein, Andrew. *Romantic Genius: The Prehistory of a Homosexual Role.* New York: Columbia University Press, 1999.

Eliot, George. *Daniel Deronda.* New York: Harper and Brothers, 1876. https:// archive.org/stream/danielderondaooelioiala#page/no/mode/2up.

Ellison, Ralph. *The Collected Essays of Ralph Ellison*, edited by John F. Callahan. New York: Modern Library, 2003 (1995, 1994).

Ellison, Ralph. *Invisible Man.* New York: Vintage Books, 1995 (1952).

Ellison, Ralph. "The Little Man at Chehaw Station: An American Artist and His Audience." *American Scholar* 47, no. 1 (1978): 25–48.

Ellison, Ralph. *The Selected Letters of Ralph Ellison*, edited by John F. Callahan and Marc C. Conner. New York: Random House, 2019.

Ellison, Ralph. *Shadow and Act.* New York: Vintage Books, 1995 (1964).

Ellsworth, Elizabeth, and Jamie Kruse. "Evidence: Making a Geologic Turn in Cultural Awareness." In *Making the Geologic Now: Responses to Material Conditions of Contemporary Life*, edited by Elizabeth Ellsworth and Jamie Kruse, 6–26. New York: Punctum Books, 2013.

El Shibli, Fatima. "Islam and the Blues." *Souls: A Critical Journal of Black Politics, Culture, and Society* 9, no. 2 (2007): 162–70.

Eng, David L. *Racial Castration: Managing Masculinity in Asian America.* Durham, NC: Duke University Press, 2001.

Eng, David L., and David Kazanjian. "Introduction—Mourning Remains." In *Loss: The Politics of Mourning*, edited by David L. Eng and David Kazanjian, 1–25. Berkeley: University of California Press, 2003.

"Ep. 21 'Falsetto Vs. Head Voice'-Voice Lessons to the World." *YouTube*, last modified July 27, 2012. https://youtu.be/qxQOespT4Bs.

Equiano, Olaudah. *The Interesting Narrative of the Life of Olaudah Equiano, Or Gustavus Vassa, The African by Himself*, edited by Brycchan Carey. New York: Oxford University Press, 2018 (1789).

"Ernest Hemingway in Africa." *ernesthemingwaycollection.com*, 2014, last modified April 1, 2022. https://www.ernesthemingwaycollection.com/about -hemingway/ernest-hemingway-in-africa.

Etoke, Nathalie. *Melancholia Africana: The Indispensable Overcoming of the Black Condition.* London: Rowman and Littlefield, 2019 (2010).

Fanon, Frantz. *Black Skin, White Masks,* translated by Richard Philcox. New York: Grove Press, 2008 (1952).

Fanon, Frantz. "The Fact of Blackness." In *Theories of Race and Racism: A Reader,* edited by Les Black and John Solomos, 257–66. New York: Routledge, 2000.

Fanon, Frantz. *The Wretched of the Earth,* translated by Richard Philcox. New York: Grove Press, 2004 (1963).

Farley, Anthony P. "Perfecting Slavery." *Loyola University Chicago Law Journal* 36, no. 1 (2005): 225–55.

Ferguson, Roderick A. *Aberrations in Black: Toward a Queer of Color Critique.* Minneapolis: University of Minnesota Press, 2004.

Fetrow, Fred M. "Minority Reporting and Psychic Distancing in the Poetry of Robert Hayden." *CLA Journal* 33, no. 2 (December 1989): 117–29.

Fetrow, Fred M. "Reading the Man: Robert Hayden and the Legacy of Frederick Douglass." *CLA Journal* 44, no. 2 (December 2000): 189–203.

Fetrow, Fred M. "Robert Hayden's 'Frederick Douglass': Form and Meaning in a Modern Sonnet." *CLA Journal* 17, no. 1 (September, 1973): 79–84.

Fisher, Rebecka Rutledge. *Habitations of the Veil: Metaphor and the Poetics of Black Being in African American Literature.* Albany: State University of New York Press, 2014.

Fishkin, Shelley Fisher. *Writing America: Literary Landmarks from Walden Pond to Wounded Knee, a Reader's Companion.* New Brunswick, NJ: Rutgers University Press, 2015.

Flory, Andrew. *I Hear a Symphony: Motown and Crossover R&B.* Ann Arbor: University of Michigan Press, 2017.

Flying Lotus. *You're Dead.* Warp, 2014.

"Flying Lotus—Never Catch Me ft. Kendrick Lamar." *YouTube,* last modified October 1, 2014. https://youtu.be/2lXDovv-ds8.

Foley, Barbara. *Wrestling with the Left: The Making of Ralph Ellison's Invisible Man.* Durham, NC: Duke University Press, 2010.

Foucault, Michel. *Discipline and Punish: The Birth of the Prison,* translated by Alan Sheridan. New York: Vintage Books, 1995 (1978, 1977, 1975).

Foucault, Michel. *The History of Sexuality, Volume I: An Introduction,* translated by Robert Hurley. New York: Vintage Books, 1990 (1978, 1976).

Foucault, Michel. *Madness and Civilization: A History of Insanity in the Age of Reason,* translated by Richard Howard. New York: Vintage Books, 1988 (1965, 1961).

Foucault, Michel. "Madness, the Absence of Work." In *Foucault and His Interlocutors,* edited by Arnold I. Davidson, 97–104. Chicago: University of Chicago Press, 1997.

Foucault, Michel. *The Order of Things: An Archaeology of the Human Sciences.* New York: Routledge, 2002 (1989, 1970, 1966).

Fought, Leigh. *Women in the World of Frederick Douglass.* New York: Oxford University Press, 2017.

Foxwell, Trish. *A Visitor's Guide to the Literary South.* Woodstock, VT: Countryman Press, 2013.

Frazier, Chelsea M. "Thinking Red, Wounds, and Fungi in Wangechi Mutu's EcoArt." In *Ecologies, Agents, Terrains,* edited by Christopher P. Heuer and Rebecca Zorach, 167–94. New Haven, CT: Yale University Press, 2018.

Freud, Sigmund. *Beyond the Pleasure Principle,* translated by James Strachey. New York: W. W. Norton, 1961 (1959).

Freud, Sigmund. "Mourning and Melancholia." In *The Standard Edition of the Complete Psychological Works of Sigmund Freud, Volume XIV (1914–1916): On the History of the Psycho-Analytic Movement, Papers on Metapsychology* and *Other Works,* translated by James Strachey, 243–58. London: Hogarth Press, 1957.

Freud, Sigmund. "A Note Upon the 'Mystic Writing-Pad.'" In *The Standard Edition of the Complete Psychological Works of Sigmund Freud, Volume XIX (1923–1925): The Ego and the Id and Other Works,* translated by James Strachey, 226–32. London: Hogarth Press, 1961.

Freud, Sigmund. *On Dreams* (unabridged), translated by M. D. Eder. New York: Dover, 2001 (1914).

Freud, Sigmund. *The Question of Lay Analysis: Conversations with an Impartial Person,* translated and edited by James Strachey. New York: W. W. Norton, 1978 (1964, 1962, 1959, 1950).

Furlonge, Nicole Brittingham. "'To Hear the Silence of Sound': Making Sense of Listening in Ralph Ellison's *Invisible Man.*" *Interference Journal* 1 (2011): 1–12. http://www.interferencejournal.org/wp-content/uploads/2011/09/Interference-Journal-Issue-1-To-Hear-the-Silence-of-Sound.pdf.

Gabriel, Charles H. "The Palms." *The National Baptist Hymnal.* Nashville, TN: National Baptist Publishing, 1977.

Gates, Henry Louis, Jr. *The Signifying Monkey: A Theory of African American Literary Criticism.* New York: Oxford University Press, 2014 (1988).

Gaye, Frankie. *Marvin Gaye, My Brother.* San Francisco: Backbeat Books, 2003.

Gaye, Jan. *After the Dance: My Life with Marvin Gaye.* New York: HarperCollins, 2015.

Gaye, Marvin. "Trouble Man." *Trouble Man Motion Picture Soundtrack.* Tamla, 1972.

Gaye, Marvin. *What's Going On.* Tamla, 1971.

Gazaway, Amerigo. *Yasiin Gaye: The Return (Side Two),* June 4, 2014. http://soulmatesproject.com/2014/06/04/download-yasiin-gaye-return-side-two/.

"genius, n. and adj." OED *Online,* last modified January 2018. Oxford University Press. http://www.oed.com.proxy.lib.duke.edu/view/Entry/77607?redirectedFrom=genius.

George, Nelson. *Buppies, B-boys, Baps, and Bohos: Notes on Post-Soul Black Culture*. Cambridge, MA: Da Capo, 2001 (1992).

George, Nelson. *Hip Hop America*. New York: Penguin, 2005 (1998).

George, Sheldon. *Trauma and Race: A Lacanian Study of African American Racial Identity*. Waco, TX: Baylor University Press, 2016.

Gerima, Haile. *Sankofa*. Mypheduh Films, 1993.

Gershwin, George. "Gone, Gone, Gone." *Porgy and Bess*. Trevor Nunn, dir. London Philharmonic. London, 1989.

Gershwin, George. "My Man's Gone Now." *Porgy and Bess*. Trevor Nunn, dir. London Philharmonic. London, 1989.

"Gershwin: Porgy and Bess—Gone Gone Gone." *YouTube*, last modified July 20, 2010. http://youtu.be/1GqoeuIvKPI.

Giles, Paul. "Douglass's Black Atlantic: Britain, Europe, Egypt." In *The Cambridge Companion to Frederick Douglass*, edited by Maurice S. Lee, 132–45. New York: Cambridge University Press, 2009.

Giles, Paul. *Virtual Americas: Transnational Fictions and the Transatlantic Imaginary*. Durham, NC: Duke University Press, 2002.

Gillespie, Michael Boyce. *Film Blackness: American Cinema and the Idea of Black Film*. Durham, NC: Duke University Press, 2016.

Gilroy, Paul. *The Black Atlantic: Modernity and Double Consciousness*. New York: Verso, 1993.

Giovanni, Nikki. *The Reason I Like Chocolate*. Folkways Records, 1976.

Glissant, Édouard. "One World in Relation: Édouard Glissant in Conversation with Manthia Diawara." *Nka: Journal of Contemporary African Art* 28 (2011): 4–19.

Glissant, Édouard. *Poetics of Relation*, translated by Betsy Wing. Ann Arbor: University of Michigan Press, 1997 (1990).

Golden, Thelma. *Freestyle: The Studio Museum in Harlem*. New York: Studio Museum in Harlem, 2001.

Goldstone, Dwonna. "Hughes, Langston (1902–1967)." In *The Frederick Douglass Encyclopedia*, edited by Julius E. Thompson, James L. Conyers, Jr., and Nancy J. Dawson, 85–86. Santa Barbara, CA: Greenwood Press, 2010.

Gordon, Lewis R. "Afro pessimism." *Contemporary Political Theory* 17, no. 1 (2017): 105–37.

Gordon, Lewis R. "Theory in Black: Teleological Suspensions in Philosophy of Culture." *Qui Parle* 18, no. 2 (Spring/Summer 2010): 193–214.

Gordon, Lewis R. "When I Was There, It Was Not: On Secretions Once Lost in the Night." *Performance Research* 12, no. 3 (2007): 8–15.

Gordy, Berry, dir. *Mahogany*. Paramount Pictures, 1975.

Grandy, Moses. *Narrative of the Life of Moses Grandy, Late a Slave in the United States of America*. Chapel Hill: University of North Carolina Press, 2011 (1843).

Grant, Jacquelyn. *White Women's Christ and Black Women's Jesus: Feminist Christology and Womanist Response*. Atlanta: Scholars Press, 1989.

Gray, Thomas R. *The Confessions of Nat Turner*. Baltimore: Lucas and Deaver, 1831. https://digitalcommons.unl.edu/cgi/viewcontent.cgi?article=1014&context=etas.

Green, Michelle Erica. "'There Goes the Neighborhood': Octavia Butler's Demand for Diversity in Utopias." In *Utopian and Science Fiction by Women: Worlds of Difference*, edited by Jane L. Donawerth and Carol A. Kolmerten, 166–89. Syracuse, NY: Syracuse University Press, 1994.

Griffin, Farah Jasmine. *In Search of Billie Holiday: If You Can't Be Free, Be a Mystery*. New York: One World Books, 2002.

Griffin, Farah Jasmine. "That the Mothers May Soar and the Daughters May Know Their Names: A Retrospective of Black Feminist Literary Criticism." *Signs: A Journal of Women in Culture and Society* 32, no. 2 (Winter 2007): 483–507.

Griffin, Farah Jasmine. "When Malindy Sings: A Meditation on Black Women's Vocality." In *Uptown Conversation: The New Jazz Studies*, edited by Robert G. O'Meally, Brent Hayes Edwards, and Farah Jasmine Griffin, 102–25. New York: Columbia University Press, 2004.

Griffin, Farah Jasmine. *"Who Set You Flowin'?": The African-American Migration Narrative*. New York: Oxford University Press, 1995.

Gumbs, Alexis Pauline, China Martens, and Mai'a Williams, eds. *Revolutionary Mothering: Love on the Front Lines*. Oakland, CA: PM Press, 2016.

Gyarkye, Lovia. "The Importance of Being Ordinary." *New Republic*, last modified July 19, 2017. https://newrepublic.com/article/143927/importance-ordinary.

Halberstam, Judith (Jack). *The Queer Art of Failure*. Durham, NC: Duke University Press, 2011.

Haley, Alex. *The Autobiography of Malcolm X*. New York: Ballantine Books, 1964.

Hall, Stuart. "What Is This 'Black' in Black Popular Culture?" *Social Justice* 20, no. 1/2 (Spring–Summer 1993): 104–14.

Hamilton, Adam. *Christianity and World Religions: Questions We Ask about Other Faiths*. Rev. ed. Nashville, TN: Abingdon Press, 2018 (2005).

Hansen, Drew. "Mahalia Jackson, and King's Improvisation." *The New York Times*, last modified August 27, 2013. http://www.nytimes.com/2013/08/28/opinion/mahalia-jackson-and-kings-rhetorical-improvisation.html.

Haraway, Donna J. *Simians, Cyborgs, and Women: The Reinvention of Nature*. New York: Routledge, 1991.

Harney, Stefano, and Fred Moten. *The Undercommons: Fugitive Planning and Black Study*. New York: Minor Compositions, 2013.

Harper, Phillip Brian. *Abstractionist Aesthetics: Artistic Form and Social Critique in African American Culture*. New York: New York University Press, 2015.

Harper, Rachel M. "Crazy." In *Black Cool: One Thousand Streams of Blackness*, edited by Rebecca Walker, 19–28. Berkeley, CA: Soft Skull, 2012.

Harry Simeone Chorale. *The Wonderful Songs of Christmas*. Mercury Records, 1962.

Hartman, Saidiya V. "The Belly of the World: A Note on Black Women's Labors." *Souls: A Critical Journal of Black Politics, Culture, and Society* 18, no. 1 (January–March 2016): 166–73.

Hartman, Saidiya V. "Intimate History, Radical Narrative." For "Online Roundtable: Saidiya Hartman's 'Wayward Lives, Beautiful Experiments.'" *Black Perspectives* (blog), May 22, 2020. https://www.aaihs.org/intimate-history-radical-narrative/.

Hartman, Saidiya V. *Lose Your Mother: A Journey along the Atlantic Slave Route.* New York: Farrar, Straus, and Giroux, 2008.

Hartman, Saidiya V. "Ralph Ellison's Letters Reveal a Complex Philosopher of Black Expression." *The New York Times,* last modified December 19, 2019. https://www.nytimes.com/2019/12/19/books/review/the-selected-letters-of -ralph-ellison.html.

Hartman, Saidiya V. *Scenes of Subjection: Terror, Slavery, and Self-Making in Nineteenth-Century America.* New York: Oxford University Press, 1997.

Hartman, Saidiya V. "Venus in Two Acts." *Small Axe* 26, 12, no. 2 (June 2008): 1–14.

Hartman, Saidiya V. *Wayward Lives, Beautiful Experiments: Intimate Histories of Social Upheaval.* New York: Norton, 2019.

Hartman, Saidiya V., and Frank B. Wilderson, III. "The Position of the Un-thought." *Qui Parle: Critical Humanities and Social Sciences* 13, no. 2 (Spring/Summer 2003): 183–201.

Hathaway, Lalah. *Self Portrait.* Stax, 2008.

Hawks, Carrie. *black enuf*.* New York: Third World Newsreel, 2016.

Hayden, Robert. "Frederick Douglass." *The Atlantic,* last modified June 28, 2020. https://www.theatlantic.com/books/archive/2020/06/frederick-douglass -poem-robert-hayden/613600/.

Hayden, Robert. "Middle Passage." *Phylon* 6, no. 3 (1945): 247–53.

Hayes, Terrance. "But There Never Was a Black Male Hysteria." In *American Sonnets for My Past and Future Assassin,* 55. New York: Penguin, 2018.

Heidegger, Martin. *Being and Time,* translated by John Macquarrie and Edward Robinson. New York: HarperCollins, 2008 (1962).

Helford, Elyce Rae. "'Would You Really Rather Die Than Bear My Young?': The Construction of Gender, Race, and Species in Octavia E. Butler's 'Bloodchild.'" *African American Review* 28, no. 2 (Summer 1994): 259–71.

Hemphill, Essex. "'In Living Color': Toms, Coons, Mammies, Faggots, and Bucks." In *Out in the Culture: Gay, Lesbian, and Queer Essays on Popular Culture,* edited by Corey K. Creekmur and Alexander Doty, 389–401. Durham, NC: Duke University Press, 1995.

Hersey, John. "'A Completion of Personality': A Talk with Ralph Ellison." In *Conversations with Ralph Ellison,* edited by Maryemma Graham and Amritjit Singh, 272–301. Jackson: University Press of Mississippi, 1995.

Hesse, Barnor. "Marked Unmarked: Black Politics and the Western Political." *South Atlantic Quarterly* 110, no. 4 (2011): 974–84.

Hill, Lauryn. "Lose Myself." *Surf's Up: Music from the Motion Picture.* Columbia Records, 2007.

Hill, Lauryn. *The Miseducation of Lauryn Hill.* Ruffhouse/Columbia, 1998.

Hinson, Maurice. *The Pianist's Dictionary.* Bloomington: Indiana University Press, 2004.

Holland, Sharon. *Raising the Dead: Readings of Death and (Black) Subjectivity.* Durham, NC: Duke University Press, 2000.

Holloway, Karla FC. *Passed On: African American Mourning Stories.* Durham, NC: Duke University Press, 2002.

Holloway, Karla FC. *Private Bodies, Public Texts: Race, Gender, and a Cultural Bioethics.* Durham, NC: Duke University Press, 2011.

Honey, Maureen, and Jean Lee Cole, eds. *Madame Butterfly / John Luther Long and A Japanese Nightingale / Onoto Watanna (Winnifred Eaton): Two Orientalist Texts.* New Brunswick, NJ: Rutgers University Press, 2002.

hooks, bell. "Representations of Whiteness." In *Black Looks: Race and Representation,* 165–78. Boston: South End Press, 1992.

Hopkins, Pauline. *The Magazine Novels of Pauline Hopkins.* New York: Oxford University Press, 1988.

"Hortence [*sic*] Spillers and Gail Lewis at the Institute of Contemporary Arts." *YouTube,* last modified June 25, 2018. https://youtu.be/tQoORQqSaWU.

Hudson, Peter James. "Frederick Douglass and American Empire in Haiti." *Boston Review,* last modified December 9, 2021. https://bostonreview.net/articles/frederick-douglass-and-american-empire-in-haiti/.

Huggins, Nathan Irvin. *Slave and Citizen: The Life of Frederick Douglass.* New York: Longman, 1980.

Hughes, Langston. *Ask Your Mama: 12 Moods for Jazz.* New York: Alfred A. Knopf, 1961.

Hughes, Langston. *The Collected Poems of Langston Hughes,* edited by Arnold Rampersad. New York: Vintage Books, 1995.

Hughes, Langston. *The Negro Mother and Other Dramatic Recitations.* New York: Golden Stair Press, 1931.

Hughes, Langston. *The Panther and the Lash: Poems of Our Times.* New York: Vintage Books, 1992 (1967).

Hull, Akasha (Gloria T.), Patricia Bell Scott, and Barbara Smith, eds. *All the Women Are White, All the Blacks Are Men, But Some of Us Are Brave: Black Women's Studies.* New York: Feminist Press, 1982.

Hurston, Zora Neale. "'Stories of Conflict,' Review of *Uncle Tom's Children* by Richard Wright." *Saturday Review of Literature* (2 April 1938): 32.

Hurston, Zora Neale. *Their Eyes Were Watching God.* New York: HarperCollins, 1998 (1937).

Hutchinson, James M. *Dubose Heyward: A Charleston Gentleman and the World of Porgy and Bess.* Jackson: University Press of Mississippi, 2000.

Ibrahim, Habiba. *Black Age: Oceanic Lifespans and the Time of Black Life.* New York: New York University Press, 2021.

India.Arie. *Acoustic Soul.* Motown, 2001.

The Isley Brothers. 3 + 3. T-Neck/Epic Records, 1973.

Iton, Richard. *In Search of the Black Fantastic: Politics and Popular Culture in the Post–Civil Rights Era.* New York: Oxford University Press, 2008.

Jackson, Lawrence. *Ralph Ellison: Emergence of Genius.* New York: John Wiley, 2002.

Jackson, Lawrence. "Ralph Ellison's Invented Life: A Meeting with the Ancestors." In *The Cambridge Companion to Ralph Ellison*, edited by Ross Posnock, 11–34. New York: Cambridge University Press, 2005.

Jackson, Michael. *HIStory: Past, Present and Future, Book I*. Epic, 1995.

Jackson, Panama. "'There Was Silence. It Was Understood': Reflections about 'Yasiin Bey: Negus,' the Listening Installation at the Brooklyn Museum." *The Root*, last modified November 25, 2019. https://verysmartbrothas.theroot.com /there-was-silence-it-was-understood-reflections-about-1840036137.

Jackson, Zakiyyah Iman. *Becoming Human: Matter and Meaning in an Antiblack World*. New York: New York University Press, 2020.

Jacobs, Harriet. *Incidents in the Life of a Slave Girl, Written by Herself*, edited by L. Maria Child. Boston: Thayer and Eldridge, 1861.

Jacobs, Michael. *D. W. Winnicott*. London: Sage, 1995.

James, Joy. "The Womb of Western Theory: Trauma, Time Theft, and the Captive Maternal." *Carceral Notebooks* 12 (2016): 253–96.

"JAMIE FOXX SINGS—FRED HAMMOND—NO WEAPON." *YouTube*, last modified September 5, 2012. https://youtu.be/HOsHA-tCqZk.

JanMohamed, Abdul R. *The Death-Bound-Subject: Richard Wright's Archaeology of Death*. Durham, NC: Duke University Press, 2005.

Jardine, Alice. *Gynesis: Configurations of Woman and Modernity*. Ithaca, NY: Cornell University Press, 1985.

Jarell, Wadsworth A. *AFRICOBRA: Experimental Art toward a School of Thought*. Durham, NC: Duke University Press, 2020.

Jarrett, Gene Andrew. *Paul Laurence Dunbar: The Life and Times of a Caged Bird*. Princeton, NJ: Princeton University Press, 2022.

Jay, Gregory S. "American Literature and the New Historicism: The Example of Frederick Douglass." *boundary 2* 17, no. 1 (1990): 211–42.

Johnson, E. Patrick. *Appropriating Blackness: Performance and the Politics of Authenticity*. Durham, NC: Duke University Press, 2003.

Johnson, James Weldon. *The Autobiography of an Ex-Colored Man*. New York: Penguin, 2011 (1927, 1912).

Johnson, James Weldon. *The Autobiography of an Ex-Colored Man*, edited by Jacqueline Goldsby. New York: Norton, 2015 (1927, 1912).

Johnson, James Weldon. *God's Trombones*. New York: Penguin, 1990 (1927).

Johnson, James Weldon. *Lift Every Voice and Sing: Selected Poems*. New York: Penguin, 2000 (1993, 1963, 1935).

Johnson, Jessica Marie. *Wicked Flesh: Black Women, Intimacy, and Freedom in the Atlantic World*. Philadelphia: University of Pennsylvania Press, 2020.

Jones, Alisha Lola. *Flaming?: The Peculiar Theopolitics of Fire and Desire in Black Male Gospel Performance*. New York: Oxford University Press, 2020.

Jordan, June. "Nobody Mean More to Me Than You and the Future Life of Willie Jordan." In *Some of Us Did Not Die: New and Selected Essays of June Jordan*, 157–73. New York: Basic Civitas Books, 2003.

Judy, R. A. T. "On the Question of Nigga Authenticity." *boundary 2* 21, no. 3 (Autumn, 1994): 211–30.

Judy, R. A. T. *Sentient Flesh: Thinking in Disorder, Poiēsis in Black*. Durham, NC: Duke University Press, 2020.

Julien, Isaac, dir. *Lessons of the Hour*. 2019. https://www.isaacjulien.com /projects/37/.

Kafka, Franz. "Before the Law." *Franz Kafka Online: The Works and Life of Franz Kafka*. Accessed April 1, 2022. http://www.kafka-online.info/before-the-law.html.

Kant, Immanuel. *The Critique of Judgment*, translated by J. H. Bernard. London: MacMillan and Co., 2015 (1914, 1892, 1790). https://www.gutenberg.org/files /48433/48433-h/48433-h.htm.

Karera, Axelle. "Paraontology: Interruption, Inheritance, or a Debt One Often Regrets." *Critical Philosophy of Race* 10, no. 2 (2022): 158–97.

Kazanjian, David. "Scenes of Speculation." *Social Text* 125 (December 2015): 77–84.

Keeling, Kara. *The Witch's Flight: The Cinematic, the Black Femme, and the Image of Common Sense*. Durham, NC: Duke University Press, 2007.

"Kendrick Lamar—God Is Gangsta." *YouTube*, last modified January 13, 2016. https://youtu.be/4wZytWFm7x0.

"Kendrick Lamar Meets Rick Rubin and They Have an Epic Conversation | GQ." *YouTube*, last modified October 20, 2016. https://youtu.be/4lPD5PtqMiE.

"Kendrick Lamar Talks 'u,' His Depression and Suicidal Thoughts (Pt. 2) | MTV News." *YouTube*, last modified April 1, 2015. https://youtu.be/Hu4Pz9PjoII.

Kernan, Mark. "In Praise of Melancholia." *opendemocracy.net*, last modified April 19, 2017. https://www.opendemocracy.net/en/transformation/in-praise -of-melancholia/.

Khan, Chaka. *What Cha' Gonna Do for Me*. Warner Bros., 1981.

Khanna, Ranjana. "Touching, Unbelonging, and the Absence of Affect." *Feminist Theory* 13, no. 2 (2012): 213–32.

Killah, Ghostface. *Supreme Clientele*. Epic Records, 2000.

Killakam. "South Africa's Influence on Kendrick Lamar's *To Pimp a Butterfly*." *okayafrica*, last modified February 11, 2016. http://www.okayafrica.com /kendrick-lamar-south-africa-to-pimp-a-butterfly/.

King, Tiffany Lethabo. "Black 'Feminisms' and Pessimism: Abolishing Moynihan's Negro Family." *Theory and Event* 21, no. 1 (January 2018): 68–87.

King, Tiffany Lethabo. *The Black Shoals: Offshore Formations of Black and Native Studies*. Durham, NC: Duke University Press, 2019.

King, Tiffany Lethabo. "The Labor of (Re)reading Plantation Landscapes Fungible(ly)." *Antipode: A Radical Journal of Cartography* 48, no. 4 (2016): 1022–39.

King, Martin Luther, Jr. "'Levels of Love,' Sermon Delivered at Ebenezer Baptist Church, September 16, 1962." In *The Papers of Martin Luther King, Jr., Volume VI: Advocate of the Social Gospel, September 1948–March 1963*, edited by Clayborne Carson, 437–44. Berkeley: University of California Press, 2007.

King, Martin Luther, Jr. "Where Do We Go from Here" (1967). In *A Testament of Hope: The Essential Writings and Speeches of Martin Luther King, Jr.*, edited by James M. Washington, 245–52. New York: HarperCollins, 1986.

Klein, Melanie. "Mourning and Its Relation to Manic-Depressive States." *The International Journal of Psycho-Analysis* 21 (1940): 125–53.

Klein, Melanie. *The Psychoanalysis of Children*, translated by Alix Strachey. New York: Grove Press, 1960 (1948, 1932).

Komunyakaa, Yusef. "A Needful Thing." *PEN America* 13 (2010): 11–12.

Komunyakaa, Yusef. "Sorrow Songs and Flying Away: Religious Influence on Black Poetry." In *Condition Red: Essays, Interviews, and Commentaries*, edited by Radiclani Clytus, 19–28. Ann Arbor: University of Michigan Press, 2017.

Konitshek, Haley. "Calling Forth History's Mocking Doubles." *Hypatia: A Journal of Feminist Philosophy* 32, no. 3 (Summer 2017): 660–78.

Kornhaber, Spencer. "The Power in Kendrick Lamar's Complexity." *The Atlantic*, last modified March 17, 2015. https://www.theatlantic.com/entertainment /archive/2015/03/kendrick-lamars-bittersweet-cacophony-to-pimp-a-butterfly /387949/.

Korsmeyer, Carolyn. *Gender and Aesthetics: An Introduction*. London: Routledge, 2004.

Kristeva, Julia. *Black Sun: Depression and Melancholia*, translated by Leon S. Roudiez. New York: Columbia University Press, 1989 (1987).

Kuryla, Pete. "A Few Thoughts on Ellison's 'Little Man at Chehaw Station' with Special Thanks to an Outlaw Philosopher." *Society for U.S. Intellectual History* (blog), May 23, 2018. https://s-usih.org/2018/05/a-few-thoughts-on-ellisons -little-man-at-chehaw-station-with-special-thanks-to-an-outlaw-philosopher/.

Lacan, Jacques. *Écrits*, translated by Bruce Fink. New York: Norton, 2006 (2002, 1999, 1971, 1970, 1966).

Lacan, Jacques. "On Jouissance." In *The Seminar of Jacques Lacan: On Feminine Sexuality, the Limits of Love and Knowledge, 1972–1973, Encore Edition, Volume Book XX*, translated by Bruce Fink and edited by Jacques-Alain Miller, 1–13. New York: W. W. Norton, 1999 (1975).

Lamar, Kendrick. *DAMN.* TDE, 2017.

Lamar, Kendrick. *good kid, m.A.A.d city*. TDE, 2012.

Lamar, Kendrick. *To Pimp a Butterfly*. TDE, 2015.

Lamar, Kendrick. *untitled unmastered*. TDE, 2016.

The Last Poets. *This Is Madness*. Douglas, 1971.

Lathan, Stan, dir. *Dave Chappelle: Sticks & Stones. Netflix*, 2019. https://www. netflix.com/title/81140577?s=i&trkid=13747225.

Latour, Bruno. "How to Talk about the Body? The Normative Dimension of Science Studies." *Body and Society* 2, no. 3 (2004): 205–29.

Lavender, Isiah, III. *Race in American Science Fiction*. Bloomington: Indiana University Press, 2011.

Lechte, John. *Julia Kristeva*. New York: Routledge, 2013 (1990).

LeClair, Thomas. "'The Language Must Not Sweat': A Conversation with Toni Morrison." *The New Republic*, March 21, 1981. https://newrepublic.com/article /95923/the-language-must-not-sweat.

Lee, Spike, dir. *Bamboozled*. New York: 40 Acres and a Mule Filmworks, 2000.

Lee, Spike, dir. *Mo' Better Blues*. New York: 40 Acres and a Mule Filmworks, 1990.

"Left of Black with Hortense Spillers and Alexis Pauline Gumbs." *YouTube*, last modified March 22, 2017. https://youtu.be/Ui-EZQ1BTfE.

Leggett, Hadley. "Butterflies Use Antenna GPS to Guide Migration." *Wired*, last modified September 24, 2009. https://www.wired.com/2009/09/monarch -migration/.

Lehman, Jessica. "Blue History." *The New Inquiry*, last modified February 6, 2017. https://thenewinquiry.com/blue-history/.

Leonard, Keith D. *Fettered Genius: The African American Bardic Poet from Slavery to Civil Rights*. Charlottesville: University Press of Virginia, 2006.

Leonard, Keith D. "First Questions: The Mission of Africana Studies: An Interview with Hortense Spillers." *Callaloo: A Journal of African Diaspora Arts and Letters* 3, no. 4 (Fall 2007): 1054–68.

Lesinrocks. "Quand Ornette Coleman improvisait avec Jacques Derrida." *Les Inrockuptibles*, no. 115 (August 20–September 2, 1997): 37–40, 43. https://www .lesinrocks.com/actu/ornette-coleman-et-jacques-derrida-la-langue-de-lautre -94053–20–08–1997/.

Lévinas, Emmanuel. *Existence and Existents*, translated by Alphonso Lingis. Pittsburgh, PA: Duquesne University Press, 1978 (1947).

Levine, Robert S. "Identity in the Autobiographies." In *The Cambridge Companion to Frederick Douglass*, edited by Maurice S. Lee, 31–45. New York: Cambridge University Press, 2009.

Levine, Robert S. "Road to Africa: Frederick Douglass's Rome." *African American Review* 34, no. 2 (Summer, 2000): 217–31.

Levine, Robert S., ed. *Martin R. Delany: A Documentary Reader*. Chapel Hill: University of North Carolina Press, 2003.

Lindsey, Kay. "The Black Woman as a Woman." In *The Black Woman: An Anthology*, edited by Toni Cade Bambara, 103–8. New York: Signet, 1970.

Lock, Graham. *Blutopia: Visions of the Future and Revisions of the Past in the Work of Sun Ra, Duke Ellington, and Anthony Braxton*. Durham, NC: Duke University Press, 1999.

"Look Closer—Kara Walker's Fons Americanus." tate.org.uk. Accessed April 1, 2022. https://www.tate.org.uk/art/artists/kara-walker-2674/kara-walkers-fons -americanus.

Lorde, Audre. *Sister Outsider*. New York: Ten Speed Press, 2007.

Lorde, Audre. *Zami: A New Spelling of My Name*. Berkeley, CA: Crossing Press, 1982.

Lordi, Emily J. *Black Resonance: Iconic Women Singers and African American Literature*. New Brunswick, NJ: Rutgers University Press, 2013.

Lordi, Emily J. *Donny Hathaway's Donny Hathaway Live*. New York: Bloomsbury, 2016.

Lubiano, Wahneema. "Like Being Mugged by a Metaphor: Multiculturalism and State Narratives." In *Mapping Multiculturalism*, edited by Avery F. Gordon and Christopher Newfield, 64–75. Minneapolis: University of Minnesota, 1996.

Lux, Thomas. *To the Left of Time*. Boston: Mariner Books, 2016.

Macharia, Keguro. "black . . . gay." *The New Inquiry* (blog), April 30, 2017. https://thenewinquiry.com/blog/black-gay/.

Macharia, Keguro. *Frottage: Frictions of Intimacy Across the Black Diaspora.* New York: New York University Press, 2019.

Mackey, Nathaniel. *Bedouin Hornbook.* Lexington: University Press of Kentucky, 1986.

Mackey, Nathaniel. *Discrepant Engagement: Dissonance, Cross-Culturality, and Experimental Writing.* New York: Cambridge University Press, 1993.

Mackey, Nathaniel. *From a Broken Bottle Traces of Perfume Still Emanate*, vols. 1–3. New York: New Directions, 2010 (2001, 1997, 1993, 1986).

Mackey, Nathaniel. *Paracritical Hinge: Essays, Talks, Notes, Interviews.* Madison: University of Wisconsin Press, 2005.

Mackey, Nathaniel. *Splay Anthem.* New York: New Directions, 2006 (2002).

Magee, Michael. *Emancipating Pragmatism: Emerson, Jazz, and Experimental Writing.* Tuscaloosa: University of Alabama Press, 2004.

Maguire, Roberta S. ed., *Conversations with Albert Murray.* Jackson: University Press of Mississippi, 1997.

Mailer, Norman. "The White Negro." *Dissent*, June 20, 2007 (Fall 1957). https://www.dissentmagazine.org/online_articles/the-white-negro-fall-1957.

Manabe, Noriko. "We Gon' Be Alright? The Ambiguities of Kendrick Lamar's Protest Anthem." *MTO* 25, no. 1 (March 2019). https://mtosmt.org/issues/mto.19.25.1/mto.19.25.1.manabe.php.

Maner, Sequoia. *Kendrick Lamar's* To Pimp a Butterfly. New York: Bloomsbury, 2022.

Manning, Erin. *Politics of Touch: Sense, Movement, Sovereignty.* Minneapolis: University of Minnesota Press, 2007.

Marable, Manning. *Malcolm X: A Life of Reinvention.* New York: Viking, 2011.

Marre, Jeremy. *What's Going On: The Life and Death of Marvin Gaye.* London, UK: Eagle Rock Entertainment, 2005.

Marriott, David. *Haunted Life: Visual Culture and Black Modernity.* New Brunswick, NJ: Rutgers University Press, 2007.

Marriott, David. "Judging Fanon." *Rhizomes: Cultural Studies in Emerging Knowledge*, no. 29 (2016). https://doi.org/10.20415/rhiz/029.e03.

Marriott, David. *On Black Men.* Edinburgh: Edinburgh Press, 2000.

Martin, Waldo E, Jr. *The Mind of Frederick Douglass.* Chapel Hill: University of North Carolina Press, 1984.

Martins, Chris. "Kendrick Lamar: 'M.A.A.d.' Stands for 'Me, an Angel on Angel Dust.'" *Spin*, October 19, 2012. https://www.spin.com/2012/10/kendrick-lamar-maad-stands-for-angel-dust/.

Masenya, Madipoane J. "African Womanist Hermeneutics: A Suppressed Voice from South Africa Speaks." *Journal of Feminist Studies in Religion* 11, no. 1 (Spring, 1995): 149–55.

Mayfield, Curtis. *Curtis.* Chicago: Curtom, 1970.

McCaffery, Larry. "An Interview with Octavia E. Butler." In *Across the Wounded Galaxies: Interviews with Contemporary American Science*

Fiction Writers, edited by Larry McCaffery, 56–70. Urbana: University of Illinois Press, 1990.

McCluskey, Paul. "The Poet and His Art: A Conversation." In Robert Hayden, *Collected Prose*, edited by Frederick Glaysher, 129–203. Ann Arbor: University of Michigan Press, 1984.

McDowell, Deborah E. "In the First Place: Making Frederick Douglass and the Afro-American Narrative Tradition." In *Critical Essays on Frederick Douglass*, edited by William L. Andrews, 192–214. Boston: G. K. Hall, 1991.

McEntyre, Marilyn Chandler. *Caring for Words in a Culture of Lies*. Grand Rapids, MI: Eerdmans, 2009.

McEwen, Mitch. "Stay Black and Die: A Possible Ethos for Architecture in a Post-Racial Imaginary." *infinite mile: a journal of art + culture(s) in Detroit* 30 (July/August 2016). https://www.infinitemiledetroit.com/Stay_Black_and_Die, _A_Possible_Ethos_for_Architecture_in_a_Post-Racial_Imaginary.html.

McFeely, William S. *Frederick Douglass*. New York: Norton, 1991.

McGowan, Todd. *Enjoying What We Don't Have: The Political Project of Psychoanalysis*. Lincoln: University of Nebraska Press, 2013.

McKay, Claude. *Harlem Shadows: The Poems of Claude McKay*. New York: Harcourt, Brace, 1922.

McKinley, Catherine. *Indigo: In Search of the Color That Seduced the World*. New York: Bloomsbury, 2011.

McKittrick, Katherine. *Demonic Grounds: Black Women and the Cartographies of Struggle*. Minneapolis: University of Minnesota Press, 2006.

McLendon, Russell. "8 Interesting Facts about Lucy the Ancient Ape." *mother nature network* (blog), July 29, 2020. https://www.treehugger.com/facts-about -lucy-australopithecine-4868785.

McLennan, John F. *Studies in Ancient History, Comprising a Reprint of Primitive Marriage: An Inquiry into the Origin of the Form of Capture in Marriage Ceremonies*. London: Macmillan, 1886. https://openlibrary.org/books /OL7003672M/Studies_in_ancient_history.

Meehan, Sean Ross. *Mediating American Autobiography: Photography in Emerson, Thoreau, Douglass, and Whitman*. Columbia: University of Missouri Press, 2008.

"melancholy, n.1." *OED Online*. Oxford University Press. http://www.oed.com .proxy.lib.duke.edu/view/Entry/116007?rskey=0VgIqP&result=1.

Mench, Chris. "Tracking the Many Voices of Kendrick Lamar," *Genius*, last modified August 1, 2017. https://genius.com/Kendrick-lamar-u-lyrics.

Messmer, David. "'If Not in the Word, in the Sound': Frederick Douglass's Mediation of Literacy Through Song." *ATQ—The American Transcendental Quarterly* 21, no. 1 (March 2007): 5–21.

Metzl, Jonathan M. *The Protest Psychosis: How Schizophrenia Became a Black Disease*. Boston: Beacon, 2009.

Miller, R. Baxter. *The Art and Imagination of Langston Hughes*. Lexington: University Press of Kentucky, 2006.

Miller, R. Baxter. "Langston Hughes, 1902–1967: A Brief Biography." In *A Histori-cal Guide to Langston Hughes*, edited by Steven C. Tracy, 23–63. New York: Oxford University Press, 2004.

Mims, Sergio. "The Very Unlikely Story of Mohamed Husen—a Black Actor of Nazi Germany." *Shadow and Act*, last modified April 20, 2017. https://shadowandact.com/the-very-unlikely-story-of-mohamed-husen-a-black-actor-of-nazi-germany-cinema.

Mingus, Charles. *Charles Mingus Presents Charles Mingus*. New York: Candid, 1961.

Mitter, Siddhartha. "Kara Walker Takes a Monumental Jab at Brittania." *The New York Times*, last modified September 30, 2019. https://www.nytimes.com/2019/09/30/arts/design/kara-walker-tate-turbine-hall.html.

Monáe, Janelle. *The ArchAndroid*. Atlanta: Bad Boy Records, 2010.

Moore, J. C. "A Meditation on Love." *Medium*, last modified April 6, 2020. https://medium.com/@justincmoore/a-meditation-on-love-e0df932105db.

Morgan, Edmund S. *Benjamin Franklin*. New Haven, CT: Yale University Press, 2002.

Morgan, Joan. "They Call Me Ms. Hill." *essence.com*, last modified January 16, 2006. http://www.essence.com/2006/01/16/they-call-me-ms-hill/.

Morrison, Toni. *Beloved*. New York: Plume, 1998 (1987).

Morrison, Toni. *The Bluest Eye*. New York: Vintage Books, 2007 (1998, 1993, 1970).

Morrison, Toni. *God Help the Child*. New York: Alfred A. Knopf, 2015.

Morrison, Toni. *Home*. New York: Alfred A. Knopf, 2012.

Morrison, Toni. "It Is Like Growing Up Black One More Time." *The New York Times*, August 11, 1974. https://www.nytimes.com/1974/08/11/archives/rediscovering-black-history-it-is-like-growing-up-black-one-more.html.

Morrison, Toni. *Playing in the Dark: Whiteness and the Literary Imagination*. New York: Vintage Books, 1993.

Morrison, Toni. "Recitatif." In *Confirmation: An Anthology of African American Women*, edited by Amiri Baraka (LeRoi Jones) and Amina Baraka, 243–61. New York: Quill, 1983.

Morrison, Toni. *Song of Solomon*. New York: Plume, 1987 (1977).

Morrison, Toni. *Song of Solomon*. New York: Vintage Books, 2004 (1977).

Morrison, Toni. *Sula*. New York: Alfred A. Knopf, 1993 (1973).

Morrison, Toni. "Unspeakable Things Unspoken: The Afro-American Presence in American Literature." *Michigan Quarterly Review* 28, no. 1 (Winter 1989): 1–34.

Morrison, Toni, and Cornel West. "'We Better Do Something': Toni Morrison and Cornel West in Conversation." *The Nation*, last modified May 6, 2004. https://www.thenation.com/article/archive/toni-morrison-cornel-west-politics/.

Mos Def (Yasiin Bey). *The New Danger*. Rawkus/Geffen, 2004.

"Moses Hogan Chorale—Elijah Rock." *YouTube*, January 1, 2007. https://youtu.be/gLR31UyuFPo.

Moten, Fred. "Black Kant (Pronounced Chant): A Theorizing Lecture at the Kelly Writers House." University of Pennsylvania, last modified February 27, 2007. https://writing.upenn.edu/pennsound/x/Moten.php#2-27-07.

Moten, Fred. "Black Op." *PMLA* 123, no. 5 (October 2008): 1743–47.

Moten, Fred. "Blackness and Nothingness (Mysticism in the Flesh)." *South Atlantic Quarterly* 112, no. 4 (2013): 737–80.

Moten, Fred. "Bridge and the One: Improvisations of the Public Sphere." In *Performing Hybridity*, edited by May Joseph and Jennifer Natalya Fink, 229–46. Minneapolis: University of Minnesota Press, 1999.

Moten, Fred. *In the Break: The Aesthetics of the Black Radical Tradition*. Minneapolis: University of Minnesota Press, 2003.

Moynihan, Daniel Patrick. "The Negro Family: The Case for National Action." Office of Policy Planning and Research. Washington, DC: United States Department of Labor, 1965.

Mulvey, Laura. "Visual Pleasure and Narrative Cinema." In *Film Theory and Criticism: Introductory Readings*, edited by Leo Braudy and Marshall Cohen, 833–44. New York: Oxford University Press, 1999.

Murillo, John. *Up Jump the Boogie*. New York: Cypher Books, 2010.

Murphy, Keith. "A Guide to Understanding D'Angelo's 'Black Messiah.'" *vibe.com*, last modified December 16, 2014. http://www.vibe.com/2014/12/guide-understanding-dangelos-black-messiah/.

Murphy, Timothy S., trans. "The Other's Language: Jacques Derrida Interviews Ornette Coleman, 23 June 1997." *Genre* 37, no. 2 (June 1, 2004): 319–29.

Murray, Albert. *Conversations with Albert Murray*, edited by Roberta S. Maguire. Jackson: University Press of Mississippi, 1997.

Murray, Albert. *Stomping the Blues*. New York: Da Capo Press, 2000 (1976).

Musser, Amber Jamilla. *Sensual Excess: Queer Femininity and Brown Jouissance*. New York: New York University Press, 2018.

Muyumba, Walton M. *The Shadow and the Act: Black Intellectual Practice, Jazz Improvisation, and Philosophical Pragmatism*. Chicago: University of Chicago Press, 2009.

"My Man's Gone Now (Old Man Sorrow)." *YouTube*, June 22, 2011. http://youtu.be/VKoTs-cH7bI.

Myrsiades, Kostas, and Linda Myrsiades, eds. *Race-ing Representation: Voice, History, and Sexuality*. Lanham, MD: Rowman and Littlefield, 1998.

Nash, Jennifer C. *Black Feminism Reimagined: After Intersectionality*. Durham, NC: Duke University Press, 2019.

Nash, Jennifer C. "Black Maternal Aesthetics." *Theory and Event* 22, no. 3 (2019): 551–75.

Ndegeocello, Meshell. *The World Has Made Me the Man of My Dreams*. Emarcy/Umgd, 2007.

Neal, Mark Anthony. *Black Ephemera: The Crisis and Challenge of the Musical Archive*. New York: New York University Press, 2022.

Neal, Mark Anthony. *New Black Man: Tenth Anniversary Edition*. New York: Routledge, 2015 (2005).

Neal, Mark Anthony. "Oddities of the Family: Toward an Intellectual Legacy." *NewBlackMan (in Exile)* (blog), January 31, 2016. http://www.newblackmaninexile.net/2016/01/oddities-of-family-toward-intellectual.html.

Neal, Mark Anthony. "Soul Train and the Desire for Black Power." *The Nation*, last modified December 22, 2021. https://www.thenation.com/article/culture/soul-train-black-power-anniversary/.

Neal, Mark Anthony. "Trouble Man: The Art and Politics of Marvin Gaye." *The Western Journal of Black Studies* 22, no. 4 (Winter 1998): 252–59.

Neal, Mark Anthony. *What the Music Said: Black Popular Music and Black Public Culture*. New York: Routledge, 1999.

Nesbitt, Nick. "The Slave-Machine: Slavery, Capitalism, and the 'Proletariat' in *The Black Jacobins* and *Capital*." *sx archipelagos* 3 (July 2019). http://smallaxe.net/sxarchipelagos/issue03/nesbitt.html.

New, Geoff. *Imaginative Preaching: Praying the Scriptures So God Can Speak Through You*. Carlisle, UK: Langham Global Library, 2015.

Niebuhr, H. Richard. *The Meaning of Revelation*. Louisville, KY: Westminster John Knox Press, 2006.

Nielsen, Cynthia R. "Resistance Is Not Futile: Frederick Douglass on Panoptic Plantations and the Un-Making of Docile Bodies and Enslaved Souls." *Philosophy and Literature* 35, no. 2 (October 2011): 251–68.

Niven, Steven J. "Cornelius Johnson and a Forgotten Protest Against Hitler at the 1936 Olympics." *The Root*, last modified February 24, 2016. https://www.theroot.com/cornelius-johnson-and-a-forgotten-us-protest-against-hi-1790854343.

Norman, Brian. "Reading a 'Closet Screenplay': Hollywood, James Baldwin's Malcolms and the Threat of Historical Irrelevance." *African American Review* 39, nos. 1–2 (Spring–Summer 2005): 103–16.

North, Michael. *The Dialect of Modernism: Race, Language, and Twentieth-Century Literature*. New York: Oxford University Press, 1994.

The Notorious B.I.G. (featuring Sadat X). "Come On." *Born Again*. Bad Boy, 1999.

NPR Staff. "Indigo: The Indelible Color That Ruled the World." *wbur.org*, last modified November 7, 2011. https://www.wbur.org/npr/142094103/indigo-the-indelible-color-that-ruled-the-world.

Nurhussein, Nadia. *Black Land: Imperial Ethiopianism and African America*. Princeton, NJ: Princeton University Press, 2019.

Nyong'o, Tavia. "Unburdening Representation." *The Black Scholar* 44, no. 2 (Summer 2014): 70–80.

O'Brien, Geoffrey. "Interrupted Symphony: A Recollection of Movie Music from Max Steiner to Marvin Gaye." In *This Is Pop: In Search of the Elusive at Experience Music Project*, edited by Eric Weisbard, 90–102. Cambridge, MA: Harvard University Press, 2004.

O'Connor, Brian. "How Maya Angelou Influenced Tupac and Hip-Hop." *Bustle*, last modified May 28, 2014. https://www.bustle.com/articles/26027-how-maya-angelou-the-godmother-of-american-hip-hop-influenced-tupac-dave-chappelle-more.

O'Hagan, Sean. "The Black Victorians: Astonishing Portraits Unseen for 120 years." *The Guardian*, last modified September 15, 2014. https://www.

theguardian.com/artanddesign/2014/sep/15/black-chronicles-ii-victorians
-photography-exhibition-rivington-place.

Okiji, Fumi. *Jazz and Critique: Adorno and Black Expression Revisited.* Stanford, CA: Stanford University Press, 2018.

Oliphant, David. *Texan Jazz.* Austin: University of Texas Press, 1996.

Ologundudu, Folasade. "Art Historian Darby English on Why the New Black Renaissance Might Actually Represent a Step Backwards." *artnet.com,* last modified February 26, 2021. https://news.artnet.com/art-world/darby-english -1947080.

O'Meally, Robert G. "Living with Music." In *Living with Music: Ralph Ellison's Jazz Writings,* edited by Robert G. O'Meally, 3–14. New York: Modern Library 2002 (2001).

O'Reilly, Andrea. *Toni Morrison and Motherhood: A Politics of the Heart.* Albany: State University of New York Press, 2004.

Owens, Ianna Hawkins. "Still, Nothing: Mammy and Black Asexual Possibility." *Feminist Review* 120, no. 1 (November 2018): 70–84.

Oyěwùmí, Oyèrónké. *The Invention of Women: Making an African Sense of Western Gender Discourses.* Minneapolis: University of Minnesota Press, 1997.

Palmer, Tyrone S. "Otherwise Than Blackness: Feeling, World, Sublimation." *Qui Parle: Critical Humanities and Social Sciences* 29, no. 2 (December 2020): 247–83.

Palmer, Tyrone S. "'What Feels More Than Feeling?': Theorizing the Unthinkability of Black Affect." *Critical Ethnic Studies* 3, no. 2 (Fall 2017): 31–56.

Palumbo-Liu, David. *Asian/American: Historical Crossings of a Racial Frontier.* Stanford, CA: Stanford University Press, 1999.

Panaram, Sasha Ann. "SayHerName: Seeking Justice for Breonna Taylor." *Black Perspectives* (blog), November 2, 2020. https://www.aaihs.org/sayhername -seeking-justice-for-breonna-taylor/.

Parrish, Tim. *Ralph Ellison and the Genius of America.* Amherst: University of Massachusetts Press, 2012.

Parrish, Tim. *Walking Blues: Making Americans from Emerson to Elvis.* Amherst: University of Massachusetts Press, 2001.

Patten, A. B., and Henri Fredrickson Hemy. "Faith of Our Mothers." In *The New National Baptist Hymnal.* Nashville, TN: National Baptist Publishing, 1977.

Pavlić, Ed. *Who Can Afford to Improvise?: James Baldwin and Black Music, the Lyric and the Listeners.* New York: Fordham University Press, 2016.

Pecou, Fahamu. *NEGUS in Paris.* Backslash Gallery. Paris, France, January 10–February 23, 2013. https://www.fahamupecouart.com/artwork/negus -in-paris.

Pecou, Fahamu. *Real Negus Don't Die.* Gallery 100. Atlanta, GA, June 11– October 11, 2019. https://www.fahamupecouart.com/real-negus-dont-die.

Peele, Jordan, dir. *Us.* Monkeypaw Productions, 2019.

Perry, Imani. *May We Forever Stand: A History of the Black National Anthem.* Chapel Hill: University of North Carolina Press, 2018.

Perry, Imani. *More Beautiful and More Terrible: The Embrace and Transcendence of Racial Inequality in the United States*. New York: New York University Press, 2011.

Perry, Imani. *Prophets of the Hood: Politics and Poetics in Hip Hop*. Durham, NC: Duke University Press, 2004.

Philip, M. NourbeSe. *Zong!* Middletown, CT: Wesleyan University Press, 2008.

Philip, Marlene Nourbese (M. NourbeSe). "She Tries Her Tongue, Her Silence Softly Breaks." In *She Tries Her Tongue, Her Silence Softly Breaks*, 69–86. Havana: Casa de las Américas, 1988.

Phillips, Adam. *Winnicott*. Cambridge, MA: Harvard University Press, 1988.

Phillips, Caryl. "Marvin Gaye." In *A New World Order*, 35–59. New York: Vintage, 2002.

Phillips, Layli. "Introduction—Womanism: On Its Own." In *The Womanist Reader*, edited by Layli Phillips, xix–lv. New York: Routledge, 2006.

Phillips, Rowan Ricardo. *When Blackness Rhymes with Blackness*. Champaign, IL: Dalkey Archive Press, 2010.

Phillips, Yoh. "The Definitive Breakdown of Kendrick Lamar's 'Alright' Video." *djbooth.com*, last modified February 12, 2018, https://djbooth.net/features/2015-07-2-breakdown-kendrick-lamar-alright-video.

Pickens, Therí Alyce. *Black Madness :: Mad Blackness*. Durham, NC: Duke University Press, 2019.

Pinsker, Joe. "The Financial Consequences of Saying 'Black,' vs. 'African American.'" *The Atlantic*, last modified December 30, 2014. https://www.theatlantic.com/business/archive/2014/12/the-financial-consequences-of-saying-black-vs-african-american/383999/.

Pollard, Sam. *Marvin Gaye: What's Going On*. May 7, 2008. http://www.pbs.org/wnet/americanmasters/episodes/marvin-gaye/exclusive-clips-from-the-program/75/.

Posnock, Ross. *Color and Culture: Black Writers and the Making of the Modern Intellectual*. Cambridge, MA: Harvard University Press, 1998.

Powery, Luke A. *Spirit Speech: Lament and Celebration in Preaching*. Nashville, TN: Abingdon Press, 2009.

Preston, Billy. *The Kids & Me*. A&M, 1974.

Price, Charles. "The Cultural Production of a Black Messiah: Ethiopianism and the Rastafari." *Journal of Africana Religions* 2, no. 3 (2014): 418–33.

Prichard, James Cowles. *The Natural History of Man; Comprising Inquiries into the Modifying Influence of Physical and Moral Agencies on the Different Tribes of the Human Family*, vol. 1. London: H. Bailliere, 1843.

Puccini, Giacomo. *Madama Butterfly*. 1904.

Quashie, Kevin. *Black Aliveness, or A Poetics of Being*. Durham, NC: Duke University Press, 2021.

Quashie, Kevin. "A Flash of Light and Life." For "Online Roundtable: Saidiya Hartman's 'Wayward Lives, Beautiful Experiments.'" *Black Perspectives* (blog), May 20, 2020. https://www.aaihs.org/a-flash-of-life-and-light/.

R. L. "Inextinguishable Fire: Ferguson and Beyond." *Mute*, last modified November 17, 2014. https://www.metamute.org/editorial/articles/inextinguishable -fire-ferguson-and-beyond.

Ramlochan, Shivanee. "Dionne Brand: The Reinvention of Poetry | Closeup." *Caribbean Beat* 159 (September/October 2019). https://www .caribbean-beat.com/issue-159/dionne-brand-the-reinvention-of-poetry -closeup#axzz62RhAlC8J.

Rampersad, Arnold. *Ralph Ellison: A Biography*. New York: Alfred A. Knopf, 2007.

Randall, Dudley. *Roses and Revolutions: The Selected Writings of Dudley Randall*, edited by Melba Joyce Boyd. Detroit, MI: Wayne State University Press, 2009.

Rankine, Patrice D. *Ulysses in Black: Ralph Ellison, Classicism, and African American Literature*. Madison: University of Wisconsin Press, 2006.

Ravens, Simon. *The Supernatural Voice: A History of High Male Singing*. Woodbridge, Suffolk, UK: Boydell Press, 2014.

Ray, Victor. "The Unbearable Whiteness of Mesearch." *insidehighered.com*, October 21, 2016. https://www.insidehighered.com/advice/2016/10/21/me-studies -are-not-just-conducted-people-color-essay.

Razinsky, Liran. *Freud, Psychoanalysis and Death*. New York: Cambridge University Press, 2013.

Rediker, Marcus. *The Amistad Rebellion: An Atlantic Odyssey of Slavery and Freedom*. New York: Penguin, 2013 (2012).

Redmond, Shana L. *Anthem: Social Movements and the Sound of Solidarity in the African Diaspora*. New York: New York University Press, 2014.

Redmond, Shana L. "Tip Toes and River Rolls: Overhearing Enslavement." *Black Camera: An International Film Journal* 7, no. 1 (Fall 2015): 150–61.

Reich, Howard. "B. B. King Teaches NU Crowd a Thing or Two about the Blues." *Chicago Tribune*, last modified February 19, 1990. https://www.chicagotribune .com/news/ct-xpm-1990–02–19–9001140942-story.html.

Reid-Pharr, Robert F. *Black Gay Man: Essays*. New York: New York University Press, 2001.

Reid-Pharr, Robert F. "Tearing the Goat's Flesh: Homosexuality, Abjection, and the Production of a Late-Twentieth-Century Black Masculinity." In *Novel Gazing: Queer Readings in Fiction*, edited by Eve Kosofsky Sedgwick, 353–76. Durham, NC: Duke University Press, 1997.

Rice, H. William. "The Invisible Man in Ralph Ellison's *Invisible Man*." In *Ralph Ellison*, edited by Harold Bloom, 113–28. New York: Infobase, 2010.

Richardson, Wyman Lewis. *Walking Together: A Congregational Reflection on Biblical Church Discipline*. Eugene, OR: Wipf and Stock, 2007.

Rinehart, Nicholas T. "Shadow Acts: On Tavia Nyong'o's 'Afro-Fabulations: The Queer Drama of Black Life' and Stephen Best's 'None Like Us: Blackness, Belonging, Aesthetic Life.'" *Los Angeles Review of Books*, last modified June 29, 2020. https://lareviewofbooks.org/article/shadow-acts-on-tavia-nyongos-afro -fabulations-the-queer-drama-of-black-life-and-stephen-bests-none-like-us -blackness-belonging-aesthetic-life/.

Riss, Arthur. "Sentimental Douglass." In *The Cambridge Companion to Frederick Douglass*, edited by Maurice S. Lee, 103–17. New York: Cambridge University Press, 2009.

Ritz, David. *Divided Soul: The Life of Marvin Gaye*. New York: Da Capo Press, 1991 (1985).

Roberson, Ed. *Voices Cast Out to Talk Us In*. Iowa City: University of Iowa Press, 1995.

Robinson, Cedric J. *Black Marxism: The Making of the Black Radical Tradition*. Chapel Hill: University of North Carolina Press, 2000 (1983).

Rocchi, Jean-Paul. "Literature and the Meta-Psychoanalysis of Race: After and With Fanon." *Palimpsest: A Journal on Women, Gender, and the Black International* 1, no. 1 (2012): 52–67.

Ross, Marlon B. *Manning the Race: Reforming Black Men in the Jim Crow Era*. New York: New York University Press, 2004.

Rowe, John Carlos. *At Emerson's Tomb: The Politics of Classic American Literature*. New York: Columbia University Press, 1997.

Royster, Francesca T. *Sounding Like a No-No: Queer Sounds and Eccentric Acts in the Post-Soul Era*. Ann Arbor: University of Michigan Press, 2013.

Rusert, Britt. "Delany's Comet: Fugitive Science and the Speculative Imaginary of Emancipation." *American Quarterly* 65, no. 4 (December 2013): 799–829.

Rusert, Britt. *Fugitive Science: Empiricism and Freedom in Early African American Culture*. New York: New York University Press, 2017.

Said, Edward W. *Freud and the Non-European*. London: Verso, 2004 (2003).

Schappell, Elissa, and Claudia Brodsky Lacour. "Toni Morrison, The Art of Fiction No. 134." *The Paris Review* 128 (Fall 1993): 83–125. https://www.theparisreview.org/interviews/1888/toni-morrison-the-art-of-fiction-no-134-toni-morrison.

Scherman, Tony. "The Omni-american." *American Heritage* 47, no. 5 (September 1996). http://www.americanheritage.com/content/omni-american?page=show.

Schreiber, Evelyn Jaffe. *Race, Trauma, and Home in the Novels of Toni Morrison*. Baton Rouge: Louisiana State University Press, 2010.

Schuessler, Jennifer. "The Term 'African-American' Appears Earlier Than Thought: Reporter's Notebook." *The New York Times*, last modified April 21, 2015. https://www.nytimes.com/times-insider/2015/04/21/the-term-african-american-appears-earlier-than-thought-reporters-notebook/.

Schuessler, Jennifer. "Use of 'African-American' Dates to Nation's Early Days." *The New York Times*, last modified April 20, 2015. http://www.nytimes.com/2015/04/21/arts/use-of-african-american-dates-to-nations-early-days.html?_r=1.

Schwenger, Peter. "Phenomenology of the Scream." *Critical Inquiry* 40, no. 2 (Winter 2014): 382–95.

Seigworth, Gregory J., and Melissa Gregg. "An Inventory of Shimmers." In *The Affect Theory Reader*, edited by Gregory J. Seigworth and Melissa Gregg, 1–25. Durham, NC: Duke University Press, 2010.

Sexton, Jared. *Black Men, Black Feminism: Lucifer's Nocturne*. London: Palgrave Macmillan, 2018.

Sexton, Jared. "The Social Life of Social Death: On Afro-Pessimism and Black Optimism." In *Tensions Journal* 5 (Fall/Winter 2011): 1–47.

Shakespeare, William. *Antony and Cleopatra*. Accessed April 1, 2022. http://shakespeare.mit.edu/cleopatra/full.html.

Shakespeare, William. *As You Like It: The Complete Works of William Shakespeare*. Accessed April 1, 2022. http://shakespeare.mit.edu/asyoulikeit/full.html.

Shange, Ntozake. *For Colored Girls Who Have Considered Suicide/When the Rainbow Is Enuf*. New York: Scribner Poetry, 2010 (1977, 1976, 1975).

Shapiro, Fred R., ed. *The Yale Book of Quotations*. New Haven, CT: Yale University Press, 2006.

Sharpe, Christina. "Beauty Is a Method." *e-flux* 105 (December 2019). https://www.e-flux.com/journal/105/303916/beauty-is-a-method/.

Sharpe, Christina. "Black Studies: In the Wake." *The Black Scholar* 44, no. 2 (Summer 2014): 59–69.

Sharpe, Christina. *In the Wake: On Blackness and Being*. Durham, NC: Duke University Press, 2016.

Sharpe, Christina. *Monstrous Intimacies: Making Post-Slavery Subjects*. Durham, NC: Duke University Press, 2010.

Sharpe, Christina. "Response to 'Ante-Anti-Blackness.'" *Lateral* 1 (2012), last modified April 1, 2022. https://doi.org/10.25158/L1.1.17.

Sheets, Hilarie M. "How Glenn Ligon Is Using Black and Blue to Begin a Dialogue." *The New York Times*, last modified June 2, 2017. https://www.nytimes.com/2017/06/02/arts/design/how-glenn-ligon-is-using-black-and-blue-to-begin-a-dialogue.html.

Sheff, David. *All We Are Saying: The Last Major Interview with John Lennon and Yoko Ono*. London: St. Martin's Griffin, 2020 (2000, 1981).

Sigelman, Lee, Steven A. Tuch, and Jack K. Martin. "What's in a Name? Preference for 'Black' versus 'African American' among Americans of African Descent." *Public Opinion Quarterly* 69, no. 3 (Autumn, 2005): 429–38.

Simone, Nina. *Forever Young, Gifted and Black: Songs of Freedom and Spirit*. RCA/Legacy, 2006.

Singleton, Jermaine. *Cultural Melancholy: Readings of Race, Impossible Mourning, and African American Ritual*. Urbana: University of Illinois Press, 2015.

Skloot, Rebecca. *The Immortal Life of Henrietta Lacks*. New York: Crown, 2010.

Slade, David, dir. "The Secret of Spoons." *American Gods*. STARZ, 2017.

Slampyak, Ted. "An Original AoM Comic: Frederick Douglass—How a Slave Was Made a Man." *The Art of Manliness*, last modified February 26, 2013. http://www.artofmanliness.com/2013/02/26/an-original-aom-comic-frederick-douglass-how-a-slave-was-made-a-man/#disqus_thread.

Snoop Doggy Dogg. *Doggystyle*. Death Row Records, 1993.

Snorton, C. Riley. *Black on Both Sides: A Racial History of Trans Identity*. Minneapolis: University of Minnesota Press, 2017.

Sounds of Blackness. *Africa to America: The Journey of the Drum*. Interscope, 1994.

Spillers, Hortense J. "'All the Things You Could Be by Now If Sigmund Freud's Wife Was Your Mother': Psychoanalysis and Race." *boundary 2* 23, no. 3 (1996): 75–141.

Spillers, Hortense J. *Black, White and in Color: Essays on American Literature and Culture*. Chicago: University of Chicago, 2003.

Spillers, Hortense J. "The Crisis of the Negro Intellectual: A Post-Date." *boundary 2* 21, no. 3 (1994): 65–116.

Spillers, Hortense J. "Ellison's 'Usable Past': Toward a Theory of Myth." *Interpretations* 9, no. 1 (1977): 53–69.

Spillers, Hortense J. "Fabrics of History: Essays on the Black Sermon," PhD diss., Brandeis University, 1974.

Spillers, Hortense J. "The Idea of Black Culture." CR: *The New Centennial Review* 6, no. 3 (Winter 2006): 7–28.

Spillers, Hortense J. "'The Little Man at Chehaw Station' Today." *boundary 2* 30, no. 2 (2003): 5–19.

Spillers, Hortense J. "Mama's Baby, Papa's, Too," *Trans-Scripts* 1 (2011): 1–4.

Spillers, Hortense J. "Mama's Baby, Papa's Maybe: An American Grammar Book." *Diacritics: A Review of Contemporary Criticism* 17, no. 2 (1987): 65–81.

Spillers, Hortense J. "Moving on Down the Line." *American Quarterly* 40, no. 1 (March 1988): 83–109.

Spillers, Hortense J. "Toward an Ontology: Women and Republican Formation." Distinguished Scholar in Residence Public Lecture, John Hope Franklin Humanities Institute, Duke University, Durham, NC.

Spivak, Gayatri Chakravorty. "Echo." *New Literary History* 24, no. 1 (Winter, 1993): 17–43.

Stadler, Gustavus. *Troubling Minds: The Cultural Politics of Genius in the United States, 1840–1890*. Minneapolis: University of Minnesota Press, 2006.

Stallings, L. H. *Funk the Erotic: Transaesthetics and Black Sexual Cultures*. Urbana: University of Illinois Press, 2015.

Stauffer, John. "Frederick Douglass and the Aesthetics of Freedom." *Raritan* 25, no. 1 (2005): 114–36.

Stauffer, John. *Giants: The Parallel Lives of Frederick Douglass and Abraham Lincoln*. New York: Twelve, 2008.

Steinberg, Michael P. "Music and Melancholy." *Critical Inquiry* 40, no. 2 (Winter 2014): 288–310.

Steiner, John. "The Conflict between Mourning and Melancholia." *Psychoanalytic Quarterly* 74 (2005): 83–104.

Stepto, Robert B. *From Behind the Veil: A Study of Afro-American Narrative*. Urbana: University of Illinois Press, 1991 (1979).

Stoever, Jennifer Lynn. *The Sonic Color Line: Race and the Cultural Politics of Listening*. New York: New York University Press, 2016.

Sumter-Freitag, Addena. *Stay Black and Die*. Vancouver, BC: Commodore Books, 2007.

Sundaresan, Mano. "The Paradox of Yasiin Bey's 'Negus,' A Rap Album Trapped in an Art Museum." *NPR*, last modified February 5, 2020. https://www.npr .org/2020/02/05/802782146/the-paradox-of-yasiin-beys-negus-a-rap-album -trapped-in-an-art-museum.

The System. *Don't Disturb This Groove.* Atlantic, 1987.

Tardio, Andres. "Exclusive: We Got All the Answers for Kendrick Lamar's "Alright" Video." *MTV*, last modified June 30, 2015. http://www.mtv.com/news /2201127/kendrick-lamar-alright-video-colin-tilley/.

Tate, Claudia. "Freud and His 'Negro': Psychoanalysis as Ally and Enemy of African Americans." *JPCS: Journal for the Psychoanalysis of Culture and Society* 1, no. 1 (Spring 1996): 53–62.

Tate, Claudia. *Psychoanalysis and Black Novels: Desire and the Protocols of Race.* New York: Oxford University Press, 1998.

Tate, Claudia. "Review: *The Song of Solomon* by Toni Morrison." *CLA Journal* 21, no. 2 (December, 1977): 327–29.

Taylor, Diana. *The Archive and the Repertoire: Performing Cultural Memory in the Americas.* Durham, NC: Duke University Press, 2003.

Taylor, Paul C. *Black Is Beautiful: A Philosophy of Black Aesthetics.* Hoboken, NJ: Wiley, 2016.

Terrefe, Selamawit D. "Speaking the Hieroglyph." *Theory and Event* 21, no. 1 (January 2018): 124–47.

Tettenborn, Éva. "Melancholia as Resistance in Contemporary African American Literature." *MELUS* 31, no. 3 (Fall, 2006): 101–21.

"Thadious Davis, NDIAS Fellow." *YouTube*, April 21, 2016. https://youtu.be /gdPWm5Dl5ik.

Thomas, Greg. "Afro-Blue Notes: The Death of Afro-pessimism (2.0)?" *Theory and Event* 21, no. 1 (January 2018): 282–317.

Tidey, Ashley. "Limping or Flying? Psychoanalysis, Afrocentrism, and *Song of Solomon. College English* 63, no. 1 (September, 2000): 48–70.

Tinsley, Justin. "How Marvin Gaye's NFL Tryout Changed His Career." *ESPN*, last modified August 20, 2015. http://www.espn.com/nfl/story/_/id/13464184 /marvin-gaye-tryout-nfl-detroit-lions.

Tompkins, Kyla Wazana. *Racial Indigestion: Eating Bodies in the 19th Century.* New York: New York University Press, 2012.

"Toni Morrison interview on 'Jazz' (1993)." *YouTube*, August 9, 2019. https:// youtu.be/lsiETgcYM7s.

Townes, Emilie M. "Womanist Theology." *Union Seminary Quarterly Review* 57 (2003): 159–76.

Trilling, Lionel. "Introduction." In Ernest Jones, *The Life and Work of Sigmund Freud,* edited by Lionel Trilling and Steven Marcus, 11–24. New York: Penguin, 1964.

Vandross, Luther. *Power of Love.* Epic, 1991.

Varga, Somogy. "From Melancholia to Depression: Ideas on a Possible Continuity." *Philosophy, Psychiatry, and Psychology* 20, no. 2 (June 2013): 141–55.

Vargas, João Costa, and Joy A. James. "Refusing Blackness-as-Victimization: Trayvon Martin and the Black Cyborgs." In *Pursuing Trayvon Martin: Historical Contexts and Contemporary Manifestations of Racial Dynamics*, edited by George Yancy and Janine Jones, 193–204. Lanham, MD: Lexington Books, 2013.

Velde, H. te. "The Cat as Sacred Animal of the Goddess Mut." In *Studies in Egyptian Religion*, edited by M. Heerma van Voss, D. J. Hoens, D. Van de Plas, G. Mussies, and H. te Velde, 127–37. Leiden, the Netherlands: E. J. Brill, 1982.

Walcott, Rinaldo. *The Long Emancipation: Moving toward Black Freedom*. Durham, NC: Duke University Press, 2021.

Walker, Alice. *The Color Purple*. Orlando, FL: Harcourt, 1982.

Walker, Alice. "Foreword: Those Who Love Us Never Leave Us Alone with Our Grief: Reading *Barracoon: The Story of the Last 'Black Cargo.'*" In Zora Neale Hurston, *Barracoon: The Story of the Last 'Black Cargo,'* edited by Deborah G. Plant, ix–xii. New York: HarperCollins, 2018.

Walker, Alice. *In Love and Trouble: Stories of Black Women*. New York: Harcourt Brace, 2001 (1973).

Walker, Alice. *In Search of Our Mothers' Gardens: Womanist Prose*. Orlando, FL: Harcourt, 2003.

Walker, Alice. *The Temple of My Familiar*. New York: First Mariner Books, 2010 (1989).

Walker, Alice. "The Unglamorous but Worthwhile Duties of the Black Revolutionary Artist, or of the Black Writer Who Simply Works and Writes." In *In Search of Our Mothers' Gardens: Womanist Prose*. Orlando, FL: Harcourt, 2003, 130–31.

Walker, David. *David Walker's Appeal, in Four Articles, Together with a Preamble, to the Coloured Citizens of the World, but in Particular, and Very Expressly, to Those of the United States of America*. New York: Hill and Wang, 1995 (1965, 1829).

Walker, David F., and Damon Smyth. *The Life of Frederick Douglass: A Graphic Narrative of a Slave's Journey from Bondage to Freedom*. New York: Ten Speed Press, 2018.

Wall, Cheryl A. *On Freedom and the Will to Adorn: The Art of the African American Essay*. Chapel Hill: University of North Carolina Press, 2018.

Wall, Cheryl A. *Worrying the Line: Black Women Writers, Lineage, and the Literary Tradition*. Chapel Hill: University of North Carolina Press, 2005.

Wallace, Maurice. *Constructing the Black Masculine: Identity and Ideality in African American Men's Literature and Culture, 1775–1995*. Durham, NC: Duke University Press, 2002.

Wallace, Maurice. "Form, Facticity, and the Struggle for Symmetry; or, Shadow and (F)Acts: A Comment on Israel Durham's 'The Interpreter of a Dream (Variations): Frederick Douglass, The (Pan)Africanist Machinist.'" A response to I. Augustus Durham's seminar paper, "The Interpreter of a Dream (Variations): Frederick Douglass, the (Pan-)African Machinist." *Slavery and the Problem of Aesthetics/Aesthetics and the Problem of Slavery*. September 23, 2013.

Wallace, Maurice. "Richard Wright's Black Medusa." *Journal of African American History* 88, no. 1 (Winter, 2003): 71–77.

Wallace, Rob. *Improvisation and the Making of American Literary Modernism.* New York: Continuum, 2010.

Wallace, William Ross. "The Hand that Rocks the Cradle Is the Hand that Rules the World." In *Beautiful Gems of Thought and Sentiment*, edited by Henry David Northrop, 248. Philadelphia: International Publishing, 1890.

Ward, David C. "What Langston Hughes' Powerful Poem 'I, Too' Tells Us About America's Past and Present." *smithsonian.com*, last modified September 22, 2016. https://www.smithsonianmag.com/smithsonian-institution/what-langston-hughes-powerful-poem-i-too-americas-past-present-180960552/.

Warren, Calvin L. *Ontological Terror: Blackness, Nihilism, and Emancipation.* Durham, NC: Duke University Press, 2018.

Warren, Kenneth W. *So Black and Blue: Ralph Ellison and the Occasion of Criticism.* Chicago: University of Chicago Press, 2003.

Washington, Dinah. *Unforgettable.* Mercury Records, 1961.

Washington, Mary Helen. "Anna Julia Cooper: The Black Feminist Voice of the 1890s." *Legacy* 4, no. 2 (Fall, 1987): 3–15.

Washington, Mary Helen. "Introduction." In *Black-Eyed Susans: Classic Stories by and about Black Women*, edited by Mary Helen Washington, ix–xxxii. New York: Anchor Books, 1975.

Washington, Mary Helen. "Introduction." In *Memory of Kin: Stories About Family by Black Writers*, edited by Mary Helen Washington, 1–8. New York: Anchor Books, 1991.

Washington, Mary Helen. "Zora Neale Hurston: A Woman Half in Shadow." In *I Love Myself When I Am Laughing . . . and Then Again When I Am Looking Mean and Impressive: A Zora Neale Hurston Reader*, edited by Alice Walker, 1–19. New York: Feminist Press, 2020 (1979).

Weheliye, Alexander G. *Habeas Viscus: Racializing Assemblages, Biopolitics, and Black Feminist Theories of the Human.* Durham, NC: Duke University Press, 2014.

Weheliye, Alexander G. *Phonographies: Grooves in Sonic Afro-Modernity.* Durham, NC: Duke University Press, 2005.

"A Well-Wisher to Great Britain." *The Then Plagues of England, of Worse Consequence Than Those of Egypt.* London: R. Withy, 1757.

West, Gerald O. *Biblical Hermeneutics of Liberation: Modes of Reading the Bible in the South African Context.* Maryknoll, NY: Orbis Books, 1995 (1991).

West, Kanye. *My Beautiful Dark Twisted Fantasy.* Roc-A-Fella/Def Jam, 2010.

West, Traci C. "Is a Womanist a Black Feminist? Marking the Distinctions and Defying Them: A Black Feminist Response." In *Deeper Shades of Purple: Womanism in Religion and Society*, edited by Stacey M. Floyd-Thomas, 291–95. New York: New York University Press, 2006.

Wexler, Laura. "'A More Perfect Likeness': Frederick Douglass and the Image of the Nation." In *Pictures and Progress: Early Photography and the Making of*

African American Identity, edited by Maurice O. Wallace and Shawn Michelle Smith, 18–40. Durham, NC: Duke University Press, 2012.

Wilderson, Frank B, III. "The Prison Slave as Hegemony's (Silent) Scandal." *Social Justice* 30, no. 2 (2003): 18–27.

Wilderson, Frank B, III. *Red, White and Black: Cinema and the Structure of U.S. Antagonisms*. Durham, NC: Duke University Press, 2010.

Williams, Delores S. *Sisters in the Wilderness: The Challenge of Womanist God-Talk*. New York: Orbis Books, 2013 (1993).

Williams, Deniece. *Let's Hear It for the Boy*. Columbia, 1984.

Williams, Raymond. "Genius." In *Keywords: A Vocabulary of Culture and Society*, 143–44. New York: Oxford University Press, 1985 (1983, 1976).

Willis, Raquel. "To Pimp the Black Woman: On Kendrick Lamar's Limited Black Liberation." *Cuepoint—Medium*, last modified April 14, 2015. https://medium .com/cuepoint/to-pimp-the-black-woman-on-kendrick-lamar-s-limited-black -liberation-26d63d94cad.

Wilson, Ronaldo V. "Lucy and All of Us." *The Black Scholar* 47, no. 1 (Spring 2017): 53–57.

Winnicott, D. W. *Playing and Reality*. New York: Routledge, 2005 (1971).

Winters, Joseph. "Beyond Flight and Containment: Kendrick Lamar, Black Study, and an Ethics of the Wound." In *Kendrick Lamar and the Making of Black Meaning*, edited by Christopher M. Driscoll, Anthony B. Pinn, and Monica R. Miller, 212–27. New York: Routledge, 2020.

Winters, Joseph. *Hope Draped in Black: Race, Melancholy, and the Agony of Progress*. Durham, NC: Duke University Press, 2016.

Winters, Joseph. "Rac(e)ing from Death: Baldwin, Bataille, and the Anguish of the (Racialized) Human." *Journal of Religious Ethics* 45, no. 2 (2017): 380–405.

Witcher, Theodore, dir. *Love Jones*. New Line Cinema, 1997.

Wonder, Stevie. *Talking Book*. Tamla, 1972.

Woodard, Vincent. *The Delectable Negro: Human Consumption and Homoeroticism within U.S. Slave Culture*, edited by Justin A. Joyce and Dwight A. McBride. New York: New York University Press, 2014.

Woods, Clyde. *Development Arrested: The Blues and Plantation Power in the Mississippi Delta*. New York: Verso, 2017 (2000, 1998).

Woubshet, Dagmawi. "Tizita: For Rafael." *Callaloo: A Journal of African Diaspora Arts and Letters* 30, no. 2 (Spring, 2007): 509–10.

Wright, John S. *Shadowing Ralph Ellison*. Jackson: University Press of Mississippi, 2006.

Wright, Nazera Sadiq. *Black Girlhood in the Nineteenth Century*. Urbana: University of Illinois Press, 2016.

Wright, Richard. *Black Boy*. New York: HarperCollins, 1993 (1945, 1944).

Wright, Richard. "Blueprint for Negro Writing." In *The Portable Harlem Renaissance*, edited by David Levering Lewis, 194–205. New York: Viking Penguin, 1994.

Wright, Richard. "Introduction." In St. Clair Drake and Horace R. Cayton, *Black Metropolis: A Study of Negro Life in a Northern City*, xvii–xxxiv. Chicago: University of Chicago Press, 1993 (1970, 1962, 1945).

Wright, Richard. "On Literature." Unpublished MSS in Wright Archive, Beinecke Library. Yale University Press, New Haven, CT.

Wright, Richard. "Psychiatry Comes to Harlem." *Free World* 28 (September 1946): 49–51.

Wynter, Sylvia. "Beyond Miranda's Meanings: Un/silencing the 'Demonic Ground' of Caliban's 'Woman.'" In *Out of the Kumbla: Caribbean Women and Literature*, edited by Carol Boyce Davies and Elaine Savory Fido, 355–72. Trenton, NJ: Africa World Press, 1990.

Yothers, Brian. *Reading Abolition: The Critical Reception of Harriet Beecher Stowe and Frederick Douglass*. Rochester, NY: Camden House, 2016.

Young, Kevin. *The Grey Album: On the Blackness of Blackness*. Minneapolis, MN: Graywolf Press, 2012.

Young, Kevin. "Ralph Ellison's Slow-Burning Art." *The New Yorker*, last modified December 2, 2019. https://www.newyorker.com/magazine/2019/12/09/ralph-ellisons-slow-burning-art.

Zafar, Rafia. *We Wear the Mask: African Americans Write American Literature, 1760–1870*. New York: Columbia University Press, 1997.

backward-gazing, 191

Bailey, Bets(e)y, 36, 40, 67–70

Bailey, Harriet, 35, 40, 42, 66–68, 70, 74, 78, 135

Baldwin, James, xvi, xvii, 105–6, 123, 127, 164–65

baptism, 190, 200, 204–5, 211

Barad, Karen, 184

Baraka, Amiri, 14, 50

bare life, 3–4, 6–8, 10, 26

the basement. *See* the underground

Battersby, Christine, 231nn58–59

Beautiful (India.Arie), 217

Bedouin Hornbook (Mackey), 144

bell hooks, 226n1

Beloved (Morrison), 2–4, 29, 127, 254n32

"Be Real Black for Me" (Flack and Hathaway), 224

Best, Stephen, 270n6

Bey, Yasiin, 127, 145, 209–11

Beyond the Pleasure Principle (Freud), 194

Billie #21 (Harris), 34

The Black Book (Morrison), 31

black boundarylessness, 128

Black Boy (Wright), 260n9

"Black Boy Fly" (Lamar), 191

"Black Boys and Native Sons" (Howe), 104–5

black cyborg, 66–68, 74, 76, 241n90

"Black English" (Jordan), 34

black fantastic, 182

black feminine/maternal: and affect, 25–26; as artistic, 171–72; background on the, 37–38; and blackness, 31–32; and the blues, 91–93, 115–16; as born again, 190, 193; as death-bearing, 5–9; and the female artist, 19; and genius, 11–12, 15, 17, 19–20, 34, 41–42, 230n47; and the groove, 36, 82–84, 92, 103, 108, 116; as grounded, 195; and handling, 214–16; and haunting, 4; and hunger, 12–13, 17, 19–20; and imagination, 189–90; and intellect, 53; and kinship, 122; and labor, 32; and labor power, 45–49; as lady in waiting, 110; and Lamar, 182; and the law, 155–56, 159–60; as living Deads, 195; and materiality, 82–84, 88, 95, 99–100, 102; and pathology, 6; as plastic, 26–27; and

poetry, 74–75, 77; and psychoanalysis, 16, 24; and the shadow, 49; and sharing love, 223; and singing, 217; and slavery, 10, 14–15; and theory, 17; and the womb, 21, 32–33, 97, 110, 113. *See also* gender; othermothers

black feminism, 4, 153–54, 182, 214, 228n29. *See also* feminism; gender; womanism

Black Is a Color (Saunders), 206

Black is Beautiful, 30–31

black jouissance, 34

black literature, 31, 48, 59, 76, 105–6, 130–31, 221–22, 228n23, 252n123

black manhood, 99–100, 213–14, 255n42

Black Messiah (D'Angelo and the Vanguard), 253n7

blackness. *See* Afro(-)pessimism; blueness; objecthood; race-ing

black optimism, 9, 16

black post-black, 182–83, 206, 209, 211–12

Black Skin, White Masks (Fanon), 29

The Black Spear (Hayden), 71–72, 75

Black Studies, 153

black women singers, 121–22

"Bloodchild" (Butler), 2, 37, 154–55, 160–78, 262n44, 263n60

Blount, Marcellus, 208

blueblackness, 2, 10–11, 14, 99, 104–5

blueness, 12–15

blueprints, 15

the blues: aesthetic performance and, 9–13, 25, 107, 164; audiences and, 214–16; epistemology of, 51–53; gender and, 91; psychoanalaytic theory and, 9, 15, 115

blues idiom, 9–10, 14–16, 25, 32–35, 50–52, 164–65, 229n41

blues music, 2, 9–12, 15–16, 50, 52–53, 75, 164–65, 215, 229n38

The Bluest Eye (Morrison), 233n92

Blyden, Edward, 71

Bodkin, Maud, 248n59

Boggs, Nicholas, 251n102

Bowen, J. W. E., 65, 240n83

braconnage, 92, 141, 247n43

Bradley, Adam, 249n64

Bradley, Margaret, 216–17

Brand, Dionne, 37

Braxton, Joanne M., 244n118

127–28, 148; the sexuality of, 36–37, 124–30, 256n48; the singing style of, 143–49, 258n88, 259n93. *See also* specific works

gender, 18–20, 43, 66–71, 77, 94, 100–101, 105–10, 123–29, 135, 208. *See also* black feminine/maternal; black feminism; the butterfly; feminism; the pimp; sexuality; transgender; womanism

Gender Trouble (Butler), 152–53, 156–59, 162, 175–76

genius: discussion of, xiii, xiv, 18–20, 231n58. *See also* black feminine/maternal; blues music; gender; specific artists

Gerima, Haile, 265n16

Gershwin, George, 37, 132, 138–45, 149

ghostolalia, 119–22, 126–27, 129, 133–36, 138, 144, 149–50, 253n7. *See also* haunting

Gillespie, Michael Boyce, 196

Glissant, Édouard, 52

glossolalia, 119, 138, 144

God-breathing machines, 61

"God is Gangsta" (Lamar), 191–93, 202–3

Golden, Thelma, 182

good kid, m.A.A.d city (Lamar), 189–91, 200–201, 206, 268n52

Gordon, Lewis R., 1

Go Tell It on the Mountain (Baldwin), 127

the grandmother, 48–50, 52, 76. *See also* black feminine/maternal

Grant, Jacquelyn, 153

Gray, Thomas R., 65

Green, Al, 144

Griffin, Farah Jasmine, 98, 115–16, 121, 146, 194

Guèbrou, Tsegué-Maryam, 210

Guggenheimer, Ida, 104

gun ownership, 173–75

hairstyle, 16, 243n112

Hammond, Fred, 138

Hansberry, Lorraine, 224

Haraway, Donna J., 241n90

Harlem, 86, 90–91, 106–7, 111

"Harlem" (Hughes), 223

"Harlem Is Nowhere" (Ellison), 106–7, 111

Harlem Renaissance, 16

Harper, Rachel M., 33

Harris, Lyle Ashton, 34

Harrison, Hazel, 36, 80–81, 84–90, 95–104, 108, 110, 115–16, 249n76

Hartman, Saidiya, 27, 79, 85, 133–34, 182, 250n91, 256n62. *See also specific works*

Hathaway, Donny, 145, 224

Hathaway, Lalah, 181, 203

haunting, 4, 17–18, 118–19, 125, 128–29, 141. *See also* ghostolalia

Hayden, Robert, 39, 63, 71–74, 204, 243n108, 244n115

Hayes, Terrance, 113–14

Heidegger, Martin, 143

Hemingway, Ernest, 106

Here, My Dear (Gaye), 145

"The Hesteriad" (Brooks), 148–49

Heyward, Edwin DuBose, 140–45, 258n79

Hill, Lauryn, 162, 222–23

The History of Sexuality, Volume I (Foucault), 44–45

Holiday, Billie, 34

Holland, Sharon Patricia, 226n1

home, 45–47, 70, 166–69, 203–7, 217, 220–21

Home (Morrison), 141

homiletics, xv

Hopkins, Gerard Manley, 244n115

Hopkins, Pauline, 207–8

Howe, Irving, 104, 247n35

Huggins, Nathan Irvin, 41, 56

Hughes, Langston, xiii–xiv, 6, 16–17, 25, 50, 56–59, 63, 65, 74, 106, 140–41, 222–23, 240n80, 248n58

humoral theory, xii, xiii, 18–19, 112–13

Hurston, Zora Neale, 79, 179–80, 260n9

Hussle, Nipsey, 210

hypocorism, 185

"i" (Lamar), 206–7

"I, Too" (Hughes), 222–23

"The Idea of Black Culture" (Spillers), 4

"If We Must Die" (McKay), 223

India.Arie, 217

indigo, 12–14, 229n41

In Search of Our Mothers' Gardens (Walker), 151–52

"Mama's Baby, Papa's Maybe" (Spillers), xi, 2, 4, 100, 119–20, 184–85, 213–14, 228n31, 265n21

Manabe, Noriko, 196–97

mania, 5–6, 32, 45, 51, 112, 159, 165, 219

manning, xv–xvi

Marriott, David, 251n110

Martin, Michel, 229n41

Martin, Trayvon, 67

maternal potency, 161–62

matricide-cum-suicide, 5–6, 34

McCune Smith, James, 36, 40, 52–53, 55, 62, 69–71, 237n45

McDowell, Deborah, 69

McKay, Claude, 223

McKinley, Catherine, 229n41

meat, 3–8, 29, 227n11. See also consumption

Meehan, Sean Ross, 239n73

melancholy: discussion of, 4–6, 9, 14, 16–17; race and, ix–xviii. See also autonomy; blues music; consumption; lost objects; mourning

memory, 21, 83–84, 95–96, 98, 101, 121, 134, 143–44. See also rememory

"Men of Color, to Arms! A Call by Frederick Douglass" (Douglass), 64–65

mesearch, 152–54, 165, 171–72

method, xiv–xv

"Middle Passage" (Hayden), 63, 204

migration, 111–13, 196

Miller, R. Baxter, 239n57

Mingus, Charles, 24–25, 30–31, 217

"A Minor Figure" (Hartman), 134, 256n62

mirror stage, 130, 191–92

mixed race, 43, 47–48, 53, 55, 66–71. See also racialization

Mo' Better Blues (Lee), 92

"Momma" (Lamar), 37, 181, 196, 203–6

Monáe, Janelle, 174

Morrison, Toni, 2–4, 17, 29–31, 127, 141, 167–68, 182, 184–90, 192–96, 205. See also specific works

"Mortal Man" (Lamar), 210

Mos Def, 127

Moten, Fred, 18, 133, 214, 255n39

Moten, Lucy Ellen, 71

the mother. See black feminine/maternal

mother-as-accident, 102, 107

Moton, Robert, 96

mourning, xii–xiii; and blackness, 219; explanation of, 4–8; and Invisible Man, 97–99; and the Maafa, 12; and pathology, 17; and slavery, 42, 49

"Mourning and Melancholia" (Freud), 4–5, 43, 68–69, 83, 112, 121, 207, 221

"Mourning Remains" (Eng and Kazanjian), xii

"The Moynihan Report," 6, 227n17

mulattos. See mixed race

multiple identities, 125

Mulvey, Laura, 191–92, 195, 204

Murillo, John, 117

Murray, Albert, 9, 31, 50

Murray, Anna, 59, 70

Musser, Amber Jamilla, 34

My Bondage and My Freedom (Douglass), 36, 39–41, 43–44, 48, 52, 60–61, 63–64, 67–68, 73, 78, 136

"My Man's Gone Now," 133, 138–45, 148–49

Mystic Writing-Pad, 83–84

The Narrative of the Life of Frederick Douglass, An American Slave, Written by Himself (Douglass), 36, 44, 50–51, 78

Nash, Howard M., 109

nationalism, 216

native daughter, 85

The Natural History of Man (Prichard), 53–56, 66

Neal, Larry, 79

"Necessity" (Hughes), xiii–xiv, 6, 17

"The Negro Mother" (Hughes), 24, 74

Negus (Bey), 209–11, 269n86

neighborhood watch, 7

"Never Catch Me" (Flying Lotus), 200–201

The New Danger (Mos Def), 127

Nielsen, Cynthia R., 239n58

noise v. sound, 93–94

nomenclature, 130, 148, 185–86, 195

nonbinary, 195, 202

Norman, Jessye, 253n12

"A Note Upon the 'Mystic Writing-Pad'" (Freud), 82–84

"No Weapon" (Hammond), 138